Linehora

D1031732

PLAUTUS

III

LCL 163

PLAUTUS

THE MERCHANT
THE BRAGGART SOLDIER
THE GHOST
THE PERSIAN

EDITED AND TRANSLATED BY

WOLFGANG DE MELO

HARVARD UNIVERSITY PRESS

CAMBRIDGE, MASSACHUSETTS
LONDON, ENGLAND
2011

Library of Congress Control Number 2010924480
CIP data available from the Library of Congress

ISBN 978-0-674-99682-3

*Composed in ZephGreek and ZephText by
Technologies 'N Typography, Merrimac, Massachusetts.
Printed on acid-free paper and bound by
The Maple-Vail Book Manufacturing Group*

CONTENTS

To my wife and daughter

PREFACE

Unlike the first two Plautus volumes, this one contains only four plays, because two of them, the *Miles gloriosus* and the *Mostellaria*, are unusually long. Both are among the best-known comedies Plautus produced. The other two plays are much less popular, but for no good reason. The *Mercator* admittedly lacks the uproarious farce characteristic of the *Casina*, another play centered around an amorous conflict between a father and a son, but its plot construction is smooth and pleasing and the characters are drawn more neatly and convincingly than those of other comedies. The *Persa*, the last play in this volume, has often been criticized as a rather tasteless piece. While this assessment is not entirely unfounded, the *Persa* does contain some remarkably lively and charming scenes, and the characters have more individual features than those of other plays.

I am fortunate to have received much help and support with this volume. J. N. Adams and Peter Brown have answered questions ranging from textual problems to stage settings. Panagiotis Filos has helped me to solve some unusual Greek problems and to consult books not available in Ghent. But as before, my greatest help came from John Trappes-Lomax, who patiently worked through the entire Latin and English texts and improved both considerably. I am immensely grateful to him; the edition would not be what it is without his generous support.

My family and friends have been kind and patient throughout. Naturally, the greatest thanks go to my wife and daughter. In the *Persa*, Toxilus has to combine the roles of clever *architectus doli* and lovesick young man, and he does not always succeed in doing so: at the beginning of the play the planning of the intrigue seems impeded by his amorous inclinations, and at the end he finds it difficult to devote himself entirely to his love because he wants to complete his coup against the pimp. I have on occasion also found it difficult to balance work and family, but my wife and daughter have always managed to steer me in the right direction, sometimes to work harder and sometimes to relax more. I dedicate this volume to them with much love.

MERCATOR

INTRODUCTORY NOTE

A number of Greek and Latin plays are named after merchants, traders, and businessmen, and such characters also appear in several Plautine plays. However, the *Mercator* is the only Plautine comedy with a title of this type. Plautus did not invent it himself; it is a literal translation of *Emporos*, "The Merchant," which, as we learn in l. 9, was the title of the Greek original by Philemon. There are in fact two merchants in the play. One of them, Demipho, is retired, while the other, his son Charinus, is just back from a business trip to Rhodes. The play centers around the conflict between father and son, both of whom love the same girl, Pasicompsa.

The comedy begins with a prologue delivered by Charinus, which sums up the necessary background information. He informs us that, much to his father's dismay, he used to squander the family money on a prostitute. Demipho got very upset about this and often contrasted his own conduct with that of his son. We hear that Demipho's father owned a farm and that Demipho had to toil on it very hard, a type of work he seems to have disliked. When Demipho's father died, he sold the farm, bought a ship, and did business, which is how he acquired his wealth. After much pressure from his father, Charinus gave up his affair and decided to follow in his father's footsteps. Demipho had a ship built for him and provided him with everything he needed in order to do business. Together with his slave Acanthio, Charinus went to Rhodes and made an enormous profit. While still in Rhodes, Charinus received an invitation from a family friend and fell in love with his slave girl Pasicompsa, whom he bought from this friend.

The action of our play unfolds when Charinus has returned to Athens. Fearing his strict father, Charinus wanted to keep it a secret that he had bought a girl. However, his father came to the ship and not only saw Pasicompsa but also flirted with her. When he inquired who she was, Acanthio, Charinus' slave, told him that Charinus had bought her as a maid for his mother. Acanthio then runs to Charinus to inform him and us of what has happened.

We first meet Demipho when he returns from the harbor. He recounts a dream that he did not understand fully. In it, he bought a beautiful she-goat, which he identifies with Pasicompsa. Since he already had a she-goat at home, namely his wife, he did not want to take this new arrival into his house. Instead, he entrusted it to a monkey, which will turn out to be his neighbor and friend Lysimachus. The monkey, however, came back to him to complain that the she-goat had eaten up his wife's dowry, a foreshadowing of a conflict between Lysimachus and his wife. Then a kid snatched the she-goat from Demipho. This kid could be Demipho's son Charinus, but it could also stand for Eutychus, the son of Lysimachus and a close friend of Charinus, who is instrumental in recovering Pasicompsa for Eutychus.

After this narrative, Demipho meets Lysimachus and confesses his love for Pasicompsa. Then he meets his son Charinus and asks him about the girl. Demipho argues that she would not make a good maid for his wife and announces that he will sell her to an old man. Charinus tries to dissuade him, saying that he wants to sell her to a young man if she is unsuitable for his mother, but the authoritarian Demipho wins the day and tells Charinus not to go to the harbor during the sale. Charinus is despondent, but is promised help by his friend Eutychus, who intends to outbid Demipho's old man.

Soon after, however, it is Lysimachus who appears with Pasicompsa. He has bought the girl in order to keep suspicion away from Demipho and now intends to put her up in his house for the day, which he thinks he can do without incurring suspicion himself, for his wife is at their country estate. Interestingly, Lysimachus seems to be attracted by Pasicompsa as well, but not as intensely as Demipho. When the latter returns, he and Lysimachus decide to hire a cook in order to have a pleasant meal with the girl. After the old men have left for the market, Eutychus comes back, meets Charinus, and tells him that the girl had already been sold to an unknown man before he got to the ship. Charinus despairs and decides to go into exile.

Dorippa, the wife of Lysimachus, found it strange that her husband had not joined her in the country. Rightly suspicious, she returns with her old servant Syra. They discover Pasicompsa in their house and are shocked. When Lysimachus comes back from the market, Dorippa confronts him. He tries to deny any inappropriate behavior. However, not only are his words unconvincing, but in addition the cook hired by Lysimachus turns up and asks him if Dorippa is his mistress. Lysimachus unsuccessfully tries to get rid of him; the cook leaves only after putting Lysimachus in the most awkward situation. The old man goes away in order to find Demipho. When Eutychus comes back, Syra informs him about the scandal. Eutychus sees the girl, finds out that she was bought for Demipho, and tries to find Charinus. He meets him as he is about to go into exile, but manages to drag him back. Eutychus and Charinus calm Dorippa down and explain to her that Pasicompsa is not the mistress of Lysimachus. The two old men return. Eutychus tells his father that Dorippa is no longer angry and he announces to Demipho that he has to give up Pasicompsa to his son, which he does with some reluctance.

As often in Plautus, the young men are portrayed in a more positive light than their fathers. Charinus may be too melodramatic for our taste, but he is genuinely in love with Pasicompsa; one can also respect him for willingness to become a merchant not out of greed but to please his father. Similarly, Eutychus is a real friend who helps and supports Charinus throughout. By contrast, Demipho is a hypocrite who disapproves of his son's former love affair and then falls in love himself, despite being married; what is more, his main reason for disliking his son's previous love affair was financial, but he himself intends to spend much money on Pasicompsa and the feast he wants to hold with her. Lysimachus is not a reliable friend. He is polite to Demipho and willing to help him, especially when he gets the chance to flirt with Pasicompsa himself, but as soon as he himself runs into problems he drops Demipho. Interestingly, when both Eutychus and Lysimachus are criticizing Demipho in the final scene, Lysimachus is much harsher; he is the one who threatens to inform Demipho's wife, whereas Eutychus lets him off the hook on condition that he give up the girl.

It is generally assumed that the *Mercator* is a play in which Plautus followed his original relatively closely. Unfortunately, even though there are many fragments of Philemon, none can be assigned to the *Emporos* with certainty. However, if the *Mercator* is close to its original, it should be relatively easy to divide the play into five acts, which was the typical Greek structure; and such a division is indeed quite straightforward. The scholars of the Renaissance assumed act breaks after ll. 224, 498, 666, and 829. Modern scholars assign act breaks in places that fulfill the so-called Webster criterion: the stage has to be empty and the offstage action must take up a significant enough amount of dramatic time to be filled by a choral interlude in the Greek original. The breaks after l. 498 and l. 666 are unproblematic. A break after l. 829 is also possible; if it was here in the Greek original, Syra's speech ending with l. 829 makes a good exit monologue and Eutychus' words beginning with l. 830 make a good entrance monologue. Alternatively we could, with Legrand, assume a Greek act break after l. 802: Syra comes back from looking for Dorippa's father in l. 803, Eutychus comes back from the city center in l. 805, and Lysimachus, who goes to the city center in l. 802, is not supposed to meet either, which means that his exit cannot be too close in dramatic time to the two arrivals. The act break in l. 224 is more problematic; the stage is empty, but hardly any action has taken place till then. This is why Lowe assumes a Greek act break after l. 334. The stage is not empty in Plautus, but there are indications that Plautus has made changes to his original here. Lysimachus goes to the harbor in l. 326, and only two lines later Demipho announces his intention to go there as well, which is awkward; and it is even more awkward that he then decides to stay and hang around during twenty-eight lines of a monologue delivered by Charinus, only to say afterward that he cannot hear what his son is saying. This clumsiness is not atypical of Plautine interventions; it is not unlikely that Philemon allowed Demipho to leave the stage after what is l. 334 in the Latin play.

There are no clear indications when the *Mercator* was first staged. The rarity of *mutatis modis cantica* points to the early phase in Plautus' career, as does the fact that he simply translated the name of the play instead of being self-confident enough to do something more creative. If the *Mercator* is as close to its Greek original as is often claimed, this would further indicate an early work. It has been noted on several occasions that the dream scene in the *Mercator* (ll. 225–70) bears a close resemblance to the dream scene in the *Rudens* (ll. 593–612). On the whole the passage in the *Mercator* is written in more banal language than that in the *Rudens*, which according to Woytek indicates that the *Mercator* passage is a reworking of the *Rudens* passage. But the matter is not so straightforward: possibly the *Rudens* passage is an improved version of the *Mercator* passage. Similarly, the possibility cannot be excluded that both Greek originals contained dreams and that one was loosely based on the other. Thus the relative chronology of these two plays must remain unclear.

8

SELECT BIBLIOGRAPHY

Editions and Commentaries

Dunsch, B. (2000), *Plautus' Mercator: A Commentary* (diss., St Andrews).

Enk, P. J. (1932), *Plauti Mercator cum prolegomenis, notis criticis, commentario exegetico* (Leiden).

Criticism

Averna, D. (1987), "La scena del sogno nel Mercator plautino," in *Pan* 8: 5–17.

––––––– (1988), "Note sull' ῎Εμπορος di Filemone," in *Dioniso* 58: 39–52.

Della Corte, F. (1952), "Philem. fr. 124 K. = Plaut. *Merc.* 404–11," in *Rivista Italiana di Filologia Classica* NS 30: 329–32.

Lefèvre, E. (1995), *Plautus und Philemon* (Tübingen).

Legrand, P.-E. (1910), *Daos: Tableau de la comédie grecque pendant la période dite nouvelle* Κωμῳδία Νέα (Lyon).

Lowe, J. C. B. (2001), "Notes on Plautus' Mercator," in *Wiener Studien* 114: 143–56.

Raffaelli, R., and Tontini, A. (eds.) (2008), *Lecturae Plautinae Sarsinates XI: Mercator (Sarsina, 29 settembre 2007)* (Urbino).

Woytek, E. (2001), "Sprach- und Kontextbeobachtung im Dienste der Prioritätsbestimmung bei Plautus: Zur Datierung von Rudens, Mercator und Persa," in *Wiener Studien* 114: 119–42.

MERCATOR

ARGVMENTVM I

Missus mercatum ab suo adulescens patre
Emit atque apportat scita forma mulierem.
Requirit quae sit, postquam eam uidit, senex;
Confingit seruos emptam matri pedisequam.
5 **A**mat senex hanc, at se simulans uendere
Tradit uicino; eum putat uxor sibi
Obduxe scortum. tum Charinum ex fuga
Retrahit sodalis, postquam amicam inuenit.

ARGVMENTVM II

mercatum asotum filium extrudit pater.
is peregre missus redimit ancillam hospitis
amore captus, aduehit. naue exsilit,
pater aduolat, ancillam uisam deperit.
5 cuius sit percontatur; seruos pedisequam
ab adulescente matri ‹ait› emptam ipsius.
senex, sibi prospiciens, ut amico suo
ueniret natum orabat, natus ut suo:

arg. 2, 4 uisam ancillam *P, transp. Lindsay*
arg. 2, 6 ait *add. Pylades*

10

THE MERCHANT

PLOT SUMMARY 1

A young man, sent as a merchant by his father, buys and brings
back a woman of beautiful appearance. After seeing her, the
old man asks who she is. The young man's slave pretends that
she was bought as an attendant for the young man's mother. The 5
old man is in love with her, but, pretending to sell her, entrusts
her to his neighbor. His neighbor's wife believes that he has
introduced a prostitute into her presence. Then a comrade of
Charinus drags him back from his flight after finding his girl-
friend.

PLOT SUMMARY 2

A father threw out his profligate son so that he should be a mer-
chant. Sent abroad, the son was overpowered by love, bought
his host's slave girl, and took her home. He disembarked. His
father rushed there, saw the slave girl, and fell in love. He asked 5
whose she was; his son's slave said she had been bought by the
young man as an attendant for his mother. Each looking out for
himself, the old man asked his son that she should be sold to a
friend of his, and the son to a friend of his. The young man had

hic filium subdiderat uicini, pater
10   uicinum; praemercatur ancillam senex.
    eam domi deprensam coniunx illius
    uicini scortum insimulat, protelat uirum.
    mercator exspes patria fugere destinat,
    prohibetur a sodale, qui patrem illius
15   orat cum suo patre ⟨una⟩ nato ut cederet.
    [apsente cum lenone perfido]

      arg. 2, 15 una *add. Ussing*
      arg. 2, 16 *del. Pius uerba ad aliud argumentum pertinentia*

taken the neighbor's son as his proxy, the father the neighbor 10
himself; the old man comes first in buying the slave girl. The
wife of that neighbor finds her at home, accuses her of being a
prostitute, and drives off her husband. Our merchant, devoid of
hope, decides to go into exile, but is prevented from doing so by
his comrade, who, together with his own father, asks the mer- 15
chant's father to give her up to his son. [absent with an untrust-
worthy pimp]

PLAUTUS

PERSONAE

CHARINVS adulescens
ACANTHIO seruos
DEMIPHO senex
LYSIMACHVS senex
LORARIVS
EVTYCHVS adulescens
PASICOMPSA meretrix
DORIPPA matrona
SYRA anus
COQVOS

SCAENA

Athenis

CHARACTERS

CHARINUS a young man; just returned from business
  abroad
ACANTHIO a slave; faithful servant of Charinus
DEMIPHO an old man; father of Charinus
LYSIMACHUS an old man; Demipho's neighbor and friend
A SLAVE belongs to Lysimachus
EUTYCHUS a young man; son of Lysimachus and friend of
  Charinus
PASICOMPSA a prostitute; belongs to her lover Charinus
DORIPPA a married woman; wife of Lysimachus
SYRA an old woman; Dorippa's servant
A COOK hired by Lysimachus

STAGING

The scene represents a street in Athens. On the left is Demi-
pho's house, on the right that of his neighbor Lysimachus. Be-
tween the houses there is an altar of Apollo. To the left, the
street leads to the harbor as well as the countryside, and to the
right, it leads to the city center.

ACTVS I

I. i: CHARINVS

CHAR duas res simul nunc agere decretum est mihi:
et argumentum et meos amores eloquar.
non ego item facio ut alios in comoediis
⟨ui⟩ uidi amoris facere, qui aut Nocti aut Dii
5 aut Soli aut Lunae miserias narrant suas:
quos pol ego credo humanas querimonias
non tanti facere, quid uelint, quid non uelint;
uobis narrabo potius meas nunc miserias.
Graece haec uocatur Ἔμπορος Philemonis,
10 eadem Latine Mercator Macci Titi.
pater ad mercatum hinc me meus misit Rhodum;
biennium iam factum est postquam abii domo.
ibi amare occepi forma eximia mulierem.
sed ea[m] ut sim implicitus dicam, si operae est auribus
15 atque aduortendum ad animum adest benignitas.
et hoc parum hercle more amatorum institi:
†per mea per conatus sum uos sumque inde exilico.†
nam amorem haec cuncta uitia sectari solent,
cura, aegritudo, nimiaque elegantia.
20 haec non modo illum qui amat sed quemque attigit

4 ui *add. Ussing*   14 eam *P*, ea *Lambinus*
17 per mea per conatus sum uos sumque inde exilico *B*, per me
perconatus sum uossumque inde exilico *CD, alii alia*

ACT ONE

Enter CHARINUS from the left.

CHAR I'm resolved to do two things at one and the same time
now: I'll tell you the plot summary and my labors in love.
I'm not behaving the same way that I have seen others
behave in comedies through the force of Love; they tell
their troubles to Night or Day or Sun or Moon. I don't be- 5
lieve that these care much about human lamentations,
what they want and what they don't want. Instead, I'll tell
you about my wretched situation. In Greek this play is
called *The Emporos*[1] of Philemon, in Latin *The Mercator* 10
of Titus Maccius. My father sent me off to do business in
Rhodes. It's already two years since I left home. There I
fell in love with a woman of outstanding beauty. But I'll
tell you how I got entangled with her, if your ears are at
leisure and you have the kindness to pay attention. I 15
haven't begun this the way lovers normally do: † . . . †
Well, normally all these vices go hand in hand with love:
worry, distress, and excessive refinement. The last of 20
these takes a full and heavy toll not only on the lover but

---

[1] Both the Greek name and the Latin mean "The Merchant."

magno atque solido multat infortunio,
nec pol profecto quisquam sine grandi malo
praequam res patitur studuit elegantiae.
sed amori accedunt etiam haec quae dixi minus:
25   insomnia, aerumna, error, [et] terror, et fuga:
ineptia ‹est›, stultitiaque adeo et temeritas[t],
incogitantia excors, immodestia,
petulantia et cupiditas, maleuolentia;
inertia, auiditas, desidia, iniuria,
30   inopia, contumelia et dispendium,
multiloquium, parumloquium: [hoc] id eo fit quia
quae nihil attingunt ad rem nec sunt usui,
tam amator profert saepe aduorso tempore;
hoc pauciloquium rursum idcirco praedico,
35   quia nullus umquam amator adeo est callide
facundus quae in rem sint suam ut possit loqui.
nunc uos mi irasci ob multiloquium non decet:
eodem quo amorem Venus mi hoc legauit die.
illuc reuorti certum est, conata eloquar.
40   principio ‹ut ex› ephebis aetate exii
atque animus studio amotus puerili est meus,
amare ualide coepi hic meretricem: ilico
res exulatum ad illam clam abibat patris.
leno importunus, dominus eius mulieris,
45   ui summa ut quicque poterat rapiebat domum.
obiurigare pater haec noctes et dies,
perfidiam, iniustitiam lenonum expromere;

25 et¹ *del. Camerarius*
26 ineptia‹st› *Lindsay*   temeritas[t] *plerique edd.*
29 ineret (inheret *C*) et iam *P*, inertia *Leo*, inerit etiam *Lindsay*
31 hoc *del. Marx*

on whomever it touches. Indeed, no one has ever striven
after refinement beyond what his means allow without
great damage. But the following things that I didn't men-
tion also go hand in hand with love: sleeplessness, toil,   25
uncertainty, fright, and flight. There's silliness, stupidity
to boot and recklessness, mindless thoughtlessness, lack
of moderation, petulance and lust, malevolence; laziness,
greed, idleness, injustice, lack, disgrace and waste, over-   30
talkativeness, under-talkativeness: this happens because
a lover often brings things up at an unsuitable time, even
though they're irrelevant to the matter at hand and use-
less; in turn I refer to it as sub-talkativeness because no   35
lover has ever been so clever at speaking that he could say
the things that benefit him. Now you ought not to be an-
gry with me because of my over-talkativeness: on the
same day that Venus endowed me with love, she also en-
dowed me with this habit. I'm resolved to return to that
topic, I'll tell you what I attempted. In the beginning,   40
when I left my teenage years[2] behind me and my mind
drifted away from childish interests, I fell madly in love
with a prostitute here. At once my father's possessions se-
cretly went into exile to her. A relentless pimp, the mas-
ter of this woman, kept dragging to his home with great-   45
est force whatever he could. My father scolded me about
this night and day and expounded the untrustworthiness
and injustice of pimps. He said his own possessions were

[2] The reference is to being an ephebe, i.e., in the Greek age class do-
ing military service (between eighteen and twenty years).

---

40 atque animus phoebus etate exiit *P*, ut ex ephebis aetate exii
Muretus

19

lacerari ualide suam rem, illius augerier.
summo haec clamore; interdum mussans colloqui:
50   abnuere, negitare adeo me natum suom.
conclamitare tota urbe et praedicere
omnes tenerent mutuitanti credere.
amorem multos illexe in dispendium:
intemperantem, non modestum, iniurium
55   trahere, exhaurire me quod quirem ab se domo;
ratione pessuma a me ea quae ipsus optuma
omnis labores inuenisset perferens
amoris ui diffunditari ac didier.
conuicium tot me annos iam se pascere;
60   quod nisi puderet, ne luberet uiuere.
sese extemplo ex ephebis postquam excesserit,
non, ut ego, amori nec desidiae in otio
operam dedisse nec potestatem sibi
fuisse; adeo arte cohibitum esse ⟨se⟩ a patre:
65   multo opere immundo rustico se exercitum
nec nisi quinto anno quoque solitum uisere
urbem atque extemplo inde, ut spectauisset peplum,
rus rursum confestim exigi solitum a patre.
ibi multo primum sese familiarium
70   laborauisse, quom haec pater sibi diceret:
"tibi aras, tibi occas, tibi seris, tibi item metis,
tibi denique iste pariet laetitiam labos."
postquam recesset uita patrio corpore,
agrum se uendidisse atque ea pecunia
75   nauim, metretas quae trecentas tolleret,

64 se *add. Camerarius*

20

being torn to pieces in a terrible way and those of that fel-
low were being increased. All this with very loud shout-
ing. From time to time he'd speak in a mutter: he'd dis- 50
own me and even deny that I'm his son. He'd shout
throughout the entire city and declare that everybody
should refrain from giving me a loan if I was trying to
borrow. Love had enticed many to waste, he'd tell me; he
said that I, an unrestrained, immoderate, unfair fellow, 55
was dragging and draining off what I could from him and
his home; through my appalling conduct the things he
himself had acquired through his excellent conduct, put-
ting up with all difficulties, would be scattered and dis-
persed by the force of love. He'd been feeding me, a dis-
grace, for so many years already; if I didn't feel any shame 60
for this, I shouldn't want to live. As soon as *he* had passed
his teenage years, he had not, like me, devoted himself to
love and laziness in leisure, nor had he had the possibil-
ity; under such tight control had he been kept by his fa-
ther: he'd been kept busy with a lot of dirty farm work, 65
and he'd visit the city only every four years, and as soon as
he'd seen the robe,[3] he'd be driven off to the country
again by his father. There he'd worked far harder than 70
any of the slaves, while his father would tell him this:
"You're plowing for yourself, harrowing for yourself,
sowing for yourself, and harvesting for yourself; finally,
that labor will give joy to you yourself." After life had left
his father's body, he'd sold the farm and with the money
for that had got a ship which could carry three hundred 75

[3] The robe is the *peplos* of Athena, the goddess guarding the Acrop-
olis of Athens. It was presented at a festival called the Panathenaea,
which took place every four years.

parasse atque ea se mercis uectatum undique,
adeo dum, quae tum haberet, peperisset bona;
me idem decere, si ut deceret me forem.
80 ego me ubi inuisum meo patri esse intellego
atque odio me esse quoi placere aequom fuit,
amens amansque ui animum offirmo meum,
dico esse iturum me mercatum, si uelit:
amorem missum facere me, dum illi opsequar.
85 agit gratias mi atque ingenium allaudat meum;
sed mea promissa non neglexit persequi.
aedificat nauim cercurum et mercis emit,
parata naui imponit, praeterea mihi
talentum argenti ipsus sua annumerat manu;
90 seruom una mittit, qui olim puero paruolo
mihi paedagogus fuerat, quasi uti mi foret
custos. his sic confectis nauim soluimus.
Rhodum uenimus, ubi quas mercis uexeram
omnis ut uolui uendidi ex sententia.
95 lucrum ingens facio praeterquam mi meus pater
dedit aestumatas mercis: ita peculium
conficio grande. sed dum in portu illi ambulo,
hospes me quidam adgnouit, ad cenam uocat.
uenio, decumbo acceptus hilare atque ampliter.
100 discubitum noctu ut imus, ecce ad me aduenit
mulier, qua mulier alia nulla est pulchrior;
ea nocte mecum illa hospitis iussu fuit.
uosmet uidete quam mi ualide placuerit:

81 esse (esset *B*) me *P, transp. Pylades*   82 ut *P*, ui *Ussing*

---

4 The metreta is a measurement for liquids corresponding to 8.5 imperial gallons or 39 liters.

metretas.[4] On this ship he'd transported goods from ev-
erywhere until he'd got the possessions he had then. I
ought to do the same if I were the way I ought to be.
When I realized that I was a nuisance to my father and   80
hated by the man I should please, I gave myself a push
and made up my mind, despite being madly in love. I said
I was going to be a merchant if he so wished; I'd let go of
my love so long as I could obey him. He thanked me and   85
praised my intentions; but he didn't fail to insist on what
I'd promised. He built a fast, light ship, bought goods,
and loaded them onto the ship once it was completed. In
addition he himself paid me out a silver talent[5] with his
own hand. Along with me he sent the slave who had long   90
ago been a tutor to me as a little boy, so as to be my guard-
ian. When this had been done in this way we set sail. We
came to Rhodes, where I sold all the goods I had trans-
ported as I wished and to my heart's content. I made an   95
enormous profit beyond the estimated value of the goods
my father gave me, so I acquired much money for my
own use.[6] But while I was walking in the harbor there, a
friend of mine recognized me and invited me to dinner. I
came and reclined at table, getting a joyful and generous
reception. As we went off to bed that night, lo and be-   100
hold, a woman came to me, the most beautiful woman in
the world; that night she was with me on my host's orders.
You yourselves can see how much I liked her: the next

---

[5] A very generous sum for an inexperienced salesman.

[6] The money slaves and children made belonged to their owners
and fathers, respectively, but some money, the *peculium*, could be set
aside for their private, independent use.

postridie hospitem adeo, oro ut uendat mihi,
105   dico eius pro meritis gratum me et munem fore.
quid uerbis opus est? ‹ab eo› emi atque aduexi heri.
eam me aduexisse nolo resciscat pater.
modo eam reliqui ad portum in naui et seruolum.
sed quid currentem seruom a portu conspicor,
110   quem naui abire uotui? timeo quid siet.

I. ii: ACANTHIO. CHARINVS

ACAN ex summis opibus uiribusque usque experire, nitere
erus ut minor opera tua seruetur: agedum, Acanthio,
abige aps te lassitudinem, caue pigritiae praeuorteris.
simul enicat suspiritus (uix suffero hercle anhelitum),
115   simul autem plenis semitis qui aduorsum eunt: aspellito,
detrude, deturba in uiam. haec disciplina hic pessuma
    est:
currenti, properanti hau quisquam dignum habet dece-
    dere.
ita tres simitu res agendae sunt, quando unam occeperis:
et currendum et pugnandum et autem iurigandum est in
    uia.
120 CHAR quid illuc est quod ille tam expedite exquirit cursuram
    sibi?
curae est negoti quid sit aut quid nuntiet.
ACAN   nugas ago.
quam restito, tam maxume res in periclo uortitur.
CHAR mali nescioquid nuntiat.

106 ab eo *add. Mueller*

day I approached my host and asked him to sell her to
me. I said I'd be grateful and obliged for his kindness.   105
What need is there for words? I bought her from him and
brought her here yesterday. I don't want my father to find
out that I brought her here. Just now I left her and my
slave at the harbor on the ship. (*looking around*) But why
do I see my slave running from the harbor? I forbade him   110
to leave the ship. I'm afraid of what this may mean.

*Enter ACANTHIO from the left, in such a hurry that he does
not notice his master.*

ACAN Keep trying and striving with all your might and main to
have your young master saved through your effort: go on,
Acanthio, drive your exhaustion away from you, make
sure that you don't devote yourself to your sloth instead
of more important things. At the same time that my dif-
ficulty in breathing is killing me (I can hardly bear the
shortness of breath), the people coming toward me on   115
the overcrowded pavements are killing me. Drive them
away, push them down, throw them down into the street.
Their conduct here is appalling: no one thinks it proper
to give way to someone who is running and rushing. You
have to do three things at the same time when you begin
one: you have to run, you have to fight, and you have to
quarrel in the street.

CHAR (*aside*) What's the reason for him to seek a space for run-   120
ning so speedily? I'm worried about what's the matter or
what his news is.

ACAN I'm not getting anywhere. The more I dawdle, the
greater is the danger our affairs are in.

CHAR (*aside*) He has some bad news.

ACAN	genua hunc cursorem deserunt;
	perii, seditionem facit lien, occupat praecordia,
125	perii, animam nequeo uortere, nimis nili tibicen siem.
127	numquam edepol omnes balineae mi hanc lassitudinem eximent.
128	domin an foris dicam esse erum Charinum?
CHAR	ego animi pendeo.
129	quid illuc sit negoti lubet scire [me], ex hoc metu uti certus sim.
130 ACAN	at etiam asto? at etiam cesso foribus facere hisce assulas?
	aperite aliquis! ubi Charinus‹t› erus? domine est an foris?
	num quisquam adire ad ostium dignum arbitratur?
CHAR	ecce me,
	Acanthio, quem quaeris.
ACAN	nusquam est disciplina ignauior.
CHAR	quae te malae res agitant?
ACAN	multae, ere, te atque me.
135 CHAR	quid est negoti?
ACAN	periimus.
135ᵃ CHAR	principium ‹id› inimicis dato.
136 ACAN	at tibi sortito id optigit.
137 CHAR	loquere id negoti quicquid est.
ACAN	placide, uolo acquiescere.
126 CHAR	at tu edepol sume laciniam atque apsterge sudorem tibi.
138 ACAN	tua causa rupi ramites, iam dudum sputo sanguinem.
139 CHAR	resinam ex melle Aegyptiam uorato, saluom feceris.

126 *post* 137 *pos. Bothe*
129 me *del. Lindsay*   ut sim certus *P*, uti certus sim *Lindsay*
131 Charinus‹t› *Lindsay*
135ᵃ id *add. Lachmann*

ACAN My knees are leaving this runner in the lurch; I'm dead, my spleen is rebelling and occupying my vitals; I'm dead, 125 I can't breathe, I'd be an awfully bad flute player. All the baths will never take this exhaustion away from me. Should I say that my master Charinus is at home or outside? (*stops in front of the door of Demipho's house*)

CHAR (*aside*) I'm in suspense. I want to know what this business is so as to be safe from this fear.

ACAN And yet I'm still standing here? And yet I'm still hesitat- 130 ing to smash this door to splinters? (*knocking*) Open up, someone! Where's my master Charinus? Is he at home or outside? Does anyone see fit to answer the door?

CHAR Here I am, Acanthio, the man you're looking for.

ACAN These are the laziest slaves in the world.

CHAR What misfortunes are upsetting you?

ACAN Many misfortunes are upsetting you and me.

CHAR What's the matter? 135

ACAN We're dead.

CHAR First of all pass that wish on to our enemies.

ACAN But it's been allotted to you.

CHAR Tell me whatever is the matter.

ACAN Gently, I want to calm down.

CHAR Do take the flap of your cloak and wipe off your sweat.

ACAN I've cracked my lungs for your sake, I've been spitting blood for a while already.

CHAR Swallow Egyptian resin dipped in honey and you'll get well.[7]

---

[7] Resin was used against chest complaints. However, it was not eaten but dissolved in liquid containing bitter almond and drunk; the taste must have been abhorrent.

140 ACAN at edepol tu calidam picem bibito, aegritudo apscesserit.
CHAR hominem ego iracundiorem quam te noui neminem.
ACAN at ego maledicentiorem quam te noui neminem.
CHAR sin saluti quod tibi esse censeo, id consuadeo?
ACAN apage istius modi salutem ‹cum› cruciatu quae aduenit.
145 CHAR dic mihi, an boni quid usquam est quod quisquam uti
     possiet
     sine malo omni, aut ne laborem capias quom illo uti uo-
     les?
ACAN nescio ego istaec: philosophari numquam didici nec scio.
     ego bonum, malum quo accedit, mihi dari hau desidero.
CHAR cedo tuam mihi dexteram, agedum, Acanthio.
ACAN   em dabitur, tene.
150 CHAR uin tu te mihi opsequentem esse an neuis?
ACAN   opera licet
     experiri, qui me rupi causa currendo tua,
     ut quae scirem scire actutum tibi liceret.
CHAR   liberum
     caput tibi faciam ‹cis› paucos mensis.
ACAN   palpo percutis.
CHAR egon ausim tibi usquam quicquam facinus falsum prolo-
     qui?
155 quin iam prius quam sum elocutus, scis si mentiri uolo.
ACAN   ah!
     lassitudinem hercle uerba tua mihi addunt, enicas.
CHAR sicin mi opsequens es?
ACAN   quid uis faciam?
CHAR   tun? id quod uolo.

144 cum *add. Pylades*
153 cis *add. Acidalius*

28

ACAN But you drink hot pitch[8] and your grief will go away. 140

CHAR I don't know anyone more prone to anger than you.

ACAN And I don't know anyone more prone to rudeness than you.

CHAR If I advise you to do what I think is good for your health?

ACAN Away with health of the type that comes with torture.

CHAR Tell me, is there any good anywhere that a man can enjoy 145
without any evil, or without undertaking toil when you
want to enjoy it?

ACAN I don't know that; I've never learned to philosophize and
I don't know how to. I have no wish to be given a good
which is accompanied by an evil.

CHAR Give me your right hand, come on, Acanthio.

ACAN (*proffering it*) There, here you are, hold it.

CHAR (*grabbing his hand*) Do you wish to be obedient to me or 150
not?

ACAN You may test it through what I've done: for your sake I've
burst myself by running, so that you could know at once
what I know.

CHAR I'll free you within a few months.

ACAN You're just sweet-talking me.

CHAR Would I ever dare to tell you some untruth? No, even be- 155
fore I've finished speaking you know if I want to lie.

ACAN Bah! Your words increase my exhaustion, you're killing
me.

CHAR Is this how you obey me?

ACAN What do you want me to do?

CHAR You? Do what I want you to do.

[8] Pitch was also used for medicinal purposes, but of course only externally.

ACAN quid \<id\> est igitur quod uis?

CHAR   dicam.

ACAN   dice.

CHAR   at enim placide uolo.

160 ACAN dormientis spectatores metuis ne ex somno excites?

CHAR uae tibi!

ACAN   tibi . . . equidem a portu apporto hoc—

CHAR   quid fers? dic mihi.

ACAN uim, metum, cruciatum, curam, iurgiumque atque ino-
       piam.

CHAR perii! tu quidem thesaurum huc mi apportauisti mali.
       nullus sum.

ACAN   immo es—

CHAR   scio iam, "miserum" dices tu.

ACAN   dixi ego tacens.

165 CHAR quid istuc est mali?

ACAN   ne rogites, maxumum infortunium est.

CHAR opsecro, dissolue iam me; nimis diu animi pendeo.

ACAN placide, multa exquirere etiam prius uolo quam uapu-
       lem.

CHAR hercle uero uapulabis nisi iam loquere aut hinc abis.

ACAN hoc sis uide, ut palpatur. nullust, quando occepit, blan-
       dior.

170 CHAR opsecro hercle oroque ut istuc quid sit actutum indices,
       quandoquidem mihi supplicandum seruolo uideo meo.

ACAN tandem indignus uideor?

CHAR   immo dignu's.

ACAN   equidem credidi.

CHAR opsecro, num nauis periit?

159 id *add. Bentley*

ACAN Then what is it you want?

CHAR I'll tell you.

ACAN Tell me.

CHAR But I want it gently.

ACAN Are you afraid of waking the sleeping spectators up from   160
their slumber?

CHAR Curse you!

ACAN No, you . . . are the one I'm bringing this news for from
the harbor—

CHAR (*interrupting*) What news are you bringing? Tell me.

ACAN Violence, fear, torture, worry, quarrel, and dearth.

CHAR I'm dead! You've brought me a storehouse of trouble. I'm
ruined.

ACAN No, you are—

CHAR (*interrupting*) I know already, you'll say "wretched."

ACAN I've said so silently.

CHAR What trouble is that?   165

ACAN Don't ask, it's an enormous disaster.

CHAR Please, relieve me now; I've been in suspense far too
long.

ACAN Gently, I still want to ask you many things before getting
a beating.

CHAR Honestly, you'll get a beating unless you tell me now or go
away.

ACAN Just look how coaxing he is! No one's more flattering once
he's started.

CHAR I beg and entreat you to inform me about what that is at   170
once, since I can see that I have to entreat my own slave.

ACAN Do I really seem not to deserve it?

CHAR No, you do deserve it.

ACAN I for one thought so.

CHAR Please, the ship isn't lost, is it?

ACAN   salua est nauis, ne time.

CHAR quid alia armamenta?

ACAN   salua et sana sunt.

CHAR   quin tu expedis

175   quid siet quod me per urbem currens quaerebas modo?

ACAN tuquidem ex ore orationem mi eripis.

CHAR   taceo.

ACAN   tace.

    credo, si boni quid ad te nuntiem instes acriter,

    qui nunc, quom malum audiendum est, flagitas me ut
        eloquar.

CHAR opsecro hercle te istuc uti tu mihi malum facias palam.

180 ACAN eloquar, quandoquidem me oras. tuos pater—

CHAR   quid meus pater?

ACAN —tuam amicam—

CHAR   quid eam?

ACAN   —uidit.

CHAR   uidit? uae misero mihi!

    hoc quod te [inter]rogo responde.

ACAN   quin tu si quid uis roga.

CHAR qui potuit uidere?

ACAN   oculis.

CHAR   quo pacto?

ACAN   hiantibus.

CHAR ine hinc dierectus? nugare in re capitali mea.

185 ACAN qui, malum, ego nugor si tibi quod me rogas respondeo?

CHAR certen uidit?

ACAN   tam hercle certe quam ego te aut tu me uides.

CHAR ubi eam uidit?

182 interrogo *P*, rogo *Bentley*

32

ACAN The ship's safe, stop being afraid.

CHAR What about the rest of the tackle?

ACAN It's safe and sound.

CHAR Why won't you explain to me why you looked for me run- 175
ning throughout the city just now?

ACAN You're snatching the speech from my mouth.

CHAR I'm quiet.

ACAN Yes, be quiet. No doubt you'd be most insistent if I were
bringing you some good news, since you're urging me to
tell you everything now that you have to hear something
bad.

CHAR I beg you to reveal that bad news to me.

ACAN I'll tell you, since you ask me. Your father— 180

CHAR (*interrupting*) What about my father?

ACAN Your girlfriend—

CHAR (*interrupting*) What about her?

ACAN He's seen her.

CHAR He's seen her? Poor, wretched me! Give me an answer to
what I ask you.

ACAN Well, if you want something, ask.

CHAR How could he see her?

ACAN With his eyes.

CHAR In what way?

ACAN They were open.

CHAR Won't you go away and be hanged? You're joking in a
matter of life and death for me.

ACAN How on earth am I joking if I give answers to what you 185
ask me?

CHAR Has he seen her for certain?

ACAN For as certain as I see you or you me.

CHAR Where did he see her?

33

ACAN   intus intra nauim, ut prope astitit;
et cum ea confabulatust.

CHAR   perdidisti me, pater.
eho tu, eho tu, quin cauisti ne eam uideret, uerbero?
190   quin, sceleste, ⟨eam⟩ apstrudebas, ne eam conspiceret
        pater?

ACAN quia negotiosi eramus nos nostris negotiis:
armamentis complicandis, [et] componendis studuimus.
dum haec aguntur, lembo aduehitur tuos pater pauxillu-
        lo,
nec quisquam hominem conspicatust, donec in nauim
        subit.

195 CHAR nequiquam, mare, supterfugi a tuis tempestatibus:
equidem me iam censebam esse in terra atque in tuto
        loco,
uerum uideo med ad saxa ferri saeuis fluctibus.
loquere porro quid sit actum.

ACAN   postquam aspexit mulierem,
rogitare occepit quoia esset.

200 CHAR   quid respondit?
ACAN   ilico
occucurri atque interpello matri te ancillam tuae
emisse illam.

CHAR   uisun est tibi credere id?
ACAN   etiam rogas?
sed scelestus subigitare occepit.

CHAR   illamne, opsecro?
ACAN mirum quin me subigitaret.

CHAR   edepol cor miserum meum,
205   quod guttatim contabescit quasi in aquam indideris sa-
        lem.
perii!

ACAN Inside on the ship, as he stood close by; and he chatted
with her.

CHAR You've ruined me, father. (*to Acanthio*) Hey you, hey
you, why didn't you guard against him seeing her, you
thug? You criminal, why didn't you hide her away so that   190
my father wouldn't spot her?

ACAN Because we were busy with our own business: we were
concentrated on folding and packing up the tackle.
While this was going on, your father came round in a tiny
boat, and no one spotted him until he went onto the ship.

CHAR In vain did I flee from your storms, o sea. I already   195
thought I was on land and in a safe place, but I can see
that I'm being flung onto the cliffs by wild waves. (*to
Acanthio*) Keep telling me what happened.

ACAN After he saw the woman, he began to ask her who she   200
belongs to.

CHAR What did she reply?

ACAN I ran toward them at once and interrupted them, saying
that you'd bought her as a maid for your mother.

CHAR Did he seem to believe you in that?

ACAN You even ask? But the criminal began to bestow his ca-
resses.

CHAR On her, please?

ACAN Strange that he didn't caress me!

CHAR My heart is really wretched; it is consumed speck by   205
speck, as if you'd put salt into water. I'm dead!

---

190 eam¹ *add. Bentley*
192 et *del. Camerarius*

ACAN   em istuc unum uerbum dixisti uerissumum.
stultitia istaec est.
CHAR   quid faciam? credo, non credet pater
si illam matri meae ‹me› emisse dicam; post autem mihi
scelus uidetur me parenti proloqui mendacium.
210   neque ille credet nec credibile est forma eximia mulie-
      rem
    eam me emisse ancillam matri.
ACAN   non taces, stultissume?
credet hercle, nam credebat iam mihi.
CHAR   metuo miser,
ne patrem prehendat ut sit gesta res suspicio.
hoc quod te rogo responde, ‹quaeso›.
ACAN   quaeso, quid rogas?
215 CHAR num esse amicam suspicari uisus est?
ACAN   non uisus est.
quin quicque ut dicebam mihi credebat.
CHAR   uerum, ut tibi quidem
uisus est.
ACAN   non, sed credebat.
CHAR   uae mi misero, nullus sum!
sed quid ego hic in lamentando pereo, ad nauim non eo?
sequere.
ACAN   si istac ibis, commodum obuiam uenies patri;
220   postea aspicit te timidum esse atque exanimatum: ilico
retinebit, rogitabit unde illam emeris, quanti emeris:
timidum temptabit te.
CHAR   hac ibo potius. iam censes patrem
abiisse a portu?

208 me *add. Acidalius*
214 quaeso *add. Ritschl*

ACAN There! That one word you've spoken absolutely truly. (*after a pause, cheerfully, realizing that the situation is not too bad*) That's nonsense!

CHAR What should I do? I don't believe my father will believe me if I say I've bought her for my mother. And then it also seems wrong to me to tell a lie to a parent. He won't 210 believe me and it isn't believable that I've bought this woman of outstanding beauty as a maid for my mother.

ACAN Won't you be quiet, you complete fool? He will indeed believe you because he has already believed me.

CHAR Poor me, I'm afraid that a suspicion will get hold of my father about how the business was done. Please give me an answer to what I ask you.

ACAN Please, what do you ask?

CHAR He didn't seem to suspect that she's my girlfriend, did 215 he?

ACAN No, he didn't. What's more, he believed me in everything that I told him.

CHAR (*unconvinced*) True, as it seemed to you.

ACAN No, he really did believe me.

CHAR Poor, wretched me, I'm done for! But why am I perishing here wailing instead of going to the ship? Follow me. (*turns to the left*)

ACAN If you go that way, you'll go exactly toward your father; then he sees that you're afraid and anxious: he'll hold you 220 back instantly and ask you who you bought her from and how much you bought her for. He'll put you to the test while you're afraid.

CHAR (*turning round*) I'll go this way instead. Do you think my father has already left the harbor?

37

ACAN   quin ea ego huc praecucurri gratia,
ne te opprimeret imprudentem atque electaret.

CHAR   optume.

ACTVS II

II. i: DEMIPHO

225   DEM   miris modis di ludos faciunt hominibus
mirisque exemplis somnia in somnis danunt.
uel ut ego nocte hac quae praeteriit proxuma
in somnis egi satis et fui homo exercitus.
mercari uisus mihi sum formosam capram;
230   ei ne noceret quam domi ante habui capram
neu discordarent si ambae in uno essent loco,
posterius quam mercatus fueram uisus sum
in custodelam simiae concredere.
ea simia adeo post hau multo ad me uenit,
235   male mi precatur et facit conuicium:
ait sese illius opera atque aduentu caprae
flagitium et damnum fecisse hau mediocriter;
dicit capram, quam dederam seruandam sibi,
suai uxoris dotem ambedisse oppido.
240   mi illud uideri mirum ut una illaec capra
uxoris simiai dotem ambederit.
instare factum simia atque hoc denique
respondet, ni properem illam ab sese abducere,
ad me domum intro ad uxorem ducturum meam.
245   atque oppido hercle bene uelle illi uisus sum,
ast non habere quoi commendarem capram;
quo magis quid facerem cura cruciabar miser.
interea ad me haedus uisust aggredirier,
infit mihi praedicare sese ab simia

ACAN Yes, I ran here before him so that he shouldn't catch you
     unawares and worm out the information.
CHAR Excellent.

Exeunt CHARINUS and ACANTHIO to the right.

ACT TWO

Enter DEMIPHO from the left.

DEM The gods make fools of men in wondrous ways and give   225
    them dreams in their sleep in strange ways. I, for in-
    stance, was agitated and troubled in my sleep last night. I
    dreamed I bought a beautiful she-goat for myself; in or-   230
    der that the she-goat I already had at home wouldn't
    harm her and that they wouldn't quarrel if they were both
    in one and the same place, I seemed to entrust the one
    I'd bought later to the care of a monkey. Now that mon-
    key came to me soon after, cursed me, and made a scene.   235
    He said that he'd incurred no small disgrace and loss
    through the doings and arrival of that goat; he said that
    the goat I'd given him to watch over had completely
    eaten up his wife's dowry. It seemed strange to me that   240
    that one goat should have eaten up the monkey's wife's
    dowry. The monkey insisted that this is what happened
    and finally replied to me that unless I took her away from
    him quickly, he'd take her to my home, to my wife inside.
    I seemed very well disposed to the monkey, but not to   245
    have anyone who I could entrust the goat to. Poor chap
    that I am, I was all the more in agony about what to do.
    Meanwhile a kid seemed to approach me. He began to

39

250 capram abduxisse et coepit irridere me;
ego enim lugere atque abductam illam aegre pati.
hoc quam ad rem credam pertinere somnium
nequeo inuenire; nisi capram illam suspicor
iam me inuenisse quae sit aut quid uoluerit.
255 ad portum hinc abii mane cum luci simul;
postquam id quod uolui transegi, atque ego conspicor
nauim ex Rhodo qua est heri aduectus filius;
collubitum est illuc mihi nescioqui uisere:
inscendo in lembum atque ad nauim deuehor.
260 atque ego illi aspicio forma eximia mulierem,
filius quam aduexit meus matri ancillam suae.
quam ego postquam aspexi, non ita amo ut sani solent
homines sed eodem pacto ut insani solent.
amaui hercle equidem ego olim in adulescentia,
265 uerum ad hoc exemplum numquam ut nunc insanio.
unum quidem hercle iam scio, periisse me;
uosmet uidete ceterum quanti siem.
nunc hoc profecto sic est: haec illa est capra;
uerum hercle simia illa atque haedus mi malum
270 apportant atque eos esse quos dicam hau scio.
sed conticiscam, nam eccum it uicinus foras.

II. ii: LYSIMACHVS. DEMIPHO. SERVOS

LYS profecto ego illunc hircum castrari uolo,
ruri qui uobis exhibet negotium.
DEM neque omen illuc mihi neque auspicium placet.
275 quasi hircum metuo ne uxor me castret mea,
atque illius hic nunc simiae partis ferat.

257 qua est (*uel* quast) heri Ω *et Prisciano*, qua heri est *Camerarius*
276 atque illius haec (hic *Thierfelder*) nunc *P*, ac metuo ne illaec *A*

tell me that he'd taken the goat away from the monkey 250
and started to laugh at me. I was sad indeed and upset
that she'd been taken away from me. I can't find out what
I should believe this dream pertains to; but I suspect I've
already found out who that goat is or what she meant. I 255
went to the harbor in the morning, at sunrise. After sort-
ing out what I wanted, I spot the ship from Rhodes on
which my son arrived yesterday. Somehow I fancy seeing
that. I go on board a boat and go to the ship. There I set 260
eyes on a woman of outstanding beauty, someone my son
brought here as a maid for his mother. After setting eyes
on her I fall in love, not the way sane men do, but the
same way that madmen do. I was indeed in love long ago,
in my youth, but never the way I'm crazy now. One thing 265
I know already, that I'm dead; as for the rest, see for your-
selves what I'm good for. Now it is indeed like this: this
woman is that goat; but that monkey and kid are bringing
me trouble and I don't know who I should say they are. 270
But I'll fall silent: look, my neighbor is coming out.

*Enter LYSIMACHUS from his house, accompanied by a
SLAVE carrying a hoe.*

LYS   (*to the slave*) That he-goat causing trouble on the farm—
       I want him castrated.
DEM   (*aside*) I like neither that omen nor the augury. I'm afraid 275
       that my wife might castrate me like the he-goat and that
       this chap is now playing the part of the monkey.

41

	LYS	i tu hinc ad uillam atque istos rastros uilico

LYS i tu hinc ad uillam atque istos rastros uilico
Pisto ipsi facito coram ut tradas in manum.
uxori facito ut nunties negotium
280 mihi esse in urbe, ne me exspectet; nam mihi
tris hodie litis iudicandas dicito.
i, et hoc memento ⟨a⟩dicere.

SER   numquid amplius?

LYS tantum est.

DEM   Lysimache, salue.

LYS   eugae, Demipho,
salueto. quid agis? quid fit?

DEM   quod miserrumus.

285 LYS di melius faxint!

DEM   di hoc quidem faciunt.

LYS   quid est?

DEM dicam, si uideam tibi operam esse aut otium.

LYS quamquam negotium est, si quid uis, Demipho,
non sum occupatus umquam amico operam dare.

DEM benignitatem tuam mi experto praedicas.

290   quid tibi ego aetatis uideor?

LYS   Acherunticus,
senex uetus, decrepitus.

DEM   peruorse uides.
puer sum, Lysimache, septuennis.

LYS   sanun es,
qui puerum te esse dicas?

DEM   uera praedico.

LYS modo hercle in mentem uenit quid tu diceres:
295 senex quom extemplo est, iam nec sentit nec sapit,
aiunt solere eum rursum repuerascere.

282 dicere *P*, adicere *Schoell*

LYS   You be off to the farmhouse and make sure that you give
      that hoe in person into the hand of our overseer Pistus
      himself. Mind you tell my wife that I have business in   280
      town, so she shouldn't expect me: tell her I have three
      lawsuits to judge today. Go and remember to add that.

SLAVE Anything else?

LYS   No, that's all.

Exit SLAVE to the left.

DEM   Lysimachus, my greetings.

LYS   Hurray, Demipho, my greetings. How are you? How are
      things?

DEM   Like a wretch, that's how I am.

LYS   May the gods give you something better!   285

DEM   No, that's what the gods are giving me.

LYS   What is it?

DEM   I'd tell you if I saw that you have time or leisure.

LYS   Although I do have business, Demipho, I'm never too
      busy to help out a friend, if you want anything.

DEM   I have experienced the kindness that you're telling me
      about. (*after a pause*) How old do you think I am?   290

LYS   Ripe for the Underworld, old and decrepit.

DEM   You see wrongly. Lysimachus, I'm a seven-year-old boy.

LYS   Are you in your right mind, calling yourself a boy?

DEM   I'm telling the truth.

LYS   It just occurred to me what you're saying: as soon as   295
      someone is an old man and no longer has his senses or
      wits about him, they say that he enters his second child-
      hood.

---

286 esse operam *P, transp. Ritschl*

DEM immo bis tanto ualeo quam ualui prius.

LYS bene hercle factum et gaudeo.

DEM   immo si scias,
    oculis quoque etiam plus iam uideo quam prius.

300 LYS bene est.

DEM   malae rei dico.

LYS   iam istuc non bene est.

DEM sed ausimne ego tibi eloqui fideliter?

LYS audacter.

DEM   animum aduorte.

LYS   fiet sedulo.

DEM hodie ire occepi in ludum litterarium,
    Lysimache. ternas scio iam.

LYS   quid, "ternas"?

DEM   "amo."

305 LYS tun capite cano amas, senex nequissume?

DEM si canum seu istuc rutilum est siue atrum est, amo.

LYS ludificas nunc tu me hic, opinor, Demipho.

DEM decide collum stanti si falsum loquor;
    uel, ut scias me amare, cape cultrum, [ac] seca

310   digitum uel aurem uel tu nasum uel labrum:
    si mouero me seu secari sensero,
    Lysimache, auctor sum ut me amando . . . enices.

LYS si umquam uidistis pictum amatorem, em illic est.
    nam meo quidem animo uetulus, decrepitus senex

315   tantidem est quasi sit signum pictum in pariete.

DEM nunc tu me, credo, castigare cogitas.

LYS egon te?

309 ac A, *om.* P

44

DEM No, I'm twice as fit as I was before.

LYS Excellent, I'm glad.

DEM No, if you knew, I already see better with my eyes than before, too.

LYS That's good.   300

DEM I mean for something naughty.

LYS Now that's not good.

DEM But may I be so bold as to tell you something in confidence?

LYS Do so boldly.

DEM Pay attention.

LYS I'll do so diligently.

DEM Today I've begun to go to primary school, Lysimachus. I already know five[9] letters.

LYS What, "five"?

DEM "I-L-O-V-E."

LYS You with your gray head are in love, you wicked old man?   305

DEM Whether that head is gray or red or black, I am in love.

LYS I think you're making fun of me now, Demipho.

DEM Cut off my head while I'm standing here if I don't speak the truth; or, so that you may know that I'm in love, take a knife and cut my finger or my ear or my nose or my lip. If 310 I move or feel that I'm being cut, Lysimachus, I give you permission to kill me . . . with love.

LYS (*to the audience*) If you've ever seen a picture of a lover, here it is: at least to my mind an old, decrepit man is 315 worth as little as if he were a picture painted on a wall.

DEM I believe you're thinking of reproaching me now.

LYS I reproach you?

[9] "Three" in Latin because "I love" is *amo*.

45

DEM   nihil est iam quod tu mihi suscenseas:
      fecere tale ante alii spectati uiri.
      ‹humanum errare est›, humanum autem ignoscere est:

320   humanum amare est atque id ui optingit deum.
      ne sis me obiurga, hoc non uoluntas me impulit.

LYS   quin non obiurgo.

DEM   at ne deteriorem tamen
      hoc facto ducas.

LYS   egon te? ah, ne di siuerint!

DEM   uide sis modo etiam.

LYS   uisum est.

DEM   certen?

LYS   perdis me.

325   hic homo ex amore insanit. numquid uis?

DEM   uale.

LYS   ad portum propero, nam ibi mihi negotium est.

DEM   bene ambulato.

LYS   bene uale.

DEM   bene sit tibi.
      quin mihi quoque etiam est ad portum negotium.
      nunc adeo ibo illuc. sed optume gnatum meum

330   uideo eccum. opperiar hominem. hoc nunc mi uiso
        opust,
      huic persuadere quo modo potis siem
      ut illam uendat neue det matri suae;
      nam ei dono aduexe audiui. sed praecauto opust,
      ne hic ‹ad› illam me animum adiecisse aliqua sentiat.

319–20 *sic ego*, humanum amarest humanum autem ignoscere est
P, humanum amarest atque id uel (= uei) optingit deum *A*
    334 ad *add. Gronovius*

DEM   There's no reason for you to be angry with me now: other respected men have done such a thing before. It is human to go astray and it is human to forgive; it is human to 320 be in love and it happens through the gods' power. Do stop castigating me, it's not my own will that drove me to it.

LYS   Well, I'm not lecturing you.

DEM   But even so, don't think less of me because of this.

LYS   I of you? Ah, may the gods forbid!

DEM   Are you quite sure?

LYS   Yes.

DEM   Definitely?

LYS   You're killing me. (*aside*) This chap is mad from love. (*to* 325 *Demipho*) Is there anything you want?

DEM   Be well.

LYS   I must go to the harbor quickly because I have business there.

DEM   Have a good walk.

LYS   Goodbye.

Exit LYSIMACHUS to the left.

DEM   (*calling after him*) Have a good time. (*to the audience*) I too have business at the harbor. Now I'll go there. But perfect, look, I can see my son. I'll wait for him. I have to 330 see now how I can persuade him to sell her and not to give her to his mother: I've heard he brought her as a present for her. But I need to be on my guard so that he doesn't realize somehow that I've fallen in love with her.

II. iii: CHARINVS. DEMIPHO

335 CHAR homo me miserior nullust aeque, opinor,
neque aduorsa quoi plura sint sempiterna;
satin quicquid est quam rem agere occepi,
proprium nequit mi quod cupio euenire?
ita mi mala res aliqua obicitur,
340 bonum quae meum comprimit consilium.
miser amicam mihi paraui, animi causa, pretio eripui,
ratus clam patrem meum posse habere;
is resciuit et uidit et perdidit me;
neque is quom roget quid loquar cogitatum est,
345 ita animi decem in pectore incerti certant.
nec quid corde nunc consili capere possim
scio, tantus cum cura meo est error animo.
dum serui mei perplacet mi consilium,
dum rursum hau placet nec pater potis uidetur
350 induci ut putet matri ancillam emptam esse illam.
nunc si dico ut res est atque illam mihi me
emisse indico, quem ad modum existumet me?
atque illam apstrahat, trans mare hinc uenum asportet;
355 scio saeuos quam sit, domo doctus. igitur
hoccine est amare? arare mauelim quam sic amare.
iam hinc olim inuitum domo extrusit ab se,
mercatum ire iussit: ibi hoc malum ego inueni.
ubi uoluptatem aegritudo uincat, quid ibi inest amoeni?
360 nequiquam abdidi, apscondidi, apstrusam habebam:
musca est meus pater, nil potest clam illum haberi,
nec sacrum nec tam profanum quicquam est, quin ibi
ilico assit.

338 euenire quod cupio *P, transp. Lindsay*
342 <me> meum *Bentley*

Enter CHARINUS from the right without noticing his father.

CHAR (*to himself*) Nobody is more wretched than me, I think, 335
or has perpetual problems in greater number. Can't any-
thing that I've begun to do turn out to my lasting advan-
tage, as I desire? No, some misfortune is thrown my way
which botches my good plan. Poor me, I bought myself a 340
girlfriend, for my enjoyment, and rescued her for a price,
believing that I could keep this secret from my father; he
has found out, seen her, and killed me. I have no idea
what to say when he asks: ten uncertain hearts are fight- 345
ing within my breast. I don't know what plan I can form in
my heart now, such great confusion is in my mind to-
gether with worry. At one time I'm very fond of my slave's
plan, at another time I'm not fond of it in turn and it
doesn't seem likely that my father can be led to believe 350
that that girl has been bought as a maid for my mother.
Now if I say how the matter is and state that I bought her
for myself, what will he think of me? And he'd drag her
off and take her across the sea to sell her. I know how 355
fierce he is, from my own experience. Is that what being
in love means then? I'd rather lead a plowman's life than
a lover's life like this. He already threw me out of the
house against my will long ago and told me to go and be a
merchant; there I found this trouble. What pleasure is
there in a situation where grief has the upper hand over
joy? In vain did I conceal her, hide her, keep her out of 360
view: my father is a fly, nothing can be kept secret from
him, and there's nothing so sacred or profane that he
wouldn't be on the spot immediately. I don't have any

> nec qui rebus meis confidam mi ulla spes in corde certa
> est.

DEM quid illuc est quod solus secum fabulatur filius?

365 sollicitus mihi nescioqua re uidetur.

CHAR   attatae!

> meus pater hicquidem est quem uideo. ibo, alloquar.
> quid fit, pater?

DEM unde incedis, quid festinas, gnate mi?

CHAR   recte, pater.

DEM ita uolo, sed istuc quid est tibi quod commutatust color?
> numquid tibi dolet?

CHAR   nescioquid meo animo est aegre, pater.

370 poste hac nocte non quieui satis mea ex sententia.

[DEM per mare ut uectu's, nunc oculi terram mirantur tui.

CHAR magis opinor—

DEM   id est profecto; uerum actutum apscesserit.]

DEM ergo edepol palles. si sapias, eas ac decumbas domi.

CHAR otium non est: mandatis rebus praeuorti uolo.

375 DEM cras agito, perendie agito.

CHAR   saepe ex te audiui, pater:
> rei mandatae omnis sapientis primum praeuorti decet.

DEM age igitur; nolo aduorsari tuam aduorsum sententiam.

CHAR saluos sum, siquidem isti dicto solida et perpetua est
> fides.

DEM quid illuc est quod a me solus se in consilium seuocat?

380 [iam] non uereor ne illam me amare hic potuerit rescis-
> cere;

371–72 *secl. Ussing*
380 iam *del. Brix*

firm hope in my heart through which I could have con-
fidence in my situation.

DEM (*aside*) What's the reason my son's talking to himself
alone? He seems to be worried about something.   365

CHAR (*spotting him*) Goodness! This is my father I can see. I'll
go and greet him. (*walking toward him*) How are you,
father?

DEM Where are you coming from and why are you in a rush,
my son?

CHAR It's okay, father.

DEM That's how I want it, but what's the reason that your color
has changed? Do you have pain anywhere?

CHAR I'm feeling somewhat awkward, father. Then last night I   370
didn't sleep as well as I'd like.

[DEM As you went across the sea, your eyes are now surprised
at the solid ground.

CHAR I rather think—

DEM (*interrupting*) That's what it is indeed; but it'll go away
soon.]

DEM That's why you're pale. You'd do well to go and lie down
at home.

CHAR I don't have leisure. I want to sort out some commissions
first.

DEM Do it tomorrow, do it the day after.   375

CHAR I've often heard it from you, father: all wise men ought to
sort out their commissions first.

DEM Go on then; I don't want to oppose your decision.

CHAR (*aside*) I'm safe if this statement can be relied on fully
and for good.

DEM (*aside*) What's the reason that he's withdrawing from me
to make his plans all by himself? I'm not afraid that he   380
could have found out here that I'm in love with that girl;

   quippe haud etiam quicquam inepte feci amantes ut so-
    lent.

CHAR res adhuc quidem hercle in tuto est, nam hunc nescire sat
    scio

   de illa amica; quod si sciret, esset alia oratio.

DEM quin ego hunc aggredior de illa?

CHAR   quin ego hinc me amolior?

385 eo ego, ut quae mandata amicum amicis tradam.

DEM   immo mane;

   paucula etiam sciscitare prius uolo.

CHAR   dic quid uelis.

DEM usquin ualuisti?

CHAR   perpetuo recte, dum quidem illic fui;

   uerum in portum huc ut sum aduectus, nescioqui animus
    mi dolet.

DEM nausea edepol factum credo; uerum actutum apscesserit.

390 sed quid ais? ecquam tu aduexti tuae matri ancillam e
   Rhodo?

CHAR aduexi.

DEM   quid? ea ut uidetur mulier?

CHAR   non edepol mala.

DEM ut morata est?

CHAR   nullam uidi melius mea sententia.

DEM mihi quidem edepol uisa est quom illam uidi—

CHAR   eho an uidisti, pater?

DEM uidi. uerum non ex usu nostro est neque adeo placet.

395 CHAR qui uero?

DEM   quia—⟨quia⟩ non nostra formam habet dignam domo.

   nihil opust nobis ancilla nisi quae texat, quae molat,

385 amicum *B*, amicus *CD*, amice *Ussing*
395 quia *add. Lindsay*

52

I haven't done anything stupid yet the way lovers normally do.

CHAR (*aside*) The matter is still safe: I know well enough that he doesn't know about that girlfriend. If he knew, he'd sing a different tune.

DEM (*aside*) Why don't I accost him about her?

CHAR (*aside*) Why don't I remove myself from here? (*to Demipho*) I'm off to execute my friends' commissions for my friends. 385

DEM No, wait; there are still a few things I want to ask you about first.

CHAR Say what you like.

DEM Have you been well throughout?

CHAR I was well all the time while I was there; but after arriving here in the harbor, I've somehow been feeling awkward.

DEM I believe it's from seasickness; but it'll go away soon. But what do you say? You brought some maid from Rhodes for your mother? 390

CHAR I did.

DEM Well then? How does this woman seem to you?

CHAR Not bad at all.

DEM What's her character like?

CHAR In my opinion I haven't seen anyone with a better character.

DEM Well, she seemed to me, when I saw her—

CHAR (*interrupting*) Oh, you've seen her, father?

DEM Yes. But she isn't of any use for us and she won't do.

CHAR How come? 395

DEM (*awkwardly*) Because—because she doesn't have the kind of appearance suitable for our house. We only need a maid to weave, to grind meal, to cut wood, to do her

53

lignum caedat, pensum faciat, aedis uorrat, uapulet,
quae habeat cottidianum familiae coctum cibum:
horunc illa nihilum quicquam facere poterit.

CHAR admodum.

400 ea causa equidem illam emi dono quam darem matri
meae.

401– DEM ne duas neu te aduexisse dixeris.

2 CHAR di me adiuuant.

DEM labefacto paulatim. uerum quod praeterii dicere,
neque illa matrem satis honeste tuam sequi poterit
comes

405 nec sinam.

CHAR qui uero?

DEM quia illa forma matrem familias
flagitium sit si sequatur; quando incedat per uias,
contemplent, conspiciant omnes, nutent, nictent, sibi-
lent,
uellicent, uocent, molesti sint; occentent ostium;
impleantur elegeorum meae fores carbonibus.

410 atque, ut nunc sunt maledicentes homines, uxori meae
mihique obiectent lenocinium facere. nam quid eo est
opus?

CHAR hercle qui tu recte dicis et tibi assentior.
sed quid illa nunc fiet?

DEM recte. ego emero matri tuae
ancillam uiraginem aliquam non malam, forma mala,

415 ut matrem addecet familias, aut Syram aut Aegyptiam;
ea molet, coquet, conficiet pensum, pinsetur flagro,
nec propter eam quicquam eueniet nostris foribus flagiti.

stint of spinning, to sweep the house, to get a beating, to have the daily food for the household ready. She won't be able to do any of these things.

CHAR Quite right. I bought her in order to give her as a present 400
to my mother.

DEM Don't give her and don't say that you brought her here.

CHAR (*aside*) The gods are helping me.

DEM (*aside*) I'm weakening his resolution a little. (*to Charinus*) But what I failed to say, she won't be able to follow
your mother decently as an attendant and I won't allow it. 405

CHAR How so?

DEM Because it would be a scandal if a woman of her appearance were to follow the mother of a household; were she
to walk through the streets, everybody would stare at her,
ogle her, nod to her, wink at her, whistle at her, pinch her,
call after her, and be a nuisance. People would serenade
the door. With their pieces of charcoal[10] my door would
be filled with ditties. And, given what crooked gossip- 410
ers people are nowadays, they would disapprove of my
wife and myself on the grounds that we were keeping a
brothel. What on earth is that necessary for?

CHAR Yes, you're speaking the truth and I agree with you. But
what will happen with her now?

DEM It's okay. I'll buy your mother some maid as strong as a
man, not bad, but with bad looks, as is appropriate for the 415
mother of a household, a woman from Syria or Egypt.
She will grind meal, cook, do her stint of spinning, be
flogged with the lash, and our door won't suffer any scandal because of her.

---

[10] Charcoal was commonly used to write gossip or insults on walls
and doors.

CHAR quid si igitur reddatur illi unde empta est?

DEM   minime gentium.

CHAR dixit se redhibere si non placeat.

DEM   nihil istoc opust:

420   litigari nolo ego usquam, tuam autem accusari fidem;

multo edepol, si quid faciendum est, facere damni mauo-
lo

quam opprobramentum aut flagitium muliebre efferri
domo.

me tibi illam posse opinor luculente uendere.

424–
25   CHAR dum quidem hercle ne minoris uendas quam ego emi,
pater.

DEM tace modo: senex est quidam qui illam mandauit mihi
ut emerem—ad istanc faciem.

CHAR   at mihi quidam adulescens, pater,
mandauit ad illam faciem, ita ut illa est, emerem sibi.

DEM uiginti minis opinor posse me illam uendere.

430 CHAR at ego si uelim, iam dantur septem et uiginti minae.

DEM at ego—

CHAR   quin ego, inquam—

DEM   ah, nescis quid dicturus sum, tace.
tris minas accudere etiam possum, ut triginta sient.

CHAR quo uortisti?

DEM   ad illum qui emit.

CHAR   ubinam est is homo gentium?

435 DEM eccillum uideo. iubet quinque me addere etiam nunc
minas.

CHAR hercle illunc diui infelicent, quisquis est.

427 ⟨aut⟩ ad *Leo*
436 dii *B*, di *CD*, diui *Seyffert*

CHAR Then how about returning her to the man I bought her from?

DEM Not at all.

CHAR He said he'd take her back if I didn't like her.

DEM That's not necessary. I don't want there to be any lawsuit 420
anywhere or your reliability to be faulted. If anything has
to be done, I'd much rather incur a loss than have a scan-
dal or disgrace on account of that woman be made public
outside the house. I think I can sell her for you with
profit.

CHAR So long as you don't sell her for less than I bought her for, 425
father.

DEM Do be quiet. There's a certain old man who charged me
with buying her—(*correcting himself*) someone of her
appearance.

CHAR But a certain young man, father, charged me with buying
him a girl of precisely her appearance.

DEM I think I can sell her for twenty minas.[11]

CHAR But if I want to, I'll be given twenty-seven now. 430

DEM But I—

CHAR (*interrupting*) No, I, I say—

DEM (*interrupting*) Ah, you don't know what I'm going to say,
be quiet. I can mint up three more minas so that it's
thirty.

CHAR Where did you turn?

DEM To the man who's buying.

CHAR Where on earth is that chap?

DEM (*pointing at the audience*) Look, I can see him. Even now 435
he tells me to add five minas.

CHAR (*aside*) May the gods give him bad luck, whoever he is.

---

[11] This is an appropriate price; the prices later on are excessive.

DEM   ibidem mihi
etiam nunc annutat addam sex minas.

CHAR   septem mihi.

DEM   numquam edepol me uincet hodie.

CHAR   commodis poscit, pater.

DEM   nequiquam poscit: ego habebo.

CHAR   at illic pollicitust prior.

440 DEM nihili facio.

CHAR   quinquaginta poscit.

DEM   non centum datur.
potine ut ne licitere aduorsum ‹mei› animi sententiam?
maxumam hercle habebis praedam: ita ille est, quoi emi-
    tur, senex;
sanus non est ex amore illius. quod posces feres.

CHAR certe edepol adulescens ille, quoi ego emo, efflictim perit
445   eius amore.

DEM   multo hercle ille magis senex, si tu scias.

CHAR numquam edepol fuit nec fiet ill' senex insanior
ex amore quam ille adulescens quoi ego do hanc operam,
    pater.

DEM   quiesce, inquam. istanc rem ego recte uidero.

CHAR   quid ais?

DEM   quid est?

CHAR non ego illam mancupio accepi.

DEM   sed ille illam accipiet. sine.

450 CHAR non potes tu lege uendere illam.

DEM   ego aliquid uidero.

441 mei *add. Scaliger*

58

DEM In the same place he's nodding to me even now to indi-
cate I should add six minas.

CHAR Seven to me.

DEM He'll never beat me today.

CHAR He's offering good, honest coin, father.

DEM He's offering it in vain: I'll have her.

CHAR But he made his offer earlier.

DEM I don't care.   440

CHAR He asks for her for fifty.

DEM He won't get her for a hundred. Can't you stop bidding
against my wishes? You'll have an enormous booty: that's
what that old man is like for whom she's being bought.
He isn't in his right mind out of love for her. What you ask
you'll get.

CHAR That young man who I am buying her for is certainly ab-
solutely mad because of his love for her.   445

DEM That old man is much more so, if only you knew.

CHAR That old man has never been and never will be madder
on account of his love than that young man for whom I'm
making this effort, father.

DEM Calm down, I'm telling you. I'll sort this business out
well.

CHAR What do you say?

DEM What is it?

CHAR I haven't bought her formally.[12]

DEM But *he* will buy her formally. Let it be.

CHAR You can't sell her legally.   450

DEM I'll find some solution.

---

[12] Formal property transactions involved *mancipatio*, the laying
hold of a person or thing in the presence of witnesses.

CHAR post autem communest illa mihi cum alio. qui scio
quid sit ei animi, uenirene eam uelit an non uelit?

DEM ego scio uelle.

CHAR   at pol ego esse credo aliquem qui non uelit.

DEM quid id mea refert?

CHAR   quia illi suam rem esse aequom est in manu.

455 DEM quid ais?

CHAR   communis mihi illa est cum illo: is hic nunc non adest.

DEM prius respondes quam rogo.

CHAR   prius tu emis quam uendo, pater.
nescio, inquam, uelit ille illam necne abalienarier.

DEM quid? illi quoidam qui mandauit tibi si emetur, tum uolet,
si ego emo illi qui mandauit, tum ille nolet? nil agis.

460   numquam edepol quisquam illam habebit potius quam
ille quem ego uolo.

CHAR certumne est?

DEM   censen certum esse? quin ad nauim iam hinc eo,
ibi uenibit.

CHAR   uin me tecum illo ire?

DEM   nolo.

CHAR   non places.

DEM meliust te quae sunt mandatae res tibi praeuortier.

CHAR tu prohibes.

DEM   at me incusato: te fecisse sedulo.

465   ad portum ne bitas dico iam tibi.

CHAR   auscultabitur.

458 illic quidam *P*, ille quidam *A*, illi quoidam *Bothe*

CHAR But then she's the joint property of myself and a third party. How do I know what his intentions are, whether he wants to sell her or not?

DEM I know that he wants to.

CHAR But *I* believe he doesn't want to.

DEM What does that matter to me?

CHAR Because he ought to have control over his own property.

DEM What do you say?[13]   455

CHAR She's shared between me and him; he isn't here now.

DEM You answer before I ask.

CHAR And you buy before I sell, father. I'm telling you, I don't know if he wants her to be sold or not.

DEM What? If she's bought for the man who commissioned you, then he'll want her sold, but if I buy her for the man who commissioned me, then he won't? Nonsense! Never   460 will anyone have her instead of the man I want to have her.

CHAR Are you resolved?

DEM Don't you think I'm resolved? More than that, I'm off to the ship now, there she'll be sold.

CHAR Do you want me to go there with you?

DEM No.

CHAR I don't like it.

DEM It's better for you to attend to your commissions first.

CHAR You don't let me.

DEM Then lay the blame on me. Say you did your best. I'm tell-   465 ing you now not to go to the harbor.

CHAR *(resigned)* I'll obey you.

---

[13] A formula to introduce a question, but Charinus takes his father literally.

DEM   ibo ad portum. ne hic resciscat cauto opust: non ipse
      emam,
      sed Lysimacho amico mandabo. is se ad portum dixerat
      ire dudum. me moror quom hic asto.

CHAR   nullus sum, occidi.

II. iv: CHARINVS. EVTYCHVS

CHAR Pentheum diripuisse aiunt Bacchas: nugas maxumas
470   fuisse credo, praeut quo pacto ego diuorsus distrahor.
      quor ego uiuo? quor non morior? quid mi est in uita
      boni?
      certum est, ibo ad medicum atque ibi me toxico morti
      dabo,
      quando id mi adimitur qua causa uitam cupio uiuere.

EVT   mane, mane opsecro, Charine.
CHAR   qui me reuocat?
EVT   Eutychus,
475   tuos amicus et sodalis, simul uicinus proxumus.
CHAR non tu scis quantum malarum rerum sustineam.
EVT   scio;
      omnia ego istaec auscultaui ab ostio, omnem rem scio.
CHAR quid id est quod scis?
EVT   tuos pater uolt uendere—
CHAR   omnem rem tenes.
EVT   —tuam amicam—
CHAR   nimium multum scis.
EVT   —tuis ingratiis.

474 qui *P*, quis *A*

---

[14] Pentheus was king of Thebes. His mother, Agave, and other
women were followers of Bacchus, the deity of wine and frenzy, and in
one such fit of frenzy they killed Pentheus.

DEM (*to himself*) I'm off to the harbor. I need to be on my guard that he won't find out; I won't buy her myself, but commission my friend Lysimachus to do so. He'd said a while ago he'd go to the harbor. I'm wasting time just standing here.

Exit DEMIPHO to the left.

CHAR I'm ruined, I'm dead.

CHAR The story goes that bacchantes tore Pentheus[14] to pieces: I think that was a mere trifle compared with how I am be- 470
ing torn apart in different directions. Why do I live? Why don't I die? What good is there in life for me? I'm re-
solved, I'll go to the doctor and kill myself with poison there, since the reason why I desire to live is being taken away from me.

Enter EUTYCHUS from his house.

EUT Wait, wait please, Charinus.

CHAR (*without looking*) Who is calling me back?

EUT Eutychus, your friend and comrade, at the same time 475
your next-door neighbor.

CHAR You don't know how much trouble I'm enduring.

EUT I do know; I've heard it all from the door, I know the whole business.

CHAR What is it you know?

EUT Your father wants to sell—

CHAR (*interrupting*) You've got the whole business.

EUT —your girlfriend—

CHAR (*interrupting*) You know far too much.

EUT —against your wishes.

63

480 CHAR plurumum tu scis. sed qui scis esse amicam illam meam?

EVT tute heri ipsus mihi narrasti.

CHAR satine ut oblitus fui
tibi me narrauisse?

EVT hau mirum est factum.

CHAR te nunc consulo.
responde: quo leto censes me ut peream potissumum?

EVT non taces? caue tu istuc dixis.

CHAR quid uis me igitur dicere?

485 EVT uin patri sublinere pulchre me os tuo?

CHAR sane uolo.

EVT uisne eam ad portum—

CHAR qui potius quam uoles?

EVT —atque eximam
mulierem pretio?

CHAR qui potius quam auro expendas?

EVT unde erit?

CHAR Achillem orabo aurum [ut] mihi det Hector qui expensus
fuit.

EVT sanun es?

CHAR pol sanus si sim, non te medicum mi expetam.

490 EVT tanti quanti poscit, uin tanti illam emi?

CHAR auctarium
adicito uel mille nummum plus quam poscet.

EVT iam tace.
sed quid ais? unde erit argentum quod des, quom poscet
pater?

CHAR inuenietur, exquiretur, aliquid fiet; enicas.

EVT iam istuc "aliquid fiet" metuo.

488 ut A, om. P

64

CHAR You know terribly much. But how do you know that she's   480
my girlfriend?

EUT You yourself told me yesterday.

CHAR Can I really have forgotten that I told you?

EUT It's no surprise.

CHAR Now I'm asking you for advice. Answer me: by which
kind of death do you think I'd best die?

EUT Won't you be quiet? Don't say that.

CHAR Then what do you want me to say?

EUT Do you want me to trick your father cleverly?   485

CHAR I do indeed.

EUT Do you want me to walk to the harbor—

CHAR *(interrupting)* Why walk rather than fly?

EUT —and take away the woman for her price?

CHAR Why this rather than weighing her with gold?

EUT Where will it come from?

CHAR I'll ask Achilles to give me the gold with which Hector
was weighed.[15]

EUT Are you in your right mind?

CHAR If I were, I wouldn't seek you as my doctor.

EUT Do you want her to be bought for as much as he asks?   490

CHAR Raise the bid by a thousand sesterces[16] more than he asks
if you like.

EUT Be quiet now. But what do you say? Where will the
money you give come from when your father asks for it?

CHAR It will be found, it will be sought, something will happen;
you're killing me.

EUT I'm afraid of that "something will happen" now.

[15] After Achilles had killed Hector, Hector's father, Priam, ran-
somed the body by paying ten talents in gold and many other precious
things.   [16] Or didrachmas; the Latin is vague.

CHAR		quin taces?
EVT		muto imperas.

495 CHAR satin istuc mandatum est?

EVT		potin ut aliud cures?
CHAR		non potest.
EVT	bene uale.	
CHAR		non edepol possum prius quam tu ad me redieris.
EVT	meliust sanus sis.	
CHAR		uale, uince et me serua.
EVT		ego fecero.
	domi maneto me.	
CHAR		ergo actutum face cum praeda recipias.

ACTVS III

III. i: LYSIMACHVS. PASICOMPSA

LYS   amice amico operam dedi: uicinus quod rogauit,
500   hoc emi mercimonium. mea es tu, sequere sane.
    ne plora: nimis stulte facis, oculos corrumpis talis.
    quin tibi quidem quod rideas magis est quam ut lamen-
       tere.

PAS   amabo ecastor, mi senex, eloquere—

LYS   exquire quiduis.

PAS   —quor emeris me.

LYS   tene ego? ut quod imperetur facias,
505   item quod tu mi si imperes, ego faciam.

PAS   facere certum est
    pro copia et sapientia quae te uelle arbitrabor.

LYS   laboriosi nil tibi quicquam operis imperabo.

497 meliust *A*, melius *P*   sis Ω, si sis *Ritschl*

CHAR Why won't you be quiet?

EUT You're commanding someone who is mute.

CHAR Is your commission clear? 495

EUT Is it possible for you to worry about something else?

CHAR No.

EUT Farewell.

CHAR I really can't fare well until you've returned to me.

EUT You'd better be in your right mind.

CHAR Farewell, be victorious and save me.

EUT I will. Wait for me at home.

CHAR Then mind you return with the booty at once.

Exeunt EUTYCHUS to the left and CHARINUS into his house.

ACT THREE

Enter LYSIMACHUS and PASICOMPSA from the left.

LYS (*to the audience*) I have done a friend a friendly turn: I bought the merchandise my neighbor asked me for. 500 (*to Pasicompsa*) You're mine, follow me, will you? Stop crying; you're behaving terribly stupidly, you're spoiling such pretty eyes. You have more reason to laugh than to lament.

PAS Please, my dear old man, tell me—

LYS (*interrupting*) Ask anything you like.

PAS —why you bought me.

LYS I you? So that you do what you're told, just as I'll do any- 505 thing should you tell me to.

PAS I'm resolved to do what I think you want as is in my power and my wisdom.

LYS I won't tell you to do any hard work.

67

PAS   namque edepol equidem, mi senex, non didici baiolare
nec pecua ruri pascere nec pueros nutricare.

510 LYS   bona si esse uis, bene erit tibi.

PAS   tum pol ego perii misera.

LYS   qui?

PAS   quia illim unde huc aduecta sum, malis bene esse solitum
est.

LYS   quasi dicas nullam mulierem bonam esse.

PAS   haud equidem dico
nec mos meust ut praedicem quod ego omnis scire cre-
dam.

LYS   oratio edepol pluris est huius quam quanti haec empta
est.

515   rogare hoc unum te uolo.

PAS   roganti respondebo.

LYS   quid ais tu? quid nomen tibi dicam esse?

PAS   Pasicompsae.

LYS   ex forma nomen inditum est. sed quid ais, Pasicompsa?
possin tu, si usus uenerit, subtemen tenue nere?

PAS   possum.

LYS   si tenue scis, scio te uberius posse nere.

520 PAS de lanificio neminem metuo, una aetate quae sit.

LYS   bonae hercle te frugi arbitror, iam inde ‹a› matura aetate
quom scis facere officium tuom, mulier.

PAS   pol docta didici.
operam accusari non sinam meam.

LYS   em istaec hercle res est.
ouem tibi eccillam dabo, natam annos sexaginta,

525   peculiarem.

521 matura iam inde aetate Ω, iam inde a matura aetate *Luchs*

PAS	Yes, my dear old man, I don't know how to carry a load or pasture livestock in the country or act as wet nurse.	
LYS	If you're willing to be good, you'll have a good time.	510
PAS	In that case I'm dead, poor me.	
LYS	How so?	
PAS	Because in the place I was brought from it was usually the bad girls who had a good time.	
LYS	As if you were to say that no woman is good.	
PAS	I'm not saying that, nor is it my habit to tell what I believe everyone knows.	
LYS	(*to the audience*) Her speech is worth more than the price she was bought for. (*to Pasicompsa*) I want to ask you this one thing.	515
PAS	When you ask I'll reply.	
LYS	What do you say? What name should I say you have?	
PAS	Pasicompsa.	
LYS	The name was given to you on account of your beauty.[17] But what do you say, Pasicompsa? Could you, if need be, spin a thin thread?[18]	
PAS	I can.	
LYS	If you know how to spin a thin one, I know you can spin a thicker one.	
PAS	As for woolmaking, I don't fear any girl of my age.	520
LYS	I think you're decent since you've known from your early youth how to do your duty, my woman.	
PAS	Yes, I've learned my lessons well. I won't let my work be faulted.	
LYS	There, this is what to do. (*pointing to Demipho's house*) Look, I'll give you that sheep, sixty years of age, all as your very own.	525

[17] The name means "pretty in every respect."
[18] Probably double entendre: the thread is a metaphor for the penis.

	PAS	mi senex, tam uetulam?
	LYS	generis Graeci est;

PAS mi senex, tam uetulam?

LYS   generis Graeci est;
eam si curabis, perbona est, tondetur nimium scite.

PAS honoris causa quicquid est quod dabitur gratum habebo.

LYS nunc, mulier, ne tu frustra sis, mea non es, ne arbitrere.

PAS dic igitur quaeso, quoia sum?

LYS   tuo ero redempta es rursum;

530 ego te redemi, ille mecum orauit.

PAS   animus rediit,
si mecum seruatur fides.

LYS   bono animo es, liberabit
ille te homo: ita edepol deperit, atque hodie primum
uidit.

PAS ecastor iam biennium est quom mecum rem coepit.
nunc, quando amicum te scio esse illius, indicabo.

535 LYS quid ais tu? iam biennium est quom tecum rem habet?

PAS   certo;

536 et inter nos coniurauimus, ego cum illo et ille mecum:

536ᵃ ego cum uiro et ill' cum muliere, nisi cum illo aut ille
mecum,

537 neuter stupri causa caput limaret.

LYS   di immortales!
etiam cum uxore non cubet?

PAS   amabo, an maritust?
neque est neque erit.

LYS   nolim quidem. homo hercle periurauit.

540 PAS nullum adulescentem plus amo.

LYS   puer est illequidem, stulta.
nam illi quidem hau sane diu est quom dentes excide-
runt.

PAS   So old, my dear old man?

LYS   It's of the Greek[19] type; if you look after it, it's very good, it can be fleeced really nicely.

PAS   In order to show you my appreciation I'll be grateful for anything I'm given.

LYS   Now, my woman, don't be mistaken, you aren't mine, so don't think you are.

PAS   Then tell me please, whose am I?

LYS   You've been bought back again for your master; I've   530
bought you back, he asked me to.

PAS   Life has returned to me, if good faith is kept with me.

LYS   Take heart, he'll free you: he's madly in love, and yet he's only seen you today.

PAS   Heavens! It's already two years since he began to be involved with me. I'll tell you now because I know you're his friend.

LYS   What do you say? He's already been involved with you for   535
two years?

PAS   Certainly; and we swore an oath together, I with him and he with me: neither of us would rub heads with another[20] for unchastity, I with a man and he with a woman, except I with him and he with me.

LYS   Immortal gods! He shouldn't even lie with his wife?

PAS   Please, is he married? He isn't and he won't be.

LYS   I wish he weren't. He's perjured himself.

PAS   There's no young man I love more.   540

LYS   He's actually a little boy, silly: he lost his teeth not long ago.

[19] Pliny (*Nat. Hist.* 8.190) also praises the breed of sheep called "Greek." There is a pun here: Demipho is Greek.

[20] I.e., kiss someone else.

PAS   quid, "dentes"?

LYS   nihil est. sequere sis. hunc me diem unum orauit
       ut apud me praehiberem locum, ideo quia uxor ruri est.

III. ii: DEMIPHO

DEM   tandem impetraui egomet me ut corrumperem:

545   empta est amica clam uxorem et clam filium.
       certum est, antiqua recolam et seruibo mihi.
       breue iam relicuom uitae spatium est: quin ego
       uoluptate, uino, et amore delectauero.
       nam hanc se bene habere aetatem nimio est aequius.

550   adulescens quom sis, tum quom est sanguis integer,
       rei tuae quaerundae conuenit operam dare;
       demum igitur quom sis iam senex, tum in otium
       te colloces, dum potest ames: id iam lucrum est
       quod uiuis. hoc ut dico, factis persequar.

555   nunc tamen interea ad me huc inuisam domum:
       uxor me exspectat iam dudum esuriens domi;
       iam iurgio enicabit, si intro rediero.
       uerum hercle postremo, utut est, non ibo tamen,
       sed hunc uicinum prius conueniam quam domum

560   redeam; ut mihi aedis aliquas conducat uolo
       ubi habitet istaec mulier. atque eccum it foras.

III. iii: LYSIMACHVS. DEMIPHO

LYS   adducam ego illum iam ad te, si conuenero.

DEM   me dicit.

LYS   quid ais, Demipho?

547 breue iam reliquom uitae spatiumst quin ego *A*, decurso in-
spatio breue quod uitae reliquumst *P*

555 *sic* Ω   *P etiam alteram recensionem exhibet*: interea tamen huc
intro ad me inuisam domum

PAS What, "his teeth"?

LYS It's nothing. Follow me, will you? He's asked me to pro-
vide him with a space in my place for only this one day
because my wife is in the country.

Exeunt LYSIMACHUS and PASICOMPSA into his house.
Enter DEMIPHO from the left.

DEM At long last I've succeeded in corrupting myself. I've   545
bought a mistress behind my wife's back and behind my
son's back. It's decided: I'll follow my old ways again and
be at my own service. Now only a brief span of life is left:
I'll enjoy myself with pleasure, wine, and love. Yes, it's
much fairer that people of *my* age should have a good
time. When you're young, when your blood is fresh, you   550
ought to look after making your fortune. Then at last,
when you're an old man, you should devote yourself to
leisure and you should love as long as you can: being alive
is already gain. As I say this, I'm following it through with
actions. Still, in the meantime I'll now have a look here at   555
home at my place. My wife has been expecting me at
home for a while, hungry. Now she'll kill me with her
nagging if I go back in. But in the end, however that may
be, I won't go in yet; instead I'll meet this neighbor of
mine before returning home. I want him to rent some   560
house for me where that woman can live. And look, he's
coming out.

Enter LYSIMACHUS from his house.

LYS (*into the house*) I'll bring him to you now if I meet him.

DEM (*aside*) He means me.

LYS (*spotting him*) What do you say, Demipho?

73

DEM   est mulier domi?

LYS   quid censes?

DEM   quid si uisam?

LYS   quid properas? ‹mane.›

565 DEM   quid faciam?

LYS   quod opust facto facito ut cogites.

DEM   quid cogitem? equidem hercle opus hoc facto existumo,
ut illo intro eam.

LYS   itane uero, ueruex? intro eas?

DEM   quid aliud faciam?

LYS   prius hoc ausculta atque ades:
prius etiam est quod te facere ego aequom censeo.

570   nam nunc si illo intro ieris, amplecti uoles,
confabulari atque osculari.

DEM   tu quidem
meum animum gestas: scis quid acturus siem.

LYS   peruorse facies.

DEM   quodne ames?

LYS   tanto minus.
iaiunitatis plenus, anima foetida,

575   senex hircosus tu osculere mulierem?
utine adueniens uomitum excutias mulieri?
scio pol te amare, quom istaec praemonstras mihi.

DEM   quid si igitur unum faciam hoc? si censes, coquom
aliquem arripiamus prandium qui percoquat

580   apud te hic usque ad uesperum.

LYS   em istuc censeo.
nunc tu sapienter loquere neque amatorie.

DEM   quid stamus? quin ergo imus atque opsonium
curamus, pulchre ut simus?

564 mane *add. Pylades*

DEM Is she in your house?

LYS What do you think?

DEM What if I have a look?

LYS Why are you in a rush? Wait.

DEM What should I do?   565

LYS Mind you think about what needs to be done.

DEM What should I think about? I believe what needs to be
     done is that I enter there.[21]

LYS Is that so, you wether? You should enter?

DEM What else should I do?

LYS First listen and pay attention. There's still something I
     think you should do first: if you enter there now, you'll   570
     want to embrace her, chat with her, and kiss her.

DEM You're completely familiar with my plan. You know what
     I'm going to do.

LYS You'll go wrong.

DEM You can go wrong with the object of your love?

LYS You should kiss her all the less. On an empty stomach,
     with stinking breath, you goaty old man would kiss a   575
     woman? In order to make her throw up when you ap-
     proach her? (*with sarcasm*) I do know that you're in love
     when you point that out to me.

DEM What if I do this one thing, then? If you think it's a good
     idea, let's get hold of some cook to cook lunch here at   580
     your place till the evening.

LYS There, that's what I think. Now you talk like a wise man
     and not like a lover.

DEM Why are we standing around? Why don't we go then and
     sort out the food in order to have a lovely time? (*turns to
     the right*)

---

[21] Double meaning: "enter the house" and "have sex."

LYS   equidem te sequor.
        atque hercle inuenies tu locum illi, si sapis:

585   nullum hercle praeter hunc diem illa apud med erit.
        metuo ego uxorem, cras si rure redierit
        ne illam hic offendat.

DEM   res parata est, sequere me.

III. iv: CHARINVS. EVTYCHVS

CHAR sumne ego homo miser, qui nusquam bene queo quies-
        cere?
        si domi sum, foris est animus, sin foris sum, animus domi
        est.

590   ita mi in pectore atque in corde facit amor incendium:
        ni ex oculis lacrumae defendant, iam ardeat credo caput.
        spem teneo, salutem amisi; redeat an non nescio:
        si opprimit pater quod dixit, exulatum abiit salus;
        sin sodalis quod promisit fecit, non abiit salus.

595   sed tamendem si podagrosis pedibus esset Eutychus,
        iam a portu rediisse potuit. id illi uitium maxumum est
        quod nimis tardus est aduorsum mei animi sententiam.

598   sed isne est quem currentem uideo? ipsus est. ibo ob-
        uiam.

[598ᵃ   diuom atque hominum quae speratrix atque era eadem
        es hominibus,

598ᵇ   spem speratam quom optulisti hanc mihi, tibi gratis ago.]

599   nunc, quod restat—ei disperii! uoltus neutiquam huius
        placet;

600   tristis cedit (pectus ardet, haereo), quassat caput.
        Eutyche!

587 est *P*, erit *Enk*
598ᵃ-98ᵇ Ω *inseruit uersus 842 et 843, quos hoc loco del. Acidalius*
600 incedit *P*, cedit *Bothe*

LYS   I'm following you. And you'll find a place for her if you're
wise: she won't be with me for a single day beyond today. 585
I'm afraid that my wife will find her here if she comes
back from the country estate tomorrow.

DEM Everything is prepared, follow me.

Exeunt DEMIPHO and LYSIMACHUS to the right.
Enter CHARINUS from his home.

CHAR Aren't I a wretch? I can't find a good rest anywhere. If I'm
at home, my mind is outside, if I'm outside, my mind is at
home. That's how love is stoking up a fire in my breast 590
and in my heart: if the tears from my eyes didn't fend it
off, I think my head would be on fire already. I have hope,
but I've lost salvation; whether it'll return or not I don't
know. If my father seizes the opportunity to do what he
said, my salvation has gone into exile; but if my comrade
has done what he promised, my salvation hasn't gone.
But even if Eutychus had gouty feet, he could have re- 595
turned from the harbor by now. It's his greatest fault that
he's too slow, against my heart's wishes.

Enter EUTYCHUS from the left.

But isn't that him who I can see running? It is. I'll go and
meet him. [You who are the engenderer of hope for
gods and men and also the mistress of men, I thank you
for bringing me this hoped-for hope.] The fact that he's
standing there now—oh no, I'm dead! I don't like his face
at all. He's walking along looking depressed (my breast is 600
on fire, I'm stuck), he's shaking his head. Eutychus!

EVT   eu, Charine!

CHAR   prius quam recipias anhelitum,
uno uerbo eloquere: ubi ego sum? hicine an apud mor-
tuos?

EVT   neque apud mortuos neque hic es.

CHAR   saluos sum, immortalitas
mihi data est: hic emit illam, pulchre os subleuit patri.

605   impetrabilior qui uiuat nullus est. dice, opsecro:
si neque hic neque Acherunti sum, ubi sum?

EVT   nusquam gentium.

CHAR disperii, illaec interemit me modo oratio.
odiosa est oratio, quom rem agas longinquom loqui.
quicquid est, ad capita rerum perueni.

EVT   primum omnium:

610   periimus.

CHAR   quin tu illud potius nuntias quod nescio?

EVT   mulier alienata est aps te.

CHAR   Eutyche, capital facis.

EVT   qui?

CHAR   quia aequalem et sodalem, liberum ciuem, enicas.

EVT   ne di sirint!

CHAR   demisisti gladium in iugulum: iam cadam.

EVT   quaeso hercle, animum ne desponde.

CHAR   nullust quem despondeam.

615   loquere porro aliam malam rem. quoi est empta?

EVT   nescio.
iam addicta atque abducta erat, quom ad portum uenio.

CHAR   uae mihi!
montis tu quidem mali in me ardentis iam dudum iacis.
perge, excrucia, carnufex, quandoquidem occepisti se-
mel.

EUT (*in low spirits*) Oh good! It's you, Charinus.

CHAR Before you catch your breath, tell me in one word: where am I? Here or among the dead?

EUT You're neither among the dead nor here.

CHAR I'm safe, I've been given immortality:[22] he's bought her, he's tricked my father beautifully. No man alive is more 605 efficient. Tell me, please: if I'm neither here nor in the Underworld, where am I?

EUT Nowhere at all.

CHAR I'm done for, that speech just killed me. A speech is hateful, talking at length when you're busy. Whatever it is, come to the main points.

EUT First of all: we're dead. 610

CHAR Why don't you announce instead what I don't know?

EUT The woman's been taken away from you.

CHAR Eutychus, you're committing a capital offense.

EUT How so?

CHAR Because you're killing your contemporary and comrade, a free citizen.

EUT May the gods forbid!

CHAR You've thrust a sword down my throat: now I'm going to fall.

EUT Please, don't give up hope.

CHAR There's none I could give up. Tell me another piece of 615 bad news. Who was she bought for?

EUT I don't know. She'd already been sold and led away when I came to the harbor.

CHAR Bad luck to me! You've been throwing burning mountains of misery onto me for a while already. Continue, torture me, you butcher, now that you've started.

---

[22] Charinus believes that if he is neither here nor in the Underworld, he must be in heaven.

[EVT non tibi istuc magis diuidiae est, quam mihi hodie fuit.
620 CHAR dic, quis emit?

EVT   nescio hercle.

CHAR   hem istucine est operam dare
      bonum sodalem?

EVT   quid me facere uis?

CHAR   idem quod me uides,
      ut pereas. quin percontatu's hominis quae facies foret
      qui illam emisset: eo si pacto posset indagarier
      mulier? heu me miserum!

EVT   flere omitte, istuc quod nunc agis.]
625 EVT quid ego feci?

CHAR   perdidisti me et fidem mecum tuam.

EVT di sciunt culpam meam istanc non esse ullam.

CHAR   eugepae!
      deos apsentis testis memoras: qui ego istuc credam tibi?

EVT quia tibi in manu est quod credas, ego quod dicam, id mi
      in manu est.

CHAR de istac re argutus es, ut par pari respondeas,
630   ad mandata claudus, caecus, mutus, mancus, debilis.
      promittebas te os sublinere meo patri: egomet credidi
      homini docto rem mandare, is lapidi mando maxumo.

EVT quid ego facerem?

CHAR   quid tu faceres? men rogas? requireres,
      rogitares quis esset aut unde esset, qua prosapia,
635   ciuisne esset an peregrinus.

EVT   ciuem esse aibant Atticum.

619–24 *secl. Leo ut a retractatore scriptum* (620–24 *iam Ritschl secluserat*)

[EUT That's no greater agony for you than it was for me today.

CHAR Tell me, who bought her?   620

EUT I really don't know.

CHAR Hey, do you call that a good comrade making an effort?

EUT What do you want me to do?

CHAR The same thing you can see me doing: perish. Why didn't you inquire what the chap who'd bought her looked like? Perhaps she could have been found this way. Poor, wretched me!

EUT Stop crying, as you are now.]

EUT What have I done?   625

CHAR You've ruined me and the confidence I had in you.

EUT The gods know that that is no fault of my own.

CHAR Goodness! You call the gods as your witnesses, even though they're absent. How can I believe you in that?

EUT Because[23] what you believe is in your hand, and what I say is in mine.

CHAR You're witty in that matter, managing to give me tit for tat, but as for my commission you're lame, blind, dumb, 630 crippled, maimed. You promised to trick my father. I believed I was putting a clever man in charge of my business, yet I put the greatest blockhead ever in charge.

EUT What should I have done?

CHAR What should you have done? You're asking me? You should have inquired and asked who he was or where he was from, from what family, and whether he was a citizen 635 or a foreigner.

EUT They said he was an Athenian citizen.

[23] Charinus asks "how" in the meaning "why" and intends the question as a rhetorical one, but Eutychus takes him literally.

81

CHAR ubi habitaret inuenires saltem, si nomen nequis.

EVT nemo aiebat scire.

CHAR   at saltem hominis faciem exquireres.

EVT feci.

CHAR   qua forma esse aiebant, ‹Eutyche›?

EVT   ego dicam tibi:

     canum, uarum, uentriosum, bucculentum, breuiculum,

640   subnigris oculis, oblongis malis, pansam aliquantulum.

CHAR non hominem mi sed thesaurum nescioquem memoras
      mali.

     numquid est quod dicas aliud de illo?

EVT   tantum, quod sciam.

CHAR edepol ne ille oblongis malis mihi dedit magnum malum.

     non possum durare, certum est exulatum hinc ire me.

645   sed quam capiam ciuitatem cogito potissumum:

     Megares, Eretriam, Corinthum, Chalcidem, Cretam,
      Cyprum,

     Sicyonem, Cnidum, Zacynthum, Lesbiam, Boeotiam?

EVT quor istuc coeptas consilium?

CHAR   quia enim me afflictat amor.

EVT quid tu ais? quid quom illuc quo nunc ire paritas ueneris,

650   si ibi amare forte occipias atque item eius sit inopia,

     iam inde porro aufugies, deinde item illinc, si item eue-
      nerit?

     quis modus tibi exilio tandem eueniet, qui finis fugae?

     quae patria aut domus tibi stabilis esse poterit? dic mihi.

     cedo, si hac urbe abis, amorem te hic relicturum putas?

---

638 Eutyche *add. Bothe*

---

[24] Lit. "a big thrashing." In the Latin there is a pun on *māla* "jaw"
and *mǎlum* "thrashing."

CHAR At least you should have found out where he lives, if you
      can't find out his name.

EUT   They all said they didn't know.

CHAR But at least you should have inquired what he looked like.

EUT   I did.

CHAR What did they say he looked like, Eutychus?

EUT   I'll tell you: gray, bowlegged, with a big belly and fat
      cheeks, shortish, with blackish eyes, long jaws, and a little   640
      splay-footed.

CHAR You're not describing a man to me, but some storehouse
      of trouble. Is there anything else you can say about him?

EUT   That's all, so far as I know.

CHAR That man with his long jaws has really given me long
      suffering.[24] I can't endure it, I'm resolved to go into ex-
      ile. But I'm not sure which state I'd best seek: Megara,   645
      Eretria, Corinth, Chalcis, Crete, Cyprus, Sicyon, Cni-
      dus, Zacynthus, Lesbos, or Boeotia?[25]

EUT   Why are you adopting this plan?

CHAR Because love is vexing me.

EUT   What do you say? When you've arrived where you're pre-
      paring to go now, what will happen if by chance you fall in   650
      love there and don't have access to the object of your
      love? Will you flee further from there, and then in the
      same way from there, if the same thing happens? What
      end will there ever be to your exile, what finish to your
      flight? What country or home can ever be stable for you?
      Tell me. Speak, if you leave this city, do you think you'll

[25] Megara lies to the west of Athens. Eretria is in Euboea, the cap-
ital of which is Chalcis. Sicyon is close to Corinth and Cnidus is in Caria.
Zacynthus, like Lesbos, is a Greek island.

655   si id fore ita sat animo acceptum est, certum id, pro certo
        si habes,
     quanto te satiust rus aliquo abire, ibi esse, ibi uiuere
     adeo dum illius te cupiditas atque amor missum facit?
CHAR iam dixisti?
EVT   dixi.
CHAR   frustra dixti. hoc mihi certissumum est.
     eo domum, patrem atque matrem ut meos salutem,
        postea
660   clam patrem patria hac effugiam aut aliquid capiam con-
        sili.
EVT   ut corripuit se repente atque abiit! heu misero mihi!
     si ille abierit, mea factum omnes dicent esse ignauia.
     certum est praeconum iubere iam quantum est condu-
        cier,
     qui illam inuestigent, qui inueniant. post ad praetorem
        ilico
665   ibo, orabo ut conquistores det mi in uicis omnibus;
     nam mihi nil relicti quicquam aliud iam esse intellego.

ACTVS IV

IV. i: DORIPPA. SYRA

DOR   quoniam a uiro ad me rus aduenit nuntius
     rus non iturum, feci ego ingenium meum,
     reueni, ut illum persequar qui me fugit.
670   sed anum non uideo consequi nostram Syram.

---

26 One of the chief legal officials at Rome.

leave your love behind here? If you feel assured that this   655
will be the case, if this is certain or as good as certain, how
much better is it for you to go somewhere in the country,
remain there, and live there until your desire and love for
her lets go of you?

CHAR Have you finished speaking now?

EUT I have finished speaking.

CHAR You've spoken in vain. This is my firm decision. I'm going
home to greet my father and mother, then I'll flee from   660
this country behind my father's back or (*darkly*) take
some other counsel.

Exit CHARINUS into his house.

EUT How suddenly he hurried off and went away! Poor,
wretched me! If he goes away, everybody will say it hap-
pened because of my idleness. I'm resolved to have all
the town criers hired so that they may look for him and
find him. Then I'll go to the praetor[26] at once and request   665
that he give me inspectors in each district: I understand
that I have nothing else left.

Exit EUTYCHUS to the right.

ACT FOUR

*Enter DORIPPA from the left, followed at some distance by
SYRA, who is carrying a big load.*

DOR As the message from my husband reached me in the
country that he wouldn't come out to our estate, I fol-
lowed my instinct and returned to get hold of the man
who is trying to avoid me. But I can't see our old servant   670

		atque eccam incedit tandem. quin is ocius?
	SYRA	nequeo mecastor, tantum hoc onerist quod fero.
	DOR	quid oneris?
	SYRA	annos octoginta et quattuor:
		et eodem accedit seruitus, sudor, sitis:
675		simul haec quae porto deprimunt.
	DOR	aliquid cedo
		qui ⟨Apollinis⟩ uicini nostri aram augeam.
		da sane hanc uirgam lauri. abi tu intro.
	SYRA	eo.
	DOR	Apollo, quaeso te ut des pacem propitius,
		salutem et sanitatem nostrae familiae,
680		meoque ut parcas gnato pace propitius.
	SYRA	disperii, perii misera, uae miserae mihi!
	DOR	satin tu sana es, opsecro? quid eiulas?
	SYRA	Dorippa, mea Dorippa.
	DOR	quid clamas? cedo.
	SYRA	nescioquae est mulier intus hic in aedibus.
685	DOR	quid, "mulier"?
	SYRA	mulier meretrix.
	DOR	ueron serio?
	SYRA	nimium scis sapere ruri quae non manseris.
687		quamuis insipiens poterat persentiscere
687ᵃ		***
688		illam esse amicam tui uiri bellissumi.
	DOR	credo mecastor.

676 hanc *P*, Apollinis *Havet*
683 obsecro *P*, cedo *Goetz*
687ᵃ *uersus deest in P, legi non potest in A*

Syra following. (*turns around*) And look, she's coming at
last. Why won't you go faster?

SYRA I really can't, the burden I bear is so great.

DOR What burden?

SYRA Eighty-four years; and to this is added slavery, sweat,
and thirst. At the same time the things I'm carrying are   675
weighing me down.

DOR Give me something to honor the altar of our neighbor
Apollo with. Do give me this branch of laurel. (*takes it*)
Go inside.

SYRA Yes.

Exit SYRA into the house of Lysimachus.

DOR (*praying at the altar*) Apollo, I ask you to give us peace in
your mercy, health and well-being for our household,
and to spare my son through your peace in your mercy.   680

Reenter SYRA from the house, agitated.

SYRA I'm dead and done for, wretch that I am, poor, wretched
me!

DOR Please, are you in your right mind? Why are you wailing?

SYRA Dorippa, my dear Dorippa!

DOR Why are you shouting? Tell me.

SYRA There's some woman inside the house here.

DOR What, "a woman"?   685

SYRA A woman who is a prostitute.

DOR Really and truly?

SYRA You've shown that you behave wisely by not staying on
the country estate. Any idiot could realize *** that she's
the mistress of your most charming husband.

DOR I do believe it.

87

SYRA   i hac mecum, ut uideas simul
690   tuam Alcumenam paelicem, Iuno mea.
DOR   ecastor uero istuc eo quantum potest.

IV. ii: LYSIMACHVS

LYS   parumne est malai rei quod amat Demipho,
        ni sumptuosus insuper etiam siet?
        decem si uocasset summos ad cenam uiros,
695   nimium opsonauit. sed coquos, quasi in mari
        solet hortator remiges hortarier,
        ita hortabatur. egomet conduxi coquom.
        sed eum demiror non uenire ut iusseram.
        sed hinc quinam a nobis exit? aperitur foris.

IV. iii: DORIPPA. LYSIMACHVS

700 DOR   miserior mulier me nec fiet nec fuit,
        tali uiro quae nupserim. heu miserae mihi!
        em quoi te et tua quae tu habeas commendes uiro,
        em quoi decem talenta dotis detuli,
        haec ut uiderem, ut ferrem has contumelias!
705 LYS   perii hercle! rure iam rediit uxor mea:
        uidisse credo mulierem in aedibus.
        sed quae loquatur exaudire hinc non queo.
        accedam propius.
DOR   uae miserae mi!
LYS   immo mihi.
DOR   disperii!

     699 quinam hinc *P, transp. Schoell*
     706 mulierem ‹illam› *Ritschl*

SYRA Come this way with me so that at the same time as me you
      may see your rival Alcumena, my Juno.[27]   690

DOR   Yes, truly, I'll go there as quickly as possible.

Exeunt DORIPPA and SYRA into their house.
Enter LYSIMACHUS from the right.

LYS   Is it not enough of a bad thing that Demipho is in love,
      without being extravagant into the bargain? Even if he'd
      invited ten dignitaries to dinner he's bought too much.   695
      But as for the cooks, he was spurring them on like a cox-
      swain spurs on rowers on the sea. I hired a cook myself.
      But I'm surprised he isn't coming as I'd told him to. But
      who is coming out from our place? The door is opening.

Enter DORIPPA and SYRA from the house without seeing any-
one.

DOR   No woman will be or has ever been more wretched than   700
      me because I married such a husband. Poor, wretched
      me! Here is the man to whom you can entrust yourself
      and your possessions! Here is the man to whom I brought
      ten talents in dowry! Just in order to see this, just in order
      to bear these humiliations!

LYS   I'm dead! My wife has already returned from our country   705
      estate. I believe she's seen the woman in the house. But I
      can't hear from here what she's talking about. I'll get
      closer.

DOR   Poor, wretched me!

LYS   (*aside*) No, me.

DOR   I'm done for!

      [27] Juno is Jupiter's wife, Alcumena was one of his mistresses.

	LYS	equidem hercle oppido perii miser!
710		uidit. ut te omnes, Demipho, di perduint!
	DOR	pol hoc est ire quod rus meus uir noluit.
	LYS	quid nunc ego faciam nisi uti adeam atque alloquar?
		iubet saluere suos uir uxorem suam.
		urbani fiunt rustici?
	DOR	pudicius
715		faciunt quam illi qui non fiunt rustici.
	LYS	num quid delinquont rustici?
	DOR	ecastor minus
		quam urbani et multo minus mali quaerunt sibi.
718	LYS	quid autem urbani deliquerunt? dic mihi,
721		cupio hercle scire.
	DOR	sed tu me temptas sciens.
719		quoia illa mulier intust?
	LYS	uidistine eam?
720	DOR	uidi.
	LYS	quoia ea sit rogitas?
	DOR	resciscam tamen.
722	LYS	uin dicam quoia est? illa—illa edepol—uae mihi!
		nescio quid dicam.
	DOR	haeres.
	LYS	hau uidi magis.
	DOR	quin dicis?
	LYS	quin si liceat—
	DOR	dictum oportuit.
725	LYS	non possum, ita instas; urges quasi pro noxio.
	DOR	scio, innoxiu's.
	LYS	audacter quam uis dicito.
	DOR	dice igitur.

721 *post* 718 *pos. Bothe*

LYS   *(aside)* And I am completely dead! She's seen her. May all   710
       the gods ruin you, Demipho!

DOR   This is the reason why my husband wouldn't go to our
       country estate.

LYS   *(aside)* What should I do now except approach and greet
       her? *(to Dorippa)* Her husband is greeting his wife. Are
       the country folks becoming city dwellers?

DOR   They behave more decently than those who don't be-   715
       come country folks.

LYS   Are the country folks committing any offenses?

DOR   Fewer than the city dwellers and they're looking much
       less for trouble.

LYS   But what offense have the city dwellers committed? Tell
       me, I really wish to know.

DOR   Well, you're testing me deliberately. Who does that
       woman inside belong to?

LYS   Have you seen her?

DOR   I have.   720

LYS   You ask who she belongs to?

DOR   I'll find out anyway.

LYS   Do you want me to say who she belongs to? She—yes,
       she—*(aside)* bad luck to me! I don't know what to say.

DOR   You're stuck.

LYS   *(trying to laugh it off)* A likely story.

DOR   Why don't you tell me?

LYS   Well, if I were allowed to—

DOR   *(interrupting)* You ought to have said it already.

LYS   I can't, what with you pushing me so much; you're pursu-   725
       ing me as if I were a delinquent.

DOR   *(with sarcasm)* I know, you're guiltless.

LYS   You can say that as boldly as you wish.

DOR   Tell me then.

LYS		dicam.
DOR		atqui dicundum est tamen.
LYS	illa est—etiam uis nomen dicam?	
DOR		nil agis,

manufesto teneo in noxia.

LYS		qua noxia?
730	istaquidem illa est.	
DOR		quae illa est?
LYS		illa—
DOR		quoia ea est?
LYS	iam—si nihil usus esset, iam non dicerem.	
732–35	DOR	non tu scis quae sit illa?
	LYS	immo iam scio:

de istac sum iudex captus.

DOR   iudex? iam scio:
nunc tu in consilium istam aduocauisti tibi.

LYS	enim sic: sequestro mihi data est.
DOR	intellego.
LYS	nihil hercle istius quicquam est.
DOR	numero purigas.
740 LYS	nimium negoti repperi. enim uero haereo.

      IV. iv: COQVOS. LYSIMACHVS. DORIPPA. SYRA

CO   agite ite actutum, nam mi amatori seni
     coquenda est cena. atque, quom recogito,
     nobis coquenda est, non <quoi con>ducti sumus.

730 iohia P, quoia east Leo   738 immo P, enim Lindsay
743 <cui con>ducti Camerarius

---

[28] She is deriding him; an arbitrator cannot ask someone for advice who is involved in the argument in any way.

LYS	I'll tell you.	
DOR	You'll have to tell me anyway.	
LYS	She is—do you also want me to tell you her name?	
DOR	You're getting nowhere, I've caught you redhanded in a crime.	
LYS	What crime? She's that one.	730
DOR	Which one?	
LYS	She—	
DOR	(*interrupting*) Who does she belong to?	
LYS	Now— (*changing tactic*) if it weren't necessary I wouldn't tell you at present.	
DOR	You don't know who she is?	735
LYS	No, I do know it now: I was appointed as arbitrator about her.	
DOR	As arbitrator? I know: now you've called on her to give you counsel.[28]	
LYS	I assure you, it's like this: she was entrusted to me in my function as depositary.[29]	
DOR	I understand.	
LYS	It's nothing of that sort.	
DOR	You're making excuses too soon.	
LYS	(*aside*) I've found too much trouble. I'm really stuck.	740

Enter a COOK from the right, followed by assistants carrying provisions and cooking utensils.

CO	(*to the assistants*) Come on, follow me this instant: I have to cook dinner for a lovesick old man. And when I think about it, I have to cook it for us, not for the man we're

---

[29] The *sequester* or depositary can watch over things as well as slaves.

		nam qui amat quod amat si habet, id habet pro cibo:
745		uidere, amplecti, osculari, alloqui;
		sed nos confido onustos redituros domum.
		ite hac. sed eccum qui nos conduxit senex.
	LYS	ecce autem perii, coquos adest!
	CO	aduenimus.
	LYS	abi.
	CO	quid, abeam?
	LYS	st! abi.
	CO	abeam?
	LYS	abi.
750	CO	non estis cenaturi?
	LYS	iam saturi sumus.
	CO	sed—
	LYS	interii!
	DOR	quid ais tu? etiamne haec illi tibi
		iusserunt ferri, quos inter iudex datu's?
	CO	haecin tua est amica quam dudum mihi
		te amare dixti, quom opsonabas?
	LYS	non taces?
755	CO	satis scitum filum mulieris. uerum hercle anet.
	LYS	abin dierectus?
	CO	hau mala est.
	LYS	at tu malu's.
	CO	scitam hercle opinor concubinam hanc.
	LYS	quin abis?
		non ego sum qui te dudum conduxi.
	CO	quid est?
		immo hercle tu istic ipsu's.
	LYS	uae misero mihi!

757 q—*A*, non abis *P* (quin abis *etiam in* 778)

94

hired for, because if a lovesick man has the object of his love, he regards it as food to look at her, embrace her, kiss 745 her, address her. But I'm confident we'll return home heavily laden. Go this way. But look, here's the old man who hired us.

LYS (*aside*) But look, I'm dead, the cook's here!

CO We've arrived.

LYS Go away.

CO What? I should go away?

LYS Hush! Go away.

CO I should go away?

LYS Go away.

CO Aren't you going to have dinner? 750

LYS We're already full.

CO But—

LYS (*interrupting*) I'm dead!

DOR (*to Lysimachus*) What do you say? Did the people between whom you were appointed as arbitrator also have all this brought to you?

CO (*to Lysimachus*) Is this your mistress whom a while ago, when you were doing the shopping, you told me you're in love with?

LYS Won't you be quiet?

CO Quite a fine figure of a woman, but she's getting on. 755

LYS Won't you go and be hanged?

CO She isn't bad.

LYS But you are bad.

CO I think she's a fine concubine.

LYS Why won't you go away? I'm not the one who hired you a while ago.

CO What's that? No, you yourself are the one.

LYS Poor, wretched me!

760 CO nempe uxor ruri est tua, quam dudum dixeras
         te odisse [aeque] atque anguis.
    LYS   egone istuc dixi tibi?
    CO   mihi quidem hercle.
    LYS   ita me amabit Iuppiter,
         uxor, ut ego illud numquam dixi.
    DOR   etiam negas?
         palam istaec fiunt te me odisse.
    LYS   quin nego.
765 CO non, non te odisse aibat sed uxorem suam;
         et uxorem suam ruri esse aiebat.
    LYS   haec ea est.
         quid mihi molestu's?
    CO   quia nouisse me negas;
         nisi metuis tu istanc.
    LYS   sapio, nam mihi unica est.
    CO   uin me experiri?
    LYS   nolo.
    CO   mercedem cedo.
770 LYS cras petito; dabitur. nunc abi.
    DOR   heu miserae mihi!
    LYS nunc ego uerum illud uerbum esse experior uetus:
         aliquid mali esse propter uicinum malum.
    CO   quor hic astamus?
    LYS   quin abis?
    CO   incommodi
         si quid tibi euenit, id non est culpa mea.
775 LYS quin me eradicas miserum.

761 aeque *AB*, aeque atque *CD*, atque *Seyffert*
773 quin abimus incommodi Ω, ‹LYS› quin abis? ‹CO› incommodi

96

CO	Surely your wife is in the country, who you said a while 760
	ago you hate as much as you hate snakes.
LYS	Did I say that to you?
CO	Yes, to me.
LYS	As truly as Jupiter will love me, my wife, I never said that.
DOR	You still deny it? It's coming out into the open that you
	hate me.
LYS	No, I deny that.
CO	(*to Dorippa*) No, he said he hated his wife, not you; and 765
	he said his wife is in the country.
LYS	This is her. Why are you being a nuisance to me?
CO	Because you say you don't know me; unless you're afraid
	of that woman.
LYS	That's wise of me: she's my one and only.
CO	Do you want me to go to law?
LYS	No.
CO	Give me my pay.
LYS	Ask for it tomorrow. You will get it. Now go away. 770
DOR	Poor, wretched me!
LYS	Now I realize that that old proverb is true: a bad neighbor
	brings bad luck.
CO	(*to his attendants*) Why are we standing here?
LYS	Why won't you go away?
CO	If you've had any inconvenience, it's not through my
	fault.
LYS	You're uprooting me totally, a poor wretch. 775

Bothe, quin abimus nos? secus *Leo* (*qui* incommodi *uariam lectionem*
ad secus *insequentis uersus ascriptam esse putat*)
    774 quid *P*, quid secus *A*

CO   scio iam quid uelis:
nemp' me hinc abire uis.

LYS   uolo inquam.

CO   abibitur.
drachmam dato.

LYS   dabitur.

CO   dari ergo sis iube.
dari potest interea dum illi ponunt.

LYS   quin abis?
potine ut molestus ne sis?

CO   agite apponite
780   opsonium istuc ante pedes illi seni.
haec uasa aut mox aut cras iubebo aps te peti.
sequimini.

LYS   fortass' te illum mirari coquom
quod uenit atque haec attulit. dicam id quid est.

DOR   non miror si quid damni facis aut flagiti.
785   nec pol ego patiar sic me nuptam tam male
measque in aedis sic scorta obductarier.
Syra, i, rogato meum patrem uerbis meis
ut ueniat ad me iam simul tecum.

SYRA   eo.

LYS   nescis negoti quid sit, uxor, opsecro.
790   conceptis uerbis iam ius iurandum dabo
me numquam quicquam cum illa—iamne abiit Syra?

CO   Now I know what you want: surely you want me to go
away.

LYS   Yes, I do!

CO   One shall go away. Give me a drachma.

LYS   You'll get one.

CO   Then give the order for me to be given one, please. I can
get it while those people are putting down their things.

LYS   Why won't you go away? Are you capable of not being a
nuisance?

CO   (*to his attendants*) Come on, put the provisions there in   780
front of the feet of that old chap. (*to Lysimachus, as they
obey*) I'll have these vessels demanded back from you a
bit later or tomorrow. (*to his attendants*) Follow me.

Exit COOK with his attendants to the right.

LYS   Perhaps you're surprised that that cook came and
brought all this here. I'll tell you what it is.

DOR   I'm not surprised if you're causing some loss or disgrace.
Goodness, I won't tolerate being married so badly and   785
prostitutes being brought into my own house before my
eyes like this. Syra, go ask my father in my name to come
to me along with you at once.

SYRA   Yes.

Exit SYRA to the right.

LYS   You don't know what's going on, my wife, please. I'll   790
swear a solemn oath now that I've never done anything
with her by way of—has Syra left already? (*looks around*)

Exit DORIPPA into her house.

perii hercle! ecce autem haec abiit. uae misero mihi!
at te, uicine, di deaeque perduint,
cum tua amica cumque amationibus!
795   suspicione impleuit me indignissume,
conciuit hostis domi: uxor acerruma est.
ibo ad forum atque Demiphoni haec eloquar,
me istanc capillo protracturum esse in uiam,
nisi hinc abducit quo uolt ex hisce aedibus.
800   uxor, heus uxor! quamquam tu irata es mihi,
iubeas, si sapias, haec intro auferrier:
eadem licebit mox cenare rectius.

IV. V: SYRA. EVTYCHVS

SYRA era quo me misit, ad patrem, non est domi:
rus abiisse aibant. nunc domum renuntio.
805 EVT defessus sum urbem totam peruenarier:
nihil inuestigo quicquam de illa muliere.
sed mater rure rediit, nam uideo Syram
astare ante aedis. Syra!
SYRA   quis est qui me uocat?
EVT erus atque alumnus tuos sum.
SYRA   salue, alumnule.
810 EVT iam mater rure rediit? responde mihi.
SYRA cum quidem salute familiai maxuma.
EVT quid istuc negoti est?

801 ⟨hinc⟩ intro *Ritschl*
809 alumne *P*, alumnule *Schoell*, alumne mi *Pylades*

100

I'm done for! (*turns back*) But look, my wife's left. Poor, wretched me! Well, may the gods and goddesses ruin you, neighbor, with your mistress and your affairs! He's 795
swamped me with suspicion in a most outrageous way, he's stirred up enemies at home; my wife is the harshest. I'll go to the market and tell Demipho that I'm going to drag her into the street by her hair unless he takes her away from this house here to wherever he wants. (*calling* 800
into the house) My wife, hey there, my wife! Even though you're angry with me, you'd do well to have this here brought inside; this way we can soon have a better dinner.

Exit LYSIMACHUS to the right.
Enter SYRA from the right.

SYRA Where my mistress sent me, to her father, well, he's not at home. They said he'd gone to the country. Now I'll bring this news back home.

Enter EUTYCHUS from the right.

EUT I'm exhausted from chasing through the whole city. 805
I can't find out anything about that woman. But my mother's come back from the country, since I can see Syra standing in front of the house. Syra!

SYRA Who is it that's calling me?

EUT It's your master and nursling.

SYRA Hello, my little nursling.

EUT Has my mother come back from the country? Answer 810
me.

SYRA Yes, and she has brought great well-being to our household.

EUT What's the trouble?

SYRA		tuos pater bellissumus
	amicam adduxit intro in aedis.	
EVT		quo modo?
SYRA	adueniens mater rure eam offendit domi.	
815 EVT	pol hau censebam istarum esse operarum patrem.	
	etiam nunc mulier intust?	
SYRA		etiam.
EVT		sequere me.

IV. vi: SYRA

SYRA ecastor lege dura uiuont mulieres
     multoque iniquiore miserae quam uiri.
     nam si uir scortum duxit clam uxorem suam,
820   id si resciuit uxor, impune est uiro;
     uxor uirum si clam domo egressa est foras,
     uiro fit causa, exigitur matrimonio.
     utinam lex esset eadem quae uxori est uiro;
     nam uxor contenta est, quae bona est, uno uiro:
825   qui minus uir una uxore contentus siet?
     ecastor faxim, si itidem plectantur uiri,
     si quis clam uxorem duxerit scortum suam,
     ut illae exiguntur quae in se culpam commerent,
     plures uiri sint uidui quam nunc mulieres.

ACTVS V

V. i: CHARINVS

830 CHAR limen superum<que> inferumque, salue, simul autem
     uale:

830 superum<que> *Ritschl*

SYRA Your terribly charming father has brought a mistress into the house.

EUT How so?

SYRA On her arrival from the country estate your mother found her at home.

EUT Goodness, I didn't think my father was one to do that sort 815 of thing. Is the woman still inside?

SYRA Yes.

EUT Follow me.

Exit EUTYCHUS into his house.

SYRA Women really do live under a harsh and much unfairer law than men: if a man hires a prostitute behind his wife's back and the wife finds out about it, the husband goes un- 820 punished. If a wife leaves the house behind her husband's back, the man thereby gets grounds to throw her out of the marriage. Would that there was the same law for the husband as for the wife: a wife who is good is content with a single husband. Why should a husband be any less con- 825 tent with a single wife? If husbands were to be punished in the same way if one hires a prostitute behind his wife's back just as guilty women are thrown out, I'd bet there would now be more divorced men than women.

Exit SYRA into the house of Lysimachus.

ACT FIVE

Enter CHARINUS from his house, wearing a travel cloak with a belt and carrying a flask and a sword.

CHAR Lintel high and threshold low, greetings and farewell at 830

103

hunc hodie postremum extollo mea domo patria pedem.
usus, fructus, uictus, cultus iam mihi harunc aedium
interemptust, interfectust, alienatust. occidi!
di Penates meum parentum, familiai Lar pater,
835   uobis mando meum parentum rem bene ut tutemini.
ego mihi alios deos Penatis persequar, alium Larem,
aliam urbem, aliam ciuitatem: ab Atticis abhorreo;
nam ubi mores deteriores increbrescunt in dies,
ubi qui amici, qui infideles sint nequeas pernoscere
840   ubique id eripiatur animo tuo quod placeat maxume,
ibi quidem si regnum detur, non cupita est ciuitas.

V. ii: EVTYCHVS. CHARINVS

EVT   diuom atque hominum quae speratrix atque era eadem
       es hominibus,
spem speratam quom optulisti hanc mihi gratis ago.
ecquisnam deus est qui mea nunc laetus laetitia fuat?
845   domi erat quod quaeritabam: sex sodalis repperi,
uitam, amicitiam, ciuitatem, laetitiam, ludum, iocum;
eorum inuentu res simitu pessumas pessum dedi,
iram, inimicitiam, maerorem, lacrumas, exilium, ino-
       piam,
849   solitudinem, stultitiam, exitium, pertinaciam.
849ᵃ   ***
850   date, di, quaeso conueniundi mi eius celerem copiam.

839 ubique *BCD*, ubi qui *Palmerius*
842 speratrix *BCD*, spectatrix ç
849 *uersum del. Ribbeck*
849ᵃ *lacunam indicat Ritschl*

---

[30] The household gods, or Penates, were originally deities of the
store cupboard, while the Lar is another protective deity associated

the same time: today I'm lifting my foot out of my father's house for the last time. The ability to use, enjoy, live in, and inhabit this house is now taken away from me, ruined, removed. I'm done for! Household gods of my parents, father Lar[30] of my household, I entrust my parents' affairs to you so that you guard them well. I'll find myself other household gods and another Lar, another city, another country: I'm shunning all things Athenian. Yes, where worse habits increase day by day, where you can't distinguish which people are friends and which are faithless, and where what most pleases your heart is stolen from you, I don't desire citizenship there even if I were given kingship. 835 840

Enter EUTYCHUS from his house without noticing anyone.

EUT You who are the engenderer of hope for gods and men and also the mistress of men,[31] I thank you for bringing me this hoped-for hope. Is there any god who is as happy as I am happy now? What I was looking for was at home. I've found six comrades: life, friendship, citizenship,[32] joy, jubilation, jest. By finding them I destroyed the greatest evils at the same time: anger, enmity, sadness, tears, exile, lack, loneliness, folly, destruction, obstinacy. *** Gods, please give me the opportunity to meet him quickly. 845 850

---

with the household. Earlier the Lares were gods of the countryside, as is apparent from l. 865, where they protect the roads.

[31] Eutychus is addressing the goddess Fortuna.

[32] Citizenship is his comrade because he is bringing back a citizen, Charinus.

CHAR apparatus sum ut uidetis: abicio superbiam;
egomet mihi comes, calator, equos, agaso, armiger,
egomet sum mihi imperator, idem egomet mihi oboedio,
egomet mihi fero quod usust. o Cupido, quantus es!
855   nam tu quemuis confidentem facile tuis factis facis,
eundem ex confidente actutum diffidentem denuo.

EVT cogito quonam ego illum curram quaeritatum.

CHAR   certa rest
me usque quaerere illam quoquo hinc abducta est gen-
    tium;
nec mihi ulla opsistet amnis nec mons neque adeo mare
860   nec calor nec frigus metuo nec uentum nec grandinem;
imbrem perpetiar, laborem sufferam, solem, sitim;
non concedam nec quiescam usquam noctu nec dius
prius profecto quam aut amicam aut mortem inuesti-
    gauero.

EVT nescioquoia uox ad auris mi aduolauit.

CHAR   inuoco
865   uos, Lares uiales, ut me bene tutetis.

EVT   Iuppiter!
estne illic Charinus?

CHAR   ciues, bene ualete.

EVT   ilico
sta, Charine.

CHAR   qui me reuocat?

EVT   Spes, Salus, Victoria.

CHAR quid me uoltis?

EVT   ire tecum.

CHAR   alium comitem quaerite,
non amittunt hi me comites qui tenent.

EVT   qui sunt ei?
870 CHAR cura, miseria, aegritudo, lacrumae, lamentatio.

106

CHAR (*to the audience*) I am prepared as you see. I'm throwing
    away my pride: I myself am my companion, attendant,
    horse, stableboy, armor bearer; I myself am my com-
    mander and I myself obey me; I myself carry for myself
    what's needed. O Cupid, how mighty you are! You easily   855
    make anyone self-confident through your actions, and
    you turn the same person from self-confident to diffident
    again immediately.

EUT I'm thinking about where I should run to search for him.

CHAR (*still to the audience*) I'm resolved to search for her con-
    tinuously wherever she's been taken. No river, no moun-
    tain, no sea will stand in my way; I fear neither heat nor   860
    cold, neither wind nor hail. I'll bear the rain, tolerate toil,
    sun, and thirst. I shan't give in or ever rest by night or day
    until I've found either my girlfriend or my death.

EUT Someone's voice has flown to my ears.

CHAR I call on you, Lares of the ways, to guard me well.   865

EUT Jupiter! Isn't that Charinus?

CHAR Farewell, citizens. (*turns to the left*)

EUT Stand where you are, Charinus.

CHAR Who is calling me back?

EUT Hope, Salvation, Victory.

CHAR What do you want from me?

EUT To go with you.

CHAR Look for another companion; the companions who are
    clinging on to me won't let go of me.

EUT Who are they?

CHAR Worry, wretchedness, grief, tears, wailing.   870

871 EVT   repudia istos comites atque huc respice et reuortere.
872 CHAR siquidem mecum fabulari uis, supsequere.
    EVT   sta ilico.
887   sta ilico, ⟨nam⟩ amicus ⟨nunc⟩ aduenio multum beneuo-
          lens.
873 CHAR male facis properantem qui me commorare. sol abit.
874 EVT   si huc item properes ut istuc properas, facias rectius:
875   huc secundus uentus nunc est; cape modo uorsoriam:
          hic fauonius serenust, istic auster imbricus;
          hic facit tranquillitatem, iste omnis fluctus conciet.
          recipe te ad terram, Charine, huc. nonne ex aduorso ui-
          des
          nubis atra imberque ⟨ut⟩ instat? aspice ad sinisteram
880   caelum ut est splendore plenum atque ut di is⟨tuc uorti
          iubent⟩.
    CHAR religionem illic ⟨mi⟩ obiecit: recipiam me illuc.
    EVT   sapis.
          o Charine, contra pariter fer gradum et confer pedem,
          porge bracchium.
    CHAR   prehende. iam tenes?
    EVT   teneo.
    CHAR   tene.
884 EVT   quo nunc ibas?
    CHAR   exulatum.
    EVT   quid ibi faceres?
    CHAR   quod miser.

    887 *post* 872 *pos. Ritschl*   nam *add. Ritschl*   nunc *scripsi*
    879 ater *BCD,* atra ꞩ ut *add. Guyet* aspice non *CD,* aspiciae non *B,*
aspice ꞩ
    880 atque ut (ut *om. B*) detis / caelum ut est splendore (splendore
est *CD*) plenum exaduorso uides *P,* ex aduorso uides *ex* 878 *illapsum et*

EUT   Reject those companions, look back here, and turn back.

CHAR If you want to speak with me, follow me. (*begins to move left*)

EUT   Stand where you are. Stand where you are: I'm coming to you now as a friend who wants your very best.

CHAR It isn't right of you to delay me in my hurry. The sun is setting.

EUT   If you were to hurry here the same way you're hurrying there, you'd behave more appropriately: in this direction   875
there's a favorable wind now; just get hold of the rope to turn your sail. Here there's the cloudless westerly, there the rainy southerly. The one here brings calm, the one there stirs up all the waves. Return here to the shore, Charinus. Can't you see how a black cloud and rain are threatening from the direction you're facing? Look to the left, how the heaven is full of brightness and how the   880
gods are telling you to turn there.

CHAR He's given me scruples; I'll return there.

EUT   You're wise. Oh Charinus, step up toward me, move your foot here, and stretch out your arm.

CHAR (*doing so*) Take it. Are you holding it now?

EUT   (*grabbing it*) Yes.

CHAR Do.

EUT   Where were you going now?

CHAR Into exile.

EUT   What would you have done there?

CHAR What a wretch does.

---

atque ut detis *suo loco motum esse putat Ritschl*, detis in dei is<tuc uorti iubent> *mutat Leo*
    881 mi *add. Ritschl*

884[a]	EVT	st!
885		ne paue, restituam iam ego te in gaudio antiquo ut sies.
886		maxume quod uis audire, id audies, quod gaudeas.
888		tuam amicam—
	CHAR	quid eam?
	EVT	ubi sit ego scio.
	CHAR	tune, opsecro?
889	EVT	sanam et saluam.
	CHAR	ubi eam saluam?
	EVT	ego scio.
	CHAR	ego me mauelim.
890	EVT	potin ut animo sis tranquillo?
	CHAR	quid si mi animus fluctuat?
	EVT	ego istum in tranquillo, quieto, tuto sistam: ne time.
	CHAR	opsecro te, loquere ⟨propere⟩ ubi sit, ubi eam uideris.
		quid taces? dice. enicas me miserum tua reticentia.
	EVT	non longe hinc abest a nobis.
	CHAR	quin [ergo] commonstras, si uides?
895	EVT	non uideo hercle nunc, sed uidi modo.
	CHAR	quin ego uideam facis?
	EVT	faciam.
	CHAR	longum istuc amanti est.
	EVT	etiam metuis? omnia
		commonstrabo. amicior mi nullus uiuit atque is est
		qui illam habet neque est quoi magis me melius uelle ae-
		quom siet.
	CHAR	non curo istunc, de illa quaero.
	EVT	de illa ergo ego dico tibi.
900		sane hoc non in mentem uenit dudum, ut ubi ⟨sit dice-
		rem.⟩

892 propere *add. Ritschl*   894 ergo *del. Guyet*

110

EUT Hush! Stop being afraid, I'll restore you to your old joy 885
now. What you want to hear most, that you shall hear,
something to be happy about. Your girlfriend—

CHAR (*interrupting*) What about her?

EUT I know where she is.

CHAR Please, you do?

EUT Safe and sound.

CHAR Where is she sound?

EUT I know where.

CHAR I'd prefer to do so myself.

EUT Can't you have a calm mind? 890

CHAR What if my mind is being tossed about by the waves?

EUT I'll place it in a calm, quiet, safe place. Stop being afraid.

CHAR I beg you, tell me quickly where she is, where you've seen
her. Why are you silent? Tell me. You're killing me, poor
me, with your silence.

EUT She isn't far away from us. (*looks at his house*)

CHAR Why don't you show me if you can see her?

EUT I can't see her now, but I just did. 895

CHAR Why won't you let me see her?

EUT I will.

CHAR For a lover that's a long time.

EUT Are you still afraid? I'll show you everything. (*after a
pause*) No one's a closer friend to me than the one who
has her, and there isn't anyone toward whom I ought to
be better disposed.

CHAR I don't care about him, I'm asking you about the girl.

EUT Well, I'm telling you about the girl. Indeed, it didn't oc- 900
cur to me until now to tell you where she is.

---

895 quem *P*, quin ς
900 sit dicerem *add. Leo*

111

CHAR dic igitur, ubi illa est?

EVT in nostris aedibus.

CHAR aedis probas,
si tu uera dicis, pulchre aedificatas arbitro.
sed quid ego istuc credam? uidisti an de audito nuntias?

EVT egomet uidi.

CHAR quis eam adduxit ad uos, inque.

EVT ⟨tu⟩ rogas?

905 CHAR uera dicis.

EVT nil, Charine, te quidem quicquam pudet.
quid tua refert qui cum istac uenerit?

CHAR dum istic siet.

EVT est profecto.

CHAR opta ergo ob istunc nuntium quid uis tibi.

EVT quid si optabo?

CHAR deos orato ut eius faciant copiam.

EVT derides.

CHAR seruata res est demum, si illam uidero.

910 sed quin ornatum hunc reicio? heus! aliquis actutum huc foras
exite, illinc pallium mi efferte.

EVT em, nunc tu mi places.

CHAR optume aduenis, puere, cape chlamydem atque istic sta ilico,
ut, si haec non sint uera, inceptum hoc itiner perficere exsequar.

EVT non mihi credis?

CHAR omnia equidem credo quae dicis mihi.

915 sed quin intro ducis me ad eam, ut uideam?

EVT paulisper mane.

902 arbitro *BC*, arbitrio *D¹*, arbitror *D²*   904 tu *add. Lindsay*

112

CHAR Tell me then, where is she?

EUT In our house.

CHAR A good house, if you're telling the truth, I think, and well built. But why should I believe you in that? Have you seen her or are you telling me on hearsay?

EUT I've seen her myself.

CHAR Tell me who took her to you.

EUT You're asking?

CHAR You're telling the truth.   905

EUT Charinus, you have no shame at all. What business of yours is it who came with her?

CHAR So long as she's there.

EUT She really is.

CHAR Then on account of that message wish what you want for yourself.

EUT What if I do?

CHAR Pray to the gods that they may procure it for you.

EUT You're mocking me.

CHAR Things are safe at last if I see her. But why don't I throw   910 off this garment? (*calling into his house*) Hey there! Someone come out here right now and bring me my cloak from there. (*a boy comes with the regular cloak of Charinus*)

EUT There, now I like you.

CHAR You've come at the right time, boy, take my cape and stand where you are, so that I may continue to travel on this journey I've begun if this isn't true. (*changes outfits*)

EUT You don't believe me?

CHAR I believe you in everything you tell me. But why don't you   915 take me inside to her so that I may see her?

EUT (*embarrassed*) Wait a little.

CHAR quid manebo?

EVT tempus non est intro eundi.

CHAR enicas.

EVT non opus est, inquam, nunc intro te ire.

CHAR responde mihi,
qua causa?

EVT operae non est.

CHAR quor?

EVT quia non est illi commodum.

CHAR itane? commodum illi non est, quae me amat, quam ego
contra amo?

920 omnibus hic ludificatur me modis. ego stultior
qui isti credam. commoratur. chlamydem sumam denuo.

EVT mane parumper atque haec audi.

CHAR cape sis, puere, hoc pallium.

EVT mater irata est patri uehementer, quia scortum sibi
ob oculos adduxerit in aedis, dum ruri ipsa abest:

925 suspicatur illam amicam esse illi.

CHAR zonam sustuli.

EVT eam rem nunc exquirit intus.

CHAR iam machaera est in manu.

EVT nam si eo ted intro ducam—

CHAR tollo ampullam atque hinc eo.

EVT mane, mane, Charine.

CHAR erras, ⟨sic⟩ me decipere hau potes.

EVT neque edepol uolo.

928 sic *add. Schoell*

---

33 In the Latin there is also a pronoun *illi*, "it's not convenient for
him/her"; Eutychus probably refers to his father, but Charinus thinks
he refers to Pasicompsa.

CHAR Why wait?

EUT It's not the right time to go in.

CHAR You're killing me.

EUT I'm telling you, it's not advisable for you to go in now.

CHAR Answer me: why?

EUT There's no time for it.

CHAR Why?

EUT Because it's not convenient.[33]

CHAR Really? It's not convenient, even though she loves me and even though I love her in return? He's tricking me in every conceivable way. I'm a fool to believe him. He's wasting my time. I'll take my cape again.   920

EUT Wait a little while and listen to this.

CHAR Boy, take this cloak, will you? (*begins to change outfits again*)

EUT My mother's terribly angry with my father because she thinks he brought a prostitute into the house for himself before her very eyes, while she herself was away on our country estate. She suspects that that woman is his mistress.   925

CHAR I've put on my belt.[34]

EUT She's inquiring about this inside now.

CHAR I already have the sword in my hand.

EUT If I were to take you in there—

CHAR (*interrupting*) I'm taking my flask and I'm leaving this place. (*moves to the left*)

EUT Wait, wait, Charinus.

CHAR You're wrong: you can't deceive me like this.

EUT I don't want to.

---

[34] The belt contains the money for the journey.

CHAR   quin tu ergo itiner exsequi meum me sinis?
930 EVT   non sino.
CHAR   egomet me moror. tu puere, abi hinc intro ocius.
        iam in currum escendi, iam lora in manus cepi meas.
EVT   sanus non es.
CHAR   quin, pedes, uos in curriculum conicitis
        in Cyprum recta, quandoquidem pater mihi exilium pa-
        rat?
EVT   stultus es, noli istuc quaeso dicere.
CHAR   certum exsequi est,
935   operam ut sumam ad peruestigandum ubi sit illaec.
EVT   quin domi est.
CHAR nam hic quod dixit id mentitust.
EVT   uera dixi equidem tibi.
CHAR iam Cyprum ueni.
EVT   quin sequere, ut illam uideas quam expetis.
CHAR percontatus non inueni.
EVT   matris iam iram neglego.
CHAR porro proficiscor quaesitum. nunc perueni Chalcidem;
940   uideo ibi hospitem Zacyntho, dico quid eo aduenerim,
        rogito quis eam uexerit, quis habeat si ibi indaudiuerit.
EVT   quin tu istas omittis nugas ac mecum huc intro ambulas?
CHAR hospes respondit Zacynthi ficos fieri non malas.
EVT   nil mentitust.
CHAR   sed de amica se indaudiuisse autumat
945   hic Athenis esse.
EVT   Calchas iste quidem Zacynthiust.

---

[35] Greek seer in the Iliad.

CHAR Then why won't you let me continue my journey?

EUT   I won't let you.   930

CHAR I'm wasting my time. You, boy, go inside quickly. (*the boy obeys*) I've already mounted my chariot, I've already taken the reins into my hands. (*pretends to be driving a chariot*)

EUT   You're not in your right mind.

CHAR My feet, why won't you start running, directly to Cyprus, since my father is imposing exile on me?

EUT   You're stupid. Please don't say that.

CHAR I'm determined to trace her, I'll make an effort to track 935 her down.

EUT   She's at home.

CHAR What this chap said was a lie.

EUT   I've told you the truth.

CHAR I've come to Cyprus now.

EUT   Do follow me so that you may see the girl you seek.

CHAR I've made inquiries, but I haven't found her.

EUT   I don't care about my mother's anger now.

CHAR I'm setting out to seek her further. Now I've arrived in Chalcis; there I can see a friend from Zacynthus. I tell 940 him why I've come there; I ask if he's heard there who brought her, who has her.

EUT   Why won't you stop that nonsense and come in here with me?

CHAR My friend has replied that there are decent figs in Zacynthus.

EUT   He hasn't lied.

CHAR But as for my girlfriend, he says he's heard that she's here 945 in Athens.

EUT   That man from Zacynthus is a Calchas.[35]

117

CHAR nauem conscendo, proficiscor ilico. iam sum domi,
iam redii ⟨ex⟩ exilio. salue, mi sodalis Eutyche:
ut ualuisti? quid parentes mei? ualent mater, pater?
bene uocas, benigne dicis: cras apud te, nunc domi.

950 sic decet, sic fieri oportet.

EVT   heia! quae mi somnias!
hic homo non sanust.

CHAR   medicari amicus quin properas ⟨mihi⟩?

EVT sequere sis.

CHAR   sequor.

EVT   clementer quaeso, calcis deteris.
audin tu?

CHAR   iam dudum audiui.

EVT   pacem componi uolo
meo patri cum matre: nam nunc est irata—

CHAR   i modo.

955 EVT —propter istanc.

CHAR   i modo.

EVT   ergo cura.

CHAR   quin tu ergo i modo.
tam propitiam reddam, quam quom propitia est Iuno
Ioui.

V. iii: DEMIPHO. LYSIMACHVS

DEM quasi tu numquam quicquam assimile huius facti feceris.

LYS edepol numquam; caui ne quid facerem. uix uiuo miser.
nam mea uxor propter illam tota in fermento iacet.

960 DEM at ego expurigationem habebo, ut ne suscenseat.

947 ex *add. Kampmann*
951 mihi *add. Ritschl*

118

CHAR I get onto the ship and leave immediately. Now I'm at home, now I've returned from my exile. My greetings, my comrade Eutychus. How have you been? What about my parents? Are my mother and father well? Thanks for the invitation, that's kind of you; tomorrow I'll dine at your place, but now at home. That is right, that is how it ought to be. 950

EUT Goodness! What are you dreaming about! This chap isn't in his right mind.

CHAR Why don't you as a friend heal me quickly?

EUT Follow me please. (*turns toward his house*)

CHAR Yes.

EUT Gently please, you're wearing down my heels. Can you hear me?

CHAR I've been hearing you for a long time already.

EUT I want peace to be settled between my father and my mother: now she's angry—

CHAR (*interrupting*) Just go.

EUT —because of that girl. 955

CHAR Just go.

EUT Take care of it then.

CHAR Then just go. I'll make her as well disposed as Juno is when she's well disposed to Jupiter.

Exeunt EUTYCHUS and CHARINUS into the house of Lysidamus.
Enter DEMIPHO and LYSIMACHUS from the right.

DEM As if you'd never done anything like this.

LYS Never; I took good care not to do it. I'm barely alive, poor me: my wife's in an awful stew because of that girl.

DEM But I'll apologize so that she won't be angry. 960

LYS   sequere me. sed exeuntem filium uideo meum.

       V. iv: EVTYCHVS. LYSIMACHVS. DEMIPHO

EVT   ad patrem ibo, ut matris iram sibi esse sedatam sciat.
          iam redeo.

LYS   placet principium. quid agis? quid fit, Eutyche?

EVT   optuma opportunitate ambo aduenistis.

LYS   quid rei est?

965   EVT   uxor tibi placida et placata est. cette dextras nunciam.

LYS   di me seruant.

EVT   tibi amicam esse nullam nuntio.

DEM   di te perdant! quid negoti est nam, quaeso, istuc?

EVT   eloquar.
          animum aduortite igitur ambo.

LYS   quin tibi ambo operam damus.

EVT   qui bono sunt genere nati, ⟨si⟩ sunt ingenio malo,

970   suapte culpa degenerascunt, genus ingenio improbant.

DEM   uerum hic dicit.

LYS   tibi ergo dicit.

EVT   eo illud est uerum magis.
          nam te istac aetate haud aequom filio fuerat tuo
          adulescenti amanti amicam eripere emptam argento suo.

DEM   quid tu ais? Charini amica est illa?

EVT   ut dissimulat malus!

---

969 si *add. Camerarius*
970 genere capiunt *P*, degenerascunt *Dunsch*

LYS   Follow me. But I can see my son coming out.

Enter EUTYCHUS from his father's house.

EUT   (*into the house*) I'm going to my father to let him know that mother's anger toward him has been calmed down. I'm returning shortly.

LYS   I like the start. (*to Eutychus*) How are you? How are things, Eutychus?

EUT   You've both come here in the nick of time.

LYS   What's the matter?

EUT   Your wife is calm and at peace with you. (*to both*) Now 965 give me your right hands.

LYS   The gods are saving me.

EUT   (*to Demipho*) My news for *you* is that you have no mistress.

DEM   May the gods ruin you! Tell me what on earth you mean by that, will you?

EUT   I'll tell you. Pay attention then, both of you.

LYS   Yes, we're both attending to you.

EUT   If those who come from a good family have a bad character, it's through their own fault that they fall short of their 970 family's standards and reject their family through their character.

DEM   What he says is true.

LYS   He's saying it to you then.

EUT   (*to Demipho*) This makes it all the more true: at your age you ought not to have stolen his girlfriend from your young, lovesick son, when he'd bought her with his own money.

DEM   What are you saying? She's Charinus' girlfriend?

EUT   How the crook is pretending not to know!

975	DEM	ille quidem illam sese ancillam matri emisse dixerat.
	EVT	propterea igitur tu mercatu's, nouos amator, uetus puer?
	LYS	optume hercle, perge, ego assistam hinc alterinsecus.
		quibus est dictis dignus usque oneremus ambo.
	DEM	nullus sum.
	LYS	filio suo qui innocenti fecit tantam iniuriam.
980	EVT	quem quidem hercle ego, in exilium quom iret, redduxi domum;
		nam ibat exulatum.
	DEM	an abiit?
	LYS	etiam loquere, larua?
		temperare istac aetate istis decet ted artibus.
983	DEM	fateor; deliqui profecto.
	EVT	etiam loquere, larua?
983ᵃ		ess' uaciuom istac ted aetate his decebat noxiis.
984		itidem ut tempus anni, aetatem aliam aliud factum condecet;
985		nam si istuc ius est, senecta aetate scortari senes,
		ubi loci est res summa nostra publica?
	DEM	ei, perii miser!
	LYS	adulescentes rei agendae isti magis solent operam dare.
	DEM	iam opsecro hercle habete uobis cum porcis, cum fiscina.
	EVT	redde illi.
	DEM	sibi habeat, iam ut uolt per me sibi habeat licet.
990	EVT	temperi edepol, quoniam ut aliter facias non est copiae.

983ᵃ uacuom esse *P*, esse uaciuom *Enk*

984 aetate *P*, aetatem ς   conuenit *P*, condecet *Lachmann*

988 uobis habete *P*, uobiscum habete *schol Verg. Georg.*, habete uobis *Acidalius*

DEM   He said that he'd bought her as a maid for his mother.   975
EUT   Is that then why you bought her, you young lover, you aged boy?
LYS   Perfect, continue, I'll assist you from the other side here. Let's both burden him with the words he deserves.
DEM   I'm dead.
LYS   To have done such an injustice to his innocent son!
EUT   A son whom I brought back when he was going into exile: 980 yes, he was going into exile.
DEM   He didn't leave, did he?
LYS   You're still speaking, you devil? At your age you should exercise moderation in that department.
DEM   I admit it. Yes, I have made a mistake.
EUT   You're still speaking, you devil? At your age you ought to be free from these offenses. Each deed befits a different age, just as it befits a different season:[36] if it's right for old   985 men to whore around in their old age, what will become of our affairs of state?
DEM   Dear me, I'm dead, poor me!
LYS   It's usually young men who are busy doing that sort of thing.
DEM   Please, have her for yourselves with the pigs and with the basket.[37]
EUT   Give her back to him.
DEM   He can have her for himself; as far as I'm concerned he may have her for himself as he wishes now.
EUT   You're acting in good time, now that you don't have a   990 chance to act differently.

---

[36] Eutychus alludes to the fact that Demipho, being old, is in the autumn or winter of his life.

[37] The exact meaning of this possibly proverbial phrase is unclear.

DEM   supplici sibi sumat quid uolt ipse ob hanc iniuriam,
        modo pacem faciatis oro, ut ne mihi iratus siet.
        si hercle sciuissem siue adeo ioculo dixisset mihi
        se illam amare, numquam facerem ut illam amanti abdu-
          cerem.

995   Eutyche, te oro, sodalis eius es, serua et subueni:
        hunc senem para [me] clientem; memorem dices bene-
          fici.

LYS   ora ut ignoscat delictis tuis atque adulescentiae.
DEM   pergin tu autem? heia! superbe inuehere. spero ego mi
          quoque
        tempus tale euenturum ut tibi gratiam referam parem.

1000 LYS missas iam ego istas artis feci.
DEM   et quidem ego dehinc iam.
EVT   nil ⟨agis⟩:
        consuetudine animus rursus te huc inducet.
DEM   opsecro,
        satis iam ut habeatis. quin loris caedite etiam, si lubet.
LYS   recte dicis. sed istuc uxor faciet, quom hoc resciuerit.
DEM   nihil opust resciscat.
EVT   quid istic? non resciscet, ne time.
1005   eamus intro, non utibilest hic locus, factis tuis,
        dum memoramus, arbitri ubi sint qui praetereant per
          uias.
DEM   hercle qui tu recte dicis: eadem breuior fabula
        erit. eamus.
EVT   hic est intus filius apud nos tuos.
DEM   optume est. illac per hortum nos domum transibimus.

996 me *del. Guyet*
1000 agis *add. Lachmann*
1006 arbitrium *B*, arbitri ut *CD*, arbitri ubi *Seyffert*

124

DEM   Let him accept as reparation for that offense anything he himself wants; all I ask you two is that you make peace between us, so that he isn't angry with me. If I'd known or if he'd told me merely in jest that he was in love with her, I would never have taken her away from her lover. Eutychus, you are his comrade: I ask you, save and help   995 me. (*pointing to himself*) Make this old man your client; you'll have occasion to say that he hasn't forgotten your kindness.

LYS   Ask him to forgive you for the follies of your youth.

DEM   (*to Lysimachus*) Are you still going on? Goodness! You're laying into me full of arrogance. I hope I too will have an opportunity to return your favor.

LYS   I've given up those arts of yours by now.   1000

DEM   And I shall do so from now on.

EUT   It's in vain: by force of habit your mind will lead you back there.

DEM   I beg you two to consider it enough now. Beat me with straps too if you want.

LYS   Quite right. But your wife will do that when she finds out about this.

DEM   She doesn't have to find out.

EUT   Have your way then. She won't find out, don't worry. Let's go in, this isn't a suitable place, as the passersby in   1005 the streets are witnesses to your deeds while we're recounting them.

DEM   You're right. We'll be making the play shorter as well. Let's go.

EUT   Your son's in here at our place.

DEM   That's splendid. We'll go to the house that way through the garden.

125

1010	LYS	Eutyche, hanc uolo prius rem agi quam meum intro refe- ro pedem.
	EVT	quid istuc est?
	LYS	suam quisque homo rem meminit. responde mihi: certon scis non suscensere mihi tuam matrem?
	EVT	scio.
	LYS	uide.
	EVT	mea fide.
	LYS	satis habeo. sed quaeso hercle, etiam uide.
	EVT	non mihi credis?
	LYS	immo credo, sed tamen metuo miser.
1015	DEM	eamus intro.
	EVT	immo dicamus senibus legem censeo prius quam abeamus, qua se lege teneant contentique sint.

annos gnatus sexaginta qui erit, si quem scibimus
si maritum siue hercle adeo caelibem scortarier,
cum eo nos hac lege agemus: inscitum arbitrabimur
1020 et per nos quidem hercle egebit qui suom prodegerit.
neu quisquam posthac prohibeto adulescentem filium
quin amet et scortum ducat, quod bono fiat modo;
si quis prohibuerit, plus perdet clam ⟨qua⟩si praehibue-
rit palam.
haec adeo ut ex hac nocte primum lex teneat senes.
1025 bene ualete; atque, adulescentes, haec si uobis lex placet,
ob senum hercle industriam uos aequom est clare plau-
dere.

1013 id *P*, sed *Ritschl*   1019 hic *P*, hac *Bothe*
1023 si prohibuerit *P*, quam si praehibuerit *Camerarius*, quasi prae-
hibuerit *Seyffert*   1024 ut *P*, uolo *Ussing*

126

LYS	Eutychus, I want this business sorted out before I set foot inside.	1010
EUT	What's the matter?	
LYS	Everybody remembers his own business. Answer me: do you know for certain that your mother isn't angry with me?	
EUT	I do.	
LYS	Check.	
EUT	On my word.	
LYS	I'm satisfied. (*after a pause*) But please, check again.	
EUT	You don't believe me?	
LYS	No, I do, but I'm afraid nevertheless, wretch that I am.	
DEM	Let's go inside.	1015
EUT	No, I think we should tell the old men our law before we leave, the law they should follow and be content with. If we find out that any sixty-year-old, married or unmarried, whores around, we shall deal with him according to the following law: we shall consider him ignorant, and as far as we're concerned when he wastes his possessions he shall reduce himself to poverty. And from now on let no one prevent his young son from being in love and hiring a prostitute, so long as it happens in moderation; if anyone prevents it, he shall lose more behind his back than if he had given it openly. This law shall apply to old men from tonight onward. Farewell. And, young men, if you like this law, it's only fair for you to give us the loud applause that the old men have earned.	1020

MILES GLORIOSUS

INTRODUCTORY NOTE

The *miles gloriosus* or "braggart soldier" is a stock character of Roman comedy. Our play, however, is the only Plautine comedy named after this role. The boastful but high-ranking soldier in it is Pyrgopolinices, whose Greek name means "capturer of towers and cities." The name is ironic, for not only is the soldier unbelievably boastful and vain, he is also a coward. We get a first insight into his character in the brief first act (ll. 1–78), in which his hanger-on Artotrogus flatters him by listing his military and amatory exploits, exploits which he tells us the soldier has never had. Artotrogus also tells us that his only reason for staying with the soldier is that he gets good food from him. The hanger-on does not appear later in the play; his only function is to introduce the soldier. A similar pair is found in Terence's *Eunuchus*, where, however, the adulatory hanger-on Gnatho has more than an expository role and where the soldier Thraso is not the central character.

We lose sight of the soldier for the entire second act (ll. 79–595). Here we first meet Palaestrio, who tells us what went on before the start of the play. He says that he used to be the slave of a very pleasant young Athenian called Pleusicles, who had a satisfying relationship of mutual love with the prostitute Philocomasium. At some point Pleusicles had to go abroad on state business and the soldier Pyrgopolinices arrived on the scene from Ephesus. He met Philocomasium, fell in love with her, and abducted her from her mother. Palaestrio tried to reach his master by ship in order to give him the news, but pirates captured the ship and took him to Ephesus, where he was given to our soldier as a present. In his house he met Philocomasium again, who told him how much she hated being with the soldier and how much she wanted to escape to Athens. Palaestrio contacted his former master Pleusicles by letter. Pleusicles is now in Ephesus and happens to lodge next door to the soldier, in the house of an old gentleman called Periplectomenus. Periplectomenus is very supportive and even came up with the plan to pierce a hole through the wall the two houses share; this can go undetected because Philocomasium has a room of her own adjacent to the house of Periplectomenus. The hole in the wall enables the lovers to meet regularly, but of course this cannot be a permanent solution.

The real action of the play begins in l. 156. Periplectomenus comes out of the house to tell us that while chasing a pet monkey on the roof, one of the soldier's slaves spotted Philocomasium and Pleusicles kissing in the house of Periplectomenus, which was possible because his house has the roof opening so common in ancient buildings. Now there is a great risk that the soldier could learn about the secret affair. Palaestrio, the chief planner of intrigues against the soldier, finds out that this slave is Sceledrus, the guard watching over Philocomasium. The girl is instructed to play herself and her imaginary twin sister called Dicaea, depending on which house she is in or comes out of. Sceledrus, at first loath to believe in the existence of such a twin sister, is gradually forced to accept that there is such a person when he sees her come out of the two houses in turn; he is finally completely convinced when Periplectomenus not only confirms the story but allows him to look at her in his own house. Sceledrus, afraid of punishment from his master for being a careless guard and causing trouble, decides to run away, but in the end changes his mind and hides in the house (l. 585).

The third act, beginning in l. 596, is the start of a second intrigue, this time against the soldier himself. The hole in the wall can hardly be satisfactory as a permanent solution to the problems. Pleusicles wants to take Philocomasium back to Athens. But before any real planning can take place, Periplectomenus describes his way of life to Pleusicles and Palaestrio. The passage is very long (ll. 627–764) and by modern standards very self-congratulatory: Periplectomenus lists the joys of bachelorhood and claims to be affable, generous, and wise. No real plan is revealed to the spectators; all we hear after the exposition of the old man's virtues is that Periplectomenus is to hire two prostitutes, one of them to be dressed as a matron in order to entice Pyrgopolinices to adultery.

The next scene (ll. 813–73), though full of Plautine humor, does not advance the action either. Palaestrio, who wants to get rid of Sceledrus to minimize any risks of discovery of the truth, finds out from the drunken slave Lucrio that Sceledrus is also drunk. Sceledrus thus poses no further risk. Palaestrio threatens to report the misbehavior to Pyrgopolinices and a timid Lucrio runs off, partly out of fear, partly because he is on an errand for Philocomasium, who was thoughtful enough to do her part in getting rid of potential dangers.

In l. 874 Periplectomenus returns with the two women,

Acroteleutium, dressed up in the distinctive outfit of a wife, and Milphidippa, her maid. The passage contains one of the standard discussions of the evil ways of women, but again the plan is not really discussed any further.

In the fourth act Palaestrio informs Pyrgopolinices that a beautiful woman, supposedly the wife of Periplectomenus, has fallen for him. She is said to have divorced her husband and to be waiting for him in the house, which is part of her dowry. The soldier is interested immediately and even keener when he sees Milphidippa, who plays the wife's maid. When she leaves, Pyrgopolinices asks Palaestrio how to solve the remaining problem: he can hardly spend his life with the beautiful new woman (whom he has yet not even seen) unless he gets rid of Philocomasium. Palaestrio has a solution; he claims that Philocomasium's twin sister and mother have arrived and advises the soldier to send her home with them; in order to have a more amicable breakup, it is suggested that he should let her keep all the expensive presents she got from him earlier. The soldier goes in to persuade the girl, who, as we know, will happily follow his command to leave. Palaestrio then tells Pleusicles to come in a captain's outfit to fetch Philocomasium. The plan is that Palaestrio will accompany them as porter and will then flee with them. Pleusicles leaves to get ready. The soldier comes out again, happy at the successful outcome of his talk with Philocomasium. Again Philocomasium is shown to support Palaestrio cleverly: we learn that she asked the soldier to give her this slave as a present, so that he can accompany her officially. Now Milphidippa returns with Acroteleutium, the supposed wife of Periplectomenus. The soldier is instantly smitten, but gives himself airs for a long time. In the end he informs

133

Acroteleutium that he is willing to spend his life with her. As the two women return to the house of Periplectomenus, Pleusicles comes, all dressed up, and takes with him Philocomasium, Palaestrio, and all the presents, carried by porters. A slave boy appears from the old man's house and beckons the soldier in.

He goes in, but after a brief noise inside the fifth act begins with his being carried out again. Periplectomenus and his slaves are beating and humiliating the soldier for his misconduct. They only let go of him when he swears that he will not take any revenge and will keep a low profile. When his slaves return, he hears that Pleusicles, now safely on board a ship with Philocomasium and Palaestrio, is the girl's lover. Pyrgopolinices admits the error of his ways and appeals to the audience for applause.

With its 1437 lines, the *Miles gloriosus* is Plautus' longest play. Leo assumed that the long second act, in which the soldier makes no appearance at all, is taken from another play in which the motif of the hole in the wall was central; this hole is irrelevant for the rest of the play. The discussion has since been very polarized, with some scholars firmly believing in the contamination hypothesis and others denying it vehemently. It has to be said that there is no reason inherent in the play that would force us to assume two originals for our Latin comedy. Of course one could argue that after the hole had been made, Philocomasium could simply have run off. But this would have put Periplectomenus in a difficult position, and what is more, the audience expects the immoral and hateful soldier to be punished more severely than simply by losing his concubine. A further argument for contamination, namely that the twin sister plays no role after the second act, is equally unconvincing; there is no real reason why she should.

Leo also argued that the long scene in which Periplectomenus praises his own lifestyle and social skills has been taken from another play. One argument in favor of this assumption is that the scene is somewhat out of place here; but to this reasoning Drexler rightly objects that such a scene would probably be out of place in any comedy. However, there are good grounds for assuming that the passage does indeed come from elsewhere; it is quite poorly integrated into the play. Thus in ll. 592–95 Periplectomenus enters his house in order to plan with Palaestrio and Pleusicles, but immediately afterward they come out to plan there. In ll. 612–13, however, Palaestrio asks if the same plan should be used that was hatched inside. Then the lengthy self-praise begins, and at its abrupt end, from l. 765 onward, it turns out that neither Periplectomenus nor Pleusicles has any idea what the plan is. Such confusions are not uncommon in places where Plautus inserts material alien to his Greek source, be it his own invention or taken from a second Greek play.

The Lucrio scene is probably also a Plautine insertion, though it is not clear whether Plautus made it up himself or took it from another play. The scene does not advance the action and is again badly integrated. It is obvious that Sceledrus needs to be got rid of. In the Greek play he probably ran off in order to avoid punishment, and in the Latin text he announces his intention to do so in l. 582. In l. 585, however, he suddenly changes his mind and goes home, as is necessary to motivate the Lucrio scene. Periplectomenus had just been speaking with him, so it is very odd that in l. 593 he states that Sceledrus is away from the house; even in the most artificial setting he would have seen him return home.

Not much is known about the Greek original. We know from l. 86 that it was called *Alazon*, "the braggart." Its author, on the other hand, remains unclear. Menander has been suggested, as well as Diphilus. Schaaf notices that the *Poenulus*, like the *Miles gloriosus*, falls into two parts, and since we know that the original of the former play was written by Alexis, he assumes the same author for the latter. Unfortunately this remains no more than one possibility among many. We are on firmer ground when it comes to establishing the date of the first performance of the Latin play. In ll. 211–12 there is a reference to an imprisoned Roman poet, who can be no other than Gnaeus Naevius. Naevius was imprisoned in 206, and since he was freed soon, our play must have been staged in 206 or shortly after. This agrees well with the fact that remarkably little use is made of song in our play; Plautus tends to use much more in his later productions.

SELECT BIBLIOGRAPHY

Editions and Commentaries

Brix, J., Niemeyer, M., and Köhler, O. (1916), *Ausgewählte Komödien des T. Maccius Plautus für den Schulgebrauch erklärt*, vol. 4: *Miles gloriosus*, 4th ed. (Leipzig).

Hammond, M., Mack, A. M., and Moskalew, W. (1963), *T. Macci Plauti Miles Gloriosus: Edited with an Introduction and Notes* (Cambridge, MA).

Criticism

Drexler, H. (1929), "Zur Interpretation des plautinischen Miles," in *Hermes* 64: 339–75.

Hall, F. W. (1923), "On Plautus, *Miles Gloriosus* 18," in *Classical Quarterly* 17: 100–102.

Haywood, R. M. (1944), "On the Unity of the *Miles gloriosus*," in *American Journal of Philology* 65: 382–86.

Questa, C. (2004), "Miles gloriosus," in C. Questa, *Sei letture Plautine* (Urbino), 77–97.

Raffaelli, R., and Tontini, A. (eds.) (2009), *Lecturae Plautinae Sarsinates XII: Miles gloriosus (Sarsina, 27 settembre 2008)* (Urbino).

Schaaf, L. (1977), *Der Miles gloriosus des Plautus und sein griechisches Original: Ein Beitrag zur Kontaminationsfrage* (Munich).

Williams, G. (1958), "Evidence for Plautus' Workmanship in the Miles gloriosus," in *Hermes* 86: 79–105.

MILES GLORIOSVS

ARGVMENTVM I

Meretricem Athenis Ephesum miles auehit.
Id dum ero amanti seruos nuntiare uolt
Legato peregre, ipsus captust in mari
Et eidem illi militi dono datust.
5 **S**uom arcessit erum ⟨priorem⟩ Athenis et forat
Geminis communem clam parietem in aedibus,
Licere ut quiret conuenire amantibus.
Obhaerentis custos hos uidet de tegulis,
Ridiculis autem, quasi sit alia, luditur.
10 **I**temque impellit militem Palaestrio
Omissam faciat concubinam, quando ei
Senis uicini cupiat uxor nubere.
Vltro abeat orat, donat multa. ipse in domo
Senis prehensus poenas pro moecho luit.

ARGVMENTVM II

meretricem ingenuam deperibat mutuo
Atheniensis iuuenis; Naupactum is domo

arg. 1, 5 priorem *add. Niemeyer*
arg. 1, 8 obh(a)erentis *P*, oberrans *Ritschl*

THE BRAGGART SOLDIER

PLOT SUMMARY 1

A soldier carries off a prostitute from Athens to Ephesus. While a slave wants to report this to his lovesick master, who is abroad on an embassy, he himself is captured at sea and given to that same soldier as a present. He summons his previous master 5 from Athens and secretly pierces through the wall shared by the two houses so that the lovers may have the opportunity to meet. From the roof tiles, a guard sees them embracing, but is tricked and hoaxed into believing that the girl is someone else. In the 10 same way Palaestrio induces the soldier to let his concubine go, on the grounds that his old neighbor's wife is keen to marry him. He asks his mistress of his own accord to go away and gives her many presents. He himself, caught in the old man's house, receives punishment as if he were an adulterer.

PLOT SUMMARY 2

A young Athenian was madly in love with a freeborn[1] prostitute, and she with him. Sent as an ambassador, he left home for

[1] Whether she is freeborn or not is unclear; the writer of the summary seems to have inferred this from l. 490, where Periplectomenus, however, is speaking of her invented twin sister. If she is indeed freeborn, she is free to marry Pleusicles.

legatus abiit. miles in eandem incidit,
deportat Ephesum inuitam. seruos Attici,
5 ut nuntiaret domino factum, nauigat.
capitur, donatur illi captus militi.
ad erum ut ueniret Ephesum scribit. aduolat
adulescens atque in proxumo deuortitur
apud hospitem paternum. medium parietem
10 perfodit seruos commeatus clanculum
qua foret amantum. geminam fingit mulieris
sororem adesse. mox ei dominus aedium
suam clientam sollicitandum ad militem
subornat. capitur ille, sperat nuptias,
15 dimittit concubinam et moechus uapulat.

140

Naupactus. A soldier met the same girl and carried her off to
Ephesus against her will. The Athenian's slave travels by ship in 5
order to report to his master what has happened. He is taken
captive and, once a captive, given to that soldier as a present.
He writes to his master to tell him to come to Ephesus. The
young man rushes there and lodges next door at his father's
friend's place. The slave pierces through the wall between the 10
houses so that the lovers would have a secret opportunity to
meet. He makes up the story that the girl's twin sister is around.
Soon after, the master of the house provides him with his pro-
tégée in order to cajole the soldier. That man is taken in; he
hopes for a wedding, lets his concubine go, and is beaten as an 15
adulterer.

PERSONAE

PYRGOPOLINICES miles
ARTOTROGVS parasitus
PALAESTRIO seruos
PERIPLECTOMENVS senex
SCELEDRVS seruos
PHILOCOMASIVM mulier
PLEVSICLES adulescens
LVCRIO puer
ACROTELEVTIVM meretrix
MILPHIDIPPA ancilla
PVER
CARIO coquos

SCAENA

Ephesi

CHARACTERS

PYRGOPOLINICES a soldier; a vain coward
ARTOTROGUS a hanger-on; flatters Pyrgopolinices
PALAESTRIO a slave; former servant of Pleusicles, but now
   in the soldier's possession
PERIPLECTOMENUS an old man; friend and host of Pleu-
   sicles
SCELEDRUS a slave; guard of the soldier's concubine
PHILOCOMASIUM a woman; loves Pleusicles but was
   forced to become the soldier's concubine
PLEUSICLES a young man; Philocomasium's lover
LUCRIO a boy; serves in the soldier's household
ACROTELEUTIUM a prostitute; a protégée of Periplecto-
   menus
MILPHIDIPPA a maid; serves Acroteleutium
SLAVE BOY works for Periplectomenus
CARIO a cook; also works for Periplectomenus

STAGING

The stage represents a street in Ephesus. On it are the houses of
Periplectomenus, to the left, and of Pyrgopolinices, to the right;
the houses share a wall. To the left, the street leads to the har-
bor, to the right, to the city center.

ACTVS I

I. i: PYRGOPOLINICES. ARTOTROGVS

PYR curate ut splendor meo sit clupeo clarior
quam solis radii esse olim quom sudum est solent,
ut, ubi usus ueniat, contra conserta manu
praestringat oculorum aciem in acie hostibus.
5 nam ego hanc machaeram mihi consolari uolo,
ne lamentetur neue animum despondeat,
quia se iam pridem feriatam gestitem,
quae misera gestit fartem facere ex hostibus.
sed ubi Artotrogus hic est?

ART   stat propter uirum
10 fortem atque fortunatum et forma regia.
tam bellatorem Mars haud ausit dicere
neque aequiperare suas uirtutes ad tuas.

PYR quemne ego seruaui in campis Curculioniis,
ubi Bumbomachides Clytomestoridysarchides
15 erat imperator summus, Neptuni nepos?

ART memini. nempe illum dicis cum armis aureis,
quoius tu legiones difflauisti spiritu,
quasi uentus folia aut peniculus tectorium.

PYR istuc quidem edepol nihil est.

ART   nihil hercle hoc quidem est
20 praeut alia dicam . . . quae tu numquam feceris.

11 tum *P*, tam *Bothe*
18 peniculum *P*, *niculum *A*, peniculus *Ussing*, paniculam *Turnebus*, paniculum *Ritschl*

---

2 Pun on the two meanings of *acies*: "sharpness of eyes" and "battle line."

MILES GLORIOSUS

ACT ONE

Enter PYRGOPOLINICES from his house, wearing a cloak and sword; he is followed by ARTOTROGUS, carrying a stylus and tablets, and attendants carrying a shield.

PYR   *(to slaves)* Take care that my shield has greater radiance than the rays of the sun can have when the sky is clear, so that when necessary it may dazzle the enemy's sharpness of sight in the sharpness of fight[2] when battle is joined. *(as they start cleaning)* Well, I want to console this sword 5 of mine so that it may not grieve or lose heart because I've been carrying it around for a long time as if it were on holiday; poor sword, it's itching to turn the enemy into mincemeat. But whereabouts is Artotrogus?

ART   He's standing next to a real man, robust, rich, and of royal 10 beauty. Mars wouldn't dare to call himself such a warrior or compare his exploits to yours.

PYR   He wouldn't, would he? After all, I saved him in the Curculionian Fields, where Bumbomachides Clytomestoridysarchides, Neptune's grandson, was commander in 15 chief.[3]

ART   I remember. You mean the one with golden armor of course, whose legions you scattered with a breath as the wind does leaves or a plasterer's brush does plaster.

PYR   That's a mere nothing.

ART   Indeed, it's a mere nothing compared with other things I 20 might mention . . . *(aside)* which you've never done. If

---

[3] Invented names. The Curculionian Fields are fields suffering from weevils (*curculiones*). The other names are Greek: Bumbomachides means "son of the man fighting with roaring noise," and Clytomestoridysarchides is the "son of the famous adviser and bad ruler."

145

periuriorem hoc hominem si quis uiderit
aut gloriarum pleniorem quam illic est,
me sibi habeto, ei ego me mancupio dabo;
nisi unum, epityra estur insanum bene.

25 PYR   ubi tu es?

ART   eccum. edepol uel elephanto in India,
quo pacto ei pugno praefregisti bracchium.

PYR   quid, "bracchium"?

ART   illud dicere uolui, "femur."

PYR   at indiligenter iceram.

ART   pol si quidem
conixus esses, per corium, per uiscera

30   perque os elephanti transmineret bracchium.

PYR   nolo istaec hic nunc.

ART   ne hercle operae pretium quidem est
mihi te narrare, tuas uirtutes qui sciam.
uenter creat omnis hasce aerumnas: auribus
peraurienda sunt, ne dentes dentiant,

35   et assentandum est quicquid hic mentibitur.

PYR   quid illuc quod dico?

ART   ehem, scio iam quid uis dicere.
factum hercle est, memini fieri.

PYR   quid id est?

ART   quicquid est.

PYR   habes—

ART   tabellas uis rogare. habeo, et stilum.

23 et *P, om. A*, ei *Wagner*
24 epytir aut *P*, epityra *Varro*, epityrum *Ritschl*
34 peraurienda *C*, peraudienda *ABD*

---

[4] Of course he cannot sell himself, as he is already a slave; the

anyone sees a man perjuring himself more than this one
or more boastful than he is, he can have me for himself,
I'll sell myself to him;[4] but there's one thing: his olive
spread[5] tastes awfully good.

PYR Where are you?   25

ART Look, here I am. Or take the elephant in India, how you
     broke its arm with your fist.

PYR What? Its "arm"?

ART I meant to say its "leg."

PYR But I only hit it casually.

ART Indeed, if you'd made an effort, your arm would have
     pierced through the elephant's skin, through its innards,   30
     and through its bones.

PYR I don't want to discuss that here now.

ART It isn't worth your while to tell me about it: I know your
     exploits. (*aside*) My belly is creating all this misery: I have
     to hear this with my ears so that my teeth won't grow
     toothy from inactivity, and I have to agree with whatever   35
     lies he dishes up.

PYR What about what I'm saying now?

ART (*eagerly*) Yes, I already know what you want to say. It did
     happen, I remember it happening.

PYR What's that?

ART (*embarrassed*) Whatever it is.

PYR Do you have—

ART (*interrupting*) You want to ask me for writing tablets. I
     do, and a pen.

---

mancupatio mentioned here is a method of sale in which the buyer puts
his hands on the goods he wishes to purchase.

5 *Epityrum* (here feminine *epityra*) consists of olives, oil, vinegar,
and herbs (Cato, *Agr.* 119).

	PYR	facete aduortis tuom animum ad animum meum.
40	ART	nouisse mores tuos me meditate decet
		curamque adhibere ut praeolat mihi quod tu uelis.
	PYR	ecquid meministi?
	ART	memini centum in Cilicia
		et quinquaginta, centum in Scytholatronia,
		triginta Sardos, sexaginta Macedones—
45		sunt homines quos tu occidisti uno die.
	PYR	quanta istaec hominum summa est?
	ART	septem milia.
	PYR	tantum esse oportet. recte rationem tenes.
	ART	at nullos habeo scriptos: sic memini tamen.
	PYR	edepol memoria es optuma.
	ART	offae monent.
50	PYR	dum tale facies quale adhuc, assiduo edes,
		communicabo semper te mensa mea.
	ART	quid in Cappadocia, ubi tu quingentos simul,
		ni hebes machaera foret, uno ictu occideras?
	PYR	at peditastelli quia erant, siui uiuerent.
55	ART	quid tibi ego dicam, quod omnes mortales sciunt,
		Pyrgopolinicem te unum in terra uiuere
		uirtute et forma et factis inuictissumis?
		amant ted omnes mulieres neque iniuria,
		qui sis tam pulcher; uel illae quae heri pallio
60		me reprehenderunt.
	PYR	quid eae dixerunt tibi?

---

6 Cilicia is a region in Asia Minor, facing Cyprus. Scytholatronia is the made-up name of a country with Scythian mercenaries. The hanger-on presumably did not mean Sardinians, but the inhabitants of Sardis in Lydia, as this would be in the region referred to.

148

PYR   You mind neatly what's on my mind.

ART   I ought to know your ways studiously and take care that I   40
get wind of what you wish in advance.

PYR   Do you remember anything?

ART   I remember one hundred and fifty in Cilicia, one hundred in Scytholatronia, thirty Sardinians, sixty Macedonians[6]—these are the men you killed in a single day.   45

PYR   What's the total body count?

ART   Seven thousand.

PYR   That's how much it ought to be. You've got the figure right.

ART   But I don't have any of them written down: I remember them all the same.

PYR   You have an excellent memory.

ART   (*aside*) The dumplings remind me.

PYR   So long as you act as you have till now, you'll be eating   50
constantly, I'll always share my table with you.

ART   How about in Cappadocia,[7] where you'd have killed five hundred at the same time, with a single stroke, if your sword hadn't been blunt?

PYR   But because they were minor infantrymen, I let them live.

ART   Why should I tell you what all mortals know, that you,   55
Pyrgopolinices, live on earth in a category of your own with regard to bravery, looks, and absolutely unbeatable deeds? All women are in love with you, and rightly so, since you're so handsome; for instance those who grabbed me by my cloak yesterday.   60

PYR   What did they say to you?

[7] Region in Asia Minor.

ART rogitabant: "hicine Achilles est?" inquit mihi.
    "immo eius frater," inquam, "est." ibi illarum altera,
    "ergo mecastor pulcher est," inquit mihi,
    "et liberalis. uide caesaries quam decet.
65   ne illae sunt fortunatae quae cum isto cubant!"
PYR itane aibant tandem?
ART   quaen me ambae opsecrauerint
    ut te hodie quasi pompam illa praeterducerem?
PYR nimia est miseria nimis pulchrum esse hominem.
ART   immo ita est.
    molestae sunt: orant, ambiunt, exopsecrant
70   uidere ut liceat, ad sese arcessi iubent,
    ut tuo non liceat dare operam negotio.
PYR uidetur tempus esse ut eamus ad forum,
    ut in tabellis quos consignaui hic heri
    latrones, ibus denumerem stipendium.
75   nam rex Seleucus me opere orauit maxumo
    ut sibi latrones cogerem et conscriberem.
    regi hunc diem mihi operam decretum est dare.
ART age eamus ergo.
PYR   sequimini, satellites.

ACTVS II

II. i: PALAESTRIO

PAL mihi ad enarrandum hoc argumentum est comitas,

78 temus (tenemus B^1, teneamus B^2) *P*, eamus ς, demus *Hasper*

---

8 Achilles, the greatest hero of Homer's Iliad, had no brother, but
the soldier would not know.

ART   They kept asking: "Is this Achilles?" says one to me. "No,"
I say, "it's his brother."[8] Then the other says to me, "That's
why he's so handsome and gracious. Look how his full
head of hair suits him. Seriously, those women who lie   65
with him are really lucky!"

PYR   Did they really say so?

ART   You ask? They both implored me to lead you past them
that way today, like a parade.

PYR   It's too wretched a thing if a man is too handsome.

ART   It is indeed. They're a nuisance: they ask, canvass, im-
plore that they may see you, and they bid me bring you to   70
them, so that one can't look after one's own business.

PYR   It seems to be time for us to go to the forum so that I can
count out the pay to the soldiers that I enlisted in my tab-
lets here yesterday. Well, King Seleucus[9] asked me as a   75
matter of great importance to muster and enroll merce-
naries for him. I'm resolved to look after the king's busi-
ness this day.

ART   Right, let's go then.

PYR   Follow me, attendants.

*Exeunt PYRGOPOLINICES, ARTOTROGUS, and the atten-
dants to the right.*

ACT TWO

Enter PALAESTRIO from the soldier's house.

PAL   I'll be so kind as to tell you the summary of this play,

[9] If the reference comes from the Greek play, this could be Seleucus
I, who was king of Syria between 306 and 281. Otherwise, it could be
Seleucus II (247–27) or Seleucus III (227–24).

80   si ad auscultandum uostra erit benignitas;
                qui autem auscultare nolet exsurgat foras,
                ut sit ubi sedeat ille qui auscultare uolt.
                nunc qua assedistis causa in festiuo loco,
                comoediai quam nos acturi sumus
85   et argumentum et nomen uobis eloquar.
                Ἀλαζών Graece huic nomen est comoediae,
                id nos Latine "gloriosum" dicimus.
                hoc oppidum Ephesust; ille est miles meus erus,
                qui hinc ad forum abiit, gloriosus, impudens,
90   stercoreus, plenus periuri atque adulteri.
                ait sese ultro omnis mulieres sectarier:
                is deridiculo est, quaqua incedit, omnibus.
                itaque hic meretrices, labiis dum ductant eum,
                maiorem partem uideas ualgis sauiis.
95   nam ego hau diu apud hunc seruitutem seruio;
                id uolo uos scire quo modo ad hunc deuenerim
                in seruitutem ab eo quoi seruiui prius.
                date operam, nam nunc argumentum exordiar.
                erat erus Athenis mihi adulescens optumus;
100   is amabat meretricem acre Athenis Atticis
                et illa illum contra; qui est amor cultu optumus.
                is publice legatus Naupactum fuit
                magnai rei publicai gratia.
                interibi hic miles forte Athenas aduenit,
105   insinuat sese ad illam amicam ⟨mei⟩ eri.
                occepit eius matri suppalparier
                uino, ornamentis opiparisque opsoniis,
                itaque intumum ibi se miles apud lenam facit.

---

93 ductant eum *Charisius*, ducant eum *P*, nictant eum *Fulgentius*, nictant ei *Lindsay*   100 matre *P*, acre *Tyrrell*

if you have the kindness to listen. But if anyone doesn't 80
want to listen, let him get up and get out, so that there
may be space to sit for someone who does want to listen.
Now as to the reason why you've sat down in this place of
joy, I'll tell you both the plot and the name of the comedy 85
we're going to stage. In Greek this comedy has the name
Alazon, which we call "The Braggart" in English.[10] This
city is Ephesus. That soldier is my master, the one who
went away to the forum, a boastful creature, shameless,
like dung, full of false oaths and adultery. He says that all 90
women are running after him of their own accord; wher-
ever he goes, he's everyone's laughingstock. That's why
the prostitutes here, while alluring him with their lips,
mostly have crooked mouths.[11] I haven't been a slave at 95
his house for long. I'd like you to know how I happened
to become this man's slave from the man whose slave I
was before. Pay attention: now I'll begin the plot sum-
mary. In Athens I had an excellent young man as master.
He was madly in love with a prostitute in Attic Athens, 100
and she in turn with him. That's the best type of love to
cultivate. He was sent to Naupactus on official business,
on a matter of great importance for the state. Meanwhile
this soldier arrives in Athens by chance and finds his way 105
to that girlfriend of my master's. He begins to wheedle
her mother with wine, jewelry, and lavish meals, and
that's how the soldier comes to be on very close terms

[10] Lit. *"gloriosus"* in Latin.
[11] Because while blowing him kisses they cannot suppress their
laughter.

---

105 meri *P* (eri *B²*), mei eri *Lindsay*

ubi primum euenit militi huic occasio,
110 sublinit os illi lenae, matri mulieris,
quam erus meus amabat; nam is illius filiam
conicit in nauem miles clam matrem suam,
eamque huc inuitam mulierem in Ephesum aduehit.
ubi amicam erilem Athenis auectam scio,
115 ego quantum uiuos possum mihi nauem paro,
inscendo, ut eam rem Naupactum ad erum nuntiem.
ubi sumus prouecti in altum, fit quod ⟨di⟩ uolunt,
capiunt praedones nauem illam ubi uectus fui:
prius perii quam ad erum ueni quo ire occeperam.
120 ill' ⟨qui⟩ me cepit dat me huic dono militi.
hic postquam in aedis me ad se deduxit domum,
uideo illam amicam erilem, Athenis quae fuit.
ubi contra aspexit me, oculis mihi signum dedit
ne se appellarem; deinde, postquam occasio est,
125 conqueritur mecum mulier fortunas suas:
ait sese Athenas fugere cupere ex hac domu,
sese illum amare meum erum, Athenis qui fuit,
nec peius quemquam odisse quam istum militem.
ego quoniam inspexi mulieris sententiam,
130 cepi tabellas, consignaui, clanculum
dedi mercatori quoidam qui ad illum deferat
meum erum, qui Athenis fuerat, qui hanc amauerat,
ut is huc ueniret. is non spreuit nuntium;
nam et uenit et is in proxumo hic deuortitur
135 apud suom paternum hospitem, lepidum senem;
itaque illi amanti suo hospiti morem gerit
nosque opera consilioque adhortatur, iuuat.
itaque ego paraui hic intus magnas machinas

113 uenit *B¹CD¹*, aduenit *B²D³*, uehit *Marx*, aduehit *Lindsay*

154

with the procuress there. As soon as the soldier gets an
opportunity, he tricks that procuress, the mother of the   110
girl my master was in love with: the soldier puts her
daughter onto a ship, behind her mother's back, and
brings her here to Ephesus, against her will. When I find
out that my master's girlfriend has been carried away
from Athens, I prepare a ship for myself as quickly as pos-   115
sible and go on board in order to bring this news to
Naupactus to my master. When we're well out to sea, the
will of the gods happens and pirates take that ship I've
been traveling on. I'm done for before reaching my mas-
ter, where I'd begun to go. The man who took me captive   120
gives me as a present to the soldier here. After he took
me into his home, I spot that girlfriend of my master, the
one who was in Athens. When she sees me face to face,
she gives me a sign with her eyes not to address her.
Then, when an opportunity arises, she complains to me   125
about her lot. She says that she wishes to flee to Athens
from this house, that she loves that master of mine, the
one who was in Athens, and that she doesn't hate anyone
more intensely than that soldier. When I saw her feel-
ings, I took tablets, sealed them, and secretly gave them   130
to a certain merchant to bring to that master of mine
who'd been in Athens and who'd loved her, telling him to
come here. He didn't despise the message: he came here
and put up next door, at his father's friend's place, a
charming old man. And so the old man humors that love-   135
sick guest of his and encourages and supports us with
help and advice. And so I've prepared great devices in

---

117 di *add. Lipsius*   120 qui *add. Beroaldus*

qui amantis una inter se facerem conuenas.
140 nam unum conclaue, concubinae quod dedit
miles, quo nemo nisi eapse inferret pedem,
in eo conclaui ego perfodi parietem
qua commeatus clam esset hinc huc mulieri;
et sene sciente hoc feci: is consilium dedit.
145 nam meus conseruos est homo hau magni preti,
quem concubinae miles custodem addidit.
ei nos facetis fabricis et doctis dolis
glaucumam ob oculos obiciemus eumque ita
faciemus ut quod uiderit ne uiderit.
150 et mox ne erretis, haec duarum hodie uicem
et hinc et illinc mulier feret imaginem,
atque eadem erit, uerum alia esse assimulabitur.
ita sublinetur os custodi mulieris.
sed foris concrepuit hinc a uicino sene;
155 ipse exit: hic ille est lepidus quem dixi senem.

II. ii: PERIPLECTOMENVS. PALAESTRIO

PER ni hercle diffregeritis talos posthac quemque in tegulis
uideritis alienum, ego uostra faciam latera lorea.
miquidem iam arbitri uicini sunt meae quid fiat domi,
ita per impluuium intro spectant. nunc adeo edico omni-
bus:
160 quemque a milite hoc uideritis hominem in nostris tegu-
lis,
extra unum Palaestrionem, huc deturbatote in uiam.

149 non Ω, ne *Priscianus*

156

here so as to enable the lovers to meet. Well, one room   140
which the soldier gave to his concubine and into which
no one except for herself could set foot, in that room I
made a hole in the wall so that the girl would have a pas-
sage from here to here in secret. (*points at the two houses
in turn*) What's more, I did this with the old man's full
knowledge: he made the suggestion. The fellow slave of   145
mine that the soldier had given his concubine as guard is
a pretty worthless chap. With our witty wiles and intelli-
gent inventions we'll cast a film over his eyes and bring it
about that he didn't see what he did see. Don't get it   150
wrong hereafter: this girl will bear the likeness of two
girls today, from here and from there, and yet she'll be
the same person, but she'll pretend to be a different one.
That's how the girl's guard will be fooled. But the door of
this house has creaked; it's the one of our neighbor, the
old man. He's coming out himself: this is that delightful   155
old man I was talking about.

Enter PERIPLECTOMENUS from his house.

PER   (*into his house*) Unless hereafter you shatter the ankles
of whatever stranger you see on our tiles, I'll turn your
sides into ribbons. The neighbors are already witnessing
what's going on in my house, judging from the way they
look in through the opening in the roof.[12] So now I an-
nounce to each and all: whoever belonging to this sol-   160
dier you see on our roof tiles, with the sole exception of
Palaestrio, you are to throw down here onto the street. As

[12] Roman houses had an opening in the roof through which rainwa-
ter could enter; this water was collected in a large basin.

quod ille gallinam aut columbam se sectari aut simiam
dicat, disperiistis ni usque ad mortem male mulcassitis.
atque adeo, ut ne legi fraudem faciant aleariae,
165   accuratote ut sine talis domi agitent conuiuium.
PAL   nescioquid malefactum a nostra hic familia est, quantum
            audio:
        ita hic senex talos elidi iussit conseruis meis.
        sed me excepit: nihili facio quid illis faciat ceteris.
        aggrediar hominem.
PER   estne aduorsum hic qui aduenit Palaestrio?
170 PAL quid agis, Periplectomene?
PER   hau multos homines, si optandum foret,
        nunc uidere et conuenire quam te mauellem.
PAL   quid est?
        quid tumultuas cum nostra familia?
PER   occisi sumus.
PAL   quid negoti est?
PER   res palam est.
PAL   quae res palam est?
PER   de tegulis
        modo nescioquis inspectauit uostrum familiarium
175   per nostrum impluuium intus apud nos Philocomasium
            atque hospitem
        osculantis.
PAL   quis homo id uidit?
PER   tuos conseruos.
PAL   quis is homo est?
PER   nescio, ita abripuit repente sese subito.
PAL   suspicor
        me periisse.

for the fact that he might say he was chasing a hen or a
dove or a monkey, you're done for unless you beat him up
dreadfully till he dies. And so that they won't break the
law against gambling with dice, make sure that they have   165
their parties at home without anklebones.[13]

PAL (*to the audience*) Some offense has been committed by
our household here, as far as I can hear: that's why this
old man has commanded that my fellow slaves' ankles
should be broken. But he's made an exception of me; I
don't care what he does with the others. I'll approach
him.

PER Isn't this Palaestrio who is coming toward me?

PAL How are you, Periplectomenus?   170

PER If there were a chance to choose, there wouldn't be any-
one I'd rather see and meet than you.

PAL Tell me, why are you ranting against our household?

PER We've been ruined.

PAL What's the matter?

PER It's out.

PAL What's out?

PER Just now one of your household saw from the tiles
through the opening in my house Philocomasium and my   175
guest kissing inside at our place.

PAL Who has seen this?

PER A fellow slave of yours.

PAL Who is that chap?

PER I don't know, he removed himself so suddenly.

PAL I suspect I'm dead.

---

[13] Roman dice were made from the anklebones of animals. Gam-
bling was popular, but at times prohibited (see Hor., *Carm.* 3.24.58).

PER   ubi abit, conclamo: "heus, quid agis tu," inquam, "in te-
          gulis?"
          ille mi abiens ita respondit, "se sectari simiam."

180   PAL   uae mi misero quoi pereundum est propter nihili bes-
          tiam!
          sed Philocomasium hicine etiam nunc est?

PER   quom exibam, hic erat.

PAL   i sis, iube transire huc quantum possit, se ut uideant domi
          familiares, nisi quidem illa nos uolt, qui serui sumus,
          propter amorem suom omnis crucibus contubernalis
          dari.

185   PER   dixi ego istuc; nisi quid aliud uis.

PAL   uolo; hoc ei dicito:

185ᵃ   profecto ut ne quoquam de ingenio degrediatur muliebri
          earumque artem et disciplinam optineat colere.

PER   quem ad modum?

PAL   ut eum, qui se hic uidit, uerbis uincat ne is se uiderit.
          siquidem centiens hic uisa sit, tamen infitias eat.

189   os habet, linguam, perfidiam, malitiam atque audaciam,
189ᵃ   confidentiam, confirmitatem, fraudulentiam.
190   qui arguat se, eum contra uincat iure iurando suo:
          domi habet animum falsiloquom, falsificum, falsiiurium,
          domi dolos, domi delenifica facta, domi fallacias.
          nam mulier holitori numquam supplicat si qua est mala:
          domi habet hortum et condimenta ad omnis mores mali-
          ficos.

195   PER   ego istaec, si erit hic, nuntiabo. sed quid est, Palaestrio,
          quod uolutas tute tecum in corde?

PAL   paulisper tace,
          dum ego mihi consilia in animum conuoco et dum con-
          sulo

PER	When he went away, I shouted: "Hey, what are you doing on our tiles?" says I. While going away he gave me the answer that "he was chasing after a monkey."	
PAL	Poor, wretched me! I have to die because of a worthless animal! But is Philocomasium still here now?	180
PER	When I came out, she was here.	
PAL	Do go, please, and tell her to cross over to here as quickly as possible, so that the members of our household can see her at home, unless she wants us, who are slaves, to be given as bedfellows to crosses because of her love affair.	
PER	I've told her that; unless you want anything else.	185
PAL	I do, actually; tell her this: under no circumstances is she to depart from her womanly ways, and she is to continue to practice their art and discipline.	
PER	How do you mean?	
PAL	With her words she should refute the man who's seen her here so as to make him believe that he hasn't seen her. Even if she's been seen here a hundred times, she should still deny it. She has a mouth, a tongue, perfidy, wickedness and boldness, self-confidence, self-assurance, and deceit. If a man accuses her, she should in turn get the better of him through her oath: she's in possession of a lying, deceiving, perjuring heart; she's in possession of tricks, in possession of wheedling ways, in possession of wiles. If a woman is bad she never needs to entreat the greengrocer: she's in possession of a garden and spices for all wicked ways.	190
PER	I'll tell her that if she's here. But what is it, Palaestrio, that you're turning over and over in your heart?	195
PAL	Be quiet for a little, while I'm assembling my wits in my mind and while I'm taking counsel as to what I should do,	

161

quid agam, quem dolum doloso contra conseruo parem,
qui illam hic uidit osculantem, id uisum ut ne uisum siet.

200 PER   quaere: ego hinc apscessero aps te huc interim. illuc sis
uide,
quem ad modum astitit, seuero fronte curans, cogitans.
pectus digitis pultat, cor credo euocaturust foras;
ecce auortit: nixus laeuo in femine habet laeuam manum,
dextera digitis rationem computat, feriens femur

205   dexterum. ita uehementer icit: quod agat aegre suppetit.
concrepuit digitis: laborat; crebro commutat status.
eccere autem capite nutat: non placet quod repperit.
quicquid est, incoctum non expromet, bene coctum
dabit.
ecce autem aedificat: columnam mento suffigit suo.

210   apage, non placet profecto mi illaec aedificatio;
nam os columnatum poetae esse indaudiui barbaro,
quoi bini custodes semper totis horis occubant.
eugae! euscheme hercle astitit et dulice et comoedice;
numquam hodie quiescet prius quam id quod petit per-
fecerit.

215   habet opinor. age si quid agis, uigila, ne somno stude,
nisi quidem hic agitare mauis uarius uirgis uigilias.
tibi ego dico. an heri adbibisti? heus te alloquor, Palaes-
trio.
uigila inquam, expergiscere inquam, lucet hoc inquam.

PAL   audio.

---

204 ferit *A*, feries *P*
217 atus uestis *P*, adbibisti *Götz*   alloqui *P*, alloquor *Beroaldus*

---

[14] The "barbarian"—i.e., Roman—poet is C. Naevius. The guards
are his chains.

what trick I should prepare against my tricky fellow slave,
who saw her kissing here, so that what's been seen won't
have been seen.

PER   Do think about it. Meanwhile I'll go away from you to   200
over here. (*moves away while Palaestrio is gesturing*)
Look at that, will you, how he's positioned himself, wor-
rying and thinking with an earnest countenance. He's
tapping his chest with his fingers, I think he's going to call
out his heart. Look, he's turned away; he has his left hand
leaning on his left thigh, with his right hand he's making   205
calculations on his fingers, beating his right thigh. He's
beating so strongly, he can hardly think of anything to do.
He's snapped his fingers; he's anxious, he's frequently
changing positions. But look, he's shaking his head: he
doesn't like what he's found. Whatever it is, he won't pro-
duce it half-baked, he'll give it done to a turn. But look,
he's building something: he's supporting his chin with a
pillar. Away with that, I don't like that sort of building   210
work at all: I've heard that a barbarian poet has a pillared
face, a man on whom two guards each always lie and
keep watch at all hours.[14] Hurray! He's set himself up in
a graceful position, right for a slave and a comedy. He'll
never rest today until he's finished what he's seeking.
He's got it, I think. (*to Palaestrio*) If you're going to do   215
anything, do it now, stay awake, stop going to sleep, un-
less you prefer to keep night watches here striped with
strokes. I'm talking to you! You didn't get drunk yester-
day, did you? Hey, I'm speaking to you, Palaestrio! Wake
up, I tell you, get up, I tell you, it's getting light, I tell you!

PAL   I can hear you.

PER   uiden hostis tibi adesse tuoque tergo opsidium? consule,
220   arripe opem auxiliumque ad hanc rem: propere hoc, non
          placide decet.
       anteueni aliqua, aliquo saltu circumduce exercitum,
       coge in opsidium perduellis, nostris praesidium para;
       interclude inimicis commeatum, tibi muni uiam
       qua cibatus commeatusque ad te et legiones tuas
225   tuto possit peruenire: hanc rem age, res subitaria est.
       reperi, comminiscere, cedo calidum consilium cito,
       quae hic sunt uisa ut uisa ne sint, facta infecta ne sient.
       magnam illic homo rem incipissit, magna munit moenia.
       tu unus si recipere hoc ad te dicis, confidentia est
230   nos inimicos profligare posse.
PAL   dico et recipio
       ad me.
PER   et ego impetrare dico id quod petis.
PAL   at te Iuppiter
       bene amet!
PER   auden participare me quod commentu's?
PAL   tace,
       dum in regionem astutiarum mearum te induco, ut scias
       iuxta mecum mea consilia.
PER   salua sumes indidem.
235 PAL   erus meus elephanti corio circumtentust, non suo, neque
          habet plus sapientiai quam lapis.
PER   ego istuc scio.
PAL   nunc sic rationem incipisso, hanc instituam astutiam,
       ut Philocomasio hanc sororem geminam germanam alte-
          ram
       dicam Athenis aduenisse cum amatore aliquo suo,
240   tam similem quam lacte lacti est; apud ⟨te⟩ eos hic
          deuortier
       dicam hospitio.

PER   Can't you see that your enemies are upon you and that
      your back is under siege? Find a solution, get hold of help   220
      and support for this business: it needs to be done quickly,
      not gently. Get ahead of them somehow, lead your army
      around them in some narrow defile, force the enemy to
      endure a siege, create help for our men. Cut off support
      from our foes, secure a path for yourself on which food
      and supplies can reach you and your legions in safety.   225
      Pay attention, it's an emergency. Find something, think
      something up, give us hot counsel quickly, so that what
      has been seen here has not been seen, yet so that what
      has been done has nevertheless been done. He's begin-
      ning something big, he's building big barricades. If only
      you say you take charge of this, I'm confident that we can   230
      crush our enemies.

PAL   I do say so and I do take charge of this.

PER   And I say that you'll be successful in what you seek.

PAL   But may Jupiter love you well!

PER   Do you wish to share with me what you've come up with?

PAL   Be quiet while I'm taking you into the realm of my mach-
      inations, so that you may know my plans as well as I do.

PER   You'll take them back from me intact.

PAL   My master is covered by elephant skin, not by his own,   235
      and he doesn't have more sense than a block of stone.

PER   I know that.

PAL   Now I'll begin my business like this, I'll set up the follow-
      ing trick: I'll say that this twin sister of Philocomasium
      has arrived from Athens with some lover of hers, a girl as   240
      similar as milk is to milk; I'll say they're staying here at
      your place as guests.

---

221 aliqua ⟨et⟩ *Müller*   229 tude unus *P*, tu oenus *Bergk*
240 te *add.* ς

PER   eugae eugae, lepide, laudo commentum tuom!

PAL ut si illic concriminatus sit aduorsum militem

meus conseruos, eam uidisse hic cum alieno osculari, eam

arguam uidisse apud te contra conseruom meum

245 cum suo amatore amplexantem atque osculantem.

PER   immo optume!

idem ego dicam si ⟨ex⟩ me exquiret miles.

PAL   sed simillumas

dicito esse, et Philocomasio id praecipiendum est ut sciat,

ne titubet si ⟨ex⟩quiret ex ea miles.

PER   nimis doctum dolum!

sed si ambas uidere in uno miles concilio uolet,

250 quid agimus?

PAL   facile est: trecentae possunt causae colligi:

"non domi est, abiit ambulatum, dormit, ornatur, lauat,

prandet, potat: occupata est, operae non est, non potest,"

quantum uis prolationis, dum modo hunc prima uia

inducamus uera ut esse credat quae mentibitur.

255 PER placet ut dicis.

PAL   intro abi ergo et, si isti est mulier, eam iube

cito domum transire, atque haec ei dice, monstra, prae-cipe,

ut teneat consilia nostra quem ad modum exorsi sumus

de gemina sorore.

PER   docte tibi illam perdoctam dabo.

numquid aliud?

PAL   intro ut abeas.

PER   abeo.

PER   Bravo, bravo, splendid! I praise your idea!

PAL   So if that fellow slave of mine accuses her in front of the soldier, saying that he's seen her kissing someone else, I'll rebut him and say that he's seen this one at your place embracing and kissing her lover.   245

PER   Perfect! I'll say the same if the soldier asks me.

PAL   But you must say that they're absolutely alike, and Philocomasium needs to be taught so that she knows, so she won't make a slip if the soldier questions her.

PER   A terribly clever trick! But if the soldier wants to see both together, what do we do?   250

PAL   That's easy: hundreds of excuses can be found: "She's not at home, she's gone for a walk, she's sleeping, she's getting dressed, she's bathing, she's having lunch, she's having drinks: she's busy, she doesn't have time, she can't," as much delay as you wish, so long as we can make him believe from the outset that the lies she'll be telling are true.

PER   I like it the way you tell me.   255

PAL   Then go in and if she's there, have her return home quickly, and tell her, show her, teach her this, so that she knows how we've established our plans about the twin sister.

PER   I'll give her to you shrewdly and thoroughly instructed. Anything else?

PAL   Yes, go in.

PER   Yes.

Exit PERIPLECTOMENUS into his house.

---

246 ex *add. Ritschl*
248 quiret *P* (queret *B²*), exquiret *Ritschl*

PAL   et quidem ego ibo domum

260   atque hominem inuestigando operam huic dissimulabili-
        ter dabo

qui fuerit conseruos qui hodie sit sectatus simiam.

nam ill' non potuit quin sermone suo aliquem familia-
        rium

participauerit de amica eri, sese uidisse eam

hic in proxumo osculantem cum alieno adulescentulo.

265   noui morem egomet: "tacere nequeo solus quod scio."

si inuenio qui uidit, ad eum uineam pluteosque agam:

res parata est, ui pugnandoque hominem capere est certa
        res.

si ita non reperio, ibo odorans quasi canis uenaticus

usque donec persecutus uolpem ero uestigiis.

270   sed fores crepuerunt nostrae, ego uoci moderabor meae;

nam illic est Philocomasio custos meus conseruos qui it
        foras.

II. iii: SCELEDRVS. PALAESTRIO

SCE   nisi quidem ego hodie ambulaui dormiens in tegulis,

certo edepol scio me uidisse hic proxumae uiciniae

Philocomasium erilem amicam sibi malam rem quae-
        rere.

275 PAL   hic illam uidit osculantem, quantum hunc audiui loqui.

SCE   quis hic est?

PAL   tuos conseruos. quid agis, Sceledre?

SCE   te, Palaestrio,

uolup est conuenisse.

PAL   quid iam? aut quid negoti est? fac sciam.

SCE   metuo—

PAL   quid metuis?

SCE   ne hercle hodie, quantum hic familiarium est,

maxumum in malum cruciatumque insuliamus.

PAL I too will go home and secretly help this old man by find- 260
ing out who this fellow slave was who chased the monkey
today. He couldn't have helped spilling the beans about
my master's girlfriend to someone or other in the house-
hold, that he's seen her here next door kissing an un-
known young man. I know the way it's done: "I can't keep 265
silent about what I alone know." If I find the one who's
seen her, I'll move all my siege equipment against him:
it's prepared, I'm determined to conquer him with force
and fighting. If I don't find him, I'll go sniffing like a hunt-
ing dog until I've reached the fox by his tracks. But our 270
door has creaked, I'll lower my voice: the chap who's
coming out is Philocomasium's guard, my fellow slave.

Enter SCELEDRUS from the soldier's house.

SCE Unless I sleepwalked on the roof today, I know for cer-
tain that I've seen Philocomasium, master's girlfriend,
looking for trouble for herself next door.

PAL (*aside*) He's the one who has seen her kissing, from what 275
I've heard him say.

SCE (*hearing something*) Who's this?

PAL Your fellow slave. How are you, Sceledrus?

SCE I'm glad I've bumped into you, Palaestrio.

PAL What's that? What's the matter? Let me know.

SCE I'm afraid—

PAL (*interrupting*) What are you afraid of?

SCE That today all the members of our household will jump
into greatest torture and the cross.

---

261 siet Ω (*scriptio plena*)

	PAL	tu sali
280		solus, nam ego istam insulturam et desulturam nil moror.
	SCE	nescis tu fortasse apud nos facinus quod natum est nouom.
	PAL	quod id est facinus?
	SCE	impudicum.
	PAL	tute scias soli tibi,
		mihi ne dixis, scire nolo.
	SCE	non enim faciam quin scias.
		simiam hodie sum sectatus nostram in horum tegulis.
285	PAL	edepol, Sceledre, homo sectatu's nihili nequam bestiam.
	SCE	di te perdant!
	PAL	te istuc aequom … quoniam occepisti, eloqui.
	SCE	forte fortuna per impluuium huc despexi in proxumum:
		atque ego illi aspicio osculantem Philocomasium cum al-
		tero
		nescioquo adulescente.
	PAL	quod ego, Sceledre, scelus ex te audio?
290	SCE	profecto uidi.
	PAL	tutin?
	SCE	egomet duobus his oculis meis.
	PAL	abi, non ueri simile dicis nec uidisti.
	SCE	num tibi
		lippus uideor?
	PAL	medicum istuc tibi meliust percontarier.
		uerum enim tu istam, si te di ament, temere hau tollas
		fabulam:
		tuis nunc cruribus capitique fraudem capitalem hinc
		creas.
295		nam tibi iam ut pereas paratum est dupliciter nisi suppri-
		mis
		tuom stultiloquium.

170

PAL You jump alone: I don't like that sort of jumping in and 280
out.

SCE Perhaps you don't know what unheard-of, wicked deed
has taken place in our midst.

PAL What wicked deed is this?

SCE A shameless one.

PAL Keep it to yourself, don't tell me, I don't want to know.

SCE I have to let you know. I chased our monkey on these
people's roof today.

PAL Goodness, Sceledrus, you, a worthless man, have chased 285
a useless beast.

SCE May the gods ruin you!

PAL No, you . . . ought to tell me now that you've begun.

SCE By pure chance I looked down through the opening in
the roof here into our neighbor's place; and there I spot
Philocomasium kissing some unknown young man.

PAL What scandal do I hear from you, Sceledrus?

SCE I've really seen her. 290

PAL You yourself?

SCE I myself with these two eyes of mine.

PAL Go away, you aren't telling a likely story and you didn't
see her.

SCE I don't seem bleary-eyed to you, do I?

PAL You'd better ask a doctor about that. But surely, if the
gods loved you, you wouldn't spread that story rashly:
now you're creating capital trouble for your shins and
head: now it's all arranged for you to die twice over unless 295
you keep your stupid talk in check.

---

282 scis *P*, scias *Gulielmius*, sci *Bentley*

SCE   qui uero dupliciter?

PAL   dicam tibi.

primumdum, si falso insimulas Philocomasium, hoc peri-
     eris;

iterum, si id uerum est, tu ei custos additus ⟨eo⟩ perieris.

SCE quid fuat me nescio: haec me uidisse ego certo scio.

300 PAL pergin, infelix?

SCE   quid tibi uis dicam nisi quod uiderim?

quin etiam nunc intus hic in proxumo est.

PAL   eho an non domi est?

SCE uise, abi intro tute, nam ego mi iam nil credi postulo.

PAL certum est facere.

SCE   hic te opperiam; eadem illi insidias dabo,

quam mox horsum ad stabulum iuuenix recipiat se ⟨e⟩
     pabulo.

305 quid ego nunc faciam? custodem me illi miles addidit:

nunc si indicium facio, interii; ⟨interii⟩ si taceo tamen,

si hoc palam fuerit. quid peius muliere aut audacius?

dum ego in tegulis sum, illaec se⟨se ex⟩ hospitio edit
     foras;

edepol facinus fecit audax. hoccin si miles sciat,

310 credo hercle has sustollat aedis totas atque hunc in cru-
     cem.

hercle quicquid est, mussitabo potius quam inteream
     male;

non ego possum quae ipsa sese uenditat tutarier.

298 eo *add. Acidalius*

304 e *add. Camerarius*

306 interii[2] *add. (post* taceo) *Camerarius*

308 sum (se *B*[2]) *P*, sese ex *Leo*

311 quidquid herclest *Bothe* (*cui* quicquid *pyrrhichicum displicet*)

SCE   What do you mean, "twice over"?

PAL   I'll tell you. First off, if you wrongly accuse Philocoma-
       sium, you'll be dead for that reason; second, if it *is* true,
       you, who were made her guard, will be dead for that
       reason.

SCE   I don't know what'll become of me; I do know for certain
       that I've seen this.

PAL   Are you persisting, unlucky creature?   300

SCE   What do you want me to tell you except what I've seen?
       Actually, she's in here next door even now.

PAL   Tell me, she's not at home?

SCE   Check, go in yourself: I don't demand to be believed any
       longer.

PAL   I'm resolved to do so.

SCE   I'll wait for you here; that way I'll also set an ambush
       here, to see how soon the heifer returns here to her
       stable from that pasture.   305

Exit PALAESTRIO into the soldier's house.

SCE   What should I do now? The soldier made me her guard.
       If I disclose it, I'm dead; I'm dead all the same if I keep
       quiet and if it comes out. What's worse or more daring
       than a woman? While I was on the roof, she slipped out-
       side, out of her quarters. She really did a daring deed. If
       the soldier finds out about this, I believe he'll crucify the 310
       entire house and this man here (*points to himself*). What-
       ever it is, I'll keep mum rather than perish miserably. I
       can't guard a woman who sells herself.

Enter PALAESTRIO from the soldier's house.

PAL   Sceledre, Sceledre, quis homo in terra te alter est auda-
         cior?

         quis magis dis inimicis natus quam tu atque iratis?

SCE   quid est?

315 PAL   iuben tibi oculos effodiri, quibus id quod nusquam est ui-
         des?

SCE   quid, nusquam?

PAL   non ego tuam empsim uitam uitiosa nuce.

SCE   quid negoti est?

PAL   quid negoti sit rogas?

SCE   quor non rogem?

PAL   non tu tibi istam praetruncari linguam largiloquam iu-
         bes?

SCE   quam ob rem iubeam?

PAL   Philocomasium eccam domi, quam in proxumo

320   uidisse aibas te osculantem atque amplexantem cum al-
         tero.

SCE   mirum est lolio uictitare te tam uili tritico.

PAL   quid iam?

SCE   quia luscitiosu's.

PAL   uerbero, edepol tu quidem
      caecus, non luscitiosu's. nam illam quidem uidi domi.

SCE   quid, domi?

PAL   domi hercle uero.

SCE   abi, ludis me, Palaestrio.

325 PAL   tum mihi sunt manus inquinatae.

SCE   quidum?

PAL   quia ludo luto.

SCE   uae capiti tuo!

315 hic *P*, (e)st �
323 illa quidem illa *P*, illam quidem uidi �

PAL   Sceledrus, Sceledrus, who on earth is bolder than you? Who was born when the gods were more hostile or angrier, than you?

SCE   What's that?

PAL   Won't you have your eyes dug out, with which you see   315 what exists nowhere?

SCE   What, nowhere?

PAL   I wouldn't buy your life for a rotten nut.

SCE   What's the matter?

PAL   You ask me what's the matter?

SCE   Why shouldn't I ask?

PAL   Won't you have that talkative tongue of yours cut off?

SCE   Why should I have that done?

PAL   Look, Philocomasium is at home, the one you claimed to   320 have seen kissing and embracing a stranger next door.

SCE   It's weird that you live on darnel[15] when wheat is so cheap.

PAL   How do you mean?

SCE   Because you're dim-sighted.

PAL   You whipping post, *you* are *blind*, not just dim-sighted: I've seen her at home.

SCE   What? At home?

PAL   Yes, at home.

SCE   Go away, you're playing games with me, Palaestrio.

PAL   Then my hands are dirty.   325

SCE   How come?

PAL   Because I'm playing with dirt.

SCE   Bad luck to you!

---

[15] A toxic weed closely resembling wheat. Ovid (*Fast*. 1.691) mentions that it is harmful to the eyes.

PAL ⟨tuo⟩ istuc, Sceledre, promitto fore
nisi oculos orationemque aliam commutas tibi.
sed fores concrepuerunt nostrae.

SCE at ego ilico opseruo fores;
nam nihil est qua hinc huc transire ea possit nisi recto
ostio.

330 PAL quin domi eccam! nescioquae te, Sceledre, scelera susci-
tant.

SCE mihi ego uideo, mihi ego sapio, ⟨mihi⟩ ego credo pluru-
mum:
me homo nemo deterrebit quin ea sit in his aedibus.
hic opsistam, ne imprudenti huc ea se surrepsit mihi.

PAL meus illic homo est, deturbabo iam ego illum de pugna-
culis.

335 uin iam faciam uti stultiuidum te fateare?

SCE age face.

PAL nec te quicquam sapere corde neque oculis uti?

SCE uolo.

PAL nemp' tu istic ais esse erilem concubinam?

SCE atque arguo
eam me uidisse osculantem hic intus cum alieno uiro.

PAL scin tu nullum commeatum hinc esse a nobis?

SCE scio.

340 PAL nec solarium neque hortum nisi per impluuium?

SCE scio.

PAL quid nunc? si ea domi est, si facio ut eam exire hinc ui-
deas domo,
dignun es uerberibus multis?

SCE dignus.

326 tuo² *add. Camerarius*
331 mihi³ *add. Pylades*

PAL   You, Sceledrus, I promise will have bad luck unless you change your eyes and speech. But our door has creaked.

SCE   (*pointing to the door of Periplectomenus*) Well, I shall watch the door here: she has no way of going from here to here (*points at the houses in turn*) except straight through the door.

PAL   Look, she's at home! Some scandals stir you, Sceledrus.   330

SCE   I see for myself, I think for myself, I believe myself most. No one will deter me from believing that she's in this house. (*points to the house of Periplectomenus*) I'll plant myself here so that she won't steal over here without me noticing it.

PAL   (*aside*) That chap is mine, I'll throw him down from the ramparts now. (*to Sceledrus*) Do you want me to make   335 you admit now that you see things foolishly?

SCE   Go ahead.

PAL   And to admit that you don't have any sense in your heart and don't use your eyes?

SCE   I do want it.

PAL   You do say that master's concubine is over there, don't you? (*points to the house of Periplectomenus*)

SCE   And I insist that I've seen her kissing a stranger in here.

PAL   Do you know that there's no way of getting there from our place?

SCE   I do.

PAL   Neither a terrace nor a garden, only through the opening   340 in the roof?

SCE   I know.

PAL   Well then? If she's at home and if I bring it about that you see her coming out from home, do you deserve a lot of blows?

SCE   I do.

PAL   serua istas fores,
ne tibi clam se supterducat istinc atque huc transeat.

SCE consilium est ita facere.

PAL   pede ego iam illam huc tibi sistam in uiam.

345 SCE agedum ergo face. uolo scire utrum egon id quod uidi ui-
      derim

an illic faciat, quod facturum dicit, ut ea sit domi.

nam ego quidem meos oculos habeo nec rogo utendos fo-
ris.

sed hic illi supparasitatur semper, hic eae proxumust,

primus ad cibum uocatur, primo pulmentum datur;

350 nam illic noster est fortasse circiter triennium

nec quoiquam quam illic in nostra meliust famulo fami-
lia.

sed ego hoc quod ago, id me agere oportet, hoc opser-
uare ostium.

sic opsistam. hac quidem pol certo uerba mihi numquam
dabunt.

II. iv: PALAESTRIO. PHILOCOMASIVM. SCELEDRVS

PAL praecepta facito ut memineris.

PHIL   totiens monere mirum est.

355 PAL at metuo ut satis sis subdola.

PHIL   cedo uel decem, edocebo

minime malas ut sint malae, mihi solae quod superfit.

age nunciam insiste in dolos; ego aps te procul recedam.

PAL quid ais tu, Sceledre?

PAL (*pointing to the door of Periplectomenus*) Guard that door so that she won't steal away from you there and come over here.

SCE It's my plan to do so.

PAL I'll have her come out here into the street in a minute.

SCE Go on then, do it.   345

Exit PALAESTRIO into the soldier's house.

SCE I want to know whether I've seen what I have seen or whether he brings about what he said he would, that she's at home. Well, I for one have my own eyes and needn't borrow them from outside. But this chap is always fawning on her, he's her closest confidant, he's invited to eat first, he's given the delicacies first. He's been one of us for   350 perhaps something like three years, and yet no servant in our household has it better than him. But I ought to be doing what I'm doing now: observing this door. I'll position myself like this. They'll never trick me this way, that's for sure. (*positions himself facing the door of Periplectomenus, hands stretched out*)

Enter PALAESTRIO and PHILOCOMASIUM from the soldier's house, unnoticed by Sceledrus.

PAL Make sure you remember my instructions.

PHIL I'm surprised that you remind me so often.

PAL But I'm afraid that you might not be wily enough.   355

PHIL Give me even ten girls and I'll make even the least naughty to be naughty by that naughtiness which I have in excess. Go on now, start to work on your tricks; I'll go away from you a little. (*does so*)

PAL (*loudly*) What do you say, Sceledrus?

SCE   hanc rem gero. habeo auris, loquere quiduis.

PAL   credo ego istoc exemplo tibi esse pereundum extra por-
          tam,

360   dispessis manibus, patibulum quom habebis.

SCE   ⟨ego?⟩ quamnam ob rem?

PAL   respicedum ad laeuam: quis illaec est mulier?

SCE   pro di immortales,
      eri concubina est haec quidem!

PAL   mi quoque pol ita uidetur.
      age nunciam, quando lubet—

SCE   quid agam?

PAL   perire propera.

PHIL ubi iste est bonus seruos qui probri me maxumi innocen-
          tem

365   falso insimulauit?

PAL   em tibi! hic mihi dixit tibi quae dixi.

PHIL tun me uidisse in proxumo hic, sceleste, ais osculantem?

PAL   ac cum alieno adulescentulo dixit.

SCE   dixi hercle uero.

PHIL tun me uidisti?

SCE   atque his quidem hercle oculis.

PHIL   carebis, credo,
      qui plus uident quam quod uident.

SCE   numquam hercle deterrebor

370   quin uiderim id quod uiderim.

PHIL   ego stulta et mora multum
      quae cum hoc insano fabuler, quem pol ego capitis per-
          dam.

SCE   noli minitari: scio crucem futuram mihi sepulcrum;
      ibi mei maiores sunt siti, pater, auos, proauos, abauos.

360 ego *add. Niemeyer*

SCE   I'm paying attention to the business at hand. I do have ears, say whatever you want.

PAL   I believe you'll have to die that way outside the Gate,[16] with your hands spread apart, when you're on the gibbet.   360

SCE   I? What for?

PAL   Just look to your left: who is that girl?

SCE   (*as he turns*) Immortal gods, this is master's concubine!

PAL   It certainly seems so to me. Go on now, since you wish—

SCE   (*interrupting*) What should I do?

PAL   Make haste to die.

PHIL Where is that good slave who is wrongly accusing me of   365 greatest disgrace, even though I'm innocent?

PAL   (*pointing to Sceledrus*) Here you go! He told me what I told you.

PHIL (*to Sceledrus*) Do you claim to have seen me here next door kissing, you criminal?

PAL   And what's more, he said you were doing so with an unknown young man.

SCE   I did indeed say so.

PHIL You've seen me?

SCE   Yes, and with these eyes.

PHIL You'll have to do without them, I believe; they see more than they see.

SCE   I'll never be deterred from having seen what I have seen.   370

PHIL It's very silly and stupid of me to speak with this madman, whom I'll have killed.

SCE   Don't threaten me: I know that the cross will be my tomb; there my ancestors have been laid to rest, my father, grandfather, great-grandfather, great-great-

---

[16] The Esquiline Gate in Rome, outside of which executions took place.

181

non possunt mihi minaciis tuis hisce oculi effodiri.
375   sed paucis uerbis te uolo, Palaestrio. opsecro te,
unde exit haec?

PAL   und' nisi domo?
SCE   domo?
PAL   me uiden?
SCE   te uideo.
nimis mirum est facinus quo modo haec hinc huc transire
    potuit;
nam certo nec solarium est apud nos neque hortus ullus
nec fenstra nisi clatrata; nam certe ego te hic intus uidi.
380 PAL   pergin, sceleste, intendere hanc arguere?
PHIL   ecastor ergo
mi hau falsum euenit somnium quod noctu hac somniaui.
PAL   quid somniasti?
PHIL   ego eloquar. sed amabo aduortite animum.
hac nocte in somnis mea soror gemina est germana uisa
uenisse Athenis in Ephesum cum suo amatore quodam;
385   i ambo hospitio huc in proxumum mihi deuortisse uisi.
PAL   Palaestrionis somnium narratur. perge porro.
PHIL   ego laeta uisa quia soror uenisset, propter eandem
suspicionem maxumam sum uisa sustinere.
nam arguere in somnis me meus mihi familiaris uisust
390   me cum alieno adulescentulo, quasi nunc tu, esse oscula-
    tam,
quom illa osculata mea soror gemina esset suompte ami-
    cum.
id me insimulatam perperam falsum esse somniaui.

376 haec *A*, hac huc *P*

grandfather. These eyes of mine cannot be dug out with
your threats. (*turning away from her*) But I want to talk   375
to you briefly, Palaestrio. Please, where did she come out
from?

PAL   From home, of course.

SCE   Home?

PAL   Can you see me?[17]

SCE   I can. It's really strange how she could cross over from
here to here: there's certainly no terrace at our place,
nor any garden or window that isn't barred. (*to Philoco-
masium*) I've definitely seen you in here.

PAL   You criminal, are you continuing to persist in accusing   380
her?

PHIL Then the dream I dreamed last night wasn't false.

PAL   What did you dream?

PHIL I'll tell you. But please pay attention, you two. Last night
I dreamed that my twin sister had come from Athens to
Ephesus with some lover of hers. Both of them appeared   385
to have put up next door.

PAL   (*aside*) Palaestrio's dream is being told. (*to Philoco-
masium*) Continue further.

PHIL I seemed happy because my sister had come, but because
of her I seemed to be under an enormous suspicion: a
household member of mine seemed to accuse me in my
dream of having kissed an unknown young man, just as   390
you're doing now, while in reality that twin sister of mine
had kissed her boyfriend. I dreamed that I'd been falsely
accused of this false charge.

---

[17] The phrase is normally used like English "trust me," but here the
literal meaning matters as much.

PAL   satin eadem uigilanti expetunt quae in somnis uisa me-
           moras?

         eu hercle praesens somnium! abi intro et comprecare.

395   narrandum ego istuc militi censebo.

PHIL   facere certum est,
         nec me quidem patiar probri falso impune insimulatam.

SCE   timeo quid rerum gesserim, ita dorsus totus prurit.

PAL   scin te periisse?

SCE   nunc quidem domi certo est. certa res est
         nunc nostrum opseruare ostium, ubiubi est.

PAL   at, Sceledre, quaeso,

400   ut ad id exemplum somnium quam simile somniauit
         atque ut tu suspicatus es eam uidisse osculantem!

SCE   nescio quid credam egomet mihi iam, ita quod uidisse
           credo
         me id iam non uidisse arbitror.

PAL   ne tu hercle sero, opinor,
         resipisces: si ad erum haec res prius praeuenit, peribis
           pulchre.

405 SCE   nunc demum experior mi ob oculos caliginem opstitisse.

PAL   dudum edepol planum est id quidem, quae hic usque
           fuerit intus.

SCE   nil habeo certi quid loquar: non uidi eam, etsi uidi.

PAL   ne tu edepol stultitia tua nos paene perdidisti:
         dum te fidelem facere ero uoluisti, apsumptu's paene.

410   sed fores uicini proxumi crepuerunt. conticiscam.

PAL   Are really the same things occurring now that you're awake which you say seemed to do so in your sleep? Goodness, there is your dream come true! Go in and pray. I should think the soldier needs to be told about this.   395

PHIL   I'm resolved to do so, and I won't let it go unpunished that I've been wrongly accused of unchastity.

Exit PHILOCOMASIUM into the soldier's house.

SCE   I'm in fear about what I may have done wrong, my entire back is itching so badly.

PAL   Do you realize that you're dead?

SCE   Now she's definitely at home. I'm resolved to guard our door now, wherever she is.

PAL   But Sceledrus, please, how similar a dream to that incident she dreamed and how corresponding to your suspicion of having seen her kissing!   400

SCE   I don't know what I should believe any longer: I don't any longer think I've seen what I believe I've seen.

PAL   You will indeed regain your senses when it's too late, I think: if this matter reaches master earlier, you'll perish prettily.

SCE   Now at last I realize that a mist had come over my eyes.   405

PAL   It's been evident for a while already since she was in here throughout.

SCE   I don't have anything definite to say: I didn't see her, even if I did.

PAL   You almost ruined us with your idiocy. While you wanted to show yourself a slave faithful to his master, you were almost ruined. But the door of our next-door neighbor has creaked. I'll fall silent.   410

II. v: PHILOCOMASIVM. SCELEDRVS. PALAESTRIO

PHIL   inde ignem in aram, ut Ephesiae Dianae laeta laudes
gratisque agam eique ut Arabico fumificem odore
amoene,
quom me in locis Neptuniis templisque turbulentis
seruauit, saeuis fluctibus ubi sum afflictata multum.

415 SCE   Palaestrio, o Palaestrio!

PAL   o Sceledre, Sceledre, quid uis?

SCE   haec mulier, quae hinc exit modo, estne erilis concubina
Philocomasium an non est ea?

PAL   hercle opinor, ea uidetur.
sed facinus mirum est quo modo haec hinc huc transire
potuit,
si quidem ea est.

SCE   an dubium tibi est eam esse hanc?

PAL   ea uidetur.

420 SCE   adeamus, appellemus. heus, quid istuc est, Philocoma-
sium?
quid tibi istic in istisce aedibus debetur, quid negoti est?
quid nunc taces? tecum loquor.

PAL   immo edepol tute tecum;
nam haec nil respondet.

SCE   te alloquor, uiti probrique plena,
quae circum uicinos uagas.

PHIL   quicum tu fabulare?

425 SCE   quicum nisi tecum?

PHIL   quis tu homo es aut mecum quid est negoti?

SCE   me rogas? hem, qui sim?

PHIL   quin ego hoc rogem quod nesciam?

PAL   quis ego sum igitur, si hunc ignoras?

Enter PHILOCOMASIUM from the house of Periplectomenus.

PHIL   *(to servants within)* Light a fire on the altar, so that I may happily give praise and thanks to Diana[18] of Ephesus and pleasantly burn Arabian incense for her, since she saved me in the stormy places and spaces of Neptune, where I suffered much from the savage waves.

SCE   Palaestrio, o Palaestrio!   415

PAL   O Sceledrus, Sceledrus, what do you want?

SCE   Is the girl who's just come out from here master's concubine, Philocomasium, or isn't she?

PAL   I think she is, she seems to be her. But it's strange how she could have got across from here to here, if indeed it's her.

SCE   You're not in doubt that it's her, are you?

PAL   It seems to be her.

SCE   *(to Palaestrio)* Let's approach and address her. *(to Philo-*   420 *comasium)* Hey, what's going on, Philocomasium? What are you owed in that house, what business do you have there? Why are you silent now? I'm talking to you.

PAL   No, to yourself; she won't answer.

SCE   *(still to Philocomasium)* I'm talking to you, you creature full of vice and disgrace, you who stray around our neighbors.

PHIL   Who are you talking to?

SCE   To you, of course.   425

PHIL   Who are you? What business do you have with me?

SCE   You ask me? Hey, you ask who I am?

PHIL   Why shouldn't I ask what I don't know?

PAL   Who am *I* then, if you don't know him?

---

[18] Diana/Artemis had a famous temple in Ephesus.

PHIL   mihi odiosus, quisquis es,
et tu et hic.

SCE   non nos nouisti?

PHIL   neutrum.

SCE   metuo maxume—

PAL   quid metuis?

SCE   enim ne ⟨nos⟩ nosmet perdiderimus uspiam;

430   nam nec te nec me nouisse ait haec.

PAL   persectari hic uolo,
Sceledre, nos nostri an alieni simus, ne dum quispiam
nos uicinorum imprudentis aliquis immutauerit.

SCE   certe equidem noster sum.

PAL   et pol ego. quaeris tu, mulier, malum.
tibi ego dico, heus, Philocomasium!

PHIL   quae te intemperiae tenent

435   qui me perperam perplexo nomine appelles?

PAL   eho!
quis igitur uocare?

PHIL   Diceae nomen est.

SCE   iniuria es;
falsum nomen possidere, Philocomasium, postulas:
ἄδικος es tu, non δικαία, et meo ero facis iniuriam.

PHIL   egone?

SCE   tu⟨ne⟩.

PHIL   quae heri Athenis Ephesum adueni uesperi

440   cum meo amatore, adulescente Atheniensi?

PAL   dic mihi,
quid hic tibi in Epheso est negoti?

429 nos *add. Reiz*
439 ne *add. Ritschl*

PHIL A man who's a nuisance to me, whoever you are; both you and him, actually.

SCE You don't know us?

PHIL Neither of you.

SCE (*to Palaestrio*) I'm terribly afraid—

PAL (*interrupting*) What are you afraid of?

SCE That we've lost ourselves somewhere; she says she knows 430
neither you nor me.

PAL Sceledrus, I want to find out if we are ourselves or other
people, in case one of our neighbors has changed us with-
out our knowledge.

SCE I am certainly one of us.

PAL (*to Sceledrus*) So am I. (*to Philocomasium*) You're look-
ing for trouble, woman. I'm talking to you, hey, Philoco-
masium!

PHIL What insanity has got you in its grip, since you wrongly 435
call me by a false name?

PAL Hey there! What are you called then?

PHIL My name is Justine.[19]

SCE You're unfair, you demand to have a false name, Philoco-
masium. You're unjust, not Justine, and you're doing my
master an injustice.

PHIL I?

SCE Yes, you.

PHIL I? I only came here to Ephesus from Athens yesterday
evening with my lover, a young Athenian. 440

PAL Tell me, what business have you here in Ephesus?

---

[19] The Greek pun is difficult to render. Philocomasium says her
name is Dicaea, which means "the just one," and Sceledrus states that
the name is inappropriate.

PHIL   geminam germanam meam
hic sororem esse indaudiui, eam ueni quaesitum.

SCE   mala es.

PHIL immo ecastor stulta multum quae uobiscum fabuler.
abeo.

SCE   abire non sinam te.

PHIL   mitte.

SCE   manufestaria es.

445   non omitto.

PHIL   at iam crepabunt mihi manus, malae tibi,
nisi me omittis.

SCE   quid, malum, astas? quin retines altrinsecus?

PAL   nil moror negotiosum mi esse tergum. qui scio
an ista non sit Philocomasium atque alia eius similis siet?

PHIL mittis me an non mittis?

SCE   immo ui atque inuitam ingratiis,

450   nisi uoluntate ibis, rapiam te domum.

PHIL   hosticum hoc mihi
domicilium est, Athenis domus est atque erus; ego istam
domum
nec moror nec uos qui homines sitis noui nec scio.

SCE   lege agito: te nusquam mittam, nisi das firmatam fidem
te huc, si omisero, intro ituram.

PHIL   ui me cogis, quisquis es.

455   do fidem, si omittis, isto me intro ituram quo iubes.

SCE   ecce omitto!

PHIL   at ego abeo missa.

451 domicilium est *B*, est domicilium *CD*

PHIL I heard that my twin sister is here and I've come to look for her.

SCE You're a bad one.

PHIL No, I'm a very stupid one because I'm talking with you two. I'm off.

SCE I won't let you go. (*grabs her*)

PHIL Let go!

SCE You're caught in the act! I won't let go.   445

PHIL But in a moment my hands and your jaws will crack together, unless you let go of me.

SCE (*to Palaestrio*) Why the blazes are you just standing around? Why don't you hold her from the other side?

PAL I don't care for having a back full of trouble. How can I be sure that she's not Philocomasium, but another girl similar to her?

PHIL (*to Sceledrus*) Will you let go of me or not?

SCE No, unless you go of your own accord, I'll drag you home 450 with force and against your wishes.

PHIL (*pointing to the house of Periplectomenus*) This is my overseas residence, my house and my procurer are in Athens. I don't care for that house of yours and I don't know or understand who you two are.

SCE Take me to court. I'll never let go of you unless you give me your firm promise that you'll go in here if I do let you go.

PHIL You're forcing me, whoever you are. I give you my prom- 455 ise that if you let go of me, I'll go in there where you tell me to.

SCE Look, I'm letting go! (*does so*)

PHIL But now that you've let go I'll go off.

Exit PHILOCOMASIUM into the house of Periplectomenus.

SCE   muliebri fecit fide.

PAL   Sceledre, manibus amisisti praedam. tam ea est quam
       potis

    nostra erilis concubina. uin tu facere hoc strenue?

SCE   quid faciam?

PAL   effer mihi machaeram huc intus.

SCE   quid facies ea?

460   PAL   intro rumpam recta in aedis: quemque hic intus uidero

    cum Philocomasio osculantem, eum ego optruncabo ex-
       tempulo.

SCE   uisane est ea esse?

PAL   immo edepol plane ea est.

SCE   sed quo modo

    dissimulabat!

PAL   abi, machaeram huc effer.

SCE   iam faxo hic erit.

PAL   neque eques nec pedes profecto est quisquam tanta au-
       dacia

465   qui aeque faciat confidenter quicquam quam mulier fa-
       cit.

    ut utrubique orationem docte diuisit suam,

    ut sublinitur os custodi cauto, conseruo meo!

    nimis beat quod commeatus transtinet trans parietem.

SCE   heus, Palaestrio, machaera nihil opust.

PAL   quid iam? aut quid est?

470   SCE   domi eccam erilem concubinam.

PAL   quid, domi?

SCE   in lecto cubat.

PAL   edepol ne tu tibi malam rem repperisti, ut praedicas.

SCE   quid iam?

PAL   quia hanc attingere ausu's mulierem hinc ex proxumo.

SCE   She's acted with all the reliability of a woman.

PAL   Sceledrus, you've lost the booty from under your hands. She's our master's concubine, sure as can be. Do you want to sort this out by force?

SCE   What should I do?

PAL   Bring me a sword from inside.

SCE   What are you going to do with it?

PAL   I'll burst directly into the house. I'll cut down at once   460 anyone I see in here kissing Philocomasium.

SCE   Did you think it's her?

PAL   Indeed, it's clearly her.

SCE   But how she pretended otherwise!

PAL   Go, bring me out the sword.

SCE   I'll make sure it's here in a second.

Exit SCELEDRUS into the soldier's house.

PAL   No soldier on foot or on horseback is indeed so bold as to   465 do anything as self-confidently as a woman. How cleverly she divided her speech for each part! How her careful guard, my fellow slave, is being tricked! I'm so happy that there's a passage through the wall.

Enter SCELEDRUS from the soldier's house.

SCE   Hey, Palaestrio, there's no need for a sword.

PAL   How come? What's the matter?

SCE   Look, master's concubine is at home.   470

PAL   What? At home?

SCE   She's lying on a couch.

PAL   You've found trouble for yourself, from what you tell me.

SCE   How so?

PAL   Because you dared to touch this girl from next door.

193

SCE magis hercle metuo.

PAL   sed numquam quisquam faciet quin soror
   istaec sit gemina huius: eam pol tu osculantem hic uide-
   ras.

475 SCE id quidem palam est eam esse, ut dicis; quid propius fuit
   quam ut perirem, si elocutus essem ero?

PAL   ergo, si sapis,
   mussitabis: plus oportet scire seruom quam loqui.
   ego abeo a te, ne quid tecum consili commisceam,
   atque apud hunc ero uicinum; tuae mi turbae non pla-
   cent.

480 erus si ueniet, si me quaeret, hic ero: hinc me arcessito.

   II. vi: SCELEDRVS. PERIPLECTOMENVS

SCE satin abiit ille neque erili negotio
   plus curat, quasi non seruitutem seruiat?
   certo illa quidem hic nunc intus est in aedibus,
   nam egomet cubantem eam modo offendi domi.

485 certum est nunc opseruationi operam dare.

PER non hercle hisce homines me marem, sed feminam
   uicini rentur esse serui militis:
   ita me ludificant. meamne hic inuitam hospitam,
   quae heri huc Athenis cum hospite aduenit meo,

490 tractatam et ludificatam, ingenuam et liberam?

SCE perii hercle! hic ad me recta habet rectam uiam.
   metuo illaec mihi res ne malo magno fuat,
   quantum hunc audiui facere uerborum senem.

488 inuitam *A*, inuita *P*, in uia ς

488 inuitam *A*, inuita *P*, in uia ϛ

SCE   I'm getting scared.

PAL   But never will anyone bring it about that she's not our girl's twin sister: she's the one you saw kissing here.

SCE   It's obvious that it's her, as you say; what was closer than   475 my end, if I'd told my master?

PAL   Then you'll keep your mouth shut if you're wise. A slave ought to know more than he says. I'm leaving you so as not to get my plans mixed up with yours, and I'll be at our neighbor's place. I don't like your troublemaking. If our   480 master comes and looks for me, I'll be here: fetch me from here.

Exit PALAESTRIO into the house of Periplectomenus.

SCE   Has he really left and doesn't care about master's business any more than if he weren't a slave? The girl is certainly in here now, in the house: I've just found her sleeping at home myself. I'm resolved to make an effort   485 to keep watch now. (*positions himself in front of the soldier's house*)

Enter PERIPLECTOMENUS from his house.

PER   (*loudly*) These people, the slaves of my neighbor, the soldier, don't think I'm a man, but a woman, to judge from how they treat me as a joke. Is it possible that my guest, who arrived here from Athens yesterday with another guest of mine, was mistreated and treated with contempt against her will, even though she's freeborn and free?   490

SCE   (*aside*) I'm dead! He's walking directly toward me. I'm afraid that that business might end up as big trouble for me, from what I've heard this old man say.

PER   accedam ad hominem. tun, Sceledre, hic, scelerum ca-
         put,
495   meam ludificauisti hospitam ante aedis modo?
SCE   uicine, ausculta quaeso.
PER   ego auscultem tibi?
SCE   [ex]purgare uolo me.
PER   tun ted expurges mihi,
        qui facinus tantum tamque indignum feceris?
        an quia latrocinamini, arbitramini
500   quiduis licere facere uobis, uerbero?
SCE   licetne?
PER   at ita me di deaeque omnes ament
        nisi mi supplicium uirgarum de te datur
        longum diutinumque, a mani ad uesperum,
        quod meas confregisti imbrices et tegulas,
505   ibi dum condignam te sectatu's simiam,
        quodque inde inspectauisti meum apud me hospitem
        amplexum amicam, quom osculabatur, suam,
        quodqu' concubinam erilem insimulare ausus es
        probri pudicam meque summi flagiti,
510   tum quod tractauisti hospitam ante aedis meas:
        nisi mi supplicium stimuleum de ‹te› datur,
        dedecoris pleniorem erum faciam tuom
        quam magno uento plenum est undarum mare.
SCE   ita sum coactus, Periplectomene, ut nesciam
515   utrum me ‹ex›postulare prius tecum aequiust—
        nisi ‹si› istaec non est haec neque ‹haec› ista est, mihi
        med expurgare haec tibi uidetur aequius;
        sicut etiam nunc nescio quid uiderim:

497 [ex]purgare *Lindsay*   511 te *add. Lambinus*
515 ‹ex›postulare *Ritschl*

PER   (*aside*) I'll approach him. (*loudly*) Have you, Sceledrus, maltreated my guest here in front of the house, you   495 source of scandals?

SCE   Neighbor, please listen.

PER   I should listen to you?

SCE   I want to apologize.

PER   You should apologize to me? You've committed such a big and disgraceful offense. Do you think that because you're mercenaries you can do anything you like, you   500 whipping-stock?

SCE   May I?

PER   As truly as all the gods and goddesses may love me, unless I'm given your punishment with rods as compensation, a long and enduring one, from dawn till dusk, because you broke my top and bottom tiles while you were chasing af-   505 ter a monkey quite worthy of yourself, and because you watched my guest from there while he was embracing and kissing his girlfriend, and because you dared to ac- cuse your master's chaste concubine of unchastity and me of the greatest wickedness, and finally because you   510 mistreated my guest in front of my house: unless I'm given your punishment with rods as compensation, I'll fill your master with more disgrace than the sea has waves when there's a strong wind.

SCE   I'm brought to such a pass, Periplectomenus, that I don't know whether I ought to argue with you first—unless, if   515 your guest isn't our girl and our girl isn't your guest, it seems fairer for me to apologize to you for this. In fact, even now I don't know what I've seen: that guest of yours

---

516 si *add. Acidalius*   haec *add. Ritschl*

		ita est ista huius similis nostrai tua,
520		siquidem non eadem est.
	PER	uise ad me intro, iam scies.
	SCE	licetne?
	PER	quin te iubeo; et placide noscita.
	SCE	ita facere certum est.
	PER	heus, Philocomasium, cito
		transcurre curriculo ad nos, ita negotium est.
		post, quando exierit Sceledrus a nobis, cito
525		transcurrito ad uos rursum curriculo domum.
		nunc pol ego metuo ne quid infuscauerit.
		si hic non uidebit mulierem—aperitur foris.
	SCE	pro di immortales! similiorem mulierem
529–		magisque eandem, ut pote quae non sit eadem, non reor
30		deos facere posse.
	PER	quid nunc?
	SCE	commerui malum.
	PER	quid igitur? eane est?
	SCE	etsi ea est, non est ea.
	PER	uidistine istam?
	SCE	uidi et illam et hospitem
		complexam atque osculantem.
	PER	eane est?
	SCE	nescio.
535	PER	uin scire plane?
	SCE	cupio.

is so similar to this girl of ours, if indeed it isn't the same 520
person.

PER Go look inside at my place, you'll know it at once.

SCE May I?

PER Yes; what's more, I order you to do it; and discover the
truth in your own time.

SCE I'm resolved to do so.

Exit SCELEDRUS into the house of Periplectomenus.

PER (*into the soldier's house*) Hey, Philocomasium, run over
to our place very quickly, that's what you have to do.
Then, when Sceledrus has come out from our place, run
over to your place again very quickly. (*to the audience*) 525
Now I'm afraid that she might have got it wrong. If he
doesn't see her—the door is opening.

Enter SCELEDRUS from the house of Periplectomenus.

SCE Immortal gods! I don't think the gods could make a more 530
similar and more identical woman, considering that she's
not the same.

PER What now?

SCE I've deserved a thrashing.

PER Well then? Is it her? (*points to the soldier's house*)

SCE Even if it's her, it's not her.

PER Have you seen that girl of ours?

SCE I've seen her embracing and kissing the guest.

PER Is she this one? (*points to the soldier's house again*)

SCE I don't know.

PER Do you want to know it plainly? 535

SCE I do.

PER   abi intro ad uos domum
continuo, uide sitne istaec uostra intus.

SCE   licet,
pulchre ammonuisti. iam ego ad te exibo foras.

PER   numquam edepol hominem quemquam ludificarier
magis facete uidi et magis miris modis.

540   sed eccum egreditur.

SCE   Periplectomene, te opsecro
per deos atque homines perque stultitiam meam
perque tua genua—

PER   quid opsecras me?

SCE   inscitiae
meae et stultitiae ignoscas. nunc demum scio
me fuisse excordem, caecum, incogitabilem.

545   nam Philocomasium eccam intus.

PER   quid nunc, furcifer?
uidistine ambas?

SCE   uidi.

PER   erum exhibeas uolo.

SCE   meruisse equidem me maxumum fateor malum
et tuae fecisse me hospitae aio iniuriam;
sed meam esse erilem concubinam censui,

550   quoi me custodem erus addidit miles meus.
nam ex uno puteo similior numquam potis
aqua aquai sumi quam haec est atque ista hospita.
et me despexe ad te per impluuium tuom
fateor.

PER   quidni fateare ego quod uiderim?
555   et ibi osculantem meum hospitem cum ista hospita
uidisti?

SCE   uidi—quor negem quod uiderim?—,
sed Philocomasium me uidisse censui.

PER   Go into your home at once and check if that girl of yours is inside.

SCE   Yes, you've given me fine advice. I'll come out to you in a moment.

Exit SCELEDRUS into the soldier's house.

PER   I've never seen anyone being made fun of more neatly and in a more amazing way. But look, he's coming out.   540

Enter SCELEDRUS from the soldier's house.

SCE   Periplectomenus, I beg you by gods and men and by my stupidity and by your knees—

PER   (*interrupting*) What are you begging me for?

SCE   Forgive me for my silliness and stupidity. Now at last I know that I was mad, blind, and thoughtless: Philoco-   545
masium is inside, look.

PER   Well then, you thug? Have you seen both?

SCE   I have.

PER   I want you to produce your master.

SCE   I admit that I've deserved greatest punishment and I say that I've done an injustice to your guest; but I did think that she's my master's concubine, whose guard my mas-   550
ter, the soldier, made me: water more similar to other wa-
ter cannot be drawn from one and the same well than our
girl is to that guest of yours. And I admit that I've looked
down into your place through your roof opening.

PER   Why shouldn't you admit what I myself have seen? And   555
have you seen my male guest kissing my female guest
there?

SCE   I have—why should I deny what I've seen?—but I did
think I'd seen Philocomasium.

	PER	ratun istic me hominem esse omnium minimi preti,
		si ego me sciente paterer uicino meo
560		eam fieri apud me tam insignite iniuriam?
	SCE	nunc demum a me insipienter factum esse arbitror
		quom rem cognosco; at non malitiose tamen
		feci.
	PER	immo indigne; nam hominem seruom suos
		domitos habere oportet oculos et manus
565		orationemque.
	SCE	egone si post hunc diem
		muttiuero, etiam quod egomet certo sciam,
		dato excruciandum me: egomet me dedam tibi;
		nunc hoc mi ignosce quaeso.
	PER	uincam animum meum,
		ne malitiose factum id esse aps te arbitrer.
570		ignoscam tibi istuc.
	SCE	at tibi di faciant bene!
	PER	ne tu hercle, si te di ament, linguam comprimes,
		posthac etiam illud quod scies nesciueris
		nec uideris quod uideris.
	SCE	bene me mones,
		ita facere certum est. sed satine oratu's?
	PER	abi.
575	SCE	numquid nunc aliud me uis?
	PER	ne me noueris.
	SCE	dedit hic mihi uerba. quam benigne gratiam
		fecit ne iratus esset! scio quam rem gerat:
		ut, miles quom extemplo a foro adueniat domum,
		domi comprehendar. una hic et Palaestrio
580		me habent uenalem: sensi et iam dudum scio.
		numquam hercle ex ista nassa ego hodie escam petam;
		nam iam aliquo aufugiam et me occultabo aliquot dies,

PER	Didn't you consider me to be the most worthless human there, if I were to tolerate, with my full knowledge, that my neighbor should suffer this injustice at my hands in such an infamous way?	560
SCE	At last I realize I've acted foolishly, now that I understand the matter. But still, I didn't act out of malice.	
PER	No, but you did act in a disgraceful way: a slave ought to have his eyes, hands, and speech under control.	565
SCE	If after this day I breathe a word, even about something I know for sure, you can hand me over for crucifixion. I will surrender myself to you. Now please forgive me for this.	
PER	I will subdue my wrath so as not to think that you've acted out of malice. I'll forgive you for this.	570
SCE	May the gods bless you!	
PER	Seriously, if the gods love you, you'll keep your tongue in check. From now on don't know even what you do know and don't see what you do see.	
SCE	You're giving me good advice, I'm resolved to do so. But have I implored you for pardon sufficiently?	
PER	Go away.	
SCE	Is there anything else you'd like from me now?	575
PER	Yes, that you don't know me. (*walks toward his house*)	
SCE	(*to the audience*) He's tricked me. How kindly he gave up being angry! I know what he's up to: as soon as the soldier returns home from the forum, I am to be seized at home. He and Palaestrio together are selling me down the river; I've felt it and I've known it for a while already. I'll never seek the bait from that fish trap[20] today: I'll flee somewhere and hide for some days until these commotions	580

---

[20] A *nassa* is a type of basket which fish can enter but not leave (Fest. p. 168 Lindsay).

PLAUTUS

dum haec consilescunt turbae atque irae leniunt.
nam uni satis populo impio merui mali.
585 uerum tamendem quicquid est, ibo hinc domum.
PER illic hinc apscessit. sat edepol certo scio
occisam saepe sapere plus multo suem:
quoin id adimatur ne id quod uidit uiderit?
nam illius oculi atque aures atque opinio
590 transfugere ad nos. usque adhuc actum est probe;
nimium festiuam mulier operam praehibuit.
redeo in senatum rursum; nam Palaestrio
domi nunc apud me est, Sceledrus nunc autem est foris:
frequens senatus poterit nunc haberier.
595 ibo intro, ne, dum apsum, alter sorti defuat.

ACTVS III

III. i: PALAESTRIO. PERIPLECTOMENVS. PLEVSICLES
PAL cohibete intra limen etiam uos parumper, Pleusicles,
sinite me prius perspectare, ne uspiam insidiae sient
concilium quod habere uolumus. nam opus est nunc tuto
loco
unde inimicus ne quis nostri spolia capiat consili.
600 nam bene consultum inconsultum est, si id inimicis usui
est,
nec potest quin, si id inimicis usui est, opsit tibi;

595 multae sortitae fiat *A*, multi (multis *B*2) sortito fuam *P*, alter sorti
defuat *Leo*

---

[21] Humorous comparison of distributing their roles with distributing tasks in the senate.

204

fall silent and these feelings of anger calm down. Yes, I've
deserved enough punishment for a whole wicked nation.
But whatever it is, I'll go home from here.   585

Exit SCELEDRUS into the soldier's house, unseen by Periplec-
tomenus.

PER   He's left. I know full well that a pig when it's been killed
often has far more sense; is it possible that he could be
robbed of having seen what he has seen? Indeed, his
eyes, ears, and thoughts have fled over to our side. Up   590
until now things have been carried out well. The girl
made a terribly amusing effort. I'm returning to the sen-
ate again: Palaestrio is at home at my place now, while
Sceledrus is outside. Now a well-attended senate meet-
ing can be held. I'll go in so that in my absence the second   595
member won't miss the drawing of the lot.[21]

Exit PERIPLECTOMENUS into his house.

ACT THREE

Enter PALAESTRIO from the house of Periplectomenus.

PAL   (*into the house*) You two, stay inside the threshold a little
longer still. Pleusicles, let me first check that there isn't
any ambush anywhere for the gathering we wish to hold:
now we need a safe place from where no enemy can make
spoils out of our plan. (*to the audience*) Indeed, a good   600
plan is no plan at all if it is of use to the enemy, and what is
of use to the enemy can only hinder you. Yes, a well-

nam bene ⟨consultum⟩ consilium surrupitur saepis-
    sume,
si minus cum cura aut cautela locus loquendi lectus est.
quippe qui, si resciuere inimici consilium tuom,
605   tuopte tibi consilio occludunt linguam et constringunt
    manus
atque eadem quae illis uoluisti facere, illi faciunt tibi.
sed speculabor nequis aut hinc aut ab laeua aut a dextera
nostro consilio uenator assit cum auritis plagis.
sterilis hinc prospectus usque ad ultumam est plateam
    probe.
610   euocabo. heus Periplectomene et Pleusicles, progredi-
    mini!

PER   ecce nos tibi oboedientes.

PAL   facile est imperium in bonis.
sed uolo scire, eodem consilio quod intus meditati sumus
gerimus rem?

PER   magis non potest esse ad rem utibile.

PAL   immo ⟨optumum est⟩.
quid tibi, Pleusicles?

PLEV   quodn' uobis placeat, displiceat mihi?
615   quis homo sit magis meus quam tu es?

PAL   loquere lepide et commode.

PER   pol ita decet hunc facere.

PLEV   at hoc me facinus miserum macerat
meumque cor corpusque cruciat.

PER   quid id est quod cruciat? cedo.

PLEV me tibi istuc aetatis homini facinora puerilia
obicere nec te decora nec tuis uirtutibus;
620   ea te expetere ex opibus summis mei honoris gratia

602 consultum *add. Bothe*

206

planned plan is very often snatched away furtively, if the
venue for the conference hasn't been chosen with care or
caution. If the enemy finds out your plan, they tie your   605
tongue and bind your hands with your own plan and do to
you what you wanted to do to them. But I'll spy about so
that no hunter having his ears as nets to snatch our plan is
here or on the left or on the right. (*looks around*) From
here up to the end of the street the view is properly
empty. I'll call them out. (*into the house*) Hey, Periplec-   610
tomenus and Pleusicles, come out!

*Enter PERIPLECTOMENUS and PLEUSICLES from the for-
mer's house.*

PER   Look, we're obeying you.

PAL   Command is easy when it's over the good. But I'd like to
know, are we acting on the same plan that we thought up
inside?

PER   It couldn't be more useful for the matter at hand.

PAL   Indeed, it's the best. What's your view, Pleusicles?

PLEU Shouldn't I like what you two like? (*to Palaestrio*) Who   615
could be more on my side than you are?

PAL   You talk nicely and pleasantly.

PER   He ought to do so.

PLEU But this fact vexes me and tortures my heart and body.

PER   What is it that tortures you? Tell me.

PLEU That I'm imposing on you, a man of your age, juvenile
concerns appropriate neither for yourself nor for your
character; and that I ask you to help me in my love with   620

607 a dext(e)ra *ACD*, dextera *B*
613 optumumst *add. Schoell*

mihique amanti ire opitulatum atque ea te facere facinora

quae istaec aetas fugere facta magis quam sectari solet:

eam pudet me tibi in senecta obicere sollicitudinem.

PAL nouo modo tu homo amas, siquidem te quicquam quod faxis pudet;

625 nihil amas, umbra es amantis magis quam amator, Pleusicles.

PLEV hancine aetatem exercere mei ‹me› amoris gratia?

PER quid ais tu? itane tibi ego uideor oppido Accherunticus?

tam capularis? tamne tibi diu uideor uitam uiuere?

nam equidem hau sum annos natus praeter quinquaginta et quattuor,

630 clare oculis uideo, pernix sum pedibus, manibus mobilis.

PAL si albicapillus hic, uidetur neutiquam ab ingenio senex.

inest in hoc emussitata sua sibi ingenua indoles.

PLEV pol id quidem experior ita esse ut praedicas, Palaestrio;

nam benignitas quidem huius oppido adulescentuli est.

635 PER immo, hospes, magis quom periclum facies, magis nosces meam

comitatem erga te amantem.

PLEV   quid opus nota noscere?

PER ut apud te exemplum experiundi habeas, ne quaeras foris:

nam nisi qui ipse amauit aegre amantis ingenium inspicit:

640 et ego amoris aliquantum habeo umorisque etiam in corpore

necdum exarui ex amoenis rebus et uoluptariis.

uel cauillator facetus uel conuiua commodus

idem ero neque ego oblocutor sum alteri in conuiuio:

incommoditate apstinere me apud conuiuas commodo

645 commemini et meam orationis iustam partem persequi

208

all your might, out of regard for me, and to do deeds
which your age normally flees rather than follows. I'm
ashamed of imposing this worry on you in your old age.

PAL   You're in love in a new way, if you're ashamed of anything
you do; you're not in love at all, you're the shadow of a   625
lover rather than a real lover, Pleusicles.

PLEU   Should I tire you out at your age for the sake of my love?

PER   What do you say? Do I seem so utterly ripe for the Un-
derworld? So fit for the coffin? Do I seem to you to have
lived such a very long life? I'm only fifty-four years old, I   630
see clearly with my eyes, am swift on my feet, agile with
my hands.

PAL   Even if he has white hair, he doesn't appear an old man in
his spirit. There's a perfect, noble character in this man.

PLEU   I realize that it is just as you say, Palaestrio: his kindness is
precisely that of a very young man.

PER   Indeed, my dear guest, when you test me more, you'll get   635
to know more of my friendliness toward you in your love.

PLEU   What need is there to get to know what's known already?

PER   That you may have a lesson of personal experience and
not seek one at second hand: unless someone's been in
love himself he hardly understands a lover's mind. I too   640
still have some love and sap in my body and haven't dried
up for all things lovely and enjoyable. I'll be a witty jester
or a tactful guest, and I'm not the type that contradicts
another in a banquet. I remember suitably to refrain
from tactlessness among guests and to stick to my fair   645
share of talking and in the same way to be silent for my

---

626 me *add. Lindemann*
637 ne itas (negis *CD*) *P*, ne quaeras *Luchs*
643 item *P*, idem *Ussing*

	et meam partem itidem tacere, quom aliena est oratio;
	minime sputator, screator sum, itidem minime mucidus:
	post Ephesi sum natus, non enim in Apulis; non sum Ani-
	mula.
PAL	o lepidum semisenem, si quas memorat uirtutes habet,
650	atque equidem plane educatum in nutricatu Venerio!
PER	plus dabo quam praedicabo ex me uenustatis tibi.
	neque ego umquam alienum scortum subigito in con-
	uiuio
	nec praeripio pulpamentum nec praeuorto poculum
	nec per uinum umquam ex me exoritur discidium in con-
	uiuio:
655	si quis ibi est odiosus, abeo domum, sermonem segrego;
	Venerem, amorem amoenitatemque accubans exerceo.
PAL	tu‹i› quidem edepol omnes mores ad uenustatem ui-
	gent;
	cedo tris mi homines aurichalco contra cum istis mori-
	bus.
PLEV	at quidem illuc aetatis qui sit non inuenies alterum
660	lepidiorem ad omnis res nec magis qui amico amicus sit.
PER	tute me ut fateare faciam esse adulescentem moribus,
	ita apud omnis comparebo tibi res benefactis frequens.
	opusne erit tibi aduocato tristi, iracundo? ecce me!
	opusne leni? leniorem dices quam mutum est mare
665	liquidiusculusque ero quam uentus est fauonius.
	uel hilarissumum conuiuam hinc indidem expromam tibi
	uel primarium parasitum atque opsonatorem optumum;
	tum ad saltandum non cinaedus malacus aeque est atque
	ego.

657 tu‹i› *Camerarius* uicet *CD*[1], uices *D*[2], uacet *B*, uigent *Ribbeck*
660 [magis] quid (qui *B*[2]) amicus amicos sint (sit *B*[2]) magis *P*, qui
amicus amico sit magis ς, magis qui amico amicus sit *Bentley*

part when someone else has the floor. I'm not one to spit, to cough, to sniffle. After all, I was born in Ephesus, not among the Apulians; I'm not from Animula.[22]

PAL   What a lovely semi-old man, if he has the qualities he's talking about, and clearly brought up in Venus' nurture!   650

PER   I'll show you more of my charm than I'll make a show of it. I never make a move on another's prostitute at a banquet, I don't snatch away the titbits, I don't take the cup out of turn, and no disagreement ever arises from me at a banquet on account of the wine. If anyone is tedious   655 there, I go home and cut off the conversation; I practice Venus, love, and loveliness while reclining at table.

PAL   All your ways are geared toward charm. Give me three men with those ways for their weight in mountain copper.[23]

PLEU   Well, you won't find another man of that age to be more   660 charming in all respects or friendlier to a friend.

PER   I'll make you yourself admit that I'm a youngster in character, so overflowing with kind acts will I appear in all things. Do you need a grim, angry advocate? Here I am! Do you need a mild one? You'll call me milder than the silent sea and I'll be gentler than the zephyr. From the   665 very same place I'll produce for you the most joyful guest or a first-rank hanger-on and perfect caterer. Next, when it comes to dancing, a catamite isn't as soft as I am.

---

[22] Apulia, a region in southern Italy, was considered backward, and Animula was a small, poor town in it (Paul. Fest. p. 23 Lindsay).

[23] *Aurichalcum*, from Greek *oreikhalkos* "brass," but with a popular connection with *aurum* "gold," refers to an invented, particularly precious metal.

PAL   quid ad illas artis optassis, si optio eueniat tibi?

670   PLEV   huius pro meritis ut referri pariter possit gratia,

tibique, quibus nunc me esse experior summae sollicitu-
dini.

at tibi tanto sumptui esse mihi molestum est.

PER   morus es.

nam in mala uxore atque inimico si quid sumas, sumptus
est,

in bono hospite atque amico quaestus est quod sumitur:

675   et quod in dinis rebus sumas sumpti sapienti lucro est.

deum uirtute est te unde hospitio accipiam apud me co-
miter:

es, bibe, animo opsequere mecum atque onera te hilari-
tudine.

liberae sunt aedes, liber sum autem ego; me uolo uiuere.

nam mi, deum uirtute dicam, propter diuitias meas

680   licuit uxorem dotatam genere summo ducere;

sed nolo mi oblatratricem in aedis intro mittere.

PAL   quor non uis? nam procreare liberos lepidum est opus.

PER   hercle uero liberum esse tete, id multo lepidiust.

PAL   tu homo et alteri sapienter potis es consulere et tibi.

685   PER   nam bona uxor suaue ductu est, si sit usquam gentium

ubi ea possit inueniri; uerum egone eam ducam domum

quae mihi numquam hoc dicat: "eme, mi uir, lanam, und'
tibi pallium

malacum et calidum conficiatur tunicaeque hibernae
bonae,

ne algeas hac hieme?"—hoc numquam uerbum ex uxore
audias—,

690   uerum prius quam galli cantent quae me e somno susci-
tet,

dicat: "da, mi uir, calendis meam qui matrem munerem,

PAL (*to Pleusicles*) What would you wish for in addition to those skills, if you got a choice?

PLEU (*to Palaestrio*) The means to give him thanks equal to his   670
merits, and you; I realize that I'm causing you two such troubles now. (*to Periplectomenus*) But I'm annoyed that I'm such an expense to you.

PER You're being silly: if you spend something on a bad wife or an enemy, it's an expense, but what's spent on a good guest and a friend is gain. Also what you spend on sacri-   675
fice is profit to a wise man. Thanks to the gods I have the means to give you a kind reception at my place. Eat, drink, enjoy yourself with me, and load yourself up with joy. The house is unengaged, and unengaged am I. I want to live. Thanks to the gods I can say, I could have married a wife with a dowry from a very high family, on account of   680
my wealth. But I don't want to allow a barking bitch into my house.

PAL Why don't you? Begetting children is a joyful business.

PER No, being free is much more joyful.

PAL You can give wise advice to another and to yourself.

PER Yes, a good wife is sweet to marry, if there were any place   685
on earth where one could be found; but should I marry one who'd never say to me: "My dear husband, buy me wool from which a soft and warm cloak can be made for you and good winter tunics, so that you won't feel cold this winter"? This word you'd never hear from a wife; in-   690
stead, before the cocks crow, she'd stir me from my sleep and say: "My dear husband, give me something to give to

da qui faciam condimenta, da quod dem quinquatrubus
praecantrici, coniectrici, hariolae atque haruspicae;
flagitium est si nil mittetur quae supercilio spicit;

695   tum plicatricem clementer non potest quin munerem;
iam pridem, quia nil apstulerit, suscenset ceriaria;
tum opstetrix expostulauit mecum, parum missum sibi;
quid? nutrici non missuru's quicquam quae uernas alit?"
haec atque huius similia alia damna multa mulierum

700   me uxore prohibent, mihi quae huius similis sermones
                sera[n]t.

PAL   di tibi propitii sunt, nam hercle si istam semel amiseris
         libertatem, hau facile in eundem rursum restitues locum.

PLEV at illa laus est, magno in genere et in diuitiis maxumis
         liberos hominem educare, generi monumentum et sibi.

705 PER   quando habeo multos cognatos, quid opus sit mihi libe-
         ris?
         nunc bene uiuo et fortunate atque ut uolo atque animo ut
         lubet.
         mea bona mea morti cognatis didam, inter eos partiam.
         ii apud me aderunt, me curabunt, uisent quid agam, quid
         uelim.
         prius quam lucet assunt, rogitant noctu ut somnum cepe-
         rim.

710   eos pro liberis habebo qui mihi mittunt munera.
        sacruficant: dant inde partem mihi maiorem quam sibi,

700 serant Ω, serat *Lambinus*
708 quid uelim *A*, hic quid u. *P*, ecquid u. ς

---

[24] Presumably the first of March, the Roman New Year. On this day
there was also the *Matronalia*, a feast at which married women gave
each other presents.

my mother on the first of the month,[24] give me something
to make preserves, give me something to give to the sor-
ceress on the festival of Minerva,[25] to the dream inter-
preter, to the clairvoyant, and to the soothsayer; it's a dis-
grace if nothing is sent to the woman who uses eyebrows
to prophesy; next, there is no way round giving a kind   695
present to the woman who folds the clothes; the woman
delivering our food[26] has been angry for a while already
for not getting any tips; then the midwife has complained
to me that she's received too little. What? You're not go-
ing to give anything to the nurse feeding the slaves born
in the house?" These losses caused by women and many
others, similar to these, keep me away from a wife who'd   700
torment me with talk of this sort.

PAL The gods are well disposed toward you: if you lose your
freedom once, you won't easily restore it to its old place
again.

PLEU But it's a source of praise to bring up children in a great
family and in greatest wealth, as a memorial to one's fam-
ily and oneself.

PER Since I have many relatives, why would I need children?   705
Now I'm living well, happily, as I want, and as it pleases
me. On my death I'll distribute my goods among my rela-
tives, I'll divide them among them. They'll be with me,
look after me, visit me to see how I am and what I want.
Before it's light they're present and ask me if I've slept
well. Those who send me gifts I treat as my children.   710
They sacrifice; from there they give a bigger part to me

---

[25] This feast began on March 19 and lasted for five days.
[26] The meaning of *ceriaria* is uncertain; I have treated it as a deriva-
tive of *Ceres*, the goddess of growth and food.

abducunt ad exta; me ad se ad prandium, ad cenam uo-
    cant;

ill' miserrumum se retur minimum qui misit mihi.

illi inter se certant donis, egomet mecum mussito:

715   "bona mea inhiant, me certatim nutricant et munerant."

PAL   nimis bona ratione nimiumque ad te et tuam uitam uides:
    et tibi sunt gemini et trigemini, si te bene habes, filii.

PER   pol si habuissem, satis cepissem miseriarum e liberis:

719–   continuo excruciarer animi: si ei fort' fuisset febris,
20   censerem emori; cecidissetue ebrius aut de equo us-
        piam,

metuerem ne ibi diffregisset crura aut ceruices sibi.

PLEV huic homini dignum est diuitias esse et diu uitam dari,
    qui et rem seruat et se bene habet suisque amicis usui
       est.

725 PAL o lepidum caput! ita me di deaeque ament, aequom fuit
    deos parauisse uno exemplo ne omnes uitam uiuerent;
    sicuti merci pretium statuit qui est probus agoranomus:
    quae proba est merx, pretium ei statuit, pro uirtute ut ue-
       neat,

quae improba est, pro mercis uitio dominum pretio pau-
       peret,

730   itidem diuos dispertisse uitam humanam aequom fuit:
    qui lepide ingeniatus esset, uitam ei longinquam darent,
    qui improbi essent et scelesti, is adimerent animam cito.
    si hoc parauissent, et homines essent minus multi mali
    et minus audacter scelesta facerent facta, et postea,

735   qui homines probi essent, esset is annona uilior.

than to themselves and bring me to the innards. They invite me to lunch and dinner. The one who's sent me least considers himself the most wretched. They're competing among each other with their gifts, and I mutter to myself: "They're staring at my possessions with mouths wide 715 open, they're cherishing me and giving me gifts as if it were a competition."

PAL   You look after yourself and your life with a tremendously good rationale. And if you enjoy yourself, you have twins and triplets.

PER   If I'd had any, I'd have had my share of afflictions from my children. I'd have had mental torture at once. If one 720 had by chance caught a fever, I'd have believed he'd die. Or if one had fallen while drunk or fallen from a horse somewhere, I'd have been afraid that he might have broken his leg or his neck there.

PLEU This man deserves to be given wealth and long life: he looks after his property, has a good time, and is useful to his relations and friends.

PAL   What a delightful creature! As truly as the gods and god- 725 desses may love me, it would have been just if the gods hadn't let all people live life in the same way; just as a good market inspector sets a price for merchandise: good merchandise he values in such a way that it might be sold for its worth, but bad merchandise is to despoil its owner in proportion to its deficiency. It would have been just if 730 the gods had allotted human life in the same way. They'd give long life to a man apt by nature and they'd take the life of rogues and criminals quickly. If they'd gone about like this, there would be fewer bad people and they'd commit their crimes less boldly, and finally, the price of 735 grain would be cheaper for decent people.

217

PER qui deorum consilia culpet stultus inscitusque sit,
quique eos uituperet. nunc [iam] istis rebus desisti decet.
nunc uolo opsonare, ut, hospes, tua te ex uirtute et mea
meae domi accipiam benigne, lepide et lepidis uictibus.

740 PLEV nil me paenitet iam quanto sumptui fuerim tibi;
nam hospes nullus tam in amici hospitium deuorti potest
quin, ubi triduom continuom fuerit, iam odiosus siet;
uerum ubi dies decem continuos sit, ea est odiorum Ilias:
tam etsi dominus non inuitus patitur, serui murmurant.

745 PER seruiendae seruituti ego seruos instruxi mihi,
hospes, non qui mi imperarent quibusue ego essem ob-
    noxius:
si illis aegre est mihi [id] quod uolup est, meo remigio
    rem gerunt,
tamen id quod odio est faciundum est cum malo atque
    ingratiis.
nunc, quod occepi, opsonatum pergam.

PLEV   si certum est tibi,
750 commodulum opsona, ne magno sumptu: mihi quiduis
    sat est.

PER quin tu istanc orationem hinc ueterem atque antiquam
    amoues?
proletario sermone nunc quidem, hospes, utere;
nam i solent, quando accubuere, ubi cena apposita est,
    dicere:
"quid opus fuit hoc ‹sumpto› sumptu tanto nostra gra-
    tia?
755 insaniuisti hercle, nam idem hoc hominibus sat erat de-
    cem."
quod eorum causa opsonatum est culpant et comedunt
    tamen.

737 iam *om.* A

PER A man who'd find fault with the plans of the gods and who'd censure them would be stupid and ignorant. Now we ought to stop such talk. Now I want to buy food, my guest, so that I can receive you kindly in my house, as befits you and me, nicely and with nice dishes.

PLEU I have put you to enough expense already: no guest can   740
put up at such a great friend's place that he wouldn't be a nuisance as soon as it's been three days in a row; but when it's ten days in a row, it's a whole Iliad[27] of hatred. Even if the master doesn't put up with it unwillingly, the slaves mutter.

PER I've schooled my slaves to serve me, my guest, not to or-   745
der me around or for me to be obliged to them. Even if they're upset at what I enjoy, they do their job under my direction and they still have to do what they hate, with beatings and against their wishes. Now I'll continue what I've begun, my shopping.

PLEU If you must, shop moderately, not with big expense; any-   750
thing is enough for me.

PER Why don't you get rid of that old, hackneyed waffle? Now you're using the poor man's way of speaking, my guest: when they've reclined at table and when the food has been placed before them, they usually say: "Why was it necessary to make such a great expense for our sake? You   755
went crazy! This same amount would have been enough for ten." They find fault with what was bought for their sake and yet they eat it up.

[27] This proverbial reference to Homer's masterpiece has less to do with its length than with the anger of the greatest hero in it, Achilles.

---

747 id A, *om.* P (*fortasse ex uersu sequente translatum*)
754 sumpto *add.* Lindsay

PAL   fit pol illuc ad illuc exemplum. ut docte et perspecte sa-
       pit!

PER   sed eidem homines numquam dicunt, quamquam appo-
       situm est ampliter:
       "iube illud demi; tolle hanc patinam; remoue pernam, nil
       moror;

760   aufer illam offam porcinam, probus hic conger frigi-
       dus‹t›,
       remoue, abi aufer": neminem eorum haec asseuerare au-
       dias,
       sed procellunt sese [et procumbunt] in mensam dimidia-
       ti, dum appetunt.

PAL   bonus bene ut malos descripsit mores!

PER   hau centesumam
       partem dixi atque, otium rei si sit, possum expromere.

765 PAL   igitur id quod agitur, ‹ei› hic primum praeuorti decet.
       nunc hoc animum aduortite ambo. mihi opus est opera
       tua,
       Periplectomene; nam ego inueni lepidam sycophantiam
       qui ammutiletur miles usque caesariatus, atque uti
       huic amanti ac Philocomasio hanc efficiamus copiam,

770   ut hic eam abducat habeatque.

PER   dari istanc rationem uolo.

PAL   at ego mi anulum dari istunc tuom uolo.

PER   quam ad rem usui est?

PAL   quando habebo, igitur rationem mearum fabricarum
       dabo.

PER   utere, accipe.

PAL   accipe a me rursum rationem doli
       quam institui.

757 illud (*bis*) P, *corr. Bothe*

PAL   That does indeed happen like that. How cleverly and intelligently he understands!

PER   But however much has been placed in front of them, the same people never say: "Have that taken away; take this platter off; remove the ham, I don't care for any; take 760 that pork dumpling away, the eel is best if it's kept cold, remove it, go on, take it away." You'd hear none of them tell you this; rather, they throw themselves down, with half their bodies hanging over the table, while grabbing things.

PAL   How well this good chap has described bad habits!

PER   I haven't said the hundredth part of what I could expound if we had leisure.

PAL   Then we should give priority here to what's being done. 765 Now pay attention, both of you. I need your help, Periplectomenus: I've found a lovely trick by which the soldier, with his full head of hair, can be fleeced thoroughly and we can create an opportunity for this lover and Philocomasium, that he may take her away and have her. 770

PER   I want to be given this scheme of yours.

PAL   But I want to be given that ring of yours.

PER   For what purpose?

PAL   When I have it, I'll give you the rationale behind my machinations.

PER   Use it, take it. (*hands over his ring*)

PAL   Take in turn from me the rationale I've thought out behind the trick.

---

760 frigidus\<t\> *Ritschl*
762 sed (*uel* se et) procumbunt *P*, sese *Ritschl*
765 ei *add. Bothe*

	PER	perpurigatis damus tibi ambo operam auribus.
775	PAL	erus meus ita magnus moechus mulierum est ut nemi-
		nem
		fuisse aeque nec futurum credo.
	PER	credo ego istuc idem.
	PAL	isque Alexandri praestare praedicat formam suam,
		itaque omnis se ultro sectari in Epheso memorat mulie-
		res.
	PER	edepol qui te de isto multi cupiunt nunc mentirier,
780		sed ego ita esse ut dicis teneo pulchre. proin, Palaestrio,
		quam potis tam uerba confer maxume ad compendium.
	PAL	ecquam tu potis reperire forma lepida mulierem
		quoi facetiarum cor pectusque sit plenum et doli?
	PER	ingenuamne an libertinam?
	PAL	aequi istuc facio, dum modo
785		eam des quae sit quaestuosa, quae alat corpus corpore,
		quoique sapiat pectus; nam cor non potest quod nulla ha-
		bet.
	PER	lautam uis an quae nondum sit lauta?
	PAL	sic consucidam,
		quam lepidissumam potis quamque adulescentem max-
		ume.
	PER	habeo eccillam meam clientam, meretricem adulescen-
		tulam.
790		sed quid ea usus est?
	PAL	ut ad te eam iam deducas domum
		itaque eam huc ornatam adducas, ex matronarum modo,

---

[28] Another name of the Homeric Paris, the Trojan who abducted Helen.

[29] The wordplay is difficult to render. The audience must have in-

PER We're both paying attention to you with thoroughly cleaned ears.

PAL My master is such a great womanizer as I don't believe 775 anyone has ever been or will ever be.

PER I believe the same.

PAL And he claims his beauty is greater than that of Alexander,[28] and he says that this is why all the women in Ephesus run after him.

PER Indeed, many people wish you were lying about that now, but I am truly aware that it is as you say. So save your 780 words as much as possible, Palaestrio.

PAL Can you find me some beautiful woman whose heart and breast are full of wit and guile?

PER Do you want a freeborn girl or one who's been freed?

PAL I don't care so long as you give me one who's good at 785 moneymaking, who feeds her body by means of her body, and who has a wise breast; after all, her heart cannot be wise since no woman has one.

PER Do you want one who is bathed or not yet bathed?[29]

PAL A juicy one like this, as charming and youthful as possible.

PER Look, I have that protégée of mine, a very young prostitute. But what do you need her for? 790

PAL So that you can take her home to your place and bring her here fitted out like this, in the style of matrons, with her

terpreted the first *lautam* as "elegant," but the second, negated *lautam* can hardly have this meaning, as the bait has to be elegant. The second *lautam* seems to be used in a mocktechnical meaning: sheep were shorn when sweaty (Varro, *Rust.* 2.11.6) and the wool was called *sucida lana*; *consucidam* is in fact the word Palaestrio uses. *Lauta/uda* and *sucida* were also used of women who were "wet" and ready for intercourse.

capite compto, crinis uittasque habeat assimuletque se
tuam esse uxorem: ita praecipiundum est.

PLEV   erro quam insistas uiam.

PAL   at scietis. sed ecqua ancilla est illi?

PER   est prime cata.

795 PAL   ea quoque opus est. ita praecipito mulieri atque ancil-
lulae,

ut simulet se tuam esse uxorem et deperire hunc mili-
tem,

quasique hunc anulum faueae suae dederit, ea porro
mihi,

militi ut darem, quasique ego rei sim interpres.

PER   audio.

799   ne me surdum uerberauit! si audes, ego recte meas

799ᵃ   auris ut⟨or⟩ ***

800 PAL   ei dabo, ⟨a⟩ tua mi uxore dicam delatum et datum,

ut sese ad eum conciliarem; ille eius modi est: cupiet mi-
ser,

qui nisi adulterio studiosus rei nulli aliae est improbus.

PER   non potuit reperire, si ipsi Soli quaerendas dares,

lepidiores duas ad hanc rem quam ego. habe animum bo-
num.

805 PAL   ergo accura, sed propere opus est. nunc tu ausculta [mi],
Pleusicles.

PLEV   tibi sum oboediens.

<hr/>

797 hoc *AB*, huc *CD*, hunc ς
799–99ᵃ meas / auris utor *Seyffert, uersum secundum om. P*
800 a *add. Camerarius*
805 mi *om. B*

hair done up; she should have plaits and ribbons and pre-
tend to be your wife.[30] That's what you have to instruct
her in.

PLEU   I fail to see what path you're taking.

PAL   But you'll both know it in time. But does she have some
maid?

PER   She does, a very clever one.

PAL   We need her as well. Instruct the woman and her maid   795
that the woman has to pretend to be your wife and to be
madly in love with this soldier, and that she's given this
ring to her favorite slave girl, and she in turn to me, so
that I should give it to the soldier, and that I am the go-
between for this.

PER   I can hear you. Goodness, he's given me an ear-bashing!
If you please, I use my ears all right ***.

PAL   I'll give it to him and say it was brought and given to me   800
by your wife, to recommend her to him. He's like this: the
poor chap will be desperate; crook that he is, he's only in-
terested in adultery.

PER   If you'd asked Sol[31] himself to look for them, he couldn't
have found two girls more lovely for this business than I
have. Be confident.

PAL   Then take care of it, but we need them quickly.   805

Exit PERIPLECTOMENUS to the right.

PAL   Now you listen, Pleusicles.

PLEU   I'm at your service.

    [30] Festus (p. 454 Lindsay) tells us that Roman matrons parted their
hair into six plaits.

    [31] The sun god, who sees everything.

PAL	hoc facito, miles domum ubi aduenerit,
	memineris ne Philocomasium nomines.
PLEV	quem nominem?
PAL	Diceam.
PLEV	nempe eandem quae dudum constituta est.
PAL	pax! abi.
PLEV	meminero. sed quid meminisse id refert, ‹rogo› ego te
	tamen.

810 PAL ego enim dicam tum quando usus poscet; interea tace;
    ut nunc etiam hic agit, actutum partis defendas tuas.

PLEV eo ego intro igitur.

PAL   et praecepta sobrie ut cures face.

III. ii: PALAESTRIO. LVCRIO

PAL quantas res turbo, quantas moueo machinas!
   eripiam ego hodie concubinam militi,

815   si centuriati bene sunt manuplares mei.
   sed illum uocabo. heus Sceledre, nisi negotium est,
   progredere ante aedis, te uocat Palaestrio.

LVC non operae est Sceledro.

PAL   quid iam?

LVC   sorbet dormiens.

PAL quid, "sorbet"?

LVC   illud "stertit" uolui dicere.

820–   sed quia consimile est, quom stertas, quasi sorbeas -
21 PAL eho an dormit Sceledrus intus?

LVC   non naso quidem,
   nam eo magnum clamat.

809 rogo *add. Brix*

PAL   Make sure that when the soldier comes home you re-
member not to call her Philocomasium.

PLEU What should I call her?

PAL   Justine.

PLEU The same we agreed on a while ago.

PAL   Enough! Off you go.

PLEU I'll remember. But all the same, I ask you what the point
of remembering is.

PAL   I'll tell you when the need arises. Meanwhile be quiet.   810
Just as this chap here is acting now, you must soon defend
your role.

PLEU I'll go in then.

PAL   And make sure you follow my orders soberly.

Exit PLEUSICLES into the house of Periplectomenus.

PAL   What great chaos I'm causing, what great machinations
I'm mobilizing! I'll rescue the concubine from the sol-
dier today, if my fellow fighters are well organized. But   815
I'll call that chap. (*into the soldier's house*) Hey, Scele-
drus, unless you're busy, come out in front of the house,
Palaestrio is calling you.

Enter LUCRIO from the soldier's house.

LUC   Sceledrus doesn't have time.

PAL   How so?

LUC   He's swigging while asleep.

PAL   What? "He's swigging"?

LUC   I meant to say "he's snoring." But because when you   820
snore it's very similar to swigging—

PAL   (*interrupting*) Tell me, is Sceledrus sleeping inside?

LUC   Well, not with his nose: with that he's shouting loudly.

227

	PAL	tetigit calicem clanculum,
		dum misit nardum in amphoram cellarius.
825		eho tu sceleste, qui illi suppromu's, eho.
	LVC	quid uis?
	PAL	qui[d] lubitum est illi condormiscere?
	LVC	oculis opinor.
	PAL	non te istuc rogito, scelus.
		procede huc. periisti iam nisi uerum scio.
		prompsisti tu illi uinum?
	LVC	non prompsi.
	PAL	negas?
830	LVC	nego hercle uero, nam ill' me uotuit dicere;
		neque equidem heminas octo exprompsi in urceum
		neque illic calidum ebibit in prandium.
	PAL	nec tu bibisti?
	LVC	di me perdant si bibi,
		si bibere potui!
	PAL	quid iam?
	LVC	quia enim opsorbui;
835		nam nimis calebat, amburebat gutturem.
	PAL	alii ebrii sunt, alii poscam potitant.
		bono suppromo et promo cellam creditam!
	LVC	tu hercle itidem faceres si tibi esset credita:
839–		quoniam aemulari non licet, nunc inuides.
40	PAL	eho an umquam prompsit antehac? responde, scelus.
		atque ut tu scire possies, dico tibi:
		si falsa dices, Lucrio, excruciabere.

824 domi sitam ardimi nam amphoram *CD*, dormis ita arcliminam phoram *B*, dum misit nardum in amphoram *Ussing*

826 quid Ω, qui *Beroaldus*

838 diem *P*, id- *A*, idem *ς*, itidem *Bergk*

PAL   He touched the wine cup in secret when he put nard[32]
      into the amphora as butler. Hey, you criminal, you who   825
      are his under-butler, hey there!

LUC   What do you want?

PAL   How could he see fit to fall asleep?

LUC   With his eyes, I think.

PAL   That's not what I'm asking you, you thug. Come here!
      You're dead this instant unless I know the truth. Did you
      draw wine for him?

LUC   No, I didn't.

PAL   You deny it?

LUC   I do indeed deny it, since he forbade me to tell. Neither   830
      did I draw two liters[33] into a pitcher, nor did he drink it
      hot for lunch.

PAL   And you didn't drink either?

LUC   May the gods ruin me if I drank, if I was able to drink!

PAL   What do you mean?

LUC   Because I gulped it down: it was too hot and was burning   835
      my throat.

PAL   Some are drunk, others drink vinegar water.[34] What a
      good under-butler and butler the cellar has been en-
      trusted to!

LUC   You would be acting in the same way if it had been en-
      trusted to you. Since you can't do like us, you're jealous   840
      now.

PAL   Hey, has he ever drawn wine before? Answer, thug. And
      so that you may know, I'm telling you: if you tell any lies,
      Lucrio, you'll be tortured.

      [32] A spice commonly used in wine and perfume.
      [33] Lit. eight heminas; a hemina is a little more than one quarter of a
liter.   [34] A common drink for slaves and soldiers.

	LVC	ita uero? ut tu ipse me dixisse delices,
845		post ⟨e⟩ sagina ego eiciar cellaria,
		ut tibi, si promptes, alium suppromum pares.
	PAL	non edepol faciam. age eloquere audacter mihi.
	LVC	numquam edepol uidi promere. uerum hoc erat:
		mihi imperabat, ego promebam postea.
850	PAL	hoc illi crebro capite sistebant cadi.
	LVC	non hercle tam istoc ualide cassabant cadi;
		sed in cella erat paulum nimis loculi lubrici,
		ibi erat bilibris aula sic propter cados,
		ea saepe deciens complebatur: uidi eam
855		plenam atque inanem fieri; opera maxuma,
		ubi bacchabatur aula, cassabant cadi.
	PAL	abi, abi intro iam. uos in cella uinaria
		bacchanal facitis. iam hercle ego illum adducam a foro.
	LVC	perii! excruciabit me erus, domum si uenerit,
860		quom haec facta scibit, quia sibi non dixerim.
		fugiam hercle aliquo atque hoc in diem extollam malum.
		ne dixeritis, opsecro, huic, uostram fidem!
	PAL	quo tu agis?
	LVC	missus sum alio: iam huc reuenero.
	PAL	quis misit?
	LVC	Philocomasium.
	PAL	abi, actutum redi.
865	LVC	quaeso tamen tu meam partem, infortunium
		si diuidetur, me apsente accipito tamen.

845 e *add. Ritschl*

---

[35] The jars (*cadi*) in the cellar were stuck in the sand. The more pots (*aulae*) were filled from them, the more the jars would lean over, until they finally lay empty in the sand.

LUC   Do you say so? So that you yourself can disclose that I told you and I can then be thrown out of my feasting in 845 the cellar, so that you can get yourself another under-butler if you become butler.

PAL   I won't do that. Go on, tell me boldly.

LUC   I never saw him draw wine. Instead it was like this: he commanded me and then *I* drew it.

PAL   That's why the jars stood on their heads there so often.[35] 850

LUC   No, that's not why the jars tottered so much; rather, in the cellar there was a small and very slippery spot. A two-pound pot stood there next to the jars like this. It was often filled ten times: I saw it getting full and empty. When 855 the pot was celebrating the rites of Bacchus,[36] the jars used to totter.

PAL   Go, go in now. *You* are celebrating the rites of Bacchus in the wine cellar. Now I'll bring our master from the forum.

LUC   (*aside*) I'm dead! Master will torture me when he comes home and finds out that this has happened, because I 860 didn't tell him. I'll flee somewhere and postpone this thrashing for another day. (*to the audience*) Don't tell him! I implore your good faith! (*moves to the left*)

PAL   Where are you going?

LUC   I've been sent elsewhere. I'll return here in a minute.

PAL   Who has sent you?

LUC   Philocomasium.

PAL   Go, return at once.

LUC   Still, please take my share in my absence if any beating is 865 being distributed.

[36] The god of wine and inebriation.

PAL   modo intellexi quam rem mulier gesserit:
         quia Sceledrus dormit, hunc succustodem suom
         foras ablegauit, dum ab se huc transiret. placet.
870   sed Periplectomenus quam ei mandaui mulierem
         nimis lepida forma ducit. di hercle hanc rem adiuuant.
         quam digne ornata incedit, hau meretricie!
         lepide hoc succedit sub manus negotium.

III. iii: PERIPLECTOMENVS. ACROTELEVTIVM.
MILPHIDIPPA. PALAESTRIO

PER   rem omnem tibi, Acroteleutium, tibique una, Milphi-
         dippa,
875   domi demonstraui in ordine. hanc fabricam fallaciasque
         minus si tenetis, denuo uolo percipiatis plane;
         satis si intellegitis, aliud est quod potius fabulemur.
ACR   stultitia atque insipientia mea istaec sit, ‹ mi patrone, ›
         me ire in opus alienum aut [t]ibi meam operam pollici-
         tari,
880   si ea in opificina nesciam aut mala esse aut fraudulenta.
PER   at meliust ‹com›monerier.
ACR   meretricem commoneri
         quam sane magni referat, nil clam est. quin egomet ultro,
         postquam adbibere aures meae tuam oram orationis,
         tibi dixi, miles quem ad modum potisset deasciari.
885 PER   at nemo solus satis sapit. nam ego multos saepe uidi
         regionem fugere consili prius quam repertam haberent.
ACR   si quid faciundum est mulieri male atque malitiose,
         ea sibi immortalis memoria est meminisse et sempiterna;

878 mi patrone *add. Leo*
879 tibi *P*, ibi *Leo*
881 ‹com›monerier *Schoell*

Exit LUCRIO to the left.

PAL   I've just realized what the girl has been doing. Because
Sceledrus is asleep, she's sent this underguard of hers
away so that meanwhile she could cross over from her
place to here. I like it. (*looks to the right*) But as for the   870
woman I told Periplectomenus to hire, he's hiring a very
pretty one. The gods are supporting our cause. How wor-
thily dressed up she comes along, not in the style of a
prostitute! This affair is shaping up well under my hands.

*Enter PERIPLECTOMENUS from the right, together with
ACROTELEUTIUM and MILPHIDIPPA.*

PER   I've shown you, Acroteleutium, and you with her, Milphi-
dippa, the whole business in order in your house. If you   875
haven't grasped this machination and these tricks, I want
you to learn them again clearly. If you understand them
sufficiently, there's something else we can talk about.

ACR   It would be stupid and daft of me, my patron, to go into
another's business or to promise you my help, if in this   880
trade I didn't know how to be bad or deceitful.

PER   But it's better to be reminded.

ACR   (*laughing*) It's not concealed from me how important it is
for a prostitute to be reminded. No, after my ears drank
up only the shore of your speech, I told you of my own ac-
cord how the soldier could be trimmed.

PER   But nobody is clever enough on his own: I've often seen   885
many run away from the land of good counsel before
they'd found it.

ACR   If a woman has to do something bad and malicious,
her memory for that is immortal and perpetual. But if

233

		sin bene quid aut fideliter faciundum est, eo deueniunt
890		obliuiosae extemplo uti fiant, meminisse nequeunt.
	PER	ergo istuc metuo, quom uenit uobis faciundum utrum-
		que:
		nam id proderit mihi, militi male quod facietis ambae.
	ACR	dum nescientes quod bonum faciamus, ne formida.
894–	PER	mala mille meres.
95	ACR	st! ne paue, peioribus conueniunt.
	PER	ita uos decet. consequimini.
	PAL	cesso ego illis obuiam ire.

uenire saluom gaudeo, lepide hercle ornatus [in]cedis.

	PER	bene opportuneque obuiam es, Palaestrio. em tibi assunt
		quas me iussisti adducere et quo ornatu.
	PAL	eu! noster esto.
900		Palaestrio Acroteleutium salutat.
	ACR	quis hic amabo est
		qui tam pro nota nominat me?
	PER	hic noster architectust.
	ACR	salue, architecte.
	PAL	salua sis. sed dic mihi, ecquid hic te
		onerauit praeceptis?
	PER	probe meditatam utramque duco.
	PAL	audire cupio quem ad modum; ne quid peccetis paueo.
905	PER	ad tua praecepta de meo nihil his nouom apposiui.

894 mala milla mer est *CD*, mala mulier est *B*, mala mille meres—st
Lindsay, mala mulier mers est *Bentley*

897 incedit *P*, cedis *Bothe*

234

| | women have to do something good or reliable, they come to be forgetful immediately and are unable to remember. | 890 |

PER Then that's what I'm afraid of, since the opportunity to do both is coming to you two: the bad both of you do the soldier will benefit me.

ACR So long as we do something good without knowing about it, you can stop being afraid.

PER You deserve a thousand bad things. 895

ACR Hush! Don't be alarmed, they're appropriate for women who are still worse.

PER The proper thing for you two! Follow me.

PAL (*aside*) I'm wasting time when I should be approaching them. (*to Periplectomenus*) I'm glad you've arrived safely, you're coming beautifully furnished.

PER You're meeting me at just the right time, Palaestrio. Here are the women for you whom you told me to bring to you and in the outfit you told me.

PAL (*to Periplectomenus*) Excellent! Be one of us. (*to Acroteleutium*) Palaestrio gives his greetings to Acroteleutium. 900

ACR (*to Periplectomenus*) Please, who is this who's calling me by name as if he knew me?

PER He's our master builder.

ACR My greetings, master builder.

PAL And mine to you. But tell me, has this chap here loaded you down with instructions at all?

PER I'm bringing them well prepared.

PAL I wish to hear how; I'm afraid that you two might make some mistake.

PER I didn't add anything new of my own to your instructions for them. 905

	ACR	nemp' ludificari militem tuom erum uis?
	PAL	elocuta es[t].
	ACR	lepide et sapienter, commode et facete res parata est.
	PAL	atque huius uxorem ‹esse› te uolo assimulare.
	ACR	fiat.
	PAL	quasi militi animum adieceris simulare.
	ACR	sic futurum est.
910	PAL	quasique ea res per me interpretem et tuam ancillam ei
		curetur.
	ACR	bonus uates poteras esse, nam quae sunt futura dicis.
	PAL	quasique anulum hunc ancillula tua aps te detulerit ad
		me
		quem ego militi ‹porro› darem tuis uerbis.
	ACR	uera dicis.
	PER	quid istis nunc memoratis opust quae commeminere?
	ACR	meliust.
915		nam, mi patrone, hoc cogitato, ubi probus est architec-
		tus,
		bene lineatam si semel carinam collocauit,
		facile esse nauem facere, ubi fundata, constituta est.
		nunc haec carina satis probe fundata et bene statuta est,
		assunt fabri architectici ad eam ‹rem› haud imperiti.
920		si non nos materiarius remoratur, quod opus‹t› qui det,
		—noui indolem nostri ingeni—cito erit parata nauis.
	PAL	nemp' tu nouisti militem meum erum?

906 es[t] *plerique editores*
908 esse *add. Camerarius*
913 porro *add. Reiz*
919 architectique *P*, architectici *Seyffert*   rem *add. Pylades*
920 opus‹t› *Lambinus*

236

ACR   (*to Palaestrio*) You want your master, the soldier, to be made a fool of?

PAL   You've said it.

ACR   The business is prepared in a lovely and clever way, properly and humorously.

PAL   And I want you to pretend to be this chap's wife.

ACR   It shall be done.

PAL   To pretend that you've fallen for the soldier.

ACR   So it shall be.

PAL   And that this is done for him through me as go-between   910
and through your slave girl.

ACR   You'd have made a good seer: you're saying what's going to happen.

PAL   And that your slave girl has brought this ring from you to me, so that I could pass it on to the soldier in your name.

ACR   You're speaking the truth.

PER   (*to Palaestrio*) What need is there to discuss the instructions now which they've memorized?

ACR   It's better to do so. Yes, my patron, think about this: 915
where there's a decent master builder, if he's set the keel well in line, it's easy to build the ship when it's laid out and set out. Now this keel has been laid out properly and set out well. The master builder's workmen, not inexperienced in this matter, are present. If the supplier of timber,[37] who should give us what we need, doesn't delay   920
us—I know what sort of characters we have—the ship will be ready quickly.

PAL   You know my master, the soldier?

[37] This is the soldier himself, who supplies the stupidity and vanity necessary for being ridiculed and tricked.

237

ACR   rogare mirum est.
populi odium quidni nouerim, magnidicum, cincinna-
tum,
moechum unguentatum?

PAL   num ille te nam nouit?

ACR   numquam uidit:
925   qui nouerit me quis ego sim?

PAL   nimis lepide fabulare;
eo pote fuerit lepidius pol fieri.

ACR   potin ut hominem
mihi des, quiescas cetera? ni ludificata lepide
ero, culpam omnem in me imponito.

PAL   age igitur intro abite,
insistite hoc negotium sapienter.

ACR   alia cura.
930 PAL   age, Periplectomene, has nunciam duc intro; ego ad fo-
rum illum
conueniam atque illi hunc anulum dabo atque praedica-
bo
a tua uxore mihi datum esse eamque illum deperire;
hanc ad nos, quom extemplo a foro ueniemus, mittitote
quasi clanculum ad ‹eum› missa sit.

PER   faciemus: alia cura.
935 PAL   uos modo curate, ego illum probe iam oneratum huc ac-
ciebo.

PER   bene ambula, bene rem geras. egone hoc si efficiam
plane,
ut concubinam militis meus hospes habeat hodie
atque hinc Athenas auehat, ‹si› hodie hunc dolum dola-
mus,
939–
40   quid tibi ego mittam muneris!

238

ACR It's strange you ask. Why shouldn't I know that object
     of popular hatred, the boastful, curly-haired, perfumed
     adulterer?

PAL He doesn't know you, does he?

ACR He's never seen me; how could he know who I am? 925

PAL You're talking very pleasantly. That's how it's become
     possible for our intrigue to be conducted more pleas-
     antly.

ACR Can't you give me the man and be silent about the rest?
     Unless I make a fool of him in fine style, you can lay all
     the blame on me.

PAL Go on then, go inside, you two, and set yourselves to
     work wisely.

ACR Worry about something else.

PAL Go on, Periplectomenus, take them in now. I'll meet the 930
     soldier at the forum and give him this ring and say that it
     was given to me by your wife and that she is madly in love
     with him. As soon as we come from the forum, send her
     (*points to Milphidippa*) to us as if she'd been sent to him
     secretly.

PER We'll do so; worry about something else.

PAL You just take care of your part; I'll fetch him here now 935
     loaded up nicely.

PER Have a good walk and be successful. If I bring it about
     that my guest has the soldier's concubine today and takes
     her away to Athens, if we hew this trick into shape today,
     what a gift I'll give you! 940

Exit PALAESTRIO to the right.

---

926 potiuerim *P*, pote fuerit *Lindsay*
934 eum *add. Pylades*   938 si *add. Camerarius*

ACR	datne ab se mulier operam?
PER	lepidissume et comissume—
ACR	confido confuturum.

ubi facta erit collatio nostrarum malitiarum,
hau uereor ne nos subdola perfidia peruincamur.

PER abeamus ergo intro, haec uti meditemur cogitate,
945 ut accurate et commode hoc quod agendum est exsequa-
mur,
ne quid, ubi miles uenerit, titubetur.

ACR tu morare.

ACTVS IV

IV. i: PYRGOPOLINICES. PALAESTRIO

PYR uolup est, quod agas, si id procedit lepide at⟨que ex⟩ sen-
tentia;
nam ego hodie ad Seleucum regem misi parasitum
meum,
ut latrones quos conduxi hinc ad Seleucum duceret,
950 qui eius regnum tutarentur, mihi dum fieret otium.

PAL quin tu tuam rem cura potius quam Seleuci, quae tibi
condicio noua et luculenta fertur per me interpretem.

PYR immo omnis res posteriores pono atque operam do tibi.
loquere: auris meas profecto dedo in dicionem tuam.

955 PAL circumspicedum ne quis nostro hic auceps sermoni siet.
nam hoc negoti clandestino ut agerem mandatum est
mihi.

PYR nemo adest.

947 at⟨que ex⟩ ς

ACR   Is the girl herself helping us?

PER   In a perfectly charming and clever way—

ACR   (*interrupting*) I trust things will turn out well. When we've brought together our resources of malice, I'm not afraid that we'll be conquered by tricky perfidy.

PER   Let's go in then to think this through thoughtfully, so that 945
we may carry out precisely and properly what needs to be done, so that no slip will be made when the soldier comes.

ACR   You are the one delaying us.

Exit PERIPLECTOMENUS into his house, followed by ACRO-TELEUTIUM and MILPHIDIPPA.

ACT FOUR

Enter PYRGOPOLINICES and PALAESTRIO from the right.

PYR   It's a pleasure if your business goes well and according to your wishes: I've sent my hanger-on to King Seleucus today to bring him the mercenaries I hired from here, so 950
that they can guard his kingdom while I have some rest.

PAL   Look after your own business rather than that of Seleucus, I mean the new and dazzling offer that's brought to you through me as go-between.

PYR   Yes, I consider everything else of secondary importance and am giving you my attention. Speak: I do indeed surrender my ears to you.

PAL   Do look around to check that there's no bird-catcher for 955
our conversation here: I was commissioned to carry out this business in secret.

PYR   (*looking around*) No one's here.

PAL	hunc arrabonem amoris primum a me accipe.
PYR	quid hic? unde est?
PAL	a luculenta ac festiua femina,

quae te amat tuamque expetessit pulchram pulchritudinem;

960 eius nunc mi anulum ad te ancilla porro ut deferrem dedit.

PYR quid ea? ingenuane an festuca facta e serua libera est?

PAL uah! egone ut ad te ab libertina esse auderem internuntius,

qui ingenuis satis responsare nequeas quae cupiunt tui?

964–
65 PYR nuptan est an uidua?

PAL et nupta et uidua.

PYR quo pacto potis

nupta et uidua esse eadem?

PAL quia adulescens nupta est cum sene.

PYR eugae!

PAL lepida et liberali forma est.

PYR caue mendacium.

PAL ad tuam formam illa una digna est.

PYR hercle pulchram praedicas.

sed quis ea est?

PAL senis huius uxor Periplectomeni e proxumo.

970 ea demoritur te atque ab illo cupit abire: odit senem.

nunc te orare atque opsecrare iussit ut eam copiam

sibi potestatemque facias.

PYR cupio hercle equidem si illa uolt.

PAL quae cupit?

PYR quid illa faciemus concubina quae domi est?

PAL	First, receive this token of love from me. (*hands over the ring*)
PYR	What's this supposed to mean? Where is it from?
PAL	From a dazzling and enjoyable woman who loves you and seeks your beautiful beauty. Now her maid has given me 960 this ring to pass on to you.
PYR	What about her? Is she freeborn or has she been freed by the rod[38] from being a slave?
PAL	Bah! Would I dare to be a go-between for you from a freedwoman? You can hardly reply to all the freeborn women who desire you.
PYR	Is she married or single? 965
PAL	Both married and single.
PYR	How can the same woman be married and single?
PAL	Because she's young, but married to an old man.
PYR	Hurray!
PAL	She has the attractive appearance worthy of a freeborn woman.
PYR	No lies to me.
PAL	She alone is worthy of your beauty.
PYR	Goodness, you say that she really is beautiful. But who is she?
PAL	The wife of this old man next door, Periplectomenus. She's dying for you and desires to leave him; she hates the 970 old man. Now she's told me to ask and beg you to give her the chance and opportunity for this.
PYR	I for one long for it if she wants to.
PAL	Wants to? She longs for it.
PYR	What will we do with that concubine who's at home?

---

38 A rod was used by the lictor in manumissions.

PAL	quin tu illam iube aps te abire quo lubet: sicut soror
975	eius huc gemina uenit Ephesum et mater, accersuntque eam.
PYR	eho tu, aduenit Ephesum mater eius?
PAL	aiunt qui sciunt.
PYR	hercle occasionem lepidam, ut mulierem excludam foras!
PAL	immo uin tu lepide facere?
PYR	loquere et consilium cedo.
PAL	uin tu illam actutum amouere, a te ut abeat per gratiam?
980 PYR	cupio.
PAL	tum te hoc facere oportet. tibi diuitiarum affatim est: iube sibi aurum atque ornamenta, quae illi instruxti mulieri,
	dono habere, ⟨abire,⟩ auferre aps te quo lubeat sibi.
PYR	placet ut dicis; sed ne istanc amittam et haec mutet fidem uide modo.
PAL	uah! delicatu's, quae te tamquam oculos amet.
985 PYR	Venus me amat.
PAL	st tace! aperiuntur fores, concede huc clanculum. haec celox illiust, quae hinc egreditur, internuntia.
PYR	quae [haec] celox?
PAL	ancillula illius est, quae hinc egreditur foras. quae anulum istunc attulit quem tibi dedi.
PYR	edepol haec quidem bellula est.

982 abire *add. Goetz*
987 haec *del. Bothe* (*ex priore uersu huc translatum*)

244

PAL	Tell her to go away wherever she wants to go. In fact, her twin sister and her mother have come here to Ephesus 975 and want to fetch her.
PYR	Tell me, has her mother come to Ephesus?
PAL	Those who know it say so.
PYR	A perfect opportunity to shut the girl out of the house!
PAL	Do you want to do so in a delightful way?
PYR	Yes, speak and tell me your plan.
PAL	Do you want to remove her immediately, yet in such a way that she leaves you amicably?
PYR	I wish for it. 980
PAL	Then you should do this. You have more than enough wealth: let the girl have the gold and jewelry you furnished her with as a present, let her go, and let her take it from you where she likes.
PYR	I like what you say. But just make sure that I don't lose the previous one while the new one breaks her promise.
PAL	Bah! You're joking. She loves you like her eyes.
PYR	Venus loves me. 985
PAL	(*listening intently*) Hush, be quiet! The door is opening, walk over here secretly. (*they step aside*)

Enter MILPHIDIPPA from the house of Periplectomenus.

PAL	The woman coming out is her speedboat, her go-between.
PYR	What speedboat?
PAL	The woman coming out is her maid. She brought that ring I gave you.
PYR	She's a pretty little thing.

PAL   pithecium haec est prae illa et spinturnicium.

990   uiden tu illam oculis uenaturam facere atque aucupium
           auribus?

IV. ii: MILPHIDIPPA. PYRGOPOLINICES. PALAESTRIO

MILPH iam est ante aedis circus ubi sunt ludi faciundi mihi.
           dissimulabo, hos quasi non uideam neque esse hic etiam-
           dum sciam.

PYR   tace, subauscultemus ecquid de me fiat mentio.

MILPH numquis[nam] hic prope adest qui rem alienam potius
           curet quam suam,

995   qui aucupet me quid agam, qui de uesperi uiuat suo?
           eos nunc homines metuo, mihi ne opsint neue opstent
           uspiam,

997   domo si bita‹n›t, dum huc transbitat, quae huius cupiens
           corporist,

997ᵃ   ‹er›a mea, quoius propter amorem cor nunc miser‹ae
           contremit›,

998   quae amat hunc hominem nimium lepidum et nimia pul-
           chritudine,
           militem Pyrgopolinicem.

PYR   satin haec quoque me deperit?

1000   meam laudat speciem. edepol huius sermo hau cinerem
           quaeritat.

PAL   quo argumento?

PYR   quia enim loquitur laute et minime sordide.

PAL   quicquid istaec de te loquitur, nihil attrectat sordidi.

---

994 nam *del. Reiz*
997 bita‹n›t *Lindsay*
997ᵃ *uersus in Palatinis non fertur*   ‹er›a, miser‹ae contremit›
Goetz

PAL   She's a little monkey, a little ugly duckling compared with
her mistress.[39] Can you see that she is hunting with her 990
eyes and catching birds with her ears?

MILPH *(to the audience)* Now the circus where I have to per-
form the games is in front of the house. I'll pretend not to
see them and not to know yet that they're here.

PYR   *(to Palaestrio)* Be quiet, let's listen if any mention is made
of me.

MILPH *(to the audience)* Is anyone near who busies himself
with someone else's business rather than his own, who 995
spies on what I'm doing, who lives on his own dinner?[40]
I'm afraid that such people might hinder me or stand in
my way if they leave home while the woman who desires
his body comes over here, my mistress. The heart of this
wretched woman is now trembling because of her love
for him; she loves this terribly lovely and terribly beauti-
ful man, the soldier Pyrgopolinices.

PYR   *(to Palaestrio)* Is she too really madly in love with me?
She's praising my appearance. Her speech needs no ash. 1000

PAL   By what token?

PYR   Because she speaks in a neat and by no means unpolished
way.[41]

PAL   She doesn't touch any unpolished topic, whatever she
speaks about you.

---

[39] Monkeys were considered ugly. It is unclear what species of bird
is referred to with the Greek-style diminutive *spinturnicium*, but ac-
cording to Festus (p. 446 Lindsay) the *spintyrnix* is an ugly type of bird.

[40] He does not have to earn his dinner from someone else and thus
has much free time.

[41] Ash was used as polish.

PYR	tum autem illa ipsa est nimium lepida nimisque nitida fe-
	mina.
	hercle uero iam allubescit primulum, Palaestrio.
1005 PAL	priusne quam illam oculis tuis—
PYR	uideone id quod credo tibi?
	tum haec celocla autem illa apsente subigit me ut amem.
PAL	hercle hanc quidem
	nil tu amassis; mi haec desponsa est: tibi si illa hodie nup-
	serit,
	ego hanc continuo uxorem ducam.
PYR	quid ergo hanc dubitas colloqui?
PAL	sequere hac me ergo.
PYR	pedisequos tibi sum.
MILPH	utinam, quoius causa foras
1010	sum egressa, ⟨eius⟩ conueniundi mihi potestas euenat.
PAL	erit et tibi exoptatum optinget, bonum habe animum, ne
	formida;
	homo quidam est qui scit quod quaeris ubi sit.
MILPH	quem ego hic audiui?
PAL	socium tuorum conciliorum et participem consiliorum.
MILPH	tum pol ego id quod celo hau celo.
PAL	immo et celas et non celas.
1015 MILPH	quo argumento?
PAL	infidos celas: ego sum tibi firme fidus.
MILPH	cedo signum, si harunc Baccharum es.
PAL	amat mulier quaedam quendam.
MILPH	pol istuc quidem multae.
PAL	at non multae de digito donum mittunt.

1006 autem *del.* Brix (*cui* celocla *displicet*)
1010 eius *add.* Spengel

PYR   But then her mistress is a terribly charming and terribly neat woman. Goodness, she already begins to please me a first little bit, Palaestrio.

PAL   Before you've set eyes on her?   1005

PYR   Doesn't my belief in you amount to seeing? Then this speedboat forces me in her mistress's absence to love her.

PAL   No, her you mustn't love; she's engaged to me. If her mistress marries you today, I'll immediately take this one as my wife.

PYR   Then why do you hesitate to address her?

PAL   Follow me then.

PYR   I'm your footman. (*they approach her, but remain unseen*)

MILPH   (*to the audience*) I hope I'll get the opportunity to meet the man for whose sake I've come out.   1010

PAL   (*to Milphidippa*) You will get it and your wish will come true. Take heart, stop being afraid. There's a man who knows where you're looking for is.

MILPH   Whom have I heard here?

PAL   A comrade in your councils and a sharer in your counsels.

MILPH   Then I'm not concealing what I'm trying to conceal.

PAL   Actually, you do conceal it and you don't conceal it.

MILPH   How do you mean?   1015

PAL   You conceal it from those deserving no trust; I deserve your complete trust.

MILPH   Give me the password, if you're one of these bacchantes.

PAL   A certain woman is in love with a certain man.

MILPH   Well, many women are.

PAL   But not many send a gift from their fingers. (*steps forward*)

MILPH enim cognoui nunc, fecisti modo mi ex procliuo pla-
num.

sed hic numquis adest?

PAL   uel adest uel non.

MILPH   cedo te mihi solae solum.

1020 PAL breuin an longinquo sermoni?

MILPH   tribus uerbis.

PAL   iam ad te redeo.

PYR quid ego? hic astabo tantisper cum hac forma et factis
frustra?

PAL patere atque asta, tibi ego hanc do operam.

PYR   propera, ⟨expecta⟩ndo excrucior.

PAL pedetemptim—tu haec scis—tractari satiust hasce huius
modi mercis.

PYR age age ut tibi maxume concinnum est.

PAL   nullum est hoc stolidius saxum.

1025 redeo ad te. quid me uoluisti?

MILPH   quo pacto hoc Ilium appelli
uelis, ut ferrem aps te consilium.

PAL   quasi hunc depereat.

MILPH   teneo istuc.

PAL collaudato formam et faciem et uirtutes commemorato.

MILPH ad eam rem habeo omnem aciem, tibi uti dudum iam
demonstraui.

1020 sermonae *B*, sermone *CD*, sermoni *Ritschl*
1021 sit frustram *B*, si sic frustram *CD*, frustra *Guyet*
1022 properando *P*, propera ⟨expecta⟩ndo *Ritschl*
1023 tractare *P*, tractari *Angelius*   sole *B*, soleet *D¹*, soles *CD²*,
satiust *Leo*   1025 apeli *CD¹*, aperi *D⁴*, accepi *B²*, appelli *Lindsay*
1026 uelis ut a—*A*, uelis ut fero ad te *B*, uaeli sit fero ad be *CD*, uelis
ut ferrem abs te *Leo*

250

MILPH Now I've recognized you, you've just made the rough places plain for me. But is anyone here?

PAL Yes and no.[42]

MILPH I want you all alone.

PAL For a short or a long talk? 1020

MILPH For three words.

PAL (*to the soldier*) I'll come back to you in a moment.

PYR What about me? Am I to stand here for so long, all for nothing, despite my beauty and deeds?

PAL Bear with me and stand here, I'm making this effort for you.

PYR Hurry up, I'm tortured by the wait.

PAL It's better—you know that—to handle such goods cautiously.

PYR All right, as it pleases you most.

PAL (*as he steps aside so as not to be overheard by the soldier*) No stone is more stupid than him. (*to Milphidippa*) I'm 1025 returning to you. What did you want from me?

MILPH To get your advice on how you want this Troy attacked.[43]

PAL As if she were dying for him.

MILPH I've got that.

PAL Praise his looks and appearance and speak about his exploits.

MILPH I have all my wits sharpened for this, as I showed you a while ago already.

---

[42] The soldier is present, but no enemy.

[43] Troy was taken through a clever trick: Greek soldiers hid in a wooden horse and only came out once the horse had been brought into Troy. Pyrgopolinices also loses his mistress through a trick.

PAL   tu cetera cura et contempla et de meis uenator uerbis.

1030 PYR   aliquam mihi partem hodie operae des denique, iam tan-
dem ades: uolo te.

PAL   assum, impera si quid uis.

PYR   quid illaec narrat tibi?

PAL   lamentari
ait illam, miseram cruciari et lacrumantem se afflictare,
quia tis egeat, quia te careat. ob eam rem huc ad te missa
est.

PYR   iube adire.

PAL   at scin quid tu facias? facito fastidi plenum,

1035   quasi non lubeat; me inclamato, quia [sic] tam te uolgo
uolgem.

PYR   memini et praeceptis parebo.

PAL   uocon ergo hanc quae te quaerit?

PYR   adeat, si quid uolt.

PAL   si quid uis, adi, mulier.

MILPH   pulcher, salue.

PYR   meum cognomentum commemorat. di tibi dent quae-
quomque optes.

MILPH tecum aetatem exigere ut liceat—

PYR   nimium optas.

MILPH   non me dico,

1040   sed eram meam quae te demoritur.

PYR   aliae multae idem istuc cupiunt
quibus copia non est.

1030 ilico *P*, uolo te *Niemeyer*, illinc *Boldrini*
1034 facito *CD*, facite *B*, face te *Pontanus*
1035 sic *del. Baier*
1038 commemorauit *P*, commemorat *Hermann*

PAL   You take care of the rest and observe and follow the track of my words.

PYR   (*calling Palaestrio*) Give me some part of your attention   1030 in the end today, now attend to me at last: I want you.

PAL   (*returning to the soldier so as not to be overheard by Milphidippa*) I am attending to you, command me if you want anything.

PYR   What does she tell you?

PAL   She says her poor mistress is lamenting, torturing herself, and wearing herself out with weeping, because she lacks you, because she's without you. That's why she was sent to you.

PYR   Have her come here.

PAL   But do you know what you should do? Be full of disdain, as if you weren't interested. Shout at me because I publi-   1035 cize you to the public like this.

PYR   I remember it and I'll obey your instructions.

PAL   Then am I to call the woman who seeks you?

PYR   Let her come if she wants to.

PAL   (*to Milphidippa*) If you want anything, come, woman.

MILPH My greetings, beautiful one.

PYR   She speaks my surname. May the gods give you everything you wish for.

MILPH Yes, that it may be possible to spend life with you—

PYR   (*interrupting*) You wish for too much.

MILPH I don't mean possible for me, but for my mistress, who   1040 is dying for you.

PYR   Many others have that same desire, yet no possibility of achieving it.

MILPH   ecastor hau mirum si te habes carum,
          hominem tam pulchrum et praeclarum uirtute et forma
             ⟨et⟩ factis.
          deus dignior fuit quisquam homo qui esset?

PAL   non hercle humanust ergo.
          nam uolturio plus humani credo est.

PYR   magnum me faciam
1045   nunc quom illaec me sic collaudat.

PAL   uiden tu ignauom ut sese infert?
          quin tu huic responde, haec illaec est ab illa quam dudum
             ⟨dixi⟩.

PYR   qua ab illarum? nam ita me occursant multae: meminisse
          hau possum.

MILPH   ab illa quae digitos despoliat suos et tuos digitos deco-
          rat.
          nam hunc anulum ⟨ego⟩ ab tui cupienti huic detuli, hic
             ⟨ad te⟩ porro.

1050 PYR   quid nunc tibi uis, mulier? memora.

MILPH   ut quae te cupit, eam ne spernas,
          quae per tuam nunc uitam uiuit: sit necn' sit spes in te
          uno est.

PYR   quid nunc uolt?

MILPH   te compellare et complecti et contrectare.
          nam nisi tu illi fers suppetias, iam illa animum desponde-
          bit.
          age, mi Achilles, fiat quod te oro, serua illam pulchram
          pulchre,
1055   exprome benignum ex te ingenium, urbicape, occisor
          regum.

1042 ⟨et⟩ factis *Camerarius*
1045 illic *P*, sic *Ritschl*

MILPH Goodness, it's no surprise if you hold yourself dear, such
a beautiful man famous for his bravery, looks, and deeds.
Has any human ever been worthier to be a god?

PAL (*aside*) Well then, he isn't human: I believe even a vulture
has more humanity.

PYR (*aside*) I'll make myself important now that she praises 1045
me like this.

PAL (*aside*) Can you see how the good-for-nothing is strutting
along? (*to the soldier*) Do give her a reply, she's that maid
from the woman I told you about some time ago.

PYR From which of them? So many approach me, I can't re-
member them all.

MILPH From the one who is robbing her fingers and adorning
yours: I brought this ring from the woman who desires
you to him, and he passed it on to you.

PYR What do you want now, woman? Tell me. 1050

MILPH That you don't spurn the woman who desires you, who
now lives through your life; whether she has hope or not
depends entirely on you.

PYR What does she want now?

MILPH To address you, embrace you, caress you; unless you
come to her help, she'll lose all hope. Go on, my dear
Achilles, fulfill my request, save that beautiful woman
beautifully, display your kind nature, you capturer of 1055
cities,[44] you slayer of kings.

[44] A reference to the soldier's Greek name, which means "capturer
of towers and cities."

1046 dixi *add. Reiz*
1049 ego *et* ad te *add. Ritschl*
1054 fiat *P,* fuat *Baier*

PYR   eu hercle odiosas res! quotiens hoc tibi, uerbero, ego in-
         terdixi,

         meam ne sic uolgo pollicitere operam?

PAL   audin tu, mulier?

         dixi hoc tibi dudum et nunc dico: nisi huic uerri affertur
         merces,

1059
–60   non hic suo seminio quemquam porclenam impertitu-
         rust.

MILPH   dabitur quantum ipsus preti poscet.

PAL   talentum Philippi huic opus auri est;
         minus ab nemine accipiet.

MILPH   eu ecastor nimis uilest tandem!

PYR   non mihi auaritia umquam innata est: satis habeo diuitia-
         rum,

         plus mi auri mille est modiorum Philippi.

PAL   praeter thesauros.

1065   tum argenti montes, non massas, habet: Aetina [mons]
         non aeque alta est.

1066 MILPH   eu ecastor hominem periurum!

PAL   ut ludo?

MILPH   quid ego? Ut
                                           sublecto?

[PAL   scite.

1067 MILPH] sed amabo, mitte me actutum.

PAL   quin tu huic responds aliquid,
         aut facturum aut non facturum?

MILPH   quid illam miseram animi excrucias,
         quae numquam male de te merita est?

1056 eu *D*, heu *B*, bu *C*
1059–60 proculem *P*, porculae nam *Priscianus*, porc(u)lenam
Merula, porcellam *Reiz*

256

PYR   (*to Palaestrio*) Goodness, what tedium! You thug, how
      often did I forbid you to promise my services to all and
      sundry like this?

PAL   Can you hear, woman? I told you this a while ago and I
      tell you now: unless this boar is given a reward, he won't   1060
      share his seed with any odd little sow.

MILPH He'll be given as much as he himself demands as his
      price.

PAL   He requires a talent of Philippic gold; he doesn't take less
      from anyone.

MILPH Goodness, he's such a bargain!

PYR   Greed has never been a trait of mine. I have wealth
      enough, I have more than a thousand pecks[45] of Philippic
      gold.

PAL   Besides his treasures. And then he has mountains of sil-   1065
      ver, not mere lumps; Etna is not so high.

MILPH (*aside to Palaestrio*) Goodness, what a perjurer!

PAL   (*aside to Milphidippa*) How am I playing my game?

MILPH (*aside to Palaestrio*) What about me? How am I cajoling
      him? (*to the soldier*) But please, send me back quickly.

PAL   (*to the soldier*) Why won't you give her an answer, a yes or
      a no?

MILPH Why are you torturing that poor woman in her heart?
      She's never deserved badly of you.

---

[45] The *modius* is a dry measure equivalent to almost nine liters.

1065 (a)ethna mons *CD*, *om. B*, Aetna [mons] *Camerarius*, Aetina
Bergk   altos *BCD¹*, altus *D³*, alta est *Camerarius*

1066 PAL scite *del. Acidalius*

1067 *forsitan* me mitte *scribendum sit quia nec* mitt' med *nec* mitte
mĕ *placet*

PYR   iube eampse exire huc ad nos.
1070   dic me omnia quae uolt facturum.
    MILPH   facis nunc ut ‹te› facere aequom,
        quom, quae te uolt, eandem tu uis—
    PYR   non [hoc] insulsum huic ingenium.
    MILPH —quomqu' me oratricem hau spreuisti sistique exorare
        ex te.
        quid est? ut ludo?
    PAL   nequeo hercle equidem risu[m] mode-
                           rarier: ‹hahahae!›
    MILPH ob eam causam huc aps te auorti.
    PYR   non edepol tu scis, mulier,
1075   quantum ego honorem nunc illi habeo.
    MILPH   scio et istuc illi dicam.
    PAL   contra auro alii hanc uendere potuit operam.
    MILPH   pol istuc tibi credo.
    PAL   meri bellatores gignuntur, quas hic praegnatis fecit,
        et pueri annos octingentos uiuont.
    MILPH   uae tibi, nugator!
    PYR   quin mille annorum perpetuo uiuont ab saeclo ad sae-
        clum.
1080 PAL   eo minus dixi ne haec censeret me aduorsum se mentiri.
    MILPH   perii! quot hic ipse annos uiuet, quoius filii tam diu
        uiuont?
    PYR   postriduo natus sum ego, mulier, quam Iuppiter ex Ope
        natust.
    PAL   si hic pridie natus foret quam ille est, hic haberet regnum
        in caelo.

1070 te *add. Ritschl*   1071 hoc *del. Ritschl*
    1073 risum ac *B*, risu meo *CD*, risu *Studemund*   moderarier *P*,
admoderarier *Camerarius*   hahahae *add. Studemund*

PYR   Tell her to come out here to us in person. Tell her that I'll   1070
do everything she wants.

MILPH   Now you're acting as you ought to, since you want the
same woman who wants you—

PYR   (*interrupting*) She has quite a witty character.

MILPH   —and since you didn't despise me when I pleaded for
her and you let me persuade you. (*aside to Palaestrio*)
Well? How am I playing my game?

PAL   (*aside to Milphidippa*) I can't control my laughter:
hahaha!

MILPH   (*aside to Palaestrio*) That's why I turned away here from
you.

PYR   Woman, you don't know how great an honor I'm doing   1075
her now.

MILPH   I do know and I shall tell her.

PAL   He could have sold this performance to another one for
gold.

MILPH   Yes, I believe you in this.

PAL   Pure warriors are born from the women he makes preg-
nant, and the boys live for eight hundred years.

MILPH   (*aside to Palaestrio*) Curse you, you clown!

PYR   No, from one generation to the next they live right on for
a thousand years.

PAL   I didn't tell her so she wouldn't believe I'm lying to her.   1080

MILPH   I'm dead! How many years will he himself live since his
sons live for so long?

PYR   Woman, I was born the day after Jupiter was born from
Ops.[46]

PAL   If he'd been born a day earlier than Jupiter, *he* would
have the kingship in heaven.

---

[46] The Latin name for Rhea, the wife of Kronos/Saturn.

MILPH iam iam sat, amabo, est. sinite abeam, si possum, uiua a
      uobis.

1085 PAL quin ergo abis, quando responsum est?

MILPH   ibo atque illam huc adducam,
      propter ⟨quam⟩ opera est mihi. numquid uis?

PYR   ne magis sim pulcher quam sum,
      ita me mea forma habet sollicitum.

PAL   quid hic nunc stas? quin abis?

MILPH   abeo.

PAL atque adeo audin [tu]? dicito docte et cordate, ut cor ei
      saliat—
      Philocomasio dic, si est istic, domum ut transeat: hunc
      hic esse.

1090 MILPH hic cum era est, ⟨ambae⟩ clam nostrum hunc sermo-
      nem sublegerunt.

PAL lepide factum est: iam ex sermone hoc gubernabunt doc-
      tius porro.

MILPH remorare, abeo.

PAL   nec te remoror nec tango nec te . . . taceo.

PYR iube maturare illam exire huc. iam istic rei praeuortemur.

IV. iii: PYRGOPOLINICES. PALAESTRIO

PYR quid nunc mi es auctor ut faciam, Palaestrio,

1095   de concubina? nam nullo pacto potest
      prius haec in aedis recipi quam illam amiserim.

PAL quid me consultas quid agas? dixi equidem tibi
      quo id pacto fieri possit clementissume.
      aurum atque uestem muliebrem omnem habeat sibi

1086 quam *add. Bentley*
1088 tu *del. Reiz*
1090 ambae *add. Ussing*

MILPH (*aside to Palaestrio*) Please, it's enough now. Let me go
away from you two alive, if possible.

PAL Then why don't you go, now that you've got your reply? 1085

MILPH (*to the soldier*) I'll go and bring the woman here on
whose behalf I'm acting. Do you want anything?

PYR Yes; that I shouldn't be more beautiful than I am, see-
ing how my appearance is the cause of so much trouble
for me.

PAL (*to Milphidippa*) Why are you standing here now? Why
don't you leave?

MILPH I'm leaving. (*turns to go*)

PAL And are you still listening? Tell her smartly and heart-
ily, so that her heart may jump— (*quietly*) tell Philoco-
masium, if she's there, that she should go home: say he's
here.

MILPH (*aside to Palaestrio*) She's here with my mistress, both 1090
have secretly been listening in on our talk.

PAL (*aside to Milphidippa*) That's excellent. They'll steer a
better course later on because of this talk.

MILPH (*aside to Palaestrio*) You're delaying me, I'm leaving.

PAL I'm not delaying you, I'm not touching you, I'm not . . .
I'm quiet.

PYR (*to Milphidippa*) Tell her to make haste to come out here.
Now we'll give our first attention to that.

Exit MILPHIDIPPA into the house of Periplectomenus.

PYR Palaestrio, what do you advise me to do now about my 1095
concubine? In no way can the new woman be received
into the house until I've let go of that other one.

PAL Why are you consulting me about what to do? I've told
you how it can be handled most amicably. Let her have all

1100	quae illi instruxisti: sumat, habeat, auferat;
	dicasque tempus maxume esse ut eat domum:
	sororem geminam adesse et matrem dicito,
	quibus concomitata recte deueniat domum.

PYR   qui tu scis eas adesse?

PAL   quia oculis meis

1105   uidi hic sororem esse eius.

PYR   conuenitne eam?

PAL   conuenit.

PYR   ecquid fortis uisa est?

PAL   omnia

     uis optinere.

PYR   ubi matrem esse aiebat soror?

PAL   cubare in naui lippam atque oculis turgidis

     nauclerus dixit, qui illas aduexit, mihi.

1110   is ad hos nauclerus hospitio deuortitur.

PYR   quid is? ecquid fortis?

PAL   abi sis hinc, nam tu quidem

     ad equas fuisti scitus ammissarius,

     qui consectare qua maris qua feminas.

     hoc age nunc.

PYR   istuc quod das consilium mihi,

1115   te cum illa uerba facere de ista re uolo;

     nam cum illa sane congruos sermo tibi.

PAL   qui potius quam tute adeas, tuam rem tute agas?

     dicas uxorem tibi necessum ducere;

     cognatos persuadere, amicos cogere.

1120 PYR   itan tu censes?

PAL   quid ego ni ita censeam?

PYR   ibo igitur intro. tu hic ante aedis interim

     speculare, ut, ubi illaec prodeat, me prouoces.

PAL   tu modo istuc cura quod agis.

the jewelry and dresses you provided her with; let her 1100
take it, have it, carry it off. And you must say it's high time
for her to go home. Tell her that her twin sister and
mother are here, in whose company she'll get home all
right.

PYR How do you know they're here?

PAL Because I've seen her sister here with my own eyes. 1105

PYR Did she meet her?

PAL She did.

PYR Did she seem good-looking?

PAL You want to get hold of everything.

PYR Where did the sister say their mother was?

PAL The captain who brought them here said she was lying on
the ship, with bleary and swollen eyes. This captain is 1110
lodging at these people's place.

PYR What about him? Is he good-looking?

PAL Go away, will you? You'd have made a proper stallion for
the mares, you who pursue both males and females. Now
pay attention.

PYR As for the advice you give me, I want you to talk to her 1115
about that: you get on really well with her.

PAL How is that preferable to you approaching her yourself
and doing your own business? Say that you have to marry;
your relatives are urging you, your friends are pushing
you.

PYR Do you think so? 1120

PAL Why shouldn't I think so?

PYR I'll go in then. You keep watch here in front of the house
in the meantime so that you can call me out when that
other woman comes out.

PAL Just take care of what you're doing.

	PYR	curatum id quidem est.
		quin si uoluntate nolet, ui extrudam foras.
1125	PAL	istuc caue faxis; quin potius per gratiam
		bonam abeat aps te. atque illaec quae dixi dato,
		aurum, ornamenta quae illi instruxisti ferat.
	PYR	cupio hercle.
	PAL	credo te facile impetrassere.
		sed abi intro. noli stare.
	PYR	tibi sum oboediens.
1130	PAL	numquid uidetur demutare ⟨alio⟩ atque uti
		dixi esse uobis dudum hunc moechum militem?
		nunc ad me ut ueniat usust Acroteleutium aut
		ancillula eius aut Pleusicles. pro Iuppiter,
		satine ut Commoditas usquequaque me adiuuat!
1135		nam quos uidere exoptabam me maxume,
		una exeuntis uideo hinc e proxumo.

IV. iv: ACROTELEVTIVM. MILPHIDIPPA. PALAESTRIO.
PLEVSICLES

	ACR	sequimini, simul circumspicite ne quis assit arbiter.
	MILPH	neminem pol uideo, nisi hunc quem uolumus conuen-
		tum.
	PAL	et ego uos.
	MILPH	quid agis, noster architecte?
	PAL	egone architectus? uah!
	MILPH	quid est?
1140	PAL	quia enim non sum dignus prae te palum ut figam in pa-
		rietem.
	ACR	heia uero!
	PAL	nimis facete nimisque facunde mala est.
		ut lepide deruncinauit militem!

1130 aut utique *P*, ⟨alio⟩ atque uti *Lachmann*

PYR   It's taken care of. If she won't go willingly, I'll throw her out of doors by force.

PAL   Guard against doing that; rather, let her go away from 1125
you amicably. And give her what I told you; let her take the gold and jewelry you furnished her with.

PYR   I'm keen on it.

PAL   I believe that you'll succeed easily. But do go in. Don't stand around.

PYR   I'm at your service.

Exit PYRGOPOLINICES into his house.

PAL   Do you think that this adulterous soldier is changing 1130
from what I told you a while ago? Now I need Acroteleutium to come to me or her maid or Pleusicles. O Jupiter! How Timeliness is supporting me throughout! I 1135
can see the people I most wished to see coming out together from next door.

Enter ACROTELEUTIUM from the house of Periplectomenus, followed by MILPHIDIPPA and PLEUSICLES.

ACR   Follow me. At the same time look around to check that no witness is present.

MILPH   I can't see anyone, except for the man we want to meet.

PAL   And I want to meet you.

MILPH   How are you, our dear master builder?

PAL   I the master builder? Bah!

MILPH   What is it?

PAL   Because compared with you I'm not worthy to pound a 1140
peg into a wall.

ACR   Come off it!

PAL   You're wicked in a wonderfully smart and wonderfully smooth way. How charmingly she trimmed the soldier!

	MILPH	at etiam parum.
	PAL	bono animo es: negotium omne iam succedit sub manus;
		uos modo porro, ut occepistis, date operam adiutabilem.
1145		nam ipse miles concubinam intro abiit oratum suam
		ab se ut abeat cum sorore et matre Athenas.
	PLEV	eu, probe!
	PAL	quin etiam aurum atque ornamenta, quae ipse instruxit, mulieri
		omnia dat dono, a se ut abeat: ita ego consilium dedi.
	PLEV	facile istuc quidem est, si et illa uolt et ille autem cupit.
1150	PAL	non tu scis, quom ex alto puteo sursum ad summum escenderis,
		maxumum periclum inde esse ab summo ne rursum cadas?
		nunc haec res apud summum puteum geritur: si praesenserit
		miles, nihil efferri poterit huius: nunc quom maxume opust dolis.
	PLEV	domi esse ad eam rem uideo siluai satis:
1155		mulieres tres, quartus tute es, quintus ego, sextus senex.
		quod apud nos fallaciarum sex situm est, certo scio,
		oppidum quoduis uidetur posse expugnari dolis.
	PAL	date modo operam.
	ACR	id nos ad te, si quid uelles, uenimus.
	PAL	lepide facitis. nunc hanc tibi ego impero prouinciam.
1160	ACR	impetrabis, imperator, quod ego potero, quod uoles.
	PAL	militem lepide et facete ‹et› laute ludificarier uolo.
	ACR	uoluptatem mecastor mi imperas.
	PAL	scin quem ad modum?

1152 prosenserit *P*, praesenserit �   1161 et² *add. Camerarius*

MILPH But still too little.

PAL Take heart; the whole business is shaping up well under
our hands. Just continue to give me your helpful atten-
tion, as you've begun. Yes, the soldier went inside himself 1145
to ask his concubine to go away from him to Athens to-
gether with her sister and mother.

PLEU Well done!

PAL What's more, he even gives her all the gold and jewelry
he himself provided her with as a present so that she may
leave him; that's how I advised him.

PLEU That's easy, if she wants it and he desires it.

PAL Don't you know that it's when you've climbed from a 1150
deep well up to the top that you're in the greatest danger
of falling back down again? Now this business is being
done at the top of the well. If the soldier gets wind of it,
none of this can be fulfilled. Now we need our tricks the
most.

PLEU I can see that there's a forest of supply for this at home:
three women, you the fourth, I the fifth, and the old man 1155
the sixth. I know for sure, with the deceptions that be-
long to the six of us any town can be taken by our trickery.

PAL Just make an effort, all of you.

ACR That's why we've come to you, to see if you want any-
thing.

PAL That's nice of you. Now I command you to undertake this
commission.

ACR You'll be successful, commander, with what I can do and 1160
what you wish.

PAL I want the soldier to be made a fool of in a lovely, amus-
ing, and neat way.

ACR Your command is a pleasure to me.

PAL Do you know how?

267

	ACR	nempe ut assimulem me amore istius differri.
	PAL	tenes.
	ACR	quasique istius causa amoris ex hoc matrimonio
1165		abierim, cupiens istius nuptiarum.
	PAL	omne ordine.

nisi modo unum hoc: hasce esse aedis dicas dotalis tuas,
hinc senem aps te abiisse, postquam feceris diuortium:
ne ille mox uereatur intro ire in alienam domum.

ACR bene mones.

PAL   sed ubi ille exierit intus, istinc te procul
1170 ita uolo assimulare, prae illius forma quasi spernas tuam
quasique eius opulentitatem reuerearis, et simul
formam, amoenitatem illius, faciem, pulchritudinem
collaudato. satin praeceptum est?

ACR   teneo. satin est, si tibi
meum opus ita dabo expolitum ut improbare non queas?

1175 PAL sat habeo. nunc tibi uicissim quae imperabo ea discito.
quom extemplo hoc erit factum, ubi intro haec abierit, ibi
tu ilico
facito uti uenias ornatu huc ad nos nauclerico;
causeam habeas ferrugineam, [et] scutulam ob oculos la-
neam,
palliolum habeas ferrugineum—nam is colos thalassi-
cust—,
1180 id conexum in umero laeuo, exfafillato bracchio,
praecinctus aliqui: assimulato quasi gubernator sies;
atque apud hunc senem omnia haec sunt, nam is piscato-
res habet.

PLEV quid? ubi ero exornatus quin tu dicis quid facturus sim?

1178 et *del. Lindsay*

ACR   I should pretend that I'm torn apart through my love for him.

PAL   You've got it.

ACR   And that for the sake of my love for him I've left this marriage, keen on marrying him.   1165

PAL   All correct; but there's one more thing: you are to say that this house is part of your dowry and that the old man left this place of yours after you divorced him; so that the soldier soon won't be afraid to enter another's house.

ACR   You're giving me good advice.

PAL   But when he's come out, I want you to pretend from 1170 there from afar that in comparison with his beauty you despise your own and that you're in awe of his splendor; at the same time you must praise his appearance, neatness, looks, and beauty. Have you been instructed sufficiently?

ACR   I've got it. Is it enough if I give you my work in such a polished state that you can't find fault with it?

PAL   Yes. (*to Pleusicles*) Now you in turn must learn what I'll 1175 command you. As soon as this is done, when she's gone in, you must instantly come here in a captain's costume. You should have a rust-colored hat, a woolen patch over your eyes, a rust-colored cloak—for this is the maritime color—and this fastened at your left shoulder, with your 1180 arm sticking out, girded with something.[47] Pretend to be a captain. And all these things are to be found with this old man because he keeps fishermen.

PLEU Well then? Why don't you say what I'm going to do when I'm dressed up?

---

[47] This is a good description of the Greek *exomis*, a man's vest leaving the right shoulder and arm bare; it was typical of the working classes.

1184 PAL   huc uenito et matris uerbis Philocomasium arcessito,
–85   ut, si itura sit Athenas, eat tecum ad portum cito
         atque ut iubeat ferri in nauim si quid imponi uelit.
         nisi eat, te soluturum esse nauim: uentum operam dare.

PLEV satis placet pictura. perge.

PAL   ille extemplo illam hortabitur

1190   ut eat, ut properet, ne matri mora sit.

PLEV   multimodis sapis.

PAL   ego illi dicam, ut me adiutorem, qui onus feram ad por-
         tum, roget.
         ill' iubebit me ire cum illa ad portum. ego adeo, ut tu
         scias,
         prorsum Athenas protinam abibo tecum.

PLEV   atque ubi illo ueneris,
         triduom seruire numquam te quin liber sis sinam.

1195 PAL   abi cito atque orna te.

PLEV   numquid aliud?

PAL   haec ut memineris.

PLEV abeo.

PAL   et uos abite hinc intro actutum; nam illum huc sat scio
         iam exiturum esse intus.

ACR   celebre apud nos imperium tuom est.

PAL   agite apscedite ergo. ecce autem commodum aperitur
         foris.
         hilarus exit: impetrauit. inhiat quod nusquam est miser.

1190 sit matri morae *P*, matri mora sit *Brix*
1193 protinus *P*, protinam *Bentley*

PAL   Come here and fetch Philocomasium in her mother's   1185
      name, saying that, if she's going to Athens, she should go
      to the harbor with you quickly and bring to the ship any-
      thing she wants to be put aboard; if she doesn't come,
      you'll set sail, the wind being favorable.

PLEU I quite like the picture. Continue.

PAL   He'll instantly encourage her to go and to hurry, so as not   1190
      to waste her mother's time.

PLEU You're terribly clever.

PAL   I'll tell her to ask for me as helper to carry the load to the
      harbor. He'll order me to go to the harbor with her. And I,
      just so that you know, will go to Athens with you straight-
      away and at once.

PLEU And when you've arrived, I'll never let you be a slave for
      as much as three days without setting you free.

PAL   Go away quickly and dress up.   1195

PLEU Anything else?

PAL   Remember this.

PLEU I'm going.

Exit PLEUSICLES to the left.

PAL   You two go in at once: I know full well that the soldier will
      come out now.

ACR   Your command is highly regarded among us.

PAL   Go on, go away then.

*Exeunt ACROTELEUTIUM and MILPHIDIPPA into the
house of Periplectomenus.*

PAL   And look, at this very moment the door is opening. He's
      coming out happy: he's been successful. He's gaping at
      something that doesn't exist anywhere, the poor wretch.

271

IV. V: PYRGOPOLINICES. PALAESTRIO

<table>
<tr><td>1200</td><td>PYR</td><td>quod uolui ut uolui impetraui, per amicitiam et gratiam,
a Philocomasio.</td></tr>
<tr><td></td><td>PAL</td><td>quid tam intus fuisse te dicam diu?</td></tr>
<tr><td></td><td>PYR</td><td>numquam ego me tam sensi amari quam nunc ab illa mu-
liere.</td></tr>
<tr><td></td><td>PAL</td><td>quid iam?</td></tr>
<tr><td></td><td>PYR</td><td>ut multa uerba feci, ut lenta materies fuit!
uerum postremo impetraui ut uolui: donaui, dedi</td></tr>
<tr><td>1205</td><td></td><td>quae uoluit, quae postulauit; ⟨te⟩ quoque ⟨ei⟩ dono
dedi.</td></tr>
<tr><td></td><td>PAL</td><td>etiam me? quo modo ego uiuam sine te?</td></tr>
<tr><td></td><td>PYR</td><td>age, animo bono es,
idem ego te liberabo. nam si possem ullo modo
impetrare ut abiret, ne te abduceret, operam dedi;
uerum oppressit.</td></tr>
<tr><td></td><td>PAL</td><td>deos sperabo teque. postremo tamen</td></tr>
<tr><td>1210</td><td></td><td>etsi istuc mi acerbum est, quia ero te carendum est op-
tumo,
saltem id uolup est quom ex uirtute formai euenit tibi
mea opera super hac uicina, quam ego nunc concilio tibi.</td></tr>
<tr><td></td><td>PYR</td><td>quid opust uerbis? libertatem tibi ego et diuitias dabo,
si impetras.</td></tr>
<tr><td></td><td>PAL</td><td>reddam impetratum.</td></tr>
<tr><td></td><td>PYR</td><td>at gestio.</td></tr>
<tr><td></td><td>PAL</td><td>at modice decet:</td></tr>
<tr><td>1215</td><td></td><td>moderare animo, ne sis cupidus. sed eccam ipsam, egre-
ditur foras.</td></tr>
</table>

1205 te, ei *add. Pylades*

---

[48] A metaphor from sawing.

Enter PYRGOPOLINICES from his house.

PYR   I've achieved from Philocomasium what I wanted the   1200
       way I wanted it, in friendship and good grace.

PAL   Why should I say you've been inside for so long?

PYR   I never realized till now that I was loved so much by that
       girl.

PAL   How so?

PYR   How many words I made, how tough the wood was![48] But
       in the end I succeeded as I wanted: I gave her and pre-
       sented her with what she wanted, what she asked for. I   1205
       also gave you to her as a present.

PAL   Me too? How should I live without you?

PYR   Go on, take heart, I'll also free you. Well, I tried to get her
       to go away without you; but she insisted.

PAL   I'll put my trust in the gods and you. But in the end, even   1210
       if it's bitter for me to have to do without you as my excel-
       lent master, at least I'm happy that through the excel-
       lence of your appearance and because of my effort you've
       got an affair with this neighbor I'm winning over for you
       now.

PYR   What need is there for words? I'll give you freedom and
       wealth if you succeed.

PAL   I shall.

PYR   Well, I'm keen.

PAL   Well, you need to be so in moderation. Control your   1215
       heart, don't be too eager. But look, she's coming out her-
       self.

*Enter MILPHIDIPPA and ACROTELEUTIUM from the house
of Periplectomenus, pretending not to see the two men. At first
the women speak quietly so as not to be overheard; the men also*

273

IV. vi: MILPHIDIPPA. ACROTELEVTIVM.
PYRGOPOLINICES. PALAESTRIO

MILPH era, eccum praesto militem.

ACR ubi est?

MILPH ad laeuam.

ACR uideo.

MILPH aspicito limis, ne ille nos se sentiat uidere.

ACR uideo. edepol nunc nos tempus est malas peiores fieri.

MILPH tuom est principium.

ACR opsecro, tute ipsum conuenisti?

1220 ne parce uocem, ut audiat.

MILPH cum ipso pol sum locuta,
placide, ipsae dum lubitum est mihi, otiose, meo arbi-
tratu.

PYR audin quae loquitur?

PAL audio. quam laeta est quia ted adiit!

ACR o, fortunata mulier es!

PYR ut amari uideor!

PAL dignu's.

ACR permirum ecastor praedicas te adiisse atque exorasse;

1225 per epistulam aut per nuntium, quasi regem, adiri eum
aiunt.

MILPH namque edepol uix fuit copia adeundi atque impe-
trandi.

PAL ut tu inclutu's apud mulieres!

PYR patiar, quando ita Venus uolt.

ACR Veneri pol habeo gratiam, eandemque et oro et quaeso
ut eius mihi sit copia quem amo quemque expetesso

1230 benignusque erga me siet, quod cupiam ne grauetur.

speak quietly when they finally hear what the women want them to hear.

MILPH Mistress, look, the soldier is here.

ACR Where is he?

MILPH   On your left.

ACR I can see him.

MILPH Look at him sideways so that he doesn't realize we can see him.

ACR I can see him. Now is the time for us bad women to become even worse.

MILPH It's your task to begin.

ACR *(loudly)* Please, did you meet him in person? *(quietly)* 1220
Don't spare your voice, make him hear you.

MILPH *(loudly)* Yes, I've spoken with him in person, calmly, as long as I myself wished, at leisure, according to my desire.

PYR *(to Palaestrio)* Can you hear what she's saying?

PAL I can. How happy she is because she has come to you!

ACR Oh, you're a lucky woman!

PYR How I appear to be loved!

PAL You deserve it.

ACR What you say is very strange, that you approached and persuaded him. They say he's approached by letter or by 1225
messenger, like a king.

MILPH It was hardly possible to approach him and succeed.

PAL How famous you are among the ladies!

PYR I'll bear it, since Venus wants it.

ACR I give thanks to Venus and I ask and entreat her that I may have the man whom I love and whom I seek, and that 1230
he may be kind to me and not grudge me what I desire.

275

MILPH spero ita futurum, quamquam eum multae sibi expe-
            tessunt:
           ille illas spernit, segregat ab se omnis, extra te unam.
ACR   ergo iste metus me macerat, quod ille fastidiosust,
           ne oculi eius sententiam mutent, ubi uiderit me,
1235   atque eius elegantia meam extemplo speciem spernat.
MILPH non faciet, ⟨modo⟩ bonum animum habe.
PYR   ut ipsa se contemnit!
ACR   metuo ne praedicatio tua nunc meam formam exsuperet.
MILPH istuc curaui, ut opinione illius pulchrior sis.
ACR   si pol me nolet ducere uxorem, genua amplectar
1240   atque opsecrabo; alio modo, si non quibo impetrare,
           consciscam letum: uiuere sine illo scio me non posse.
PYR   prohibendam mortem mulieri uideo. adibon?
PAL   minime.
           nam tu te uilem feceris, si te ultro largiere:
           sine ultro ueniat; quaeritet, desideret, exspectet
1245   sine: perdere istam gloriam uis quam habes? caue sis
           faxis.
           nam nulli mortali scio optigisse hoc nisi duobus,
           tibi et Phaoni Lesbio, tam mulier se ut amaret.
ACR   eo intro an tu illunc euocas foras, mea Milphidippa?
MILPH immo opperiamur dum exeat aliquis.
ACR   durare nequeo
1250   quin eam intro.

1231 illum *P*, eum *Bentley*
1232 hasce *CD*, hec *B*, ab se ꙅ
1236 modo *add. Leo*

MILPH I hope it'll come true, although there are many who
       seek him for themselves. He despises them and keeps
       them all away from him, except for you.

ACR Well then, since he's choosy, the fear is wearing me out
       that his eyes might change his decision when he's seen
       me, and that his fine taste might instantly despise my   1235
       looks.

MILPH He won't do so, do take heart.

PYR How she looks down on herself!

ACR I'm afraid that your praise will now surpass my appear-
       ance.

MILPH I've taken care to understate your beauty.

ACR If he doesn't want to marry me, I'll clutch his knees and   1240
       entreat him. Otherwise, if I can't achieve it, I'll commit
       suicide. I know I can't live without him.

PYR I can see that I have to prevent her from dying. Shall I
       approach her?

PAL Certainly not: you'll make yourself cheap if you give
       yourself away of your own accord. Let her come of her
       own accord; let her seek, desire, await you. Do you want   1245
       to throw the reputation you have away? Don't do it. I
       know that no mortal has succeeded in making a woman
       love him like this, except for two: you and Phaon of
       Lesbos.[49]

ACR Am I going in or are you calling him out, my dear Mil-
       phidippa? (*approaches the soldier's door*)

MILPH No, let's wait till someone comes out.

ACR I can't handle not going in.   1250

---

[49] Tradition has it that Sappho, the great poetess of Lesbos, fell in
love with Phaon, who did not requite her love; she then committed sui-
cide by jumping off the Leucadian rock.

MILPH   occlusae sunt fores.

ACR   effringam.

MILPH   sana non es[t].

ACR   si amauit umquam aut si parem sapientiam [hic] habet ac
        formam,

        per amorem si quid fecero, clementi ⟨hic⟩ animo ignos-
         cet.

PAL   ut, quaeso, amore perdita est te misera!

PYR   mutuom fit.

PAL   tace, ne audiat.

MILPH   quid astitisti opstupida? quor non pultas?

1255 ACR   quia non est intus quem ego uolo.

MILPH   qui scis?

ACR   scio de olefactu;

        nam odore nasum sentiat, si intus sit.

PYR   hariolatur.

        quia me amat, propterea Venus fecit eam ut diuinaret.

ACR   nescio ubi hic prope adest quem expeto uidere: olet pro-
        fecto.

PYR   naso pol iam haec quidem plus uidet quam oculis.

PAL   caeca amore est.

1260 ACR   tene me opsecro.

MILPH   quor?

ACR   ne cadam.

MILPH   quid ita?

ACR   quia stare nequeo,

        ita animus per oculos meos ⟨meus⟩ defit.

MILPH   militem pol
        tu aspexisti.

ACR   ita.

1250 es[t] *Pylades*   1251 hic *del. Bentley*

MILPH   (*as she checks*) The door is locked.

ACR   I'll break it open.

MILPH   You aren't in your right mind.

ACR   If he's ever been in love or if he has as much wisdom as beauty, he'll benevolently forgive me if I do anything out of love.

PAL   Please, how the poor woman is besotted with you!

PYR   It's mutual.

PAL   Be quiet so that she doesn't hear you.

MILPH   Why have you stopped, stupefied? Why won't you knock?

ACR   Because the man I want isn't inside.   1255

MILPH   How do you know?

ACR   I know it from the smell: my nose would feel it from the fragrance if he were inside.

PYR   She's a clairvoyant. Because she loves me, Venus made her prophesy.

ACR   The man I'm keen to see is somewhere near. I can indeed scent him out.

PYR   She now sees more with her nose than with her eyes.

PAL   She's blinded with love.

ACR   (*walking unsteadily*) Hold me, please.   1260

MILPH   Why?

ACR   So that I won't fall.

MILPH   How so?

ACR   Because I'm unable to stand, my mind becomes so weak because of my eyes.

MILPH   You've spotted the soldier.

ACR   Yes.

1252 hic *add. Lindsay ex priore uersu*
1261 meus *add. Haupt*

MILPH   non uideo. ubi est?

ACR   uideres pol, si amares.

MILPH   non edepol tu illum magis amas quam ego, mea, si per
      te liceat.

PAL   omnes profecto mulieres te amant, ut quaeque aspexit.

1265 PYR   nescio tu ex me hoc audiueris an non: nepos sum Veneris.

ACR   mea Milphidippa, adi opsecro et congredere.

PYR   ut me ueretur!

PAL   illa ad nos pergit.

MILPH   uos uolo.

PYR   et nos te.

MILPH   ut iussisti,
      eram meam eduxi foras.

PYR   uideo.

MILPH   iube ergo adire.

PYR   induxi in animum ne oderim item ut alias, quando orasti.

1270 MILPH   uerbum edepol facere non potis, si accesserit prope ad
      te.
      dum te optuetur, interim linguam oculi praeciderunt.

PYR   leuandum morbum mulieri uideo.

MILPH   ut tremit atque extimuit,
      postquam te aspexit.

PYR   uiri quoque armati idem istuc faciunt,
      ne tu mirere mulierem. sed quid ‹est quod› uolt me fa-
      cere?

1275 MILPH   ad se ut eas: tecum uiuere uolt atque aetatem exigere.

PYR   egone ad illam eam quae nupta sit? uir eius me ut pre-
      hendat?

MILPH   quin tua causa exegit uirum ab se.

1274 est quod *add. Lindsay*
1276 me—dat *A,* metuere hendast (metuendus est *B*) *P,* med ut
prendat *Goetz,* me deprehendat *Loewe*

MILPH   I can't see him. Where is he?

ACR   You would see him if you were in love.

MILPH   You don't love him more than I do, my dear, if you al-
lowed me to do so.

PAL   Indeed, all women love you, as soon as they see you.

PYR   I don't know if you've heard this from me or not: I'm the   1265
grandson of Venus.[50]

ACR   My dear Milphidippa, please go and approach him.

PYR   How she's in awe of me!

PAL   She's coming toward us.

MILPH   (*to the men*) I want to speak to you.

PYR   And we to you.

MILPH   I've brought my mistress out, as you told me to.

PYR   I can see her.

MILPH   Then tell her to come here.

PYR   I've persuaded myself not to hate her like the others,
since you pleaded with me.

MILPH   She won't be able to utter a word if she comes close to   1270
you. While she was looking at you, her eyes cut off her
tongue.

PYR   I can see that I have to alleviate the woman's illness.

MILPH   How she's been trembling and how afraid she's become
since spotting you!

PYR   Armed men do the same too, so don't be surprised that a
woman does. But what is it that she wants me to do?

MILPH   To go to her place. She wants to live and spend her life   1275
with you.

PYR   I should go to the place of a woman who's married? So
that her husband should get hold of me?

MILPH   No, she put him out of her place for your sake.

---

[50] Venus, the goddess of love, is Jupiter's daughter, whose brother
the soldier claims to be in l. 1082.

PYR   qui id facere potuit?
MILPH [quia] aedes dotalis huius sunt.
PYR   itane?
MILPH   ita pol.
PYR   iube domum ire.
     iam ego illi ero.
MILPH   uide ne sies in exspectatione,
1280   ne illam animi excrucies.
PYR   non ero profecto. abite.
MILPH   abimus.
PYR   sed quid ego uideo?
PAL   quid uides?
PYR   nescioquis eccum incedit
     ornatu quidem thalassico.
PAL   it ad nos, uolt te profecto.
     nauclerus hicquidem est.
PYR   uidelicet accersit hanc iam.
PAL   credo.

IV. vii: PLEVSICLES. PALAESTRIO. PYRGOPOLINICES

PLEV alium alio pacto propter amorem ni sciam
1285   fecisse multa nequiter, uerear magis
     me amoris causa hoc ornatu incedere.
     uerum quom multos multa ammisse acceperim
     inhonesta propter amorem atque aliena a bonis:
1290   mitto iam, ut occidi Achilles ciuis passus est—
     sed eccum Palaestrionem, stat cum militi:

1278 quia *del. Reiz*

---

[51] Achilles stopped fighting when Chryseis was taken away from him; the Greeks suffered until he started again.

PYR How could she do it?

MILPH The house is part of her dowry.

PYR Really?

MILPH Yes.

PYR Tell her to go home. I'll be there in a moment.

MILPH Make sure you don't keep her waiting, so as not to tor- 1280
ture her in her mind.

PYR I shan't. Go away, you two.

MILPH Yes.

*Exeunt MILPHIDIPPA and ACROTELEUTIUM into the
house of Periplectomenus.*

PYR But what do I see?

PAL What do you see?

PYR Look, someone's strutting along in a maritime outfit.

PAL He's coming to us, he actually wants to speak to you. This
is the captain.

PYR Of course, he's fetching her now.

PAL I believe so.

*Enter PLEUSICLES from the left, in a captain's outfit and with
his left eye covered.*

PLEU (*to the audience*) If I didn't know that other men had
done many bad things in one way or another on account 1285
of their love, I'd be more hesitant to parade myself in this
getup for the sake of my love. But since I've heard that
many people have committed many dishonorable things
because of their love and have done what's improper
for good men—I won't mention how Achilles allowed
his fellow citizens to be slaughtered[51]—(*looking around*) 1290

283

oratio alio mihi demutanda est mea.
mulier profecto nata est ex ipsa Mora;
nam quaeuis alia, quae mora est aeque, mora
minor ea uidetur quam quae propter mulierem est.
1295   hoc adeo fieri credo consuetudine.
nam ego hanc accerso Philocomasium. sed fores
pultabo. heus, ecquis hic est?

PAL   adulescens, quid est?
     quid uis? quid pultas?

PLEV   Philocomasium quaerito.
     a matre illius uenio. si itura est, eat.
1300   omnis moratur: nauim cupimus soluere.

PYR   iam dudum res parata est. i, Palaestrio,
     aurum, ornamenta, uestem, pretiosa omnia
     duc adiutores tecum ad nauim qui ferant.
     omnia composita sunt quae donaui: auferat.

1305 PAL   eo.

PLEV   quaeso hercle propera.

PYR   non morabitur.
     quid istuc, quaeso? quid oculo factum est tuo?

PLEV habeo equidem hercle oculum.

PYR   at laeuom dico.

PLEV   eloquar.
     amoris causa hercle hoc ego oculo utor minus,
     nam si apstinuissem amorem, tamquam hoc uterer.
1310   sed nimis morantur me diu.

PYR   eccos exeunt.

---

[52] The soldier is to understand that he lost his eye in a fight for a girl, but Pleusicles also means that he is covering his eye as part of the plot to get Philocomasium back.

but here's Palaestrio standing with the soldier; I have to change my way of speaking. (*loudly*) Woman was indeed born of Delay herself: any other delay that's equally much of a delay seems smaller than that which one has on account of a woman. What's more, I believe they do it as 1295 a matter of custom. As for me, I'm fetching Philocomasium here. But I'll knock at the door. (*does so*) Hey, is anyone here?

PAL   Young man, what is it? What do you want? Why are you knocking?

PLEU I'm looking for Philocomasium. I've come from her mother. If she's going to go, let her go. She's wasting 1300 everybody's time; we're keen to set sail.

PYR   (*to Pleusicles*) It's all been ready for a long time. (*to Palaestrio*) Go, Palaestrio, and take helpers with you to take the gold, jewelry, clothing, and all the valuables to the ship. Everything I gave her has been assembled. Let her take it away.

PAL   I'm going. 1305

PLEU Please hurry.

Exit PALAESTRIO into the soldier's house.

PYR   He won't delay you. What's that, please? What happened to your eye?

PLEU I do have an eye.

PYR   But I mean the left one.

PLEU I'll tell you. I don't have use of this eye because of love:[52] if I'd kept away from love, I'd use it like this one. But 1310 they're keeping me waiting for too long.

PYR   Look, they're coming out.

IV. viii: PALAESTRIO. PHILOCOMASIVM.
PYRGOPOLINICES. PLEVSICLES

PAL   quid modi flendo quaeso hodie facies?

PHIL   quid ego ni fleam?
ubi pulcherrume egi aetatem, inde abeo.

PAL   em hominem tibi
qui a matre et sorore uenit.

PHIL   uideo.

PYR   audin, Palaestrio?

PAL   quid uis?

PYR   quin tu iubes efferri omnia quae isti dedi?

1315 PLEV   Philocomasium, salue.

PHIL   et tu salue.

PLEV   materque et soror
tibi salutem me iusserunt dicere.

PHIL   saluae sient.

PLEV   orant te ut eas, uentus operam dum dat, ut uelum expli-
cent;
nam matri oculi si ualerent, mecum uenissent simul.

PHIL   ibo; quamquam inuita facio, impietas sit nisi eam.

PLEV   sapis.

1320 PYR   si non mecum aetatem egisset, hodie stulta uiueret.

PHIL   istuc crucior, a uiro me tali abalienarier,
nam tu quemuis potis es facere ut afluat facetiis;
et quia tecum eram, propterea animo eram ferocior:
eam nobilitatem amittendam uideo.

PYR   a! ne fle.

PHIL   non queo,

1325   quom te uideo.

PYR   habe bonum animum.

PHIL   scio ego quid doleat mihi.

1319 omni pietas sit eo (scio *B*) PL sapis *P, corr. Brix*

Enter PALAESTRIO and PHILOCOMASIUM from the soldier's house.

PAL   Please, what end will you put to your crying today?

PHIL   Why shouldn't I cry? I'm leaving the place where I've lived my life most agreeably.

PAL   Here's your man, the one who has come from your mother and sister.

PHIL   I can see him.

PYR   Can you hear me, Palaestrio?

PAL   What do you want?

PYR   Why won't you have all that I gave her taken out?

PLEU   Philocomasium, my greetings.   1315

PHIL   And mine to you.

PLEU   Your mother and sister have told me to pass on their greetings to you.

PHIL   I hope they're well.

PLEU   They ask you to go while the wind is favorable, so that they can set sail: if your mother's eyes were well, they'd have come along with me.

PHIL   I'll go. Even though I'm doing so unwillingly, it would be a breach of family duty if I didn't go.

PLEU   You're sensible.

PYR   If she hadn't spent time with me, she'd be an idiot today.   1320

PHIL   I'm in agony because I'm being taken away from such a man: you can make anyone overflow with wit; and because I was with you, I was more confident in my heart. I can see that I have to give up that renown.

PYR   Ah! Stop crying.

PHIL   I can't when I see you.   1325

PYR   Take heart.

PHIL   I know what makes me suffer.

PAL   nam nil miror, si lubenter, Philocomasium, hic eras,
         ⟨si⟩ forma huius, mores, uirtus, attinuere animum hic
            tuom,
         quom ego seruos quando aspicio hunc, lacrumo quia
            diiungimur.

PHIL   opsecro licet complecti prius quam proficisco?

PYR   licet.

1330   PHIL   o mi ocule, o mi anime.

PAL   opsecro, tene mulierem,
         ne affligatur.

PYR   quid istuc quaeso est?

PAL   quia aps te abit, animo male
         factum est huic repente miserae.

PYR   curre intro atque efferto aquam.

PAL   nil aquam moror, quiescat malo. ne interueneris,
         quaeso, dum resipiscit.

PYR   capita inter se nimis nexa hisce habent.

1335   non placet. labra ab labellis aufer, nauta, caue malum.

PLEV   temptabam spirarent an non.

PYR   aurem ammotam oportuit.

PLEV   si magis uis, eam omittam.

PYR   nolo: retineas.

PAL   fio miser.

PYR   exite atque efferte huc intus omnia quae isti dedi.

PAL   etiam nunc saluto te, ⟨Lar⟩ familiaris, prius quam eo.

1340   conserui conseruaeque omnes, bene ualete et uiuite,
         bene quaeso inter uos dicatis et med apsenti tamen.

1327 si *add. Bugge*   attinere P, attinuere *Pylades*
1339 Lar *add. Bothe*

---

[53] A protective deity.

PAL   I'm not surprised if *you* enjoyed being here, Philoco-
     masium, if his beauty, character, and bravery have held
     your mind here, since when I, a mere slave, see him, I cry
     because we're being torn apart.

PHIL   (*to the soldier*) Please, may I embrace you before leav-
     ing?

PYR   You may.

PHIL   O apple of my eye, o my soulmate. (*begins to faint*)   1330

PAL   (*to Pleusicles*) Please hold her so that she won't fall down.
     (*Pleusicles grabs her*)

PYR   What's going on, please?

PAL   Because she's leaving you, the poor girl has suddenly felt
     faint.

PYR   Run in and bring out water.

PAL   I don't care for water, I prefer her to rest. Please don't go
     near her while she's recovering.

PYR   (*as Pleusicles leans over her and kisses her*) These two
     have their heads too closely together. I don't like it.   1335
     Sailor, take your lips away from hers, watch out for trou-
     ble.

PLEU   I was checking if they're breathing or not.

PYR   You should have moved your ear to them.

PLEU   If you prefer it, I'll let go of her.

PYR   No, keep hold of her.

PAL   (*aside*) I'm becoming wretched.

PYR   (*calling for servants*) Come out and bring out everything
     I gave her. (*porters, including Sceledrus, enter from the
     soldier's house*)

PAL   And now once more, Lar[53] of the household, I give you
     my greetings before I go. All my fellow servants, male   1340
     and female, goodbye and farewell, please speak well of
     me even in my absence.

PYR age, Palaestrio, bono animo es.

PAL   eheu! nequeo quin fleam,
quom aps ted abeam.

PYR   fer animo aequo.

PAL   scio ego quid doleat mihi.

PHIL sed quid hoc? quae res? quid uideo? lux, salue. ‹ubi sum
gentium?›

1345 PLEV ‹et tu salue›. iam resipisti?

PHIL   opsecro, quem amplexa sum
hominem? perii! sumne ego apud me?

PLEV   ne time, uoluptas mea.

PYR quid istuc est negoti?

PAL   animus hanc modo hic reliquerat.
metuoque et timeo, ne hoc tandem propalam fiat, nimis.

PYR quid id est?

PAL   nos secundum ferri nunc per urbem haec omnia,

1350   ne quis tibi hoc uitio uortat.

PYR   mea, non illorum dedi:
parui ego illos facio. agite, ite cum dis bene uolentibus.

PAL tua ego hoc causa dico.

PYR   credo.

PAL   iam uale.

PYR   et tu bene uale.

PAL ite cito, iam ego assequar uos: cum ero pauca uolo loqui.

1343 te . . . aequo animo *P*, ted . . . animo aequo *Guyet*
1344 ubi sum gentium *add. Niemeyer*
1345 et tu salue *add. Niemeyer*

---

[54] She refers to the daylight, which she can now see again, and, as a
term of endearment, to Pleusicles. The soldier does not notice the dou-
ble meaning.

PYR   Come on, Palaestrio, cheer up.

PAL   Dear me! I can't refrain from crying because I'm leaving you.

PYR   Bear it stoically.

PAL   I know what makes me suffer.

PHIL   (*recovering*) But what's this? What? What do I see? My greetings, light.[54] Where on earth am I?

PLEU   And my greetings to you. Have you recovered now?   1345

PHIL   Please, what man did I embrace? I'm dead! Am I in my right mind?

PLEU   Stop being afraid, my darling.

PYR   (*sternly*) What business is that?

PAL   She's just lost conscience here. (*aside*) I'm terribly scared and afraid that this might come out at last.

PYR   (*overhearing him*) What do you mean?

PAL   (*improvising*) All this stuff now being carried behind us throughout the city, I'm afraid that someone might find   1350 fault with you for it.

PYR   I gave what's mine, not what's theirs; I care little about them. Come on, go with the gods' favor.

PAL   I'm saying this for your sake.

PYR   I believe you.

PAL   Goodbye now.

PYR   And goodbye to you.

PAL   (*to Pleusicles and Philocomasium*) Go quickly, I'll follow you in a moment. I want to have a few words with my master.

Exeunt PLEUSICLES, PHILOCOMASIUM, and the porters to the left.

quamquam alios fideliores semper habuisti tibi,
1355 quam me, tamen tibi habeo magnam gratiam rerum om-
nium;
et, ita si sententia esset, tibi seruire malui
multo quam alii libertus esse.

PYR   habe animum bonum.

PAL eheu, quom uenit mi in mentem ut mores mutandi sient,
muliebres mores discendi, obliscendi stratiotici!

1360 PYR fac sis frugi.

PAL   iam non possum, amisi omnem lubidinem.

PYR i, sequere illos, ne morere.

PAL   bene uale.

PYR   et tu bene uale.

PAL quaeso memineris, si forte liber fieri occeperim
—mittam nuntium ad te—, ne me deseras.

PYR   non est meum.

PAL cogitato identidem tibi quam fidelis fuerim.
1365 si id facies, tum demum scibis tibi qui bonus sit, qui ma-
lus.

PYR scio et perspexi saepe.

PAL   uerum quom antehac, hodie maxume
scies: immo hodie uerum factum faxo post dices magis.

PYR uix reprimor quin te manere iubeam.

PAL   caue istuc feceris:
dicant te mendacem nec uerum esse, fide nulla esse te,
1370 dicant seruorum praeter me ess' fidelem neminem.
nam si honeste censeam te facere posse, suadeam;
uerum non potest. caue faxis.

1356 si ita *P, transp. Lachmann*
1367 meorum (eorum *B*) *P,* uerum *Camerarius*

PAL   Even though you always considered others more faithful
to you than me, I'm still very grateful to you for every-   1355
thing. And if it were your decision, I'd much rather be
your slave than another's freedman.

PYR   Cheer up.

PAL   Dear me! When I think about how I shall have to change
my ways! I shall have to learn women's ways and forget
the military ones.

PYR   Do be a good fellow, will you?   1360

PAL   I can't any longer, I've lost all my desire.[55]

PYR   Go, follow them, don't waste time.

PAL   Farewell.

PYR   And farewell to you.

PAL   Please remember not to desert me if by chance I begin
the life of a free man; I'll send you a message.

PYR   It isn't my way.

PAL   Think again and again how faithful I've been to you. If   1365
you do this, you will at last know who is good to you and
who is bad.

PYR   I know and I've often come to understand it.

PAL   But even though you've known it before, you'll know it
best today. Indeed, I'll bring it about later today that
you'll say even more that it's turned out true.

PYR   I can barely refrain from ordering you to stay.

PAL   Don't do that. People would say that you're a liar and
not truthful, that you're absolutely faithless; they'd say   1370
none of the slaves apart from me is faithful. Indeed, if I
thought you could do so honorably, I'd advise you to; but
it's impossible. Don't do it.

---

[55] Double meaning. The soldier is to understand that Palaestrio is
dejected because he cannot stay with him, while the audience under-
stands that he has no intention of helping the soldier.

PYR	abi iam.
PAL	patiar quicquid est.
PYR	bene uale igitur.
PAL	ire meliust strenue.
PYR	etiam nunc uale.

PYR ante hoc factum hunc sum arbitratus semper seruom
pessumum:
1375 eum fidelem mi esse inuenio. quom egomet mecum co-
gito,
stulte feci qui hunc amisi. ibo hinc intro nunciam
ad amores meos. sed, sensi, hinc sonitum fecerunt fores.

IV. ix: PVER. PYRGOPOLINICES

PVER ne me moneatis, memini ego officium meum,
ego iam conueniam illum, ubiubi est gentium;
1380 inuestigabo, operae non parco meae.
PYR me quaerit illic. ibo huic puero obuiam.
PVER ehem, te quaero. salue, uir lepidissume,
cumulate commoditate, praeter ceteros
duo di quem curant.
PYR qui duo?
PVER Mars et Venus.
1385 PYR facetum puerum!
PVER intro te ut eas opsecrat,
te uolt, te quaerit, teque exspectans expetit.
amanti fer opem. quid stas? quin intro is?
PYR eo.

1379 nam *P*, iam *Camerarius*

PYR Go now.

PAL I'll bear whatever may befall.

PYR Farewell then.

PAL It's better to go quickly.

PYR Once more, farewell.

Exit PALAESTRIO to the left.

PYR Before this I always considered him to be my worst slave. Now I discover that he's faithful to me. Now I come to think of it, it was stupid of me to let him go. Now I'll go in to my love. But I've heard something, the door has made a noise.   1375

Enter a BOY from the house of Periplectomenus.

BOY (*into the house*) Don't remind me, I remember my duty. I'll meet him wherever he may be. I'll find him, I won't spare my effort.   1380

PYR (*aside*) He's looking for me. I'll approach this boy.

BOY Oh, I've been looking for you. My greetings, most charming man, teeming with timeliness, whom two gods favor beyond the others.

PYR Which two?

BOY Mars and Venus.

PYR A smart boy!   1385

BOY She entreats you to go in. She wants you, she seeks you, she looks for you longingly. Bring help to a lovesick woman. Why are you standing here? Why won't you go in?

PYR I'm going.

Exit PYRGOPOLINICES into the house of Periplectomenus.

PVER ipsus illic sese iam impediuit in plagas;
      paratae insidiae sunt: in statu stat senex,
1390   ut adoriatur moechum, qui forma est ferox,
      qui omnis se amare credit, quaeque aspexerit
      mulier: eum oderunt qua uiri qua mulieres.
      nunc in tumultum ibo: intus clamorem audio.

ACTVS V

V. i: PERIPLECTOMENVS. PYRGOPOLINICES.
CARIO. LORARII. SCELEDRVS

PER ducite istum; si non sequitur, rapite sublimem foras,
1395   facite inter terram atque caelum ut siet, discindite.
PYR opsecro hercle, Periplectomene, te.
PER   nequiquam hercle opsecras.
      uide ut istic tibi sit acutus, Cario, culter probe.
CAR quin iam dudum gestit moecho hoc abdomen adimere,
      ut faciam quasi puero in collo pendeant crepundia.
1400 PYR perii!
PER   haud etiam, numero hoc dicis.
CAR   iamne ‹ego› in hominem inuolo?
1401 PER immo etiam prius uerberetur fustibus.
CAR   multum quidem.
1401ᵃ agi *** c *** ams *** s *** f *** m ***
1402 PER quor es ausus subigitare alienam uxorem, impudens?
PYR ita me di ament, ultro uentum est ad me.
PER   mentitur, feri.

1400 ego *add. Fleckeisen*
1401ᵃ *uersus in Palatinis deest*

BOY He's entangled himself in the net now. The ambush is
prepared. The old man stands at his post ready to attack 1390
the adulterer, who is fierce only in his beauty and who be-
lieves that all women who see him fall in love him. Both
men and women hate him. Now I'll enter the uproar: I
can hear shouting inside.

ACT FIVE

*Enter PERIPLECTOMENUS from his house, followed by
slaves, CARIO, carrying a large knife, and PYRGOPOLINI-
CES, tied up and half naked.*

PER (*to slaves*) Bring him along; if he doesn't follow, lift him
up and carry him out, make sure that he's between earth 1395
and heaven, tear him apart.

PYR I entreat you, Periplectomenus!

PER (*to the soldier*) You're entreating me in vain. (*to Cario*)
Make sure that that knife is properly sharp, Cario.

CAR Indeed, it's been keen for a long time now to cut off the
adulterer's lower parts, so that I can make them hang
round his neck like a child's rattle.

PYR I'm dead! 1400

PER Not yet, you're saying this too early.

CAR Am I to fly upon him now?

PER No, first he should be beaten with cudgels.

CAR And a lot. ***

PER (*to the soldier*) Why did you dare to make a move on an-
other's wife, you shameless creature?

PYR As truly as the gods may love me, advances were made to
me without encouragement on my part.

PER (*to a slave*) He's lying, hit him.

	PYR	mane dum narro.
	PER	quid cessatis?
	PYR	non licet mi dicere?
1405	PER	dice.
	PYR	oratus sum ad eam ut irem.
	PER	quor ire ausu's? em tibi!
	PYR	oiei! satis sum uerberatus. opsecro.
	CAR	quam mox seco?
	PER	ubi lubet: dispennite hominem diuorsum et distendite.
	PYR	opsecro hercle te ut mea uerba audias prius quam secat.
	PER	loquere.
	PYR	non de nihilo factum est: uiduam hercle esse censui,
1410		itaque ancilla, conciliatrix quae erat, dicebat mihi.
	PER	iura te non nociturum esse homini de hac re nemini,
		quod tu hodie hic uerberatu's aut quod uerberabere,
		si te saluom hinc amittemus Venerium nepotulum.
	PYR	iuro per Iouem et Mauortem me nociturum nemini,
1415		quod ego hic hodie uapularim, iureque id factum arbitror;
		et si intestatus non abeo hinc, bene agitur pro noxia.
	PER	quid si id non faxis?
	PYR	ut uiuam semper intestabilis.
	CAR	uerberetur etiam, postibi amittendum censeo.
	PYR	di tibi bene faciant semper, quom aduocatus mihi bene es.

1407 dispendite hominem *AB*, distendite h. *CD*, dispennite h.
Nonius

---

[56] *Intestatus* literally means "without the power to bear witness,"

PYR   Wait while I'm telling you.

PER   (*to the servants*) Why are you hesitating?

PYR   Am I not allowed to speak?

PER   Speak.   1405

PYR   I was begged to go to her.

PER   Why did you dare to go? Take that! (*hits him*)

PYR   Ow! I've been beaten enough. I entreat you!

CAR   (*to Periplectomenus*) How soon am I to cut him?

PER   As soon as you like. (*to servants*) Spread him out and stretch him.

PYR   I beg you to listen to my words before he cuts me!

PER   Speak.

PYR   It didn't happen out of nowhere; I thought she was divorced, that's what her maid, who was the go-between, 1410 told me.

PER   Swear that you won't harm anyone for having been beaten here today and for being beaten later on, if we let you go away from here safely, you little grandson of Venus.

PYR   I swear by Jupiter and Mars that I won't harm anyone for 1415 having been beaten here today, and I think it serves me right. And if I don't go away from here without the power to bear witness as a man,[56] I'm getting off lightly.

PER   What if you don't keep your word?

PYR   Then may I always live without that power.

CAR   (*to Periplectomenus*) Let him get another beating; after that I think he ought to be let off the hook.

PYR   May the gods always do you good for being a good advocate for me.

but also puns on *testes* "testicles"; the soldier is not threatened with losing legal powers, but with being castrated as punishment.

1420	CAR	ergo des minam auri nobis.
	PYR	quam ob rem?
	CAR	saluis testibus
		ut ted hodie hinc amittamus Venerium nepotulum;
		aliter hinc non ibis, ne sis frustra.
	PYR	dabitur.
	CAR	magis sapis.
		de tunica et chlamyde et machaera ne quid speres, non feres.
	LOR	uerberone etiam, an iam mittis?
	PYR	mitis sum equidem fustibus.
1425		opsecro uos.
	PER	soluite istunc.
	PYR	gratiam habeo tibi.
	PER	si posthac prehendero ego te hic, carebis testibus.
	PYR	causam hau dico.
	PER	eamus intro, Cario.
	PYR	seruos meos
		eccos uideo. Philocomasium iam profecta est? dic mihi.
	SCE	iam dudum.
	PYR	ei mihi!
	SCE	magis dicas, si scias quod ego scio.
1430		nam ill' qui lanam ob oculum habebat ⟨laeuom⟩ nauta non erat.
	PYR	quis erat igitur?
	SCE	Philocomasio amator.
	PYR	qui tu scis?

1430 qui ob oculum habebat l- *A*, qui lanam ob oculum habebat *P*, q. lan. ob ⟨laeuom⟩ oc. h. *Hasper*, q. lan. ob oc. h. ⟨laeuom⟩ *Leo*

CAR   Then give us a mina of gold.   1420

PYR   What for?

CAR   So that we let you go away today with your testicles intact, you, the little grandson of Venus. Otherwise you won't get away, don't fool yourself.

PYR   You'll get it.

CAR   That's more sensible of you. As for your tunic, cloak, and sword, don't fool yourself, you won't take them with you.

SLAVE   (*to Periplectomenus*) Am I to beat him once more or are you letting him off in peace now?

PYR   (*to Periplectomenus*) I'm in pieces from the cudgels. I 1425 entreat you!

PER   (*to the slaves*) Untie him.

PYR   Thank you.

PER   If hereafter I catch you here, you'll be without testicles.

PYR   I have no objection.

PER   Let's go in, Cario.

Exit PERIPLECTOMENUS into his house, followed by CARIO and the servants. Enter SCELEDRUS with the now empty-handed porters from the right.

PYR   Look, I can see my slaves. Has Philocomasium left already? Tell me.

SCE   Already long ago.

PYR   Dear me!

SCE   You'd say that all the more if you knew what I know: that 1430 chap who had a patch on his left eye was not a sailor.

PYR   Who was he, then?

SCE   Philocomasium's lover.

PYR   How do you know?

SCE   scio.

    nam postquam porta exierunt, nil cessarunt ilico

    osculari atque amplexari inter se.

PYR   uae misero mihi!

    uerba mihi data esse uideo. scelus uiri Palaestrio,

1435   is me in hanc illexit fraudem. iure factum iudico;

    si sic aliis moechis fiat, minus hic moechorum siet,

    magis metuant, minus has res studeant. eamus ad me.

      plaudite.

SCE I know; after they left the gate, they didn't hesitate at all to kiss on the spot and to embrace each other.

PYR Poor, wretched me! I can see that I've been tricked. That scoundrel of a man, Palaestrio, lured me into this decep- 1435 tion. I judge it serves me right. If it happened like this to other adulterers, there would be fewer of them here, they'd be more afraid and would be less keen on these things. (*to the servants*) Let's go in to my house. (*to the audience*) Give us your applause.

MOSTELLARIA

INTRODUCTORY NOTE

The name *Mostellaria*, like *Asinaria* and *Aulularia*, contains the suffix *-aria*, which indicates what the comedy is about. Just as the *Asinaria* is about *asini*, "asses," and the *Aulularia* is about an *aulula*, "a little pot," the *Mostellaria* is about a *mostellum*. This at first sight curious word is the regular diminutive of *mo(n)strum*, "ghost" or "apparition."

Festus cites two passages of the *Mostellaria*, saying that they come from Plautus' *Phasma*, "The Ghost" (pp. 158 and 394 Lindsay). As it was common practice to cite a Latin play under the name of the Greek original, the Greek comedy must have been called *Phasma*. Its author remains unclear, for there were at least three plays of that name: one by Menander, one by Philemon, and one by Theognetus. As the Menandrian play seems to have been rather different in its plot, modern scholars typically assign the original to Philemon or Theognetus, though there may have been other, lesser-known figures who had composed plays called *Phasma*. Ritschl and Leo were quite certain that Plautus had used Philemon's play, while Della Corte tended toward Theognetus. From the limited evidence available to us, the question cannot be resolved satisfactorily. The fact that in l. 1149 an old man is told that he should narrate to Diphilus or Philemon the way he was fooled, so that they may have better plots, has been used to

307

argue both for and against Philemon as author of the origi-
nal; obviously, evidence of this kind is inconclusive at best.
It is equally unclear when the *Mostellaria* was first staged.
There are no indications in the play and connections with
other comedies remain elusive. It is generally assumed
that the play is one of Plautus' later creations, perhaps
written in the first decade of the second century. The large
amount of song, so typical of the later plays, also supports
this theory.

But now we must turn to the plot of the comedy. The
ghost in our story is an invention of the slave Tranio, the
main character. At the very beginning of the play we get to
know him in a dialogue with Grumio, another slave of the
same master, Theopropides. Grumio, who does not appear
later in the play, works on his master's farm and is an honest
servant, while Tranio lives in his city mansion and is a
crook. Partly in this dialogue and partly in an ensuing
monologue by Philolaches, the son of Theopropides, we
hear that Theopropides has been away on business for
three years. Philolaches, until his father's departure a mod-
est, hardworking young man, has fallen in love with the
prostitute Philematium, bought her, and freed her. In ad-
dition he has spent large sums of money on parties, which
his friend Callidamates attends with his girlfriend Del-
phium on a regular basis.

We meet Philematium for the first time in a scene
which has been considered problematical on account of
its sheer length. In l. 157 Philematium comes out of her
lover's house accompanied by her maid Scapha. Philema-
tium begins to make herself up and discusses with Scapha
her relationship with Philolaches. Philematium is por-

trayed as a sweet-natured, slightly naive girl who is truly in love with Philolaches, while Scapha, whose only function is to emphasize the young girl's decency, is presented as a cunning old woman. Philolaches overhears the discussion, but only approaches the pair in l. 292. This lengthy passage probably goes back to the original but is likely to have been expanded considerably by Plautus. The joke in ll. 267–71, for instance, bears all the hallmarks of Plautine humor. Probably also Plautine is the invective against rich, ugly old women using ointments but still smelling terrible (ll. 272–81); some parallels can be found in Greek Old Comedy, but not in New Comedy. If the rather crude ll. 282–89 are also Plautine rather than Greek, and if we delete ll. 290–91, which seem to be a post-Plautine addition, l. 292 makes more sense than it would do otherwise. The Greek text presumably contained the equivalent of ll. 265–66, in which Philematium kisses her mirror and Philolaches becomes jealous of it; in the Greek text, l. 292 must have followed immediately, and now Philolaches' statement there fits with what was going on before: *nimis diu apstineo manum* is best interpreted as his wish to harm the personified mirror.

Applying makeup outside one's house may strike us as unnatural, but as indoor scenes could not be staged in Roman comedy, the shift to outside the house is unavoidable. The outdoor banquet that follows is far more natural. In ll. 313–47 Callidamates and Delphium join Philolaches and Philematium for a drinks party outside Philolaches' house. Callidamates is already drunk. His portrayal as stammering and unable to walk in a straight line (ll. 319–35ᵃ) is probably owed to Plautus: until l. 318 his behavior is still entirely normal, and the complete absence of any words coming from Philolaches or Philematium in the stammering passage would be odd in a Greek play. The words of Philolaches in l. 336–38 are somewhat incongruous as well because he does not comment on the drunkenness at all. Were we to cut out the Plautine expansion consisting of ll. 319–35ᵃ, the scene would lose much of its humor, but ll. 318 and 336 would fit together nicely.

In l. 348 Tranio arrives with the news that his master, the father of Philolaches, is back. He tells Philolaches to move the tables, couches, and guests inside and to continue the party there. Tranio promises to frighten the father of Philolaches so much that he will not enter the house but run away. When Theopropides arrives at his house, Tranio tells him that the house is haunted by a ghost. He claims that Philolaches had been visited in his dreams by the ghost of a man murdered in the house by the previous owner. Because of the curse that the house is under, the family had to move out. In l. 528 Theopropides runs away, frightened by Tranio's story.

It is likely that the second act in the Greek play ended where Renaissance scholars posited an act break in the Latin play, namely after l. 531. Theopropides is offstage and interviews the man who sold him his house and who naturally denies the alleged crime. In the Greek play Tranio presumably went into the house and then came out again later, after a choral interlude, ready to meet Theopropides. This meeting must have been followed by another one with Misargyrides, the moneylender who provided Philolaches with the money for Philematium. Plautus, who does not have choral interludes, keeps Tranio onstage after Theopropides has left. Since Theopropides cannot come back immediately, Tranio spots the money-lender before Theopropides returns. The consequence of this rearrangement is the somewhat awkward inactivity of Misargyrides in ll. 541–59; Misargyrides stands around idly while Tranio and Theopropides discuss the latter's meeting with the previous owner of their house. When Tranio finally talks with the moneylender, the result is an even longer and more awkward period of inactivity for Theopropides (ll. 562–614, interrupted only by Theo-propides' aside in l. 609ᵃ–10). This time, the idle period for Theopropides has to do with Plautine expansions in the exchange between Tranio and Misargyrides; the passage contains the typically Roman way of demanding one's rights, the *flagitatio* (ll. 575–609).

Tranio pretends that the money was borrowed in order to buy a house since the old one was cursed. Theopropides is overjoyed that his son shows an interest in business and is more than willing to pay off the moneylender. When he asks Tranio which house they bought, he replies that it is their neighbor Simo's. More difficulties are in store for Tranio when Theopropides expresses his desire to inspect the house. Tranio tells Simo that Theopropides plans to enlarge his own house and for this reason wants to look at his neighbor's. Simo does not object.

Naturally, Tranio does not want Theopropides to state in Simo's presence that he has a claim to his house. Therefore he tells his master that Simo is unhappy about selling his house and that it is more humane not to mention the purchase. Theopropides agrees. In ll. 797–98 an interesting difference between Greek and Roman legal practice

311

emerges. In Greek law a part payment such as that supposedly given to Simo by Philolaches does not force the owner to give up his property; he can still return the money and render the purchase null and void. In our passage, on the other hand, the part payment results in a legally binding contract to hand over the house.

Theopropides inspects the house, at first in Simo's presence and then, when Simo leaves, only with Tranio. While they are inside, two of Callidamates' slaves appear to fetch him. They knock at Theopropides' door, but to no avail. Tranio is sent away to bring back Philolaches from the family farm, where he is supposedly working, and Theopropides encounters the two slaves on his own. They tell him how his son has behaved in his absence. Theopropides, deeply disturbed but still not fully convinced that he has been tricked, meets Simo, who confirms what the two slaves have already said, namely that Simo's house has never been sold. Theopropides wants to take revenge on Tranio, who takes refuge on an altar. Luckily, Callidamates appears and manages to persuade Theopropides to forgive everyone, including Tranio.

Like the *Bacchides*, the *Miles gloriosus*, and the *Pseudolus*, the *Mostellaria* has a cunning slave as a main character. But the *Mostellaria* is different in one crucial respect. In the other plays the slaves' intrigues are successful; in the *Mostellaria*, Tranio's goal is to prevent Theopropides from finding out the truth, and it is clear from the start that he can achieve this for only a very limited time. Tranio's escapades are enjoyable, but the happy ending of the comedy is the result of Callidamates' intervention, not of Tranio's cleverness.

SELECT BIBLIOGRAPHY

Editions and Commentaries

Bertini, F. (1970), *Plauto: Mostellaria* (Turin).

Sonnenschein, E. A. (1907), *T. Macci Plauti Mostellaria: Edited with Notes Explanatory and Critical*, 2nd ed. (Oxford).

Sturtevant, E. H. (1925), *T. Macci Plauti Mostellaria: Edited with an Introduction and Notes* (New Haven).

Criticism

Della Corte, F. (1952), "La commedia della fantasima," in *Dioniso* NS 15: 49–55.

Fuchs, H. (1944), "Zur Putzszene der Mostellaria," in *Hermes* 79: 127–48.

Lowe, J. C. B. (1985), "Plautine Innovations in *Mostellaria* 529–857," in *Phoenix* 39: 6–26.

Raffaelli, R., and Tontini, A. (eds.) (2010), *Lecturae Plautinae Sarsinates XIII: Mostellaria (Sarsina, 26 settembre 2009)* (Urbino).

Weide, I. (1961), "Der Aufbau der Mostellaria des Plautus," in *Hermes* 89: 191–207.

MOSTELLARIA

ARGVMENTVM

Manu misit emptos suos amores Philolaches
Omnemque apsente rem suo apsumit patre.
Senem, ut reuenit, ludificatur Tranio:
Terrifica monstra dicit fieri in aedibus
5 **E**t inde pridem emigratum. interuenit
Lucripeta faenus faenerator postulans,
Ludosque rursum fit senex; nam mutuom
Acceptum dicit, pignus emptis aedibus.
Requirit quae sint. ait uicini proxumi.
10 **I**nspectat illas. post se derisum dolet,
Ab sui sodale gnati exoratur tamen.

THE GHOST

PLOT SUMMARY

Philolaches buys his sweetheart, frees her, and uses up the entire wealth in his father's absence. When the old man returns, Tranio makes a fool of him: he says that terrible apparitions take place in the house and that they moved out long ago. A greedy 5 moneylender arrives in the meantime, demanding his interest, and again the old man is fooled: the slave says his young master took up a loan as deposit for a house. The old man asks which house it is. The slave says it is the one belonging to their next-door neighbor. The old man inspects it. Later he is upset that he 10 was made fun of, but is nevertheless appeased by his son's chum.

PLAUTUS

PERSONAE

GRVMIO seruos
TRANIO seruos
PHILOLACHES adulescens
PHILEMATIVM meretrix
SCAPHA ancilla
CALLIDAMATES adulescens
DELPHIVM meretrix
THEOPROPIDES senex
MISARGYRIDES danista
SIMO senex
PHANISCVS seruos
PINACIVM seruos
SPHAERIO seruos

SCAENA

Athenis

CHARACTERS

GRUMIO a slave; a farmhand of Theopropides

TRANIO a slave; also belongs to Theopropides, but lives in
the city

PHILOLACHES a young man; son of Theopropides

PHILEMATIUM a prostitute; bought and freed by
Philolaches

SCAPHA a female servant; Philematium's attendant

CALLIDAMATES a young man; close friend of Philolaches

DELPHIUM a prostitute; girlfriend of Callidamates

THEOPROPIDES an old man; has just returned from
abroad

MISARGYRIDES a moneylender; has lent money to Philo-
laches

SIMO an old man; neighbor of Theopropides

PHANISCUS a slave boy; favorite of his master Callidamates

PINACIUM a slave boy; colleague of Phaniscus

SPHAERIO a slave; works in the household of Theopropides

STAGING

The stage represents a street in Athens. On it are the houses of
Theopropides, to the left, and of Simo, to the right; they are
separated by a small alley. In front of the house of Theopropi-
des there is an altar. On the right the street leads into the city
center. On the left it leads to the harbor as well as the country-
side.

317

PLAUTUS

ACTVS I

GRV	exi e culina sis foras, mastigia,
	qui mi inter patinas exhibes argutias.
	egredere, erilis permities, ex aedibus.
	ego pol te ruri, si uiuam, ulciscar probe.
5	exi, inquam, nidor, e culina. quid lates?
TRA	quid tibi, malum, hic ante aedis clamitatio est?
	an ruri censes te esse? apscede ab aedibus.
	abi rus, abi directe, apscede ab ianua.
9–10	em, hoccin uolebas?
GRV	perii! quor me uerberas?
TRA	quia uiuis.
GRV	patiar. sine modo adueniat senex.
	sine modo uenire saluom quem apsentem comes.
TRA	nec ueri simile loquere nec uerum, frutex,
	comesse quemquam ut quisquam apsentem possiet.
15 GRV	tu urbanus uero scurra, deliciae popli,
	rus mihi tu obiectas? sane hoc, credo, Tranio,
	quod te in pistrinum scis actutum tradier.
	cis hercle paucas tempestates, Tranio,
	augebis ruri numerum, genus ferratile.
20	nunc, dum tibi lubet licetque, pota, perde rem,
	corrumpe ⟨porro⟩ erilem adulescentem optumum;
	dies noctesque bibite, pergraecamini,
	amicas emite, liberate: pascite
	parasitos: opsonate pollucibiliter.
25	haecin mandauit tibi, quom peregre hinc it, senex?

5 nidore cupinam (culinae *B*²) *P*, nidor e culina *Pylades*
6 clamatiosi *P*, clamitatiost *Acidalius*   21 porro *add. Leo*

ACT ONE

GRUMIO is banging at the door of the house of Theopropides.

GRU   Come out of the kitchen, you whipping post, will you? You're showing me your glib tongue among the platters. Come out of the house, ruin of our master! I'll take revenge on you properly at the farm, as truly as I live. Come   5 out of the kitchen, I insist, you stench! Why are you hiding?

Enter TRANIO from the house of Theopropides.

TRA   Damn it, what right do you have to bawl here in front of the house? Do you think you're on the farm? Go away from the house. Go to the farm, go be hanged, go away from the door. (*hits him*) There, did you want this?   10

GRU   I'm dead! What are you hitting me for?

TRA   For being alive.

GRU   I'll put up with it. Just let the old man come. Just let the man that you're eating up in his absence return safely.

TRA   You aren't telling a true or a likely story, you blockhead, that anyone could eat up anyone else in his absence.

GRU   What? You city loafer, you darling of the streets, you are   15 throwing the farm in my face? I do believe, Tranio, that you know you'll be thrown into the mill soon. Before long, Tranio, you'll increase the farm population, the folks that work in iron fetters. Now, while you wish and   20 are able to do so, drink, squander our wealth, continue to corrupt master's fine young son. Do drink day and night, live in Greek style, buy girlfriends and free them; feed hangers-on; buy sumptuous amounts of food. Is this what   25 the old man told you to do when he went abroad? Is this

hocin modo hic rem curatam offendet suam?
hoccin boni esse officium serui existumas
ut eri sui corrumpat et rem et filium?
nam ego illum corruptum duco quom his factis studet.
30   quo nemo adaeque iuuentute ex omni Attica
antehac est habitus parcus nec magis continens,
is nunc in aliam partem palmam possidet.
uirtute id factum tua et magisterio tuo.

TRA quid tibi, malum, me aut quid ego agam curatio est?
35   an ruri, quaeso, non sunt quos cures boues?
lubet potare, amare, scorta ducere.
mei tergi facio haec, non tui fiducia.

GRV quam confidenter loquitur [fue]!

TRA   at te Iuppiter
dique omnes perdant! ⟨fu!⟩ oboluisti alium,
40   germana illuuies, rusticus, hircus, hara suis,
caenum κόπρῳ commixtum.

GRV   quid uis fieri?
non omnes possunt olere unguenta exotica,
si tu oles, nec superiores accumbere
44– nec tam facetis quam tu uiuis uictibus.
45
tu tibi istos habeas turtures, piscis, auis,
sine me aliato fungi fortunas meas.
tu fortunatu's, ego miser: patiunda sunt.
49– meum bonum me, te tuom maneat malum.
50 TRA quasi inuidere mi hoc uidere, Grumio,
quia mi bene est et tibi male est; dignissumum est:
decet me amare et te bubulcitarier,
me uictitare pulchre, te miseris modis.

38–39 fu(e) *transp. Ritschl*   41 canem capram commixtam *P*,
caenum κόπρῳ commixtum *Schoell*

320

how he'll find his business looked after? Is this what you
consider the duty of a good servant, to ruin his master's
wealth and son? Yes, I do consider him ruined now that
he goes in for this sort of thing. Before, no one among all   30
the youth in Attica was deemed equally thrifty or more
restrained; now he bears the palm for the very opposite.
This happened thanks to you and your teaching.

TRA Damn it, what do you care about me or what I do? Aren't   35
there any cattle for you to care about on the farm, please?
I wish to drink, to love, to keep company with prostitutes.
I do so relying on my own back, not on yours.

GRU With what self-confidence he speaks!

TRA But may Jupiter and all the gods ruin you! Yuck! I've
caught a whiff of garlic on your breath, you native filth,   40
peasant, goat, pigsty, mire mixed with manure.

GRU What do you expect? Not everybody can smell of exotic
ointments even if you do, or have the more honorable
places at table, or live on such dainty dishes as you do.   45
Have those turtledoves, fish, and birds for yourself, but
leave me to my lot fed on garlic dishes. You are lucky, I
am wretched; I have to bear it. So long as my good for-   50
tune awaits me and your bad fortune you.

TRA You seem to kind of envy me, Grumio, because I am hav-
ing a good time and you a bad one. It's fully deserved. It's
appropriate that I should look after the ladies and you
after the cattle, and that I should live beautifully and you
wretchedly.

55	GRV	o carnuficium cribrum, quod credo fore,
		ita te forabunt patibulatum per uias
		stimulis ⟨carnufices⟩, huc si reueniat senex.
	TRA	qui scis an tibi istuc eueniat prius quam mihi?
	GRV	quia numquam merui, tu meruisti et nunc meres.
60	TRA	orationis operam compendi face,
		nisi te mala re magna mactari cupis.
	GRV	eruom daturi ⟨si⟩ estis bubus quod feram,
		date; si non estis, agite, porro pergite
		quoniam occepistis: bibite, pergraecamini,
65		este, effercite uos, saginam caedite.
	TRA	tace atque abi rus. ego ire in Piraeum uolo,
		in uesperum parare piscatum mihi.
		eruom tibi aliquis cras faxo ad uillam afferat.
		quid est quod tu me nunc optuere, furcifer?
70	GRV	pol tibi istuc credo nomen actutum fore.
	TRA	dum interea sic sit, istuc "actutum" sino.
	GRV	ita est. sed unum hoc scito, nimio celerius
		uenit quod molest⟨um est⟩ quam illud quod cupide pe-
		tas.
	TRA	molestus ne sis nunciam, i rus, te amoue.
75		ne tu hercle praeterhac mi non facies moram.
	GRV	satin abiit nec quod dixi flocci existumat?

57 carnufices *add. Leo* si huc *P, transp. Guyet*
62 ⟨si⟩ *add. Sonnenschein*
63 data es in(h)onestis (-ste *C*) *P,* date aes *B²in margine,* date si non estis *Sonnenschein*
73 uenire quod moleste *P,* uenit quod molest⟨um est⟩ *Bentley*

GRU You hangman's sieve! At any rate that's what I believe 55
you'll be if the old man returns here, so thoroughly will
the hangmen pierce you with cattle prods while you carry
the crossbar through the streets.

TRA How do you know that won't happen to you rather than
to me?

GRU Because I've never deserved it; you have deserved it and
do so now.

TRA Spare yourself the trouble of a speech, unless you want to 60
be favored with a fine flagellation.

GRU If you're going to give me the fodder to bring to the
cattle, do so; if not, go on, continue further, since you've
begun: drink, live in Greek style, eat, stuff yourselves, 65
devour your filling meals.

TRA Be quiet and go to the farm. I want to go to the Piraeus[1] in
order to buy fish for our dinner. I'll have someone bring
you your fodder to the farmhouse tomorrow. What do
you mean by staring at me now, you jailbird?

GRU Goodness, I believe *you* will have that epithet soon.   70

TRA So long as it's like this in the meantime, I don't mind your
"soon."

GRU Quite. But you should know this one thing: what's un-
pleasant comes a lot more quickly than what you're
keen on.

TRA Don't be a nuisance now, go to the farm, remove yourself.
You certainly won't waste my time any more.   75

Exit TRANIO to the left.

GRU Has he positively gone and doesn't care a straw about

<hr />

[1] The Athenian harbor.

pro di immortales, opsecro uostram fidem!
facite huc ut redeat noster quam primum senex,
triennium qui iam hinc abest, priusquam omnia
80 periere, et aedes et ager; qui nisi nunc redit,
paucorum mensum sunt relictae reliquiae.
nunc rus abibo. nam eccum erilem filium
uideo, corruptum ex adulescente optumo.

I. ii: PHILOLACHES

PHILO recordatus multum et diu cogitaui
85 argumentaque in pectus multa institui
ego, atque in meo corde, si est quod mihi cor,
eam rem uolutaui et diu disputaui,
hominem quoius rei, quando natus est
similem esse arbitrarer simulacrumque habere.
90 id repperi iam exemplum.
nouarum aedium esse arbitro similem ego hominem
quando [hic] natus est. ei rei argumenta dicam.
[atque hoc hau uidetur ueri simile uobis,
at ego id faciam esse ita ut credatis.
95 profecto esse ita ut praedico uera uincam.]
atque hoc uosmet ipsi, scio, proinde uti nunc
ego esse autumo, quando dicta audietis
mea, haud aliter id dicetis.
auscultate, argumenta dum dico ad hanc rem:
100 simul gnaruris uos uolo esse hanc rem mecum.
aedes quom extemplo sunt paratae, expolitae,
factae probe examussim,
laudant fabrum atque aedes probant, sibi quisque inde
    exemplum expetunt,
sibi quisque similis uolt suas, sumptum, operam ⟨non⟩
    parcunt suam.
105 atque ubi illo immigrat nequam homo, indiligens[que]

324

what I said? Immortal gods, I implore your protection!
Let our old master return as quickly as possible—he's
been away for three years already—before everything is   80
ruined, both house and land. Unless he returns now, the
remaining remains will be finished in a few months. Now
I'll go off to the country: I can see master's son, corrupted
after being an excellent fellow.

Exit GRUMIO to the left.
Enter PHILOLACHES from his house.

PHILO Pondering much, I've thought long and searched my   85
heart thoroughly, and I've turned this matter around and
long discussed it in my mind, if indeed I do have a mind,
what thing I should consider man to be similar to and
what he is like when he's born. I've found this parallel   90
now. I think man resembles a new house when he's born.
I'll give the proofs that confirm the matter. [And this
doesn't seem likely to you, but I'll make sure that you be-
lieve it. Indeed I'll convince you that it's just as I say.] And   95
I know, when you hear my words, you yourselves will say
that it's just the same as I say it is. Listen while I'm telling
you the arguments bearing upon this matter; I want you   100
to know this matter as well as I do. The moment a house
has been finished, polished, built to perfection, people
praise the builder and commend the house; everyone
wants one like it for himself, wants his own to be similar,
and doesn't spare expense and trouble. And when a use-   105

---

80 huc *P*, nunc *Ritschl*   92 hic *del. Lorenz*
93–95 *uersus del. Ritschl*   98 mea *del. Hermann*
104 simile suo is *B*, similesuo is *CD*, similes uolt *Ritschl* non *add.*
Hermann   105 que *del. Pylades*

325

cum pigra familia, immundus, instrenuos,
hic iam aedibus uitium additur, bonae quom curantur
    male;
atque illud saepe fit: tempestas uenit,
confringit tegulas imbricesque: ibi
110   dominus indiligens reddere alias neuolt;
uenit imber, lauit parietes, perpluont,
tigna putrefacit, perdit operam fabri:
nequior factus iam est usus aedium.
atque haud est fabri culpa, sed magna pars
115   morem hunc induxerunt: si quid nummo sarciri potest,
usque mantant neque id faciunt donicum
parietes ruont: aedificantur aedes totae denuo.
haec argumenta ego aedificiis dixi; nunc etiam uolo
dicere uti homines aedium esse similis arbitremini.
120   primumdum parentes fabri liberum sunt:
i fundamentum supstruont liberorum;
extollunt, parant sedulo in firmitatem,
et ut ‹et› in usum boni et in speciem
poplo sint sibique, hau materiae reparcunt
125   nec sumptus ibi sumptui esse ducunt;
expoliunt: docent litteras, iura, leges,
sumptu suo et labore
nituntur ut alii sibi esse illorum similis expetant.
ad legionem quom ita ‹paratos mittunt› amminiclum is
    danunt
130   tum iam, aliquem cognatum suom.
ea tenus; abeunt a fabris. unum ubi emeritum est stipen-
    dium,
igitur tum specimen cernitur quo eueniat aedificatio.
nam ego ad illud frugi usque et probus fui

less and careless man moves in there, a slovenly slacker,
together with a lazy household, then the house gets dam-
aged, being a good house but badly looked after. And that
sort of thing happens a lot: a storm comes and breaks all
the tiles; then the careless owner doesn't want to replace   110
them. Rain comes and soaks the walls; they let in water;
the rain rots the timbers and destroys the builder's work.
The utility of the house has already been diminished.
And this is not the builder's fault, but most people have   115
adopted this custom: if something can be fixed for a trifle,
they keep waiting and don't do it until the walls come
down; the entire house has to be rebuilt. So much for
buildings; now I also want to say how you should consider
man to be similar to a house. First, parents are the build-   120
ers of their children: they lay their children's foundation.
They raise them, eagerly prepare them to be strong, and
do not spare their building materials so that they're good
for use and an ornament for the people and for them-
selves; and they don't consider an expense to be an ex-   125
pense in that case. They polish them: they teach them lit-
erature, laws, and statutes, and with their expense and
hard work it's their ambition that others should want to
have children similar to those. When they send them to
the army prepared like this, they give them support at   130
once, some relative of theirs. So far, so good. They leave
the builders. When one campaign has been served, then
one can see an example of how the building is to turn out.
I, for instance, was good and decent as long as I was un-

---

123 et *add. Schoell*
129 *lacuna in P*, paratos mittunt *add. Leo*

in fabrorum potestate dum fui.
135   postea quom immigraui ingenium in meum,
perdidi operam fabrorum ilico oppido.
uenit ignauia, ea mi tempestas fuit,
mi aduentu suo grandinem imbrem[que] attulit;
haec uerecundiam mi et uirtutis modum
140   deturbauit [texit] detexitque a med ilico;
postilla optigere me neglegens fui.
continuo pro imbre amor aduenit, pluit in corpus meum;
is usque in pectus permanauit, permadefecit cor meum.
nunc simul res, fides, fama, uirtus, decus[que]
145   deseruerunt: ego sum in usu factus nimio nequior.
atque edepol ita haec tigna umide ⟨iam⟩ putent: non
    uideor mihi
sarcire posse aedis meas quin totae perpetuae ruant,
[quin] cum fundamento perierint nec quisquam esse
    auxilio queat.
cor dolet quom scio ut nunc sum atque ut fui,
150   quo neque industrior de iuuentute erat
*** arte gymnastica:
disco, hastis, pila, cursu, armis, equo
uictitabam uolup,
parsimonia et duritia discipulinae aliis eram,
155   optumi quique expetebant a me doctrinam sibi.
nunc, postquam nihili sum, id uero meopte ingenio rep-
    peri.

138 que *del. Bothe*
140 texit *del. Camerarius*
141 eam *P*, me *Lambinus*
142 in cor meum *P*, pluit in corpus meum *Sonnenschein*
144 que *del. Bothe*

der the influence of the builders. Thereafter, when I took   135
up abode in my natural disposition, I immediately ruined
the work of the builders utterly. Laziness came: she was
my storm, she brought me hail and rain when she arrived.
She tore my sense of shame and my virtuous self-control   140
away from me and unroofed me. Thereafter I didn't
bother to reroof myself. At once Love arrived in place
of the downpour and rained into my body. He trickled
right into my breast and soaked my heart. Now wealth,
trustworthiness, reputation, manliness, and respectabil-
ity have deserted me all at the same time; I am nothing   145
like so valuable in use. And these timbers are already so
wet and rotting that I don't think I can repair my house
without its collapsing entirely from top to bottom, with-
out its perishing with its foundations, and without anyone
being able to help. My heart aches since I know how I am
now and how I used to be. None of the young men   150
worked harder than me *** in athletics: I lived joyfully
with the discus, javelins, the ball, running, weapons, and
riding. With my thrift and self-discipline I was an exam-
ple for others: all the best sought a model in me. Now   155
that I'm worthless I've found this state through my own
character.

Enter PHILEMATIUM and SCAPHA from the house of Theo-
propides, the latter carrying a mirror, jewelry, and makeup.
PHILOLACHES stands at a distance, unseen and unheard, but
observing the goings-on.

---

146 iam *add. Hermann*
148 quin *del. Ritschl*

I. iii: PHILEMATIVM. SCAPHA. PHILOLACHES

PHILE iam pridem ecastor frigida non laui magis lubenter
    nec quom me melius, mea Scapha, rear esse deficatam.

SCA euentus rebus omnibus, uelut horno messis magna

160   fuit.

PHILE   quid ea messis attinet ad meam lauationem?

SCA nihilo plus quam lauatio tua ad messim.

PHILO   o Venus uenusta,
    haec illa est tempestas mea, mihi quae modestiam om-
        nem
    detexit, tectus qua fui, quom mihi Amor et Cupido
    in pectus perpluit meum, nec iam umquam optegere
    possum:

165   madent iam in corde parietes, periere haec oppido ae-
        des.

PHILE contempla, amabo, mea Scapha, satin haec me uestis
    deceat.
    uolo me placere Philolachi, meo ocello, meo patrono.

SCA quin tu te exornas moribus lepidis, quom lepida tute es?
    non uestem amatores amant mulieris, sed uestis fartim.

170 PHILO ita me di ament, lepida ‹est› Scapha, sapit scelesta mul-
    tum.
    ut lepide omnis ‹mo›res tenet sententiasque amantum!

PHILE quid nunc?

SCA   quid est?

PHILE   quin me aspice et contempla ut haec me deceat.

SCA uirtute formae id euenit te ut deceat quicquid habeas.

170 lepida‹st› *Gruterus*
171 ‹mo›res *Bergk*
172 decet *P*, deceat *Camerarius*

PHILE For a long time now I haven't had a more pleasant bath
in cold water and haven't had a more thorough scouring,
I should think, my dear Scapha.

SCA There's an outcome for all things, as for example there's
been a huge harvest this year.   160

PHILE What does this harvest have to do with my bath?

SCA No more than your bath has to do with the harvest.[2]

PHILO O lovely Venus, this is that storm of mine that has taken
away the roof of all my modesty, the roof that I was cov-
ered with, when Love and Passion rained into my breast,
and I can't reroof myself ever again: the walls in my heart   165
are already soaked, this house is utterly destroyed.

PHILE Look me over, please, my dear Scapha, to see if this
dress suits me nicely. I want to please Philolaches, my
darling and my patron.

SCA Why don't you adorn yourself with pretty ways, since you
are pretty yourself? Lovers don't love a woman's dress,
but its stuffing.

PHILO As truly as the gods may love me, Scapha is lovely, she   170
knows a lot, the hussy. In what a lovely way she under-
stands all the ways and sentiments of lovers!

PHILE Well then?

SCA What is it?

PHILE Do look at me and see how this suits me.

SCA Thanks to your beauty whatever you wear suits you.

---

[2] Everything must be judged by its outcome, like the harvest; the
bath is a preparation for harvesting a lover's money.

PHILO ergo ob istuc uerbum te, Scapha, donabo ego hodie . . .
aliqui
175 nec patiar te istanc gratiis laudasse, quae placet mi.
PHILE nolo ego te assentari mihi.
SCA   nimis tuquidem stulta es mulier.
eho, mauis uituperarier falso quam uero extolli?
equidem pol uel falso tamen laudari multo malo
179–
80 quam uero culpari aut meam speciem alios irridere.
PHILE ego uerum amo, uerum uolo dici mi: mendacem odi.
SCA ita tu me ames, ita Philolaches tuos te amet, ut uenusta
es.
PHILO quid ais, scelesta? quo modo adiurasti? ita ego istam
amarem?
quid "istaec me," id quor non additum est? infecta dona
facio.
185 periisti: quod promiseram tibi dono perdidisti.
SCA equidem pol miror tam catam, tam doctam te et bene
eductam
nunc stultam stulte facere.
PHILE   quin mone quaeso, si quid erro.
SCA tu ecastor erras quae quidem illum exspectes unum at-
que illi
morem praecipue sic geras atque alios aspernaris.
190 matronae, non meretricium, est unum inseruire aman-
tem.
PHILO pro Iuppiter! nam quod malum uorsatur meae domi
illud?
di deaeque omnes me pessumis exemplis interficiant,
nisi ego illam anum interfecero siti fameque atque algu.
PHILE nolo ego mihi male te, Scapha, praecipere.

189 asperneres (asperneris B^1) P (= aspernere?)

332

PHILO Very well then, because of this word of yours, Scapha,
today I'll give you . . . something or other and I won't let 175
you have praised the girl I love without reward.

PHILE I don't want you to flatter me.

SCA You're a very stupid woman. Tell me, do you prefer be-
ing run down undeservedly to being praised deservedly?
I for one prefer to be complimented, even if undeserv-
edly, to being criticized deservedly or having others 180
laugh about my appearance.

PHILE I love the truth, I want to be told the truth; I hate a liar.

SCA As truly as you love me and as truly as your Philolaches
loves you, you're pretty.

PHILO What do you say, you criminal? How did you swear? As
truly as I love her? What about "she me," why wasn't that
added? I revoke my presents. You're done for: you've lost 185
what I promised you as a gift.

SCA I'm really surprised that you, such a smart, such a clever,
such a well-brought-up girl, are now behaving so terribly
stupidly.

PHILE Do give me advice, please, if I'm making a mistake.

SCA You're indeed making a mistake by waiting on him alone,
showing him your special favor like this, and despising
others. It's appropriate for a married woman, not for a 190
prostitute, to be at the beck of a single lover.

PHILO O Jupiter! What crooked creature is this living in my
house? May all the gods and goddesses kill me in the
most horrible way if I don't kill that old woman with
thirst, hunger, and cold.

PHILE I don't want you to give me crooked advice, Scapha.

SCA   stulta es plane
195   quae illum tibi aeternum putes fore amicum et beneuo-
              lentem.
         moneo ego te: te ille deseret aetate et satietate.
PHILE non spero.
SCA   insperata accidunt magis saepe quam quae speres.
         postremo, si dictis nequis perduci ut uera haec credas
         mea dicta, ex factis nosce rem. uides quae sim et quae fui
              ante.
200   nilo ego quam nunc tu ***
200ᵃ   *** amata sum; atque uni modo gessi morem:
201   qui pol me, ubi aetate hoc caput colorem commutauit,
         reliquit deseruitque me. tibi idem futurum credo.
PHILO uix comprimor quin inuolem illi in oculos stimulatrici.
PHILE solam ille me soli sibi suo ⟨sumptu⟩ liberauit:
205   illi me soli censeo esse oportere opsequentem.
PHILO pro di immortales, mulierem lepidam et pudico inge-
              nio!
         bene hercle factum et gaudeo mihi nil esse huius causa.
SCA   inscita ecastor tu quidem es.
PHILE   quapropter?
SCA   quae istuc ⟨cures⟩,
         ut te ille amet.
PHILE   quor opsecro non curem?
SCA   libera es iam.
210   tu iam quod quaerebas habes: ill' te nisi amabit ultro,
         id pro tuo capite quod dedit perdiderit tantum argenti.
PHILO perii hercle, ni ego illam pessumis exemplis enicasso!
         illa hanc corrumpit mulierem malesuada cantilena.

200–200ᵃ *unus uersus in P, lacunam statuit Leo*
204 sumptu *add. Bentley*

334

SCA You're plain stupid for believing that he'll remain your 195
    friend and benefactor for ever. I remind you: he'll leave
    you when you're older and he's colder.

PHILE I hope not.

SCA Things you don't hope for happen more often than things
    you do hope for. Finally, if you can't be led to believe
    through words that these words of mine are true, learn
    reality from facts. You can see who I am and who I was
    before. No less than you now I *** I was loved; and I de- 200
    voted myself to just one man. When this head changed
    color because of old age, he left and deserted me. I be-
    lieve the same will happen to you.

PHILO I can barely refrain from flying into the eyes of that
    temptress.

PHILE He freed me alone for himself alone at his own expense;
    I think I ought to please him alone. 205

PHILO Immortal gods, a lovely woman with a pure heart! Well
    done, and I'm happy to have nothing because of her.

SCA You really are silly.

PHILE How so?

SCA Because you concern yourself with making him love you.

PHILE Why, please, should I not concern myself with that?

SCA You're already free. You already have what you were 210
    looking for; unless he loves you into the bargain, he'll
    have wasted the money he gave for you.

PHILO I'm dead if I don't kill her in the harshest way! That
    witch is spoiling this lady with her bad advice.

---

205 *ante* 204 *P, transp. Ritschl*
208 cures *add. Pylades*
211 capite tuo *P, transp. Bentley*
213 uitilena *B,* uttilena *C,* utilena *D,* cantilena *Ussing*

PHILE numquam ego illi possum gratiam referre ut meritust
    de me.
215   Scapha, id tu mihi ne suadeas ut illum minoris pendam.
SCA   at hoc unum facito cogites: si illum inseruibis solum
    dum tibi est nunc haec aetatula, in senecta male querere.
PHILO in anginam ego nunc me uelim uorti, ut ueneficae illi
    fauces prehendam atque enicem scelestam stimulatri-
    cem.
220 PHILE eundem animum oportet nunc mihi esse gratum, ut im-
    petraui,
    atque olim, prius quam id extudi, quom illi subblandie-
    bar.
PHILO di⟨ui⟩ me faciant quod uolunt, ni ob istam orationem
    te liberasso denuo et ni Scapham enicasso.
SCA   si tibi sat acceptum est fore tibi uictum sempiternum
225   atque illum amatorem tibi proprium futurum in uita,
    soli gerundum censeo morem et capiundas crinis.
PHILE ut fama est homini, exin solet pecuniam inuenire.
    ego si bonam famam mihi seruasso, sat ero diues.
PHILO siquidem hercle uendundust pater, uenibit multo po-
    tius
230   quam te me uiuo umquam sinam egere aut mendicare.
SCA   quid illis futurum est ceteris qui te amant?
PHILE   magis amabunt,
    quom ⟨me⟩ uidebunt gratiam referre ⟨bene mere⟩nti.
PHILO utinam meus nunc mortuos pater ad me nuntietur,
    ut ego exheredem me meis bonis faciam atque haec sit
    heres.

217 tibi nunc haec aetatula est *P, transp. Klotz*
222 di⟨ui⟩ *Bothe*

PHILE I can never repay him the way he's deserved of me.
Scapha, don't advise me to value him less highly.   215

SCA But do think about this one thing: if you serve only him
while you have this youth of yours now, you'll be com-
plaining bitterly in your old age.

PHILO I'd like to turn into a quinsy right now so as to grab that
witch by her throat and kill the crooked propagandist.

PHILE I ought to have the same attitude now that I've got what 220
I wanted as I used to have back then, before I succeeded,
when I was making myself pleasant to him.

PHILO May the gods do with me what they want if I don't free
you anew because of that speech of yours and if I don't
kill Scapha.

SCA If you feel assured that you'll have food for good and that 225
he'll be your own lover throughout life, I think you ought
to humor only him and assume the matron's plaits.[3]

PHILE As one's reputation is, so one usually finds money. If I
preserve my good reputation, I shall be rich enough.

PHILO If my father has to be sold, he'll be sold much rather
than that I ever let you be poor or beg while I'm alive.   230

SCA What's going to happen to those others who love you?

PHILE They'll love me more when they see me grateful to the
man who deserves so well of me.

PHILO I'd like to get news of my father's death now, so that I
could disinherit myself of my property and she could be
the heir.

---

[3] At marriage a Roman girl's hair was divided into six plaits.

---

232 me *add. Gruterus* referenti P, referre bene merenti *Camerarius*
234 meis me P, *transp. Schoell*

235 SCA iam istaquidem apsumpta res erit: dies noctesque estur,
  bibitur,
  nec quisquam parsimoniam adhibet: sagina plane est.

PHILO in te hercle certum est principe ut sim parcus experiri,
  nam neque edes quicquam nec bibes apud me his decem
  diebus.

PHILE si quid tu in illum bene uoles loqui, id loqui licebit:
240 nec recte si illi dixeris, iam ecastor uapulabis.

PHILO edepol si summo Ioui bo‹ui eo› argento sacruficassem,
  pro illius capite quod dedi, numquam aeque id bene lo-
  cassem.
  uideas eam medullitus me amare. oh! probus homo sum:
  quae pro me causam diceret, patronum liberaui.

245 SCA uideo [enim] te nihili pendere prae Philolache omnis ho-
  mines.
  nunc, ne eius causa uapulem, tibi potius assentabor,
  si acceptum sat habes, tibi fore illum amicum sempiter-
  num.

PHILE cedo mi speculum et cum ornamentis arculam actutum,
  Scapha,
  ornata ut sim, quom huc ‹ad›ueniat Philolaches uoluptas
  mea.

250 SCA mulier quae se suamque aetatem spernit, speculo ei usus
  est:
  quid opust speculo tibi quae tute speculo speculum es
  maxumum?

PHILO ob istuc uerbum, ne nequiquam, Scapha, tam lepide
  dixeris,
  dabo aliquid hodie peculi . . . tibi, Philematium mea.

237 principium *P*, principe *Bentley*
241 iouiuo (ioui uiuo *B²*) *P*, ioui boui eo *Leo*

SCA That wealth will be used up in no time: day and night 235
there's eating and drinking and no one shows any thrift:
it's plain gluttony.

PHILO I've decided that you are going to be the first to experi-
ence how thrifty I can be: you won't eat or drink anything
at my place for the next ten days.

PHILE If you want to say anything nice about him, you'll be al-
lowed to say it. If you abuse him, you'll get a thrashing. 240

PHILO If I'd sacrificed an ox to great Jupiter with that money I
gave for her, I'd never have invested it equally well. You
can see that she loves me dearly. Oh! I'm a fine fellow:
I've freed an advocate to plead my cause.

SCA I can see that you consider all men as worthless com- 245
pared with Philolaches. Now I'll agree with you rather
than get a beating for his sake, if you're fully convinced
that he'll be your friend for good.

PHILE Give me the mirror and the jewel casket at once,
Scapha, so that I can be made up when my darling Philo-
laches arrives.

SCA A woman who is dissatisfied with herself and her age 250
needs a mirror. Why do you need a mirror? You yourself
are the best possible mirror for the mirror.[4] (*hands it over
nevertheless*)

PHILO Because of this word, Scapha, so that you haven't spo-
ken so nicely for nothing, I'll give some money today . . .
to you, my dear Philematium.

---

[4] A compliment on her complexion and especially her clear eyes;
she can show the mirror more than the mirror can show her.

---

245 enim *Varro, om. P*   247 *uersum del. Acidalius*
249 ueniat *P*, adueniat *Ritschl*

PHILE suo quique loco uide capillum, satin compositust commode.

255 SCA ubi tu commoda es, capillum commodum esse credito.

PHILO uah! quid illa pote peius quicquam mulieri memorarier?

nunc assentatrix scelesta est, dudum aduorsatrix erat.

PHILE cedo cerussam.

SCA   quid cerussa opust nam?

PHILE   qui malas oblinam.

SCA una opera ebur atramento candefacere postules.

260 PHILO lepide dictum de atramento atque ebore. eugae! plaudo Scaphae.

PHILE tum tu igitur cedo purpurissum.

SCA   non do. scita es tu quidem.

noua pictura interpolare uis opus lepidissumum?

non istanc aetatem oportet pigmentum ullum attingere,

nec cerussam nec Melinum neque aliam ullam offuciam.

265 PHILE cape igitur speculum.

PHILO   ei mi misero! sauium speculo dedit.

nimis uelim lapidem qui ego illi speculo dimminuam caput.

SCA linteum cape atque exterge tibi manus.

PHILE   quid ita, opsecro?

SCA ut speculum tenuisti, metuo ne olant argentum manus:

ne usquam argentum te accepisse suspicetur Philolaches.

270 PHILO non uideor uidisse lenam callidiorem ullam alteras.

ut lepide atque astute in mentem uenit de speculo malae!

PHILE etiamne unguentis unguendam censes?

254 uiden capillus satis compositust *P*, uide capillum satin compositum sit *Nonius*, uide capillum satin compositust *Sonnenschein*

PHILE Look if my hair is all put up attractively enough, all in its proper place.

SCA If you are attractive, believe your hair to be attractive, too. 255

PHILO Wow! What can be mentioned that's worse than that woman? Now the criminal is constantly agreeing, a moment ago she was constantly disagreeing.

PHILE Give me the white lead.

SCA What do you need the white lead for?

PHILE To paint my cheeks.

SCA You might just as well expect to whiten ivory with ink.

PHILO A lovely saying about the ink and the ivory. Bravo! I applaud Scapha. 260

PHILE Then give me the rouge.

SCA I won't. (*with irony*) You are a clever one! Do you want to touch up a perfect picture with new brushwork? Girls of your age shouldn't touch any color, neither white lead nor Melian clay,[5] or any other makeup.

PHILE Take the mirror then. (*kisses and returns it*) 265

PHILO Poor me! She's given the mirror a kiss. I'd really like a stone to smash the mirror's head with.

SCA Take a towel and wipe your hands.

PHILE Why, please?

SCA (*jokingly*) I'm afraid that after holding the mirror your hands might smell of silver; Philolaches shouldn't suspect that you've taken money somewhere.

PHILO I don't think I've seen a cleverer procuress anywhere. In what a smart and lovely way the witch got the idea with the mirror! 270

PHILE Do you think I should also apply ointments?

[5] White in color.

SCA   minime feceris.

PHILE quapropter?

SCA   quia ecastor mulier recte olet ubi nil olet.
      nam istae ueteres, quae se unguentis unctitant, interpo-
        les,

275   uetulae, edentulae, quae uitia corporis fuco occulunt,
      ubi sese sudor cum unguentis consociauit, ilico
      itidem olent quasi quom una multa iura confudit coquos.
      quid olant nescias, nisi id unum ut male olere intellegas.

PHILO ut perdocte cuncta callet! nihil hac docta doctius.

280   uerum illuc est: maxuma adeo pars uostrorum intellegit,
      quibus anus domi sunt uxores, quae uos dote meruerunt.

PHILE agedum contempla aurum et pallam, satin haec ⟨me⟩
      deceat, Scapha.

SCA non me istuc curare oportet.

PHILE   quem opsecro igitur?

SCA   eloquar:

284–   Philolachem, is ne quid emat, nisi quod sibi placere cen-
85   seat.
      [nam amator meretricis mores sibi emit auro et purpura.]
      quid opust, quod suom esse nolit, ei ultro ostentarier?
      purpura aetati occultandae est, aurum turpi mulieri.
      pulchra mulier nuda erit quam purpurata pulchrior:

290   [poste nequiquam exornata est bene, si morata est male.
      pulchrum ornatum turpes mores peius caeno collinunt.]
      nam si pulchra est nimis ornata est.

PHILO   nimis diu apstineo manum.
      quid hic uos [diu] agitis?

    278 ni *P*, ut *Camerarius*   282 me *add. Camerarius*
    284–85 tibi *P*, sibi *Schoell*   286 *uersum secl. Ritschl*
    290–91 *uersus del. Ritschl*   293 diu *del. Weise*

SCA Don't do that.

PHILE Why?

SCA Because a woman smells right when she doesn't smell of anything: as for those old women who apply ointments, furbishing themselves up, toothless crones who conceal 275 their poor physical shape with makeup, when their sweat mingles with the ointments, they instantly smell the same way as when a cook mixes many sauces together. What they smell of you can't tell, except for this one thing: you know they smell bad.

PHILO How cleverly she knows everything! Nothing's cleverer than this clever one. That's true; and most of you know it, 280 you who have old women as wives at home, who bought you with their dowries.

PHILE Go on, look if the jewelry and gown suit me well enough, Scapha.

SCA I shouldn't be the one to care about that.

PHILE Who, then, should, please?

SCA I'll tell you: Philolaches, so that he doesn't buy anything 285 except what he thinks he'll like. [Yes, a lover buys a prostitute's favors with jewelry and purple-dyed clothes.] What's the point of showing him unasked what he doesn't want to be his? Purple is there for concealing old age, jewelry for concealing an ugly woman. A beautiful woman will be more beautiful naked than dressed in purple. [What's more, if a woman has a bad character she's 290 adorned for nothing. An ugly character besmirches beautiful adornment worse than dung.] Yes, if she's beautiful she's adorned more than enough.

PHILO It's high time to go and address them. (*advancing*) What are you two doing here?

343

PHILE   tibi me exorno ut placeam.

PHILO   ornata es satis.

       abi tu hinc intro atque ornamenta haec aufer. sed, uoluptas mea,

295   mea Philematium, potare tecum collubitum est mihi.

PHILE et edepol mihi tecum, nam quod tibi lubet idem mi lubet,

       mea uoluptas.

PHILO   em istuc uerbum uile est uiginti minis.

PHILE cedo, amabo, decem: bene emptum tibi dare hoc uerbum uolo.

PHILO etiam nunc decem minae apud te sunt; uel rationem puta.

300   triginta minas pro capite tuo dedi.

PHILE   quor exprobras?

PHILO egone id exprobrem, qui mihimet cupio id opprobrarier?

       nec quicquam argenti locaui iam diu usquam aeque bene.

PHILE certe ego, quod te amo, operam nusquam melius potui ponere.

PHILO bene igitur ratio accepti atque expensi inter nos conuenit:

305   tu me amas, ego te amo; merito id fieri uterque existumat.

       haec qui gaudent, gaudeant perpetuo suo semper bono;

       qui inuident, ne umquam eorum quisquam inuideat prorsus commodis.

PHILE age accumbe igitur. cedo aquam manibus, puere, appone hic mensulam.

       uide tali ubi sint. uin unguenta?

PHILE I'm making myself up for you so as to please you.

PHILO You're made up enough. (*to Scapha*) You go inside and take this frippery away.

Exit SCAPHA into the house, carrying the mirror and jewelry.

PHILO (*to Philematium*) But, my darling, my dear Philema- 295
tium, the fancy has caught me to drink with you.

PHILE And me to drink with you: what you fancy I fancy too, my darling.

Enter servants with tables and couches.

PHILO There now! That word is cheap at twenty minas.

PHILE Give me ten, please: I want to give you this word inexpensively.

PHILO Even now ten minas are with you; if you like, balance the account. I paid thirty minas for you. 300

PHILE Why are you casting it in my teeth?

PHILO I casting it in your teeth? I desire to have it cast in *my* teeth. I haven't invested any money equally well anywhere for a long time.

PHILE Surely I couldn't have invested my services better than by loving you.

PHILO Then the account of receipt and expenditure balances admirably between us: you love me, I love you; each of us 305
believes that this is only what we deserve. May those who are happy about it always be happy about their own everlasting joy; and may no one ever envy the advantages of those who envy us.

PHILE Go on, recline at table then. (*to a servant*) Give me water for my hands, boy, put the little table here. Check where the dice are. (*to Philolaches*) Do you want ointments?

345

PHILO   quid opust? cum stacta accubo.

310   sed estne hic meus sodalis qui huc incedit cum amica
                  sua?
                is est, Callidamates cum amica incedit. eugae! oculus
                  meus,
                conueniunt manuplares eccos: praedam participes pe-
                  tunt.

I. iv: CALLIDAMATES. DELPHIVM.
PHILOLACHES. PHILEMATIVM

CAL   aduorsum ueniri mihi ad Philolachem
          uolo temperi. audi, em tibi imperatum est.
315   nam illi ubi fui, inde effugi foras,
          ita me ibi male conuiui sermonisque taesum est.
          nunc comissatum ibo ad Philolachetem,
          ubi nos hilari ingenio et lepide accipient.
          ecquid tibi uideor mammamadere?
320 DEL   semper istoc modo
          moratu's ‹tu te. ire huc› debebas.
     CAL   uisne ego te ac tu me amplectare?
     DEL   si tibi cordi est, facere licet.
     CAL   lepida es.
          duc me amabo.
     DEL   caue ne cadas, asta.
325 CAL   o . . . o . . . ocellus es meus;
325ᵃ   tuos sum alumnus, mel meum.
326 DEL   caue modo ne prius in uia accumbas
          quam illi, ubi lectus est stratus, concumbimus.

318 accipiet *P*, accipient *Lorenz*
321 uite *P*, tu te. ire huc *Leo*
327 coimus (cotmus *D¹*) *P*, concumbimus *Leo*

346

PHILO What for? I'm already lying next to oil of myrrh. But 310
isn't this my chum who is coming here with his girl-
friend? It's him, Callidamates is coming with his girl-
friend. Hurray! Apple of my eye, our comrades in service
are coming, look; our fellows are demanding their share
of the booty.

*Enter CALLIDAMATES and DELPHIUM from the right, the
latter carrying a little parcel and supporting her drunken lover.
They are accompanied by PHANISCUS.*

CAL (*to Phaniscus*) I want to be fetched early at Philolaches'
place. Listen, there! You've got your orders.

Exit PHANISCUS to the right.

CAL Well, I escaped from where I was: I was terribly fed up 315
with the company and conversation there. Now I'll go to
Philolaches to have a good time, where they'll receive us
with merry humor and in a lovely way. Do I seem to be ti-
ti-tipsy to you?

DEL You've always wasted time like that. You should have 320
gone straight here. (*points to the house of Philolaches*)

CAL Do you want me to embrace you and you me?

DEL If it pleases you, we can do so. (*they embrace*)

CAL You're a darling. Guide me, please.

DEL Watch out so you don't fall, stand up.

CAL You're the a-a-apple of my eye; I'm your baby, my honey. 325

DEL Just watch out so you don't lie down in the street before
we lie together[6] there, where a couch has been made
ready for us.

[6] *Concumbere* is used euphemistically in the meaning "have inter-
course."

347

	CAL	sine, sine cadere me.
	DEL	sino, sed hoc quod mi in manust:
		si cades, non cades quin cadam tecum.
330	CAL	iacentis tollet postea nos ambos aliquis.
	DEL	madet homo.
	CAL	tun me ais mammamadere?
	DEL	cedo manum, nolo equidem te affligi.
	CAL	em tene.
	DEL	age, i simul.
	CAL	quo ego eam?
	DEL	an nescis?
334	CAL	scio, in mentem uenit modo:
335		nemp' domum eo comissatum.
335ᵃ	DEL	immo istuc quidem.
	CAL	iam memini.
336	PHILO	num non uis me obuiam his ire, anime mi?
		illi ego ex omnibus optume uolo.
		iam reuortar.
	PHILE	diu est "iam" id mihi.
	CAL	ecquis hic est?
	PHILO	adest.
	CAL	eu, Philolaches,
340		salue, amicissume mi omnium hominum.
	PHILO	di te ament. accuba, Callidamates.
		unde agis te?
	CAL	unde homo ebrius probe.
	PHILE	quin amabo accubas, Delphium mea?
		da illi quod bibat.

328 sinos et *B¹CD¹*, sino set et *B⁴*, sines et *D³*, sino sed *Leo*

CAL   Let go of me, let me fall.

DEL   I will let go, but of what I have in my hand. (*drops her parcel*) If you fall, you shan't fall without me falling with you.

CAL   Someone will pick the two of us up later where we lie.   330

DEL   The chap's tipsy.

CAL   Are you saying that I'm ti-ti-tipsy?

DEL   Give me your hand, I don't want you to get hurt.

CAL   Here, take it. (*offers it*)

DEL   Go on, walk with me.

CAL   Where should I walk?

DEL   You don't know?

CAL   I do know, it just occurred to me: surely I'm going home   335 to have a party.

DEL   No, you're going there. (*points to the house of Philolaches*)

CAL   Now I remember.

PHILO   (*to Philematium*) You don't mind me going and meeting them, do you, my darling? He's the dearest of all my friends. I'll come back in a minute.

PHILE   This "minute" is a long time for me.

CAL   (*not yet seeing his hosts*) Is anyone here?

PHILO   Yes, there is.

CAL   Excellent, Philolaches, greetings, my best friend among   340 all men.

PHILO   May the gods love you. Do recline at table, Callidamates. Where are you coming from?

CAL   (*as he lies down*) Where a properly drunken fellow comes from.

PHILE   Please, why don't you recline at table, my dear Delphium? (*as she does so, to a servant standing beside Callidamates*) Give him something to drink.

CAL	dormiam ego iam.

345 PHILO num mirum aut nouom quippiam facit?

DEL quid ego hoc faciam postea?

PHILE   mea, sic sine eumpse.

       age tu interim da ab Delphio cito cantharum circum.

ACTVS II

II. i: TRANIO. PHILOLACHES. CALLIDAMATES.
DELPHIVM. PHILEMATIVM. PVER

TRA Iuppiter supremus summis opibus atque industriis

       me periisse et Philolachetem cupit erilem filium.

350   occidit spes nostra, nusquam stabulum est confidentiae,

       nec Salus nobis saluti iam esse, si cupiat, potest:

       ita mali maeroris montem maxumum ad portum modo

       conspicatus sum: erus aduenit peregre, periit Tranio.

       ecquis homo est qui facere argenti cupiat aliquantum lu-

         cri,

355   qui hodie sese excruciari meam uicem possit pati?

       ubi sunt isti plagipatidae, ferritribaces uiri,

       uel isti qui hosticas trium nummum causa subeunt sub

         falas,

       ubi quinis aut denis hastis corpus transfigi solet?

       ego dabo ei talentum primus qui in crucem excucurrerit;

360   sed ea lege ut offigantur bis pedes, bis bracchia.

       ubi id erit factum, a me argentum petito praesentarium.

       sed ego, sumne infelix qui non curro curriculo domum?

    358 aliqui quique *P*, quinis aut *Leo*

CAL   Now I'll sleep. (*puts down his head*)
PHILO Is he doing anything strange or new?   345
DEL   What should I do with him after this?
PHILE My dear, leave him like this. (*to Philolaches*) Go on,
      in the meantime pass round the jar, beginning with Del-
      phium.

ACT TWO

Enter TRANIO from the left.

TRA   With all his might and main Jupiter above wishes me and
      Philolaches, master's son, to be dead. Our hope has per-   350
      ished, nowhere can optimism find a home, nor can Salva-
      tion be of salvation to us, even if she should desire to be
      so: I've spotted a mighty mountain of monstrous misery
      at the harbor; master has come from abroad and Tranio is
      dead. Is there anyone who'd like to earn some money,
      who could bear to be tortured instead of me today?   355
      Where are those sons of the whip, the men who wear out
      iron chains, or rather those who go underneath the en-
      emy's towers for the sake of three sesterces,[7] where their
      bodies are generally pierced with five or ten spears?[8] I'll
      give a talent to the chap who first makes a sally onto the
      cross; but on condition that his feet and arms are nailed   360
      down double. When this is done, let him ask me for the
      money in cash. But as for me, aren't I a wretch since I'm
      not running home at full speed?

      [7] Roughly equivalent to the tetrobol, the daily pay of a Greek mer-
cenary.
      [8] The first group are slaves, the second soldiers.

PHILO ⟨adest⟩, adest opsonium. eccum Tranio a portu redit.
TRA   Philolaches!
PHILO   quid est?
TRA   ⟨et⟩ ego et tu—
PHILO   quid "et ego et tu"?
TRA   periimus.
365 PHILO quid ita?
TRA   pater adest.
PHILO   quid ego ex te audio?
TRA   apsumpti sumus.
      pater inquam tuos uenit.
PHILO   ubi is est, opsecro?
TRA   ⟨in portu iam⟩ adest.
PHILO quis id ait? quis uidit?
TRA   egomet, inquam, uidi.
PHILO   uae mihi!
      quid ego ago?
TRA   nam quid tu, malum, me rogitas quid agas? accubas.
PHILO tutin uidisti?
TRA   egomet, inquam.
PHILO   certe?
TRA   ⟨certe⟩, inquam.
PHILO   occidi,
370   si tu uera memoras.
TRA   quid mi sit boni, si mentiar?
PHILO quid ego nunc faciam?
TRA   iube haec hinc omnia amolirier.
      quis istic dormit?
PHILO   Callidamates. suscita istum, Delphium.

363 adest *add. Gruterus*   364 et *add. Dousa*
366 in portu iam *add. Ritschl*

PHILO It's here, food's here! Look, Tranio's returning from the
     harbor.

TRA Philolaches!

PHILO What's the matter?

TRA You and I—

PHILO (*interrupting*) What, "you and I"?

TRA We've died.

PHILO How so?   365

TRA Your father's back.

PHILO What must I hear from you?

TRA We're done for. I'm telling you, your father has come.

PHILO Where is he, please?

TRA He's at the harbor already.

PHILO Who says so? Who has seen him?

TRA I myself have seen him, I'm telling you.

PHILO Bad luck to me! What do I do now?

TRA Why the blazes are you asking me what you're doing?[9]
     You're reclining at table.

PHILO Have you seen him yourself?

TRA Yes, I have, I'm telling you.

PHILO Certainly?

TRA Certainly, I'm telling you.

PHILO I'm dead, if you're speaking the truth.   370

TRA What would be the point of lying?

PHILO What should I do now?

TRA Have all this removed from here. Who's sleeping there?

PHILO Callidamates. Wake him up, Delphium.

[9] Philolaches asks for advice, but Tranio deliberately misunder-
stands him.

---

369 certe *add. Camerarius*

DEL Callidamates, Callidamates, uigila!

CAL   uigilo, cedo [ut] bibam.

DEL uigila. pater aduenit peregre Philolachei.

CAL   ualeat pater.

375 PHILO ualet illequidem atque ⟨ego⟩ disperii.

CAL   bis periisti? qui potest?

PHILO quaeso edepol, exsurge; pater aduenit.

CAL   tuos uenit pater?

iube abire rursum. quid illi reditio etiam huc fuit?

PHILO quid ego agam? pater iam hic me offendet miserum
       adueniens ebrium,

aedis plenas conuiuarum et mulierum. miserum est opus

380 igitur demum fodere puteum, ubi sitis faucis tenet;

sicut ego aduentu patris nunc quaero quid faciam miser.

TRA ecce⟨re⟩ autem hic deposiuit caput et dormit. suscita.

PHILO etiam uigilas? pater, inquam, aderit iam hic meus.

CAL   ain tu, pater?

cedo soleas mi, ut arma capiam. iam pol ego occidam pa-
       trem.

385 PHILO perdis rem.

DEL   tace, amabo.

PHILO   abripite hunc intro actutum inter manus.

CAL iam hercle ego uos pro matula habebo, nisi mihi matulam
       datis.

PHILO perii!

373 ut *del. Bentley*   375 ego *add. Pylades*
377 iu-iube, et-etiam *Sonnenschein*
382 ecce⟨re⟩ *Ritschl*

[10] Philolaches uses the verb *disperire*, "die completely," but Callidamates mishears it as *bis perire*, "die twice."

DEL Callidamates, Callidamates, wake up!

CAL I'm awake, give me something to drink.

DEL Wake up. The father of Philolaches has arrived from abroad.

CAL I bid his father farewell.

PHILO My father certainly does fare well and I will be dead in a   375
second's time.

CAL You'll be dead a second time?[10] How is that possible?

PHILO Please, do get up. My father's arrived.

CAL Your father's come? Tell him to go away again. Why did
he have to come back here?

PHILO What should I do? On his arrival, my father will find me
drunk here now, wretch that I am, and the house full of
guests and women. It's a wretched business to start dig-   380
ging a well only when thirst has got you by the throat. In
just the same way I'm asking what to do, now that my
father has arrived, wretch that I am.

TRA Look, though, this chap's put his head down and is sleep-
ing. Wake him up.

PHILO (*shaking Callidamates*) Will you wake up? I'm telling
you, my father will be here in a moment.

CAL Do you say so, your father? Give me my sandals so that I
may take up arms. I'll slay your father right now.

PHILO You're ruining everything.   385

DEL (*to Callidamates*) Be quiet, please.

PHILO (*to the slaves*) Catch hold of him and carry him off in-
side instantly. (*they obey and also begin to carry away the
table and couches*)

CAL This minute I'll use you as my night pot, unless you give
me a night pot.

PHILO I'm dead!

TRA   habe bonum animum: ego istum lepide medicabo me-
tum.

PHILO nullus sum!

TRA   taceas: ego qui istaec sedem meditabor tibi.
satin habes si ego aduenientem ita patrem faciam tuom,

390   non modo ne intro eat, uerum etiam ut fugiat longe ab
aedibus?

uos modo hinc abite intro atque haec hinc propere amoli-
mini.

PHILO ubi ego ero?

TRA   ubi maxume esse uis: cum hac, cum istac eris.

DEL quid si igitur abeamus hinc nos?

TRA   non hoc longe, Delphium.
nam intus potate hau tantillo hac quidem causa minus.

395 PHILO ei mihi! quom istaec blanda dicta quo eueniant madeo
metu.

TRA potin ut animo sis quieto et facias quod iubeo?

PHILO   potest.

TRA omnium primum, Philematium, intro abi, et tu, Del-
phium.

DEL morigerae tibi erimus ambae.

TRA   ita ille faxit Iuppiter!
animum aduorte nunciam tu quae uolo accurarier.

400   omnium primumdum ‹haec› aedes iam fac occlusae
sient;

intus caue muttire quemquam siueris.

PHILO   curabitur.

TRA tamquam si intus natus nemo in aedibus habitet.

396 animo ut *P, transp. Bentley*
400 haec *add. Ritschl*

TRA   Take heart. I'll find a lovely remedy for your fear.

PHILO   I'm gone!

TRA   Be quiet. I'll come up with some way to settle your business quietly. Are you content if I make sure that on his arrival your father does not only not go in, but even runs far 390
away from the house? You just go in and take these things away quickly.

PHILO   Where will I be?

TRA   Where you want to be most: you'll be with this girl and with that. (*points at Philematium and Delphium*)

DEL   Hadn't we better go away?

TRA   Not an inch, Delphium: don't drink one drop less inside because of this.

PHILO   Poor me! I sweat with fear at the thought of what those 395
coaxing words of yours will lead to.

TRA   Can't you have a calm mind and do what I tell you?

PHILO   Yes.

TRA   First of all, Philematium, go inside, and you too, Delphium.

DEL   We'll both obey you.

Exeunt DELPHIUM and PHILEMATIUM into the house of Philolaches.

TRA   May great Jupiter grant that it should be so![11] (*to Philolaches*) You, pay attention now to what I want sorted out. First of all make sure this house is locked up now. Let no 400
one breathe a word inside.

PHILO   It shall be seen to.

TRA   As if no one lived inside in the house.

---

[11] Tranio interprets the obedience in a sexual way.

PHILO   licet.

TRA   neu quisquam responset quando hasce aedis pultabit se-
         nex.

PHILO numquid aliud?

TRA   clauem mi harunc aedium Laconicam

405   iam iube efferri intus: hasce ego aedis occludam hinc fo-
         ris.

PHILO in tuam custodelam meque et meas spes trado, Tranio.

407– TRA   pluma haud interest patronus an cliens probior siet.
8   homini, quoi nulla in pectore est audacia,

410   [nam quoiuis homini uel optumo uel pessumo,]
         quamuis desubito facile est facere nequiter:
         uerum id uidendum est, id uiri docti est opus,
         quae dissignata sint et facta nequiter,
         tranquille cuncta ut proueniant et sine malo,

415   ne quid potiatur quam ob rem pigeat uiuere.
         sic ut ego efficiam, quae facta hic turbauimus,
         profecto ut liqueant omnia et tranquilla sint
         nec quicquam nobis pariant ex se incommodi.
         sed quid tu egredere, Sphaerio?

SPHAE   em clauim.

TRA   optume

420   praeceptis paruisti.

SPHAE   iussit maxumo
         opere orare ut patrem aliquo apsterreres modo
         ne intro iret ad se.

TRA   quin etiam illi hoc dicito,
         facturum <me> ut ne etiam aspicere aedis audeat,
         capite obuoluto ut fugiat cum summo metu.

---

   410 *uersum secl. Ritschl*
   414 et ut proueniant *P, transp. Bentley*   416 turbabimus *P*

PHILO Okay.

TRA And no one is to answer when the old man knocks at this house.

PHILO Anything else?

TRA Have the outdoor key of this house brought out to me this   405
instant; I'll lock this house from here, from the outside.

PHILO I put myself and my hopes under your protection, Tranio.

TRA There's not a feather's weight of difference whether the
protector or the protégé is cleverer. A man who has no
daring in his breast [anyone, the best or the worst] can   410
easily mess things up on however short notice. But this
requires seeing to, this is the work of a clever man, to
make sure that what has been boldly schemed and craft-
ily executed has a happy and harmless ending, so that he   415
doesn't come in for anything to make him sorry that he
was born. Thus I shall bring it about that the mess we've
created here will actually end in clear and calm weather
and won't create any trouble for us.

Enter SPHAERIO from the house of Philolaches with a key.

TRA But what are you coming out for, Sphaerio?

SPHAE Here's the key.

TRA You've obeyed my commands excellently.   420

SPHAE He told me to do my best to beg you to frighten away his
father somehow so that he won't go inside.

TRA Yes; tell him I'll make sure that he won't even dare to look
at the house and that he'll run away with covered head in

---

419 iamiam *P*, em clauim *Seyffert* (*qui haec uerba Sphaerioni dat*)
422 adest *P*, ad se *Pylades*   423 me *add. Pylades*

425   clauim cedo atque abi [hinc] intro atque occlude ostium,
        et ego hinc occludam. iube uenire nunciam.
        ludos ego hodie uiuo praesenti hic seni
        faciam, quod credo mortuo numquam fore.
        concedam a foribus huc, hinc speculabor procul,
430   unde aduenienti sarcinam imponam seni.

      II. ii: THEOPROPIDES. TRANIO

THEO habeo, Neptune, gratiam magnam tibi,
        quom me amisisti a te uix uiuom domum.
        uerum si posthac me pedem latum modo
        scies imposisse in undam, hau causa est ilico
435   quod nunc uoluisti facere quin facias mihi.
        apage, apage te a me nunciam post hunc diem!
        quod crediturus tibi fui, omne credidi.
TRA edepol, Neptune, peccauisti largiter
        qui occasionem hanc amisisti tam bonam.
440 THEO triennio post Aegypto aduenio domum;
        credo exspectatus ueniam familiaribus.
TRA nimio edepol ille potuit exspectatior
        uenire qui te nuntiaret mortuom.
THEO sed quid hoc? occlusa ianua est interdius.
445   pultabo. heus, ecquis intust? aperitin fores?
TRA quis homo est qui nostras aedis accessit prope?

425 hinc *ex insequenti uersu uidetur uenisse*
432 modo *P*, domum *P. Thomas*
445 ist *P*, intust *Leo*

12 A pun; *ludi* can refer to funeral games, but also to the ridicule
someone is exposed to unwittingly.

greatest fear. Give me the key, go inside, and lock the   425
door; and I shall lock it from here.

SPHAERIO hands over the key, then returns into the house.

TRA (*as he locks the door*) Let him come now. I'll play a com-
edy for the old man today, while he's alive and present,
which I believe will never happen after his death.[12] (*mov-
ing out of sight*) I'll go away from the door to this place,
from here from a distance I'll observe by what means I   430
can cajole the old man on his arrival.

*Enter THEOPROPIDES from the left, accompanied by two
slaves.*

THEO I'm very grateful to you, Neptune, for letting me get back
home from you, even if barely alive. But if hereafter you
hear that I have set one foot's breadth into the deep, I
give you leave to do to me instantly what you wanted to   435
do just now. Go away, go away from me now after this
day! Everything I meant to entrust you with I have en-
trusted you with already.

TRA (*aside*) Goodness, Neptune, you made an enormous mis-
take by letting go of such a good opportunity.

THEO After three years I'm returning home from Egypt; I be-   440
lieve I'll be a welcome visitor to those in my household.

TRA (*aside*) Someone with news of your death would have
come as a much more welcome visitor.

THEO (*inspecting the door*) But what's this? The door's locked
in broad daylight. I'll knock. (*does so*) Hey there, is any-   445
one inside? Won't you open the door?

TRA (*going toward the house*) Who is this who has approached
our house?

THEO meus seruos hicquidem est Tranio.

TRA   o Theopropides,

ere, salue, saluom te aduenisse gaudeo.

usquin ualuisti?

THEO   usque, ut uides.

TRA   factum optume.

450 THEO quid uos? insanine estis?

TRA   quidum?

THEO   sic, quia

foris ambulatis, natus nemo in aedibus

seruat nec qui recludat nec [qui] respondeat.

pultando [pedibus] paene confregi hasce ambas ⟨fores⟩.

454– TRA eho an tu tetigisti has aedis?

55 THEO   quor non tangerem?

quin pultando, inquam, paene confregi fores.

TRA tetigistin?

THEO   tetigi, inquam, et pultaui.

TRA   uah!

THEO   quid est?

TRA male hercle factum.

THEO   quid est negoti?

TRA   non potest

dici quam indignum facinus fecisti et malum.

460 THEO quid iam?

TRA   fuge, opsecro, atque apscede ab aedibus.

fuge huc, fuge ad me propius. tetigistin fores?

THEO quo modo pultare potui, si non tangerem?

TRA occidisti hercle—

THEO   quem mortalem?

TRA   —omnis tuos.

THEO di te deaeque omnes cum istoc omine—

THEO This is my slave Tranio.

TRA O Theopropides, my master, greetings, I'm happy that you've returned safely. Have you been well throughout?

THEO Yes, as you can see.

TRA Excellent.

THEO What about you? Are you all mad?   450

TRA Why?

THEO Well, because you're strolling about outside and no one's keeping watch in the house, neither to open the door nor to answer. I almost broke both halves of the double door with my knocking.

TRA Hey there, have you touched this house?   455

THEO Why shouldn't I have touched it? I'm telling you, I almost broke the door with my knocking.

TRA You've touched it?

THEO I'm telling you, I've touched it and I've knocked.

TRA Oh no!

THEO What is it?

TRA It's a disaster.

THEO What's the matter?

TRA It can't be said what an evil and wicked deed you've done.

THEO How so?   460

TRA Run, I entreat you, and get away from the house. Run here, run closer to me. Did you touch the door?

THEO How could I have knocked without touching it?

TRA You've killed—

THEO (*interrupting*) Whom?

TRA —all your household members.

THEO With that omen may all the gods and goddesses—

---

452 qui² *del. Bothe*   453 pedibus *del. Bothe* foris *add. Ritschl*

465	TRA	metuo te atque istos expiare ut possies.
466	THEO	quam ob rem? aut quam subito rem mihi apportas nouam?
466ᵃ	TRA	***
467		et heus, iube illos illinc ambo apscedere.
	THEO	apscedite.
	TRA	aedis ne attigatis. tangite uos quoque terram.
	THEO	opsecro hercle, quin eloquere ⟨rem⟩.
470	TRA	quia septem menses sunt quom in hasce aedis pedem nemo intro tetulit, semel ut emigrauimus.
	THEO	eloquere, quid ita?
	TRA	circumspicedum: numquis est sermonem nostrum qui aucupet?
	THEO	tutum probe est.
	TRA	circumspice etiam.
	THEO	nemo est. loquere nunciam.
475	TRA	capitalis caedis facta est.
	THEO	[quid est?] non intellego.
	TRA	scelus, inquam, factum est iam diu, antiquom et uetus.
	THEO	antiquom?
	TRA	id adeo nos nunc factum inuenimus.
	THEO	quid istuc est sceleris? aut quis id fecit? cedo.
	TRA	hospes necauit hospitem captum manu;
480		iste, ut ego opinor, qui has tibi aedis uendidit.
	THEO	necauit?
	TRA	aurumque ei ademit hospiti eumque hic defodit hospitem ibidem in aedibus.
	THEO	quapropter id uos factum suspicamini?

466ᵃ *lacunam statuit* Leo
469 rem *add.* Bothe

TRA (*interrupting*) I fear that you may not be able to purify   465
yourself and them.

THEO Why? Or what new problem are you suddenly bringing
me?

TRA *** and hey, have those two go away from there.

THEO (*to the slaves*) Go away.

TRA Do not touch the house. You too touch the earth. (*they
obey*)

THEO Please, tell me all about it.

TRA Because it's seven months since anyone put a foot into   470
this house once we'd moved out.

THEO Tell me, why?

TRA Do look around: is there anyone who might overhear us?

THEO It's perfectly safe.

TRA Do look around again.

THEO There's no one. Now speak.

TRA An atrocious murder has been committed.   475

THEO I don't understand.

TRA I'm telling you, a crime was committed, long ago already,
an old and ancient one.

THEO Ancient?

TRA That's what we've now found out has been committed.

THEO What crime is that? Or who committed it? Tell me.

TRA A host overpowered his guest and murdered him; the   480
one, I think, who sold you this house.

THEO He murdered him?

TRA And he took away this guest's gold and buried the guest
right here in the house.

THEO Why do you suspect this has happened?

---

475 capitali scedis facta est *P*, capitale scelus factumst *Bergk* quid
est *del. Camerarius*   478 sceleste *P*, sceleris *Bentley*

TRA	ego dicam, ausculta. ut foris cenauerat
485	tuos gnatus, postquam rediit a cena domum,
	abimus omnes cubitum; condormiuimus:
	lucernam forte oblitus fueram exstinguere;
	atque ille exclamat derepente maxumum.
THEO	quis homo? an gnatus meus?
TRA	st! tace, ausculta modo.
490	ait uenisse illum in somnis ad se mortuom.
THEO	nempe ergo in somnis?
TRA	ita. sed ausculta modo.
	ait illum hoc pacto sibi dixisse mortuom—
THEO	in somnis?
TRA	mirum quin uigilanti diceret
	qui abhinc sexaginta annis occisus foret.
495	interdum inepte stultus es, ⟨Theopropides.⟩
THEO	taceo.
TRA	sed ecce quae illi in ⟨somnis mortuos⟩:
	"ego transmarinus hospes sum Diapontius.
	hic habito, haec mi dedita est habitatio.
	nam me Accheruntem recipere Orcus noluit,
500	quia praemature uita careo. per fidem
	deceptus sum: hospes me hic necauit isque me
	defodit insepultum clam [ibidem] in hisce aedibus,
	scelestus, auri causa. nunc tu hinc emigra.
	scelestae [hae] sunt aedes, impia est habitatio."
505	quae hic monstra fiunt anno uix possum eloqui.
THEO	st, st!
TRA	quid, opsecro hercle, factum est?
THEO	concrepuit foris.

495 Theopropides *add. Ritschl* 496 somnis mortuos *add.*
Schoell   502 ibidem *del. Bentley*   504 hae *del. Lindsay*

TRA I'll tell you, listen. When your son had dined out, we all 485
     went to bed after he returned home from dinner. We fell
     asleep. I'd accidentally forgotten to put out the lamp.
     And suddenly he lets out an enormous shout.

THEO Who? My son?

TRA Hush! Be quiet, just listen. He said that that dead man 490
     had come to him in his sleep.

THEO It was in his sleep then?

TRA Yes. But just listen. He said that that dead man had spo-
     ken to him in the following way—

THEO (*interrupting*) In his sleep?

TRA Strange that he didn't speak to him while he was awake,
     given that he'd been killed sixty years ago. Sometimes 495
     you really are incredibly stupid, Theopropides.

THEO I'll keep quiet.

TRA But look what the dead man said to him in his sleep: "I
     am a guest from overseas, Diapontius.[13] I live here, this
     dwelling place has been allotted to me: Orcus[14] did not
     want to receive me into the Underworld because I lost 500
     my life before my time. I was deceived in violation of the
     obligations of hospitality: my host murdered me here and
     he secretly put me underground in this house without
     due rites, for the sake of gold, the criminal. Now move
     out from here. This house is under a curse, this dwelling
     place is defiled." I could barely tell you in a year what 505
     apparitions take place here.

THEO (*listening intently*) Hush, hush!

TRA Please, what's happened?

THEO The door has creaked.

---

13 The name fittingly means "man from overseas."
14 The god of the Underworld.

TRA   hicin percussit!

THEO   guttam haud habeo sanguinis,

               uiuom me accersunt Accheruntem mortui.

510   TRA   perii! illisce hodie hanc conturbabunt fabulam.

               nimis quam formido ne manufesto hic me opprimat.

THEO   quid tute tecum loquere?

TRA   apscede ab ianua.

               fuge, opsecro hercle.

THEO   quo fugiam? etiam tu fuge.

TRA   nil ego formido, pax mihi est cum mortuis.

515   INTVS heus, Tranio!

TRA   non me appellabis si sapis.

               nil ego commerui neque istas percussi fores.

THEO   quaeso—

⟨TRA   caue uerbum faxis.

THEO   dic⟩ quid segreges

        ⟨sermonem.

TRA   apage hinc te.

THEO   quae r⟩es te agitat, Tranio?

               quicum istaec loquere?

TRA   an quaeso tu appellaueras?

520   ita me di amabunt, mortuom illum credidi

               expostulare quia percussisses fores.

               sed tu, etiamne astas nec quae dico optemperas?

THEO   quid faciam?

TRA   caue respexis, fuge, [atque] operi caput.

THEO   quor non fugis tu?

TRA   pax mihi est cum mortuis.

525   THEO   scio. quid modo igitur? quor tanto opere extimueras?

512 te tu cum (tu tecum B^2) *P*, tute tecum *Merula*
517 ⟨TRA caue uerbum faxis. THEO dic⟩ *Leo*

TRA It was he who knocked!

THEO I don't have a drop of blood! The dead are taking me to the Underworld while I'm still alive!

TRA (*aside*) I'm done for! They'll upset this story today. I'm 510 terribly afraid that he'll catch me red-handed.

THEO What are you talking to yourself about?

TRA Go away from the door. Run, I entreat you.

THEO Where should I run? You run as well.

TRA I'm not afraid at all, I'm at peace with the dead.

FROM INSIDE Hey, Tranio! 515

TRA (*to the voice inside*) You'd do well not to address me. I haven't done anything wrong and I haven't knocked on the door.

THEO Please—

TRA (*ignoring Theopropides*) Don't utter a word.

THEO Tell me why you're breaking off the conversation.

TRA (*still to the voice inside*) Away with you from here.

THEO What's the matter with you, Tranio? Who are you saying this to?

TRA Please, was it you that called? As truly as the gods will 520 love me, I believed it was that dead man complaining because you'd knocked on the door. But you, are you still standing here and not obeying my commands?

THEO What should I do?

TRA Don't look back, run, and cover your head.

THEO Why don't you run?

TRA I'm at peace with the dead.

THEO (*doubtfully*) I see. Then what about just now? Why were 525 you so afraid?

---

518 ‹sermonem. TRA apage hinc te. THEO quae r›es *Leo*
523 atque *del. Guyet*

TRA   nil me curassis, inquam, ego mi prouidero:
        tu, ut occepisti, tantum quantum quis fuge
        atque Herculem inuoca.

THEO   Hercules, ted inuoco.

TRA   et ego . . . tibi hodie ut det, senex, magnum malum.
530   pro di immortales, opsecro uostram fidem!
        quid ego hodie negoti confeci mali.

ACTVS III

III. i: DANISTA. TRANIO. THEOPROPIDES

MIS   scelestiorem ego annum argento faenore
        numquam ullum uidi quam hic mihi annus optigit.
        a mani ad noctem usque in foro dego diem,
535   locare argenti nemini nummum queo.

TRA   nunc pol ego perii plane in perpetuom modum.
        danista adest qui dedit ⟨argentum faenore⟩,
        qui amica est empta quoque ⟨opus in sumptus fuit⟩.
        manufesta res est, nisi quid occurro prius,
540   hoc ne senex resciscat. ibo huic obuiam.
        sed quidnam hic sese tam cito recipit domum?
        metuo ne de hac re quippiam indaudiuerit.
        accedam atque appellabo. ei, quam timeo miser!
        nihil est miserius quam animus hominis conscius,

537 argentum faenori *add. Camerarius*
538 opus in sumptus fuit *add. Camerarius*
540 ne hoc P, *transp. Bothe*

TRA   Don't worry about me, I tell you, I'll look out for myself;
you, as you've begun, must run as fast as you can and in-
voke Hercules.

THEO Hercules, I invoke you!

Exit THEOPROPIDES to the left, followed by his slaves.

TRA   And so do I . . . that he may give you a big thrashing to-
day, old chap. Immortal gods, I implore your protection!   530
What bad business I've done today!

ACT THREE

Enter MISARGYRIDES from the right.

MIS   I've never seen a worse year for money put out at interest
than this year has been. I spend my entire day in the fo-
rum, from morning till night, yet I can't lend as much as a   535
silver coin to anyone.

TRA   (*spotting him in the distance*) Now every inch of me is
certainly dead. The moneylender is here, the one who
loaned that money on interest with which the girlfriend
was bought and which we needed for our spending. The
cat's out of the bag unless I'm beforehand with some
move to prevent the old man from finding out about this.   540
I'll go and meet him.

Enter THEOPROPIDES from the left.

TRA   (*as he spots him*) But why is he coming back home so
soon? I'm afraid he might have got wind of this business.
I'll approach and address him. Dear me, how scared I
am, poor wretch that I am! Nothing's more wretched

371

545   sicut me ‹male› habet. uerum utut res sese habet,
        pergam turbare porro: ita haec res postulat.
        unde is?

THEO   conueni illum unde hasce aedis emeram.

TRA numquid dixisti de illo quod dixi tibi?

THEO dixi hercle uero omnia.

TRA   ei misero mihi!

550   metuo ne techinae meae perpetuo perierint.

THEO quid tute tecum?

TRA   nihil enim. sed dic mihi,
        dixtine quaeso?

THEO   dixi, inquam, ordine omnia.

TRA etiam fatetur de hospite?

THEO   immo pernegat.

TRA negat ‹scelestus?

THEO   negitat in›quam.

TRA   cogita:

555   ‹non confitetur?›

THEO   dicam si confessus sit.
        quid nunc faciundum censes?

TRA   egon? quid censeam?
        cape, opsecro hercle, cum eo ‹tu› una iudicem
        (sed eum uideto ut capias, qui credat mihi):
        tam facile uinces quam pirum uolpes comest.

560 MIS sed Philolachetis seruom eccum Tranium,
        qui mihi nec faenus nec sortem argenti danunt.

THEO quo te agis?

    545 male *add. Niemeyer*
    554 ‹scelestus? THEO negitat in›quam *Leo*
    555 non confitetur *add. Leo*
    557 tu *add. Lindsay*

than a man's guilty conscience, just as mine's torturing 545
me. But no matter what's up, I'll carry on causing trouble:
this situation demands it. (*to Theopropides*) Where are
you coming from?

THEO (*angrily*) I met the man I'd bought this house from.

TRA Did you tell him what I told you?

THEO Yes, I told him everything.

TRA (*aside*) Poor me! I'm afraid that my tricks have perished 550
utterly.

THEO What are you saying to yourself?

TRA Nothing, I assure you. But tell me, did you tell him,
please?

THEO I told him everything from beginning to end, I assure
you.

TRA Does he now admit it about the guest?

THEO No, he denies it absolutely.

TRA The criminal denies it?

THEO He does, I'm telling you.

TRA Think about it: he won't admit it? 555

THEO I'd tell you if he'd admitted it. What do you think should
be done now?

TRA I? What should I think? Please, choose an arbitrator to-
gether with him— (*aside*) but make sure that you choose
one who believes me: (*to Theopropides again*) you'll win
as easily as a fox eats a pear.

MIS (*aside*) But look, I can see the slave of Philolaches, 560
Tranio; they're giving me neither my interest nor the
principal.

THEO (*as Tranio begins to move toward Misargyrides*) Where
are you going?

	TRA	nec quoquam abeo. ne ego sum miser,
		scelestus, natus dis inimicis omnibus.
		iam illo praesente adibit. ne ego homo sum miser,
565		ita et hinc et illinc mi exhibent negotium.
		sed occupabo adire.
	MIS	hic ad me it, saluos sum,
		spes est de argento.
	TRA	hilarus est: frustra est homo.
		saluere iubeo te, Misargyrides, bene.
	MIS	salue et tu. quid de argento est?
	TRA	abi sis, belua.
570		continuo adueniens pilum iniecisti mihi.
	MIS	⟨certe⟩ hic homo inanis est.
	TRA	hic homo est certe hariolus.
	MIS	quin tu istas mittis tricas?
	TRA	quin quid uis cedo.
	MIS	ubi Philolaches est?
	TRA	numquam potuisti mihi
		magis opportunus aduen⟨ire quam⟩ aduenis.
575	MIS	quid est?
	TRA	concede huc.
	MIS	⟨quin mihi faenus red⟩ditur?
	TRA	scio te bona esse uoce, ne clama nimis.
	MIS	ego hercle uero clamo.
	TRA	ah, gere morem mihi.
	MIS	quid tibi ego morem uis geram?
	TRA	abi quaeso hinc domum.
	MIS	abeam?
	TRA	redito huc circiter meridie.

571 certe *add. Seyffert*   574 aduen⟨ire quam⟩ ς
575 ⟨quin mihi faenus red⟩ditur ς

374

TRA   I'm not going anywhere. (*aside*) I really am a wretched, unlucky fellow, born when all the gods were hostile. In a moment he'll come to me when the old man is present. I really am wretched, judging from how they're troubling 565 me from this side and from that. But I'll be first to go and address him.

MIS   (*aside*) He's coming toward me, I'm safe, there's hope about the money.

TRA   (*aside*) He's cheerful: the chap's mistaken. (*aloud*) My greetings to you, Misargyrides.

MIS   And mine to you. What about the money?

TRA   Go away, will you, you animal? As soon as you arrived you 570 cast a javelin on me.

MIS   (*half aside*) This chap is certainly empty-handed.

TRA   (*overhearing him*) This chap is certainly a soothsayer.

MIS   Why don't you stop that nonsense?

TRA   Why don't you tell me what you want?

MIS   Where's Philolaches?

TRA   You could never have come to me at a better time than this.

MIS   How so? 575

TRA   Come over here.

MIS   (*very loudly*) Why aren't I paid my interest?

TRA   I know that you have a powerful voice, stop shouting so much.

MIS   But I will shout.

TRA   Ah, do me a favor.

MIS   How do you want me to do you a favor?

TRA   Please go home.

MIS   I should go?

TRA   Return here around midday.

580 MIS   reddeturne igitur faenus?

TRA   reddet: nunc abi.

MIS   quid ego huc recursem aut operam sumam aut conte-
          ram?

        quid si hic manebo potius ad meridie?

TRA   immo abi domum, uerum hercle dico, abi modo domum.

⟨MIS⟩ at nolo ⟨priusqua⟩m ⟩faenus—

⟨TRA   i, i⟩nqu⟨am, i mo⟩do.

585 MIS   quin uos mihi faenus date. quid hic nugamini?

TRA   eu hercle, ne tu—abi modo, ausculta mihi.

MIS   iam hercle ego illunc nominabo.

TRA   eugae strenue;

        beatus uero es nunc quom clamas.

MIS   meum peto.

        multos me hoc pacto iam dies frustramini.

590   molestus si sum reddite argentum: abiero.

        responsiones omnis hoc uerbo eripis.

TRA   sortem accipe.

MIS   immo faenus, id primum uolo.

TRA   quid ais tu? ⟨tun,⟩ hominum omnium taeterrume,

        uenisti huc te extentatum? agas quod in manu est.

595   non dat, non debet.

MIS   non debet?

TRA   ne[c] frit quidem

        ferre hinc potes. an metuis ne quo abeat foras

        urbe exsulatum faenoris causa tui,

        quoi sortem accipere iam lice[bi]t?

---

580 reddetur nunc abi *P*, reddet nunc abi *Guyet*, reddeturne abi *Leo*
    583 modo *P*, domum *A*, modo domum *Ritschl*   584 *uersus non
fertur in P, suppl. Sonnenschein*   593 tun *add. Ritschl* hominem
(hominum *B²*) omnium *P*, omnium kominum *A*

MIS	Will I be paid the interest then?	580
TRA	He'll pay; now go away.	

MIS   Why should I run back here or make or waste an effort? What if instead I remain here till midday?

TRA   No, go home, I'm telling the truth, just go home.

MIS   But I don't want to before the interest—

TRA   (*interrupting*) Go, I'm telling you, just go.

MIS   No, give me my interest. Why are you trifling here?   585

TRA   Goodness, you—just go away, listen to me.

MIS   I'll call him by name right now. (*begins to shout the name Philolaches*)

TRA   Bravo, well done! Now that you're shouting you're happy.

MIS   I'm demanding what's mine. You've been tricking me like this for many days already. If I'm a nuisance, pay the   590 money: I'll be gone. With a word to this effect you can shut me up.

TRA   Take the principal.[15]

MIS   No, the interest is what I want first.

TRA   What do you say? Have you, most disgusting of all men, come here to inflate your lungs? Do what's in your power. He won't pay, he doesn't owe you anything.   595

MIS   He doesn't owe me anything?

TRA   You can't even get an atom out of him. You aren't afraid, are you, that he might go into exile somewhere outside the town because of your interest? You can get the principal now.

---

[15] If the principal has been returned, the interest need not be paid.

---

594 manu *P*, manum *A*
595 nec erit *P*, ne frit *Ellis*
598 licebit Ω, licet *Studemund*

	MIS	quin non peto
599–		sortem: illuc primum, faenus, reddundum est mihi.
600	TRA	molestus ne sis. nemo dat, age quidlubet.
		tu solus, credo, faenore argentum datas.
	MIS	cedo faenus, redde faenus, faenus reddite.
		daturine estis faenus actutum mihi?
605		datur faenus mi?
	TRA	faenus illic, faenus hic!
		nescit quidem nisi faenus fabularier.
		ultro te! neque ego taetriorem beluam
		uidisse me umquam quemquam quam te censeo.
609	MIS	non edepol tu nunc me istis uerbis territas.
609ᵃ	THEO	calidum hoc est: etsi procul abest, urit male.
610		quod illuc est faenus, opsecro, quod illic petit?
	TRA	pater eccum aduenit peregre non multo prius
		illius, is tibi et faenus et sortem dabit,
		ne inconciliare quid nos porro postules.
		uide num moratur.
	MIS	quin feram, si quid datur?
615	THEO	quid ais tu?
	TRA	quid uis?
	THEO	quis illic est? quid illic petit?
		quid Philolachetem gnatum compellat ⟨meum⟩
		sic et praesenti tibi facit conuicium?
		quid illi debetur?
	TRA	opsecro hercle, ⟨tu⟩ iube
		obicere argentum ob os impurae beluae.
620	THEO	iubeam?
	TRA	iuben homini argento os uerberarier?

616 meum *add. Camerarius*   618 tu *add. Schoell*
619 obici ς, obicere *Mueller*

378

MIS   But I'm not asking for the principal: first I have to be paid   600
the interest.

TRA   Don't be a nuisance. No one will give it to you, you can do
whatever you like. You're the only one, I believe, giving
money on interest.

MIS   Give me my interest, pay my interest, you two should pay
my interest! Are you not going to give me my interest this
instant? Am I given my interest?   605

TRA   Interest here, interest there! He can only talk about in-
terest. Away with you! I don't think I've ever seen any
more revolting beast than you.

MIS   You don't frighten me with your words now.

THEO (*approaching*) This is warm work: even if it doesn't touch
me, I feel it pretty hot. (*to Tranio*) Please, what's that   610
interest he's demanding?

TRA   (*to Misargyrides*) Look, his father came from abroad not
long ago; he'll give you both interest and principal, so
don't insist on trying to defraud us further. See if he
keeps you waiting.

MIS   Why shouldn't I take anything if it's offered?

THEO (*to Tranio*) I say!   615

TRA   What do you want?

THEO Who is that? What's he demanding? Why is he dunning
my son Philolaches like this and loudly abusing you in
your presence? What's he owed?

TRA   Please, have money thrown into the face of this disgust-
ing creature.

THEO I should have that done?   620

TRA   Won't you have his face smashed with money?

---

620 iuben *B²*, iube in *ceteri Palatini*

621	MIS	perfacile ego ictus perpetior argenteos.
625	TRA	audin? uidetur⟨ne⟩, opsecro hercle, idoneus
626		danista qui sit, genus quod improbissumum est?
627	THEO	non ego istuc curo qui sit, ⟨quid sit,⟩ unde sit;
628		⟨id⟩, id uolo mi dici, id me scire expeto:
622		quod illuc argentum est?
	TRA	est—huic debet Philolaches
623		paullum.
	THEO	quantillum?
	TRA	quasi—quadraginta minas;
624		ne sane id multum censeas.
	THEO	paullum id quidem est.
629		adeo etiam argenti faenus creditum audio?
630	TRA	quattuor quadraginta illi debentur minae;
		et sors et faenus.
	MIS	tantum est, nihilo plus peto.
	TRA	uelim quidem hercle ut uno nummo plus petas.
		dic te daturum, ut abeat.
	THEO	egon dicam dare?
	TRA	dice.
	THEO	egone?
	TRA	tu ipsus. dic modo, ausculta mihi.
635		promitte, age inquam: ego iubeo.
	THEO	responde mihi:
		quid eo est argento factum?
	TRA	saluom est.
	THEO	soluite
		uosmet igitur si saluom est.
	TRA	aedis filius
		tuos emit.

625–28 *post 621 posuit Ritschl*

MIS   I can easily bear beatings with money.

TRA   Do you hear him? Please, doesn't he seem the ideal man   625
to be a moneylender, which is the worst type of person?

THEO   I don't care who he is, what he is, where he's from. This is
what I want to be told, this is what I demand to know:
what money is that?

TRA   It's—well, Philolaches owes him a little.

THEO   How little?

TRA   As it were—forty minas; really, don't consider that a lot.

THEO   (*with sarcasm*) Yes, it's very little. Besides, I hear that in-
terest is due to him?

TRA   He's owed forty-four minas, both principal and interest.   630

MIS   That's the sum, I don't ask for more.

TRA   I'd like you to ask for one single coin more.[16] Say that
you're going to give it to him to make him go away.

THEO   I should say that I'm giving it?

TRA   Do say so.

THEO   I?

TRA   Yes, you. Just say it, listen to me. Promise, go on, I'm tell-   635
ing you; I'm commanding you.

THEO   Answer me: what's been done with that money?

TRA   It's safe.

THEO   Then you pay him if it's safe.

TRA   Your son's bought a house.

---

[16] If a plaintiff demands more than he has a right to, he is liable to be
cast in his suit.

---

625 ne *add. Camerarius*   627 quid sit *add. Leo*
628 id *add. Lindsay*
623 paulum *CD*, paululum *B*
631–32 *post* 652ᵃ *P, post* 630 Ritschl

THEO	aedis?
TRA	aedis.
THEO	eugae! Philolaches

patrissat: iam homo in mercatura uortitur.

640   ain tu, aedis?

TRA	aedis inquam. sed scin quoius modi?
THEO	qui scire possum?
TRA	uah!
THEO	quid est?
TRA	ne me roga.
THEO	nam quid ita?
TRA	speculoclaras, candorem merum.
THEO	bene hercle factum. quid? eas quanti destinat?
TRA	talentis magnis totidem quot ego et tu sumus.

645   sed arraboni has dedit quadraginta minas;
   hinc sumpsit quas ei dedimus. satin intellegis?
   nam postquam haec aedes ita erant, ut dixi tibi,
   continuo est alias aedis mercatus sibi.

649–51 THEO	bene hercle factum.
MIS	heus, iam appetit meridie.
652 TRA	apsolue hunc quaeso, uomitu[m] ne hic nos enicet.
652ᵃ	quattuor quadraginta illi debentur minae.
653 THEO	adulescens, mecum rem habe.
MIS	nempe aps te petam?
THEO	petito cras.
MIS	abeo: sat habeo si cras fero.
655 TRA	malum quod isti di deaeque omnes duint!

   ita mea consilia perturbat paenissume.
   nullum edepol hodie genus est hominum taetrius
   nec minus bono cum iure quam danisticum.

652 uomitu[m] *Bothe*

382

THEO A house?

TRA Yes, a house.

THEO Hurray! Philolaches is taking after his father; the boy's
     already taking to business. Do you say so, a house?   640

TRA Yes, a house. But do you know what it's like?

THEO How can I know?

TRA Goodness!

THEO What is it?

TRA Stop asking me.

THEO Why?

TRA A mirror-bright one, pure candor.

THEO Excellent. Well then? What's the agreed price?

TRA As many Attic talents as you and I added together. But 645
     these forty minas he's given as deposit; he's taken from
     this chap what we gave the vendor. Do you understand?
     Well, after our house was the way I told you, he immedi-
     ately bought himself another.

THEO Excellent.   650

MIS Hey, midday is already approaching.

TRA Please pay him off so that he won't kill us with his verbal
     vomiting. Forty-four minas are owed to him.

THEO (to Misargyrides) Young man, you may deal with me.

MIS Am I to ask for it from you?

THEO Ask for it tomorrow.

MIS I'm going away; I'm satisfied if I get it tomorrow.

Exit MISARGYRIDES to the right.

TRA (aside) May all the gods and goddesses give him a real 655
     thrashing! He came within an inch of messing up my
     plans. No type of person is more disgusting today or
     more unreasonable than the moneylender type.

THEO qua in regione istas aedis emit filius?

660 TRA ecce autem perii!

THEO   dicisne hoc quod te rogo?

TRA dicam. sed nomen domini quaero quid siet.

THEO age comminiscere ergo.

TRA   quid ego nunc agam
       nisi ut in uicinum hunc proxumum ⟨rem conferam⟩,
       eas emisse aedis huius dicam filium?

665   calidum hercle esse audiui optumum mendacium.

667   quicquid di dicunt, id decretum est dicere.

THEO quid igitur? iam commentu's?

TRA   di istum perduint -
       immo istunc potius—de uicino hoc proxumo

670   tuos emit aedis filius.

THEO   bonan fide?

TRA siquidem tu argentum reddituru's, tum bona,
       si redditurus non es, non emit bona.

THEO non in loco emit perbono?

TRA   immo in optumo.

THEO cupio hercle inspicere hasce aedis. pultadum fores

675   atque euoca aliquem intus ad te, Tranio.

TRA ecce autem perii! nunc quid dicam nescio.
       iterum iam ad unum saxum me fluctus ferunt.

THEO quid nunc?

TRA   non hercle quid nunc faciam reperio:
       manufesto teneor.

THEO   euocadum aliquem ocius,

680   roga circumducat.

663 mendatium *P*, d*rdiem *A*, rem conferam *Ritschl*

THEO In what area did my son buy that house?

TRA *(aside)* Look now, I'm dead!   660

THEO Won't you tell me what I'm asking you?

TRA I will. But I'm trying to remember what the owner's name is.

THEO Come on, try and think then.

TRA *(aside)* What should I do now other than refer the business to our next-door neighbor and say that this is the house his son bought? I've heard your best lie is one that's 665
served up piping hot. I'm resolved to tell him whatever the gods tell me.

THEO Well then? Have you remembered?

TRA May the gods kill that chap— *(aside, with a nod toward Theopropides)* no, rather this one here— *(clearly again)*
your son bought this house from his next-door neighbor. 670

THEO Honestly?

TRA Well, if you're going to pay the money, then yes, if you're not going to pay it, then no.[17]

THEO Didn't he buy it in an excellent location?

TRA Yes, in the best.

THEO I do wish to inspect this house. Knock at the door and call 675
someone out, Tranio.

TRA *(aside)* Look there, I'm dead! I don't know what to say now. Yet again the waves are carrying me to one and the same cliff.

THEO Well then?

TRA *(aside)* I really can't come up with what I should do now: I'm caught in the act.

THEO Do call someone quickly, ask him to take us around. 680

[17] A deliberate misunderstanding. Theopropides means *bonan fide hoc dixisti*, "did you say that in earnest," while Tranio interprets it as *bonan fide aedis emit*, "did he act in earnest when he bought the house."

TRA   heus tu, at hic sunt mulieres:
      uidendum est primum utrum eae uelintne an non uelint.

THEO bonum aequomque oras. i, percontare et roga.
      ego hic tantisper, dum exis, te opperiar foris.

TRA di te deaeque omnes funditus perdant, senex,
685   ita mea consilia undique oppugnas male.
      eugae! optume eccum aedium dominus foras
      Simo progreditur ipsus. huc concessero,
      dum mihi senatum consili in cor conuoco.
      igitur tum accedam hunc, quando quid agam inuenero.

III. ii: SIMO. TRANIO. THEOPROPIDES

690 SIMO melius anno hoc mihi non fuit domi
      nec quod una esca me iuuerit magis.
      prandium uxor mihi perbonum dedit,
      nunc dormitum iubet me ire: minime.
      non mihi forte uisum ilico fuit,
695   melius quom prandium quam solet dedit:
      uoluit in cubiculum abducere me anus.
      non bonust somnus de prandio. apage.
      clanculum ex aedibus me edidi foras.
      tota turget mihi uxor, scio, domi.

700 TRA res parata est mala in uesperum huic seni.
      nam et cenandum et cubandum est ei male.

SIMO quom magis cogito cum meo animo:
      si quis dotatam uxorem atque anum habet,
      neminem sollicitat sopor: omnibus
705   ire dormitum odio est, ueluti nunc mihi
      exsequi certa res est ut abeam
      potius hinc ad forum quam domi cubem.
      atque pol nescio ut moribus sient
709   uostrae: haec sat scio quam me habeat male

TRA   Listen, though, there are women here. We have to see first whether they're willing to let us in or not.

THEO What you ask is good and proper. Go and make your request. I'll wait here outside for you until you come out. (*walks out of earshot*)

TRA   May all the gods and goddesses kill you entirely, old man: you assault my plans from all sides. (*as the door of Simo's* 685 *house opens*) Hurray! Look, the owner of the house, Simo, is coming out himself in the nick of time. I'll walk over here while I'm calling a senate meeting of good counsel in my heart. I'll go and address him when I've come up with what to do. (*moves away*)

Enter SIMO from his house, followed by a slave.

SIMO I haven't been so well entertained at home for this whole 690 year nor has any single meal given me more pleasure. My wife gave me a very good lunch. Now she tells me to go to bed: no way. I immediately realized it wasn't due to chance when she gave me a better lunch than usual: the 695 old lady wanted to get me into bed. Sleep after lunch is no good. Away with you! I sneaked out of the house on the quiet. My wife's in a perfect fury at home, I know that.

TRA   (*aside*) There's a rod in pickle for this old man tonight: 700 he'll have to have a bad dinner and a bad night.

SIMO The more carefully I think about this in my mind, sleep allures nobody, if he has a wife with a dowry, and an old one at that; they all hate to go to bed. I, for instance, am 705 now resolved to go away from here rather than to go to bed at home. And I don't know what character yours have; how badly mine treats me I know well enough ***

709ᵃ   ***

710   peius posthac fore quam fuit mihi.

TRA   abitus tuos tibi, senex, fecerit male:

nil erit quod deorum nullum accusites;

te ipse iure optumo merito incuses licet.

tempus nunc est senem hunc alloqui mihi.

715   hoc habet! repperi qui senem ducerem,

quo dolo a me dolorem procul pellerem.

accedam. di te ament plurumum, Simo.

SIMO   saluos sis, Tranio.

TRA   ut uales?

SIMO   non male.

quid agis?

TRA   hominem optumum teneo.

SIMO   amice facis

720   quom me laudas.

TRA   decet certe.

SIMO   quin hercle te [habeo]

721   hau bonum teneo seruom.

721ᵃ   [THEO heia! mastigia, ad me redi.

TRA   iam isti ero.]

722 SIMO quid nunc? quam mox—?

TRA   quid est?

SIMO   quod solet fieri hic

intus.

TRA   quid id est?

SIMO   scis iam quid loquar. sic decet.

*** morem geras.

725   uita quam sit breuis simul cogita.

709ᵃ *lacunam statuit Leo*   720 habeo *del. Camerarius*
721ᵃ uersum *del. Schoell*

that I'll have a worse time later than I had before.   710

TRA   (*aside*) Your going away will cause you trouble, old man.
There will be no reason for you to find fault with any of
the gods; you're perfectly entitled to find fault with your-
self. Now's the time for me to address this old man. He's   715
had it![18] I've found a way to lead the old man by the nose,
a plan with which I can drive the pain far away from me.
I'll go and address him. (*loudly*) May the gods love you
greatly, Simo. (*grabs his hand*)

SIMO   My greetings to you, Tranio.

TRA   How are you?

SIMO   Not bad. What are you up to?[19]

TRA   I'm holding the hand of an excellent fellow.

SIMO   Very kind of you to praise me.   720

TRA   You certainly deserve it.

SIMO   Well, and I am holding your hand, the hand of not a good
slave at all.

[THEO   Goodness! Return to me, whip-fodder.

TRA   I'll be with you in a moment.]

SIMO   Well then? How soon—?

TRA   What do you mean?

SIMO   What usually happens inside here.

TRA   What do you mean?

SIMO   You already know what I mean. It's proper. *** humor
***. At the same time think about how short life is.   725

---

[18] A gladiatorial metaphor; he has been struck.

[19] Tranio takes the inquiry after his well-being literally, as a question
about his activities.

TRA	*** quid? *** ehem,
	uix tandem percepi super his rebus nostris te loqui.
SIMO	musice hercle agitis aetatem, ita ut uos decet,
	uino et uictu probo, piscatu electili
	uitam ⟨uos⟩ colitis.
TRA	immo uita antehac erat:
	nunc nobis comia haec exciderunt.
SIMO	quidum?
TRA	ita oppido occidimus omnes, Simo.
SIMO	non taces? prospere uobis cuncta usque adhuc
	processerunt.
TRA	ita ut dicis facta hau nego.
	nos profecto probe ut uoluimus uiximus.
	sed, Simo, ita nunc uentus nauem
	deseruit.
SIMO	quid est? quo modo?
TRA	pessumo.
SIMO	quaene subducta erat tuto in terra?
TRA	ei!
SIMO	quid est?
TRA	me miserum, occidi!
SIMO	qui?
TRA	quia uenit nauis nostrae naui quae frangat ratem.
SIMO	uellem ut tu uelles, Tranio. sed quid est negoti?
TRA	eloquar.
	erus peregre uenit.
SIMO	tunc ⟨malum corio tuo⟩ portenditur,
	ind' ferriterium, postea ⟨crux⟩.

729–30
30

735

739
739ᵃ

740

729–30 piscatu probo *P, transp. Gulielmus*
731 uos *add. Spengel*   741 uelim *P,* uellem *Lipsius*
742 malum corio tuo *add. Sonnenschein*

TRA *** what? *** Oh, only now have I understood that you're talking about our business here.

SIMO You spend your time stylishly, as you should, you're leading your lives with decent wine and food and fine fish. 730

TRA No, life is what we had before: now these entertainments have gone from us.

SIMO How so?

TRA All of us have died completely, Simo.

SIMO Won't you be quiet? Up until now everything's gone successfully for you. 735

TRA I don't deny what you say. We did indeed have a decent life, the way we liked it. But, Simo, now the wind has deserted our ship.

SIMO What's that? In what way?

TRA In the worst possible way.

SIMO A ship which had been brought to shore safely?

TRA Dear me!

SIMO What is it?

TRA Poor me, I'm dead!

SIMO How come? 740

TRA Because a ship has come to smash the timbers of our ship.

SIMO I sympathize with you, Tranio. But what's the matter?

TRA I'll tell you. Master's come from abroad.

SIMO Then there's a thrashing in prospect for your hide, then the place where fetters are worn away,[20] at last the cross.

---

[20] The workhouse, where the slaves are in shackles.

---

743 crux *et* per tua te *add. Ussing*

TRA ⟨per tua te⟩ genua opsecro,

744–45 ne indicium ero facias meo.

SIMO e me, ne quid metuas, nil sciet.

TRA patrone, salue.

SIMO nil moror mi istius modi clientes.

TRA nunc hoc quod ad te noster me misit senex—

SIMO hoc mihi responde primum quod ego te rogo:
iam de istis rebus uoster quid sensit senex?

750 TRA nil quicquam.

SIMO numquid increpitauit filium?

TRA tam liquidust quam liquida esse tempestas solet.
nunc te hoc orare iussit opere maxumo,
ut sibi liceret inspicere hasce aedis tuas.

SIMO non sunt uenales.

TRA scio equidem istuc. sed senex

755 gynaeceum aedificare uolt hic in suis
et balineas et ambulacrum et porticum.

SIMO quid ergo somniauit?

TRA ego dicam tibi.
dare uolt uxorem filio quantum potest,
ad eam rem facere uolt nouom gynaeceum.

760 nam sibi laudauisse hasce ait architectonem
nescioquem exaedificatas insanum bene;
nunc hinc exemplum capere uolt, nisi tu neuis.
nam ille eo maiore hinc opere ex te exemplum petit,
quia isti umbram aestate tibi esse audiuit perbonam

765 sub diuo columine usque perpetuom diem.

SIMO immo edepol uero, quom usquequaque umbra est, ta-
men
sol semper hic est usque a mani ad uesperum:

757 consomniauit *P*, ergo somniauit *Leo*

TRA I'm imploring you by your knees not to betray us to my 745
master.

SIMO Don't be afraid, he won't learn anything from me.

TRA Greetings, my patron.

SIMO I don't care for clients of your caliber.

TRA Now what our old man has sent me to you for—

SIMO (*interrupting*) First answer the question I'm asking you:
does your old master already know anything about those
goings-on?

TRA Nothing at all. 750

SIMO Has he shouted at his son?

TRA He's as unclouded as fine weather is unclouded. Now he
told me to ask you earnestly to be allowed to inspect this
house of yours.

SIMO It's not for sale.

TRA I know that. But the old man wants to build women's 755
quarters here in his own house and baths and a vestibule
and a portico.

SIMO What's he dreamed about then?

TRA I'll tell you. He wants to give his son a wife as soon as
possible, and for this purpose he wants to build new
women's quarters. Well, he said some architect or other 760
had praised your house to him as being built awfully well.
Now he wants to take it as a model, if that's okay by you:
he's all the keener on taking it as a model because he's
heard that you have excellent shade there the entire day
in the summer, even under a cloudless sky. 765

SIMO No, not at all; even when there's shade everywhere the
sun's always here from morning till evening. Like a dun it

393

quasi flagitator astat usque ad ostium,
nec mi umbra hic usquam est nisi si in puteo quaepiam
est.

770 TRA quid? Sarsinatis ecqua est, si Vmbram non habes?
SIMO molestus ne sis. haec sunt sicut praedico.
TRA at tamen inspicere uolt.
SIMO inspiciat, si lubet;
si quid erit quod illi placeat, de exemplo meo
ipse aedificato.
TRA eon, uoco huc hominem?
SIMO i, uoca.
775 TRA Alexandrum Magnum atque Agathoclem aiunt maxumas
duo res gessisse: quid mihi fiet tertio,
qui solus facio facinora immortalia?
uehit hic clitellas, uehit hic autem alter senex.
nouicium mi quaestum institui non malum:
780 nam muliones mulos clitellarios
habent, at ego habeo homines clitellarios.
magni sunt oneris: quicquid imponas uehunt.
nunc hunc hau scio an colloquar. congrediar.
heus Theopropides!
THEO hem quis hic nominat me?
785 TRA ero seruos multimodis fidus.
THEO unde is?
TRA quod me miseras, affero omne impetratum.

785 multimodis *A*, multum suo *P*, multis modis *Leo*

---

[21] The double meaning of *umbra* ("shade"/"woman from Umbria")
leads to the joke about the woman from Sarsina, which is actually in
Umbria.

394

	stands outside the door and I don't have shade anywhere here, unless there's some in the well.	
TRA	Well then? If you don't have any shade, perhaps you have a shady lady from Sarsina?[21]	770
SIMO	Don't be a nuisance. It's the way I tell you.	
TRA	But he still wants to inspect it.	
SIMO	He's welcome to inspect it if he so wishes; if there's anything that catches his fancy, he can build it himself following my model.	
TRA	Am I to go and call him here?	
SIMO	Go call.	
TRA	(*walking away, toward Theopropides*) They say Alexander the Great and Agathocles[22] were two men who did enormous deeds; how about me for a third? I singlehandedly do immortal deeds. Here's one old fellow heavily saddled, here's another. I've begun a new trade that's not bad: mule drivers have pack mules, whereas I have pack humans. They're beasts of great burden: whatever you load onto them, they carry it. Now I don't know if I should talk to him. I'll go and address him. (*loudly*) Hey, Theopropides!	775

780 |
THEO	Oh, who is calling me?	
TRA	A slave who is very reliable to his master.	785
THEO	Where are you coming from?	
TRA	About the business you sent me for, I bring it back all sorted out.	

---

[22] Agathocles (361–289), the tyrant of Syracuse and king of Sicily, fought against Carthage, but was hardly the equal of Alexander the Great (356–323).

THEO quid illic, opsecro, tam diu destitisti?

TRA seni non erat otium, id sum opperitus.

THEO antiquom optines hoc tuom, tardus ut sis.

790 TRA heus tu, si uoles uerbum hoc cogitare,
    simul flare sorbereque hau factu facile est.
    ego hic esse et illi simitu hau potui.

THEO quid nunc?

TRA   uise, specta tuo usque arbitratu.

THEO age, duce me.

TRA   num moror?

THEO   supsequor te.

795 TRA senex ipsus te ante ostium eccum opperitur.
    sed ut maestus est sese hasc' uendidisse!

THEO quid tandem?

TRA   orat ut suadeam Philolacheti
    ut istas remittat sibi.

THEO   haud opinor.
    sibi quisque ruri metit. si male emptae

800   forent, nobis istas redhibere hau liceret.
    lucri quicquid est, id domum trahere oportet.
    misericordia s‹e apstinere› hominem oportet.

TRA morare hercle, ‹uerba ut› facis. supsequere.

THEO   fiat.
    do tibi ego operam.

TRA   senex illic est. em, tibi adduxi hominem.

805 SIMO saluom te aduenisse peregre gaudeo, Theopropides.

THEO di te ament.

SIMO   inspicere te aedis has uelle aiebat mihi.

THEO nisi tibi est incommodum.

787 illic Ω, illi *Bothe*   802 s‹e apstinere› *Leo*
803 uerba ut *add. Camerarius*

THEO Why did you absent yourself there for so long, please?

TRA The old man didn't have time, that's what I waited for.

THEO You stick to your old habit of being slow.

TRA Hey you, if you'd like to bear this saying in mind, whis- 790
tling and drinking at the same time is a difficult thing to
do. I couldn't have been here and there at the same time.

THEO Well then?

TRA Look about you and inspect it without interrupion, at
your own discretion.

THEO Go on, take me there.

TRA Am I wasting time?

THEO I'm following you.

TRA Look, the old man himself is waiting for you in front of 795
the door. But how sad he is about having sold this house!

THEO What's the matter now?

TRA He asks me to advise Philolaches to let him have it back.

THEO I don't think so. In the country each farmer brings in the
harvest for his own benefit. If it had been bought for too 800
high a price, we wouldn't be allowed to back out. One
ought to keep for oneself whatever profit there is. One
ought not to be sentimental.

TRA You're wasting our time with your talk. Follow me.

THEO Yes. I'm at your service. (*they walk over*)

TRA (*to Theopropides*) There's the old man. (*to Simo*) Here
you go, I've brought him to you.

SIMO I'm happy that you've returned safely from abroad, 805
Theopropides.

THEO May the gods love you.

SIMO He said to me you wanted to inspect this house.

THEO Unless it's not convenient for you.

SIMO   immo commodum. i intro atque inspice.

THEO at enim mulieres—

SIMO   caue tu ullam flocci faxis mulierem.
qualubet perambula aedis oppido tamquam tuas.

810 THEO "tamquam"?

TRA   ah, caue tu illi obiectes nunc in aegritudine
te has emisse. non tu uides hunc uoltu uti tristi est senex?

THEO uideo.

TRA   ergo irridere ne uideare et gestire admodum;
noli facere mentionem te ⟨has⟩ emisse.

THEO   intellego
et bene monitum duco, atque esse existumo humani in-
geni.

815 quid nunc?

SIMO   quin tu is intro? atque otiose perspecta ut lubet.

816 THEO bene benigneque arbitror te facere.

SIMO   factum edepol uolo.

816ᵃ [uin qui perductet?

THEO   apage istum perductorem, non placet.

816ᵇ quicquid est, errabo potius quam perductet quispiam.]

817 TRA uiden uestibulum ante aedis hoc et ambulacrum, quoius
modi?

THEO luculentum edepol profecto.

TRA   age specta postis, quoius modi,
quanta firmitate facti et quanta crassitudine.

820 THEO non uideor uidisse postis pulchriores.

813 has *add. Guyet*
816ᵃ–16ᵇ *uersus secl. Seyffert*

[23] Tranio pretends to be talking about two old wooden posts but in
reality means the two old men. When he later talks about coating the

SIMO No, it's perfectly convenient. Come in and inspect it.

THEO But the women—

SIMO (*interrupting*) Don't give a damn about any woman. Walk around throughout the entire house as if it were yours.

THEO (*aside, to Tranio*) "As if"? 810

TRA (*quietly*) Ah, don't cast it into his teeth now in his sadness that you've bought it. Can't you see what a sad face this old chap has?

THEO (*quietly*) Yes, I can.

TRA (*quietly*) Then don't give the appearance of laughing at him and being altogether triumphant. Don't mention that you've bought it.

THEO (*quietly*) I understand. I believe you've given me good advice and I think this is a sign of a humane spirit. What 815 now?

SIMO Why don't you go inside? Examine it at your leisure just as you please.

THEO I think you're acting well and kindly.

SIMO I really want it done. [Do you want someone to take you in?

THEO Away with that person taking me in, I don't like it. Whatever it is, I'd rather take a wrong turning than have someone take me in.]

TRA (*to Theopropides*) Can you see the forecourt and the space to walk in front of the house, what they're like?

THEO Splendid indeed.

TRA Go on, look at the doorposts, what they're like, how strong and how thick.[23]

THEO I don't think I've ever seen more beautiful posts. 820

"posts" with tar, he alludes to the *tunica molesta*, a layer of tar put on criminals and then set aflame.

399

SIMO   pol mihi
eo pretio empti fuerant olim.

TRA   audin "fuerant" dicere?
uix uidetur continere lacrumas.

THEO   quanti hosce emeras?

SIMO tris minas pro istis duobus praeter uecturam dedi.

THEO hercle qui multo improbiores sunt quam a primo credidi.

825 TRA quapropter?

THEO   quia edepol ambo ab infumo tarmes secat.

TRA intempestiuos excisos credo, id is uitium nocet.
atque etiam nunc satis boni sunt, si sunt inducti pice;
non enim haec pultiphagus opifex opera fecit barbarus.
uiden coagmenta in foribus?

THEO   uideo.

TRA   specta quam arte dormiunt.

830 THEO "dormiunt"?

TRA   illud quidem "ut coniuent" uolui dicere.
satin habes?

THEO   ut quicquid magis contemplor, tanto magis placet.

TRA uiden pictum, ubi ludificat una cornix uolturios duos?

THEO non edepol uideo.

TRA   at ego uideo. nam inter uolturios duos
cornix astat, ea uolturios duo uicissim uellicat.

835   quaeso huc ad me specta, cornicem ut conspicere pos-
sies.
iam uides?

824 multum *P*, multo ꜱ

---

[24] I.e., Roman; the Romans ate a type of spelt porridge called *puls*.

SIMO I had bought them for this much long ago. (*makes a hand gesture indicating a large sum*)

TRA (*aside, to Theopropides*) Can you hear him say "had"? He seems hardly able to hold back his tears.

THEO (*to Simo*) How much did you buy them for?

SIMO I paid three minas for those two, transport excluded.

THEO (*examining them more closely*) Goodness, they're in a far worse condition than I thought at first.

TRA Why?   825

THEO Because a worm has been gnawing at both of them from below.

TRA I think they were cut out of season, that's the only thing that's the matter with them. And even now they're good enough if they're coated with tar; no porridge-eating barbarian[24] workman has made them. Can you see the door joints?

THEO Yes.

TRA Look how fast they're asleep.

THEO "Asleep"?   830

TRA I meant to say "how fast they're shut."[25] Are you satisfied?

THEO The more I look at everything, the more I like it.

TRA Can you see the fresco where one crow is making fun of two vultures?[26]

THEO No, I can't.

TRA But I can: the crow is standing between the two vultures and is pecking at the two in turn. Please look in my direc- 835
tion so that you can see the crow. Do you see it now?

[25] The pun is hard to reproduce; *coniuere* means "to be shut," but is mostly used of eyes, hence virtually equivalent to "being asleep."

[26] The clever crow is Tranio; the stupid vultures are Theopropides and Simo.

401

THEO   profecto nullam equidem illic cornicem intuor.

TRA   at tu isto ad uos optuere, quoniam cornicem nequis
        conspicari, si uolturios forte possis contui.

THEO omnino, ut te apsoluam, nullam pictam conspicio hic
        auem.

840 TRA   age, iam mitto, ignosco: aetate non quis optuerier.

THEO haec, quae possum, ea mi profecto cuncta uehementer
        placent.

SIMO latius demum est operae pretium iuisse.

THEO   recte edepol mones.

SIMO eho istum, puere, circumduce hasce aedis et conclauia.
        nam egomet ductarem, nisi mi esset apud forum nego-
        tium.

845 THEO apage istum a me perductorem, nil moror ductarier.

846–
47   quicquid est, errabo potius quam perductet quispiam.

SIMO aedis dico.

THEO   ergo intro eo igitur sine perductore.

SIMO   ilicet.

THEO ibo intro igitur.

TRA   mane sis uideam, ne canes—

THEO   agedum uide.

850 TRA   st! abi, canes. st! abin dierecta? abin hinc in malam cru-
        cem?
        at etiam restas? st! abi istinc.

SIMO   nil pericli est, age ⟨modo⟩.
        tam placida est quam feta quaeuis. ire intro audacter li-
        cet.
        eo ego hinc ad forum.

THEO   fecisti commode, bene ambula.

851 modo *add. Ritschl*

THEO I really can't spot any crow there.

TRA But since you can't see the crow, look in your own direction, toward the two of you, to see if you can spot the vultures.

THEO To have done with you, I can't see any painted bird here at all.

TRA Well, well, I'll stop now, I make allowances for you: 840 you're too old to see clearly.

THEO But everything I *can* see I like terribly well.

SIMO You really need to go right in; otherwise it's not worth your while.

THEO You're giving me good advice.

SIMO (*to his slave*) Hey there, boy, take him around the house and rooms. (*to Theopropides*) I would have taken you in myself if I didn't have business in the forum.

THEO Away with that chap taking me in, I don't want to be led 845 up the garden path. Whatever it is, I'll take a wrong turning rather than have someone take me in.

SIMO I mean into the house.

THEO Well then, I'll go in without someone to take me in.

SIMO Do go.

THEO I'll go in then.

TRA (*peeping into the door*) Wait, please, let me see that the dog doesn't—

THEO (*interrupting*) Go on, look.

TRA Sh! Go away, dog. Sh! Won't you go and be hanged? 850 Won't you go off to terrible torture? You're still hanging around? Sh! Go away from there.

SIMO There's no danger, just get on with it. She's as calm as any bitch in pup. You can go in boldly. I'm off to the forum.

THEO You've been kind, have a good walk.

Tranio, age, canem istam a foribus ⟨aliquis⟩ abducat
    face,

855   etsi non metuenda est.

TRA   quin tu illam aspice ut placide accubat;
    nisi molestum uis uideri te atque ignauom.

THEO   iam ut lubet.
    sequere hac me igitur.

TRA   equidem haud usquam a pedibus apscedam tuis.

ACTVS IV

IV. i: PHANISCVS

PHAN serui qui quom culpa carent tamen malum metuont,
    i solent esse eris utibiles.

860   nam illi qui nil metuont, postquam sunt malum meriti,
    stulta sibi expetunt consilia:

    exercent sese ad cursuram, fugiunt, sed i si reprehensi
        sunt,

    faciunt de malo peculium quod nequeunt ⟨de bono⟩;

864–   augent ex pauxillo, ⟨thesaurum in⟩d' parant.
65

    mihi in pectore consili⟨um est cauere⟩ malam rem prius
    quam ut meum ⟨tergum doleat⟩.

    ut adhuc fuit mi, corium esse oportet,
    sincerum; atque ut uotem uerberari,

870   si huic imperabo, probe tectum habebo,
    malum quom impluit ceteris, ne impluat mi.
    nam, ut serui uolunt esse erum, ita solet.

---

854 aliquis *add.* Weise   863 a *P*, de *Gulielmus* peculio *P*, pecu-
lium *Pylades* de bono *add.* Ritschl   864–65 ⟨thesaurum in⟩de
Camerarius   866 consili⟨um est cauere⟩ *Ussing*
    867 tergum doleat *add.* Ritschl

Exit SIMO to the right, accompanied by his slave.

THEO Tranio, go on, have someone remove that dog from the
door, even if it's one not to be afraid of.   855

TRA Just look at how quietly it's lying there; unless you want to
give the impression of being a nuisance and a coward.

THEO Okay, as you like. Follow me this way then.

TRA I won't go away from your feet anywhere.

Exeunt THEOPROPIDES and TRANIO into Simo's house.

ACT FOUR

Enter PHANISCUS from the right.

PHAN Those slaves who fear a thrashing even when they're free
from guilt are generally useful to their masters; those   860
who don't fear anything, even after deserving a thrashing,
are seeking stupid counsel for themselves. They practice
running and flee, but when they're caught and brought
back they get private funds[27] in the shape of beatings
which they couldn't get in the shape of tips. They in-   865
crease their funds from very little and create a treasure
from it. I for one have the plan in my heart to be on my
guard against a beating rather than that my back should
feel pain. My hide should be as I've had it so far, un-
broken; and so as to prevent myself from being beaten,
(*looking at his left hand, the one for stealing*) if I com-   870
mand this one, I'll have my hide protected properly, so
that when it rains blows on others it won't rain on me.
Yes, a master is usually the way slaves want him to be. If

[27] The *peculium* is the money a slave can have for himself.

boni sunt, ‹bonust›; improbi sunt, malus fit.
nam nunc domi nostrae tot pessumi uiuont,

875   peculi sui prodigi, plagigeruli.
ubi aduorsum ut eant uocantur ero: "non
eo, molestus ne sis.
scio quod properas: gestis aliquo . . . ; iam hercle ir' uis,
    mula, foras pastum."
bene merens hoc preti inde apstuli. abii foras.

880   solus nunc eo aduorsum ero ex plurumis seruis.
hoc die crastini quom erus resciuerit,

882   mane castigabit eos
882ᵃ   bubulis exuuiis.
883   postremo minoris pendo tergum illorum quam meum:
illi erunt bucaedae multo potius quam ego sim restio.

IV. ii: PINACIVM. PHANISCVS

885   PIN   mane tu atque assiste ilico,
886   Phanisce. etiam respicis?
886ᵃ   PHAN   mihi molestus ne sies.
887   PIN   uide ut fastidit simia!
887ᵃ   manesne ilico, impure parasite?
       PHAN   ‹dic tu,›
888   qui parasitus sum?
       PIN   ego enim dicam: cibo perduci poteris quouis.
       PHAN   mihi sum, lubet esse. quid id curas?
890   PIN   ferocem facis, quia te erus amat.
       PHAN   uah!
              oculi dolent.
       PIN   quor?
       PHAN   quia fumus molestust.

they are good, he is good; if they are useless, he becomes
bad. Yes, now a lot of terribly bad slaves live in our house,
wasting their private funds and having to bear beatings. 875
When they're called to fetch their master they say: "I
won't go, don't be a nuisance. I know what you're in such
a hurry for: you're itching after some favorite haunt . . .
now you want to go out to pasture, you female ass." For
my good services I've got this reward. I've left. Now I'm 880
fetching my master, I alone out of a great number of
slaves. When master finds out about this tomorrow, he'll
chastise them early with cowhide. In a word, I care less
for their backs than for my own. They shall go in for a tan-
ning much sooner than I take up the rope business.

Enter PINACIUM from the right.

PIN Wait and stop at once, Phaniscus! Look back, will you? 885
PHAN Don't be a nuisance to me.
PIN Look how the monkey is giving himself airs! Won't you
     stop at once, you dirty hanger-on?
PHAN Tell me, how am I a hanger-on?
PIN Yes, I'll tell you: with food you can be enticed anywhere.
PHAN That's my own business, I like to be one. Why do you
     care?
PIN You're playing the hard man because master loves you. 890
PHAN Bah! My eyes hurt.
PIN Why?
PHAN Because your gas is a nuisance.

---

878 quod *P*, quo *Merula*
880 ⟨ego⟩ eo *Studemund ut uersus Reizianus fiat*
887ª dic tu *add. Leo*

PIN   tace sis, faber, qui cudere soles plumbeos nummos.
PHAN non potes tu cogere me ut tibi male dicam.

894–
95   nouit erus me.
PIN   suam quidem pol culcitulam oportet.
PHAN si sobrius sis, male non dicas.
PIN   tibi optemperem, quom tu mi nequeas?
    at tu mecum, pessume, ito aduorsus.
PHAN   quaeso hercle apstine
    iam sermonem de istis rebus.
PIN   faciam et pultabo fores.
    heus, ecquis hic est, maxumam qui his iniuriam
900   foribus defendat? ecquis has aperit fores?
    homo nemo hinc quidem foras exit.
902   ut esse addecet nequam homines, ita sunt.
902ᵃ sed eo magis cauto est opus
903   ne huc exeat qui male me mulcet.

      IV. iii: THEOPROPIDES. TRANIO

TRA quid tibi uisum est mercimoni?
THEO   ⟨totus⟩, totus gaudeo.
905 TRA num nimio emptae tibi uidentur?
THEO   nusquam edepol ego me scio
    uidisse umquam abiectas aedis nisi modo hasce.
TRA   ecquid placent?
THEO ecquid placeant me rogas? immo hercle uero perplacent.
TRA quoius modi gynaeceum? quid porticum?
THEO   insanum bonam.
    non equidem ullam in publico esse maiorem hac existu-
    mo.

904 totus *add. Gruterus*

PIN   Be quiet, you moneyer who always mints base coin.[28]

PHAN   You can't force me to insult you. Master knows me.   895

PIN   He ought to know his own little pillow.

PHAN   If you were sober, you wouldn't insult me.

PIN   Should I obey you when you can't obey me? But do go
        with me and fetch him, you worst of all creatures.

PHAN   Please keep the conversation away from those topics.

PIN   I'll do so and knock at the door. (*loudly, banging at the
        door*) Hey, is there anyone to ward off a huge assault from   900
        this door? Is anyone going to open this door? No one's
        coming out. They're just the way useless people can be
        expected to be.[29] But I'll need to be all the more careful
        that no one comes out here to give me a bad beating.

Enter THEOPROPIDES and TRANIO from Simo's house.

TRA   What did you make of the purchase?

THEO   I'm overjoyed.

TRA   It doesn't seem overpriced to you, does it?   905

THEO   I know I've never seen a house thrown away anywhere if
        not this one now.

TRA   Do you like it?

THEO   Do I like it, you ask me? Yes, I absolutely love it.

TRA   What are the women's quarters like? What about the por-
        tico?

THEO   Awfully good. I don't think there's any bigger than this on
        the public street.

[28] I.e., his jokes are stale.
[29] I.e., drunk.

910	TRA	quin ego ipse et Philolaches in publico omnis porticus sumus commensi.
	THEO	quid igitur?
	TRA	longe omnium longissuma est.
	THEO	di immortales, mercimoni lepidi! ⟨si⟩ hercle nunc ferat sex talenta magna argenti pro istis praesentaria, numquam accipiam.
	TRA	si hercle accipere cupies, ego numquam sinam.
915	THEO	bene res nostra collocata est istoc mercimonio.
	TRA	me suasore atque impulsore id factum audacter dicito, qui subegi faenore argentum ab danista ut sumeret, quod isti dedimus arraboni.
	THEO	seruauisti omnem ratem. nempe octoginta debentur huic minae?
	TRA	hau nummo amplius.
920	THEO	hodie accipiat.
	TRA	ita enim uero, ne qua causa supsiet. uel mihi denumerato, ego illi porro denumerauero.
	THEO	at enim ne quid captioni mihi sit, si dederim tibi.
	TRA	egone te ioculo modo ausim dicto aut facto fallere?
	THEO	egone aps te ausim non cauere, ne quid committam tibi?
925	TRA	quid? tibi umquam quicquam, postquam tuos sum, uerborum dedi?
	THEO	ego enim caui recte: eam mi habeas gratiam atque animo meo! sat sapio si aps te modo uno caueo.
	TRA	tecum sentio.

912 si *add. Camerarius*
925 quia Ω, quid *Bothe*
926 eam dehis (debes *B²*) *P*, *ambis *A*, eam mi habeas *Sonnenschein*

410

TRA Yes, I myself and Philolaches measured all the porticos 910
     on the street.

THEO And?

TRA It's by far the longest of them all.

THEO Immortal gods, a lovely purchase! If he were to bring me
     six Attic silver talents cash down for it now, I'd never
     accept.

TRA Even if you desire to accept, I'll never allow you to.

THEO Our money is well invested with that purchase. 915

TRA You may boldly say that it was done on my advice and
     urging; it was I who forced him to take money from the
     moneylender at interest, which we gave to that chap as
     deposit.

THEO You've saved the whole ship. So eighty minas are owed to
     him?

TRA Not a coin more.

THEO He shall get it today. 920

TRA By all means, so that he doesn't have any excuse for back-
     ing out. If you wish, count it out to me, I'll then count it
     out to him.

THEO But I'm afraid there's a trap in store for me, if I give it to
     you.

TRA Would I dare to deceive you in word or deed, even in
     jest?

THEO Would I dare not to be on my guard against you, against
     trusting you in anything?

TRA What? Have I ever deceived you in anything since be- 925
     coming your slave?

THEO Well, I was on my guard properly; you can be grateful for
     this situation to me and my watchfulness! I show good
     sense enough if I'm on my guard against you alone.

TRA (*aside*) I agree with you.

411

THEO nunc abi rus, dic me aduenisse filio.

TRA   faciam ut iubes.

929– THEO curriculo iube in urbem ueniat iam simul tecum.
30 TRA   licet.

      nunc ego me illac per posticum ad congerrones confe-
         ram.

      dicam ut hic res sint quietae atque hunc ut hinc amoue-
         rim.

IV. iv: PHANISCVS. THEOPROPIDES. PINACIVM

PHAN hic quidem nec conuiuarum sonitus, item ut antehac fuit,
     nec tibicinam cantantem neque alium quemquam audio.

935 THEO quae illaec res est? quid illisce homines quaerunt apud
         aedis meas?

      quid uolunt? quid intro spectant?

PHAN   pergam pultare ostium.
     heus, reclude, heus, Tranio, etiamne aperis?

THEO   quae haec est fabula?

PHAN etiamne aperis? Callidamati nostro aduorsum uenimus.

THEO heus uos, pueri, quid istic agitis? quid istas aedis frangi-
         tis?

940 PIN heus senex, quid tu percontare ad te quod nihil attinet?

THEO nihil ad me attinet?

PIN   nisi forte factu's praefectus nouos,
     qui res alienas procures, quaeras, uideas, audias.

THEO non sunt istae aedes ubi statis.

PIN   quid ais? an iam uendidit
     aedis Philolaches? aut quidem iste nos defrustratur se-
         nex.

933 itidem Ω, item *Bothe*

412

THEO Now go to the farm and tell my son that I've arrived.

TRA I'll do as you tell me.

THEO Tell him to come swiftly to the city along with you.　930

TRA Yes. (*aside*) Now I'll go that way to my boon companions through the back door. I'll tell them how quiet things are here and how I removed this chap from here.

Exit TRANIO through the alley between the houses of Simo and Theopropides.

PHAN There's no noise from guests here, as there was before, and I can't hear a flutist playing or anyone else.

THEO (*aside*) What's that? What are those people looking for at　935 my house? What do they want? What are they peeping inside for?

PHAN I'll carry on knocking at the door. (*loudly, banging at the door*) Hey there, open up, hey there, Tranio, will you open up now?

THEO (*aside*) What's this farce?

PHAN Will you open now? We've come to fetch our master Callidamates.

THEO Hey there, you, boys, what are you doing there? What are you breaking this house for?

PIN Hey there, old man, why are you inquiring about what　940 has nothing to do with you?

THEO It has nothing to do with me?

PIN Unless perhaps you've been made a new magistrate, since you're taking care of others' business, asking about it, spying on it, and listening to it.

THEO That house where you're standing is not others' business.

PIN What do you mean? (*to Phaniscus*) Has Philolaches already sold the house? Otherwise that old chap's fooling us.

945 THEO uera dico. sed quid uobis est negoti hic?
PHAN   eloquar.
      erus hic noster potat.
THEO   erus hic uoster potat?
PHAN   ita loquor.
THEO puere, nimium delicatu's.
PIN   ei aduorsum uenimus.
THEO quoi homini?
PIN   ero nostro. quaeso, quotiens dicendum est tibi?
THEO puere, nemo hic habitat. nam te esse arbitror puerum
      probum.
950 PHAN non hic Philolaches adulescens habitat hisce in aedibus?
THEO habitauit, uerum emigrauit iam diu ex hisce aedibus.
PHAN senex hic elleborosust certe. erras peruorse, pater.
      nam nisi hinc hodie emigrauit aut heri, certo scio
      hic habitare.
THEO   quin sex menses iam hic nemo habitat.
PIN   somnias.
955 THEO egone?
PIN   tu.
THEO   tu ne molestu's. sine me cum puero loqui.
      nemo habitat.
PHAN   habitat profecto, nam heri et nudiustertius,
      quartus, quintus, sextus, usque postquam hinc peregri
          eius pater
      abiit, numquam hic triduom unum desitum est potarier.
THEO quid ais?
PHAN   triduom unum est haud intermissum hic esse et bibi,
960   scorta duci, pergraecari, fidicinas, tibicinas
      ducere.
THEO   quis istaec faciebat?

THEO I'm telling the truth. But what business have you here? 945

PHAN I'll tell you. Our master's drinking here.

THEO Your master's drinking here?

PHAN Yes, I say so.

THEO You're joking, boy.

PIN We've come to fetch him.

THEO To fetch whom?

PIN Our master. Please, how often do you have to be told?

THEO (*to Phaniscus*) Boy, no one lives here: I think you are a decent boy.

PHAN Doesn't young Philolaches live here in this house? 950

THEO He did, but he moved house long ago.

PHAN (*aside, to Pinacium*) This old boy is certainly a confirmed maniac. (*to Theopropides*) You're completely mistaken, father: I know for sure that he lives here, unless he moved out from here today or yesterday.

THEO No, no one's lived here for the last six months.

PIN You're dreaming.

THEO I? 955

PIN Yes, you.

THEO (*to Pinacium*) Stop being a nuisance, you. Let me talk with the boy. (*to Phaniscus*) No one lives here.

PHAN He does: yesterday, the day before yesterday, three days ago, four days ago, five days ago, continuously after his father went abroad, they've never stopped drinking here for three days at a time.

THEO What do you say?

PHAN They've never stopped eating and drinking here for three days at a time, and the same goes for keeping company 960 with prostitutes, living in Greek style, and hiring girls to play the lyre and the flute.

THEO Who did that?

PHAN	Philolaches.
THEO	qui Philolaches?

PHAN quoius patrem Theopropidem esse opinor.

THEO   ei ‹mihi›, occidi,
        si haec hic uera memorat! pergam porro percontarier.
        ain tu istic potare solitum Philolachem istum, quisquis
            est,

965   cum ero uostro?

PHAN   aio, inquam.

THEO   puere, praeter speciem stultus es,
        uide sis ne forte ad merendam quopiam deuorteris
        atque ibi ampliuscule quam satis fuerit biberis.

PHAN   quid est?

THEO ita dico, ne ad alias aedis perperam deueneris.

PHAN scio qua me ire oportet et quo uenerim noui locum.

970   Philolaches hic habitat, quoius est pater Theopropides.
        qui, postquam pater ad mercatum hinc abiit, hic tibici-
            nam
        liberauit.

THEO   Philolachesne ergo?

PHAN   ita, Philematium quidem.

973 THEO quanti?

PHAN   triginta—

THEO   talentis?

PHAN   μὰ τὸν Ἀπόλλω, sed minis.

973ᵃ THEO liberauit?

PHAN   liberauit ualide, triginta minis.

974 THEO ain minis triginta amicam destinatam Philolachem?

975 PHAN aio.

THEO   atque eam manu emisisse?

962 mihi *add. Camerarius*

PHAN Philolaches.

THEO Which Philolaches?

PHAN The one whose father I believe to be Theopropides.

THEO (*aside*) Dear me, I'm dead if he's speaking the truth! I'll carry on investigating. (*to Phaniscus*) Do you say that that Philolaches, whoever he is, used to drink there with your 965 master?

PHAN Yes, I do, I assure you.

THEO Boy, you're more of a fool than you look. I suspect that you called in somewhere for a snack and that you drank a little more there than was good for you.

PHAN What's that?

THEO That's what I'm saying, I suspect that you've come to the wrong house by mistake.

PHAN I know what street to take and I recognize the place I've come to. Philolaches lives here, whose father is Theo- 970 propides. After his father went off on business, he freed a flute girl here.

THEO You mean Philolaches?

PHAN Yes, and she is called Philematium.

THEO For how much?

PHAN Thirty—

THEO (*interrupting*) Talents?

PHAN No, by Apollo,[30] minas of course.

THEO He's freed her?

PHAN Yes, very much so, for thirty minas.

THEO Do you say that Philolaches bought his girlfriend for thirty minas?

PHAN I do. 975

THEO And that he freed her?

[30] A Greek oath by the god of oracles.

PHAN   aio.
THEO   et, postquam eius hinc pater
sit profectus peregre, perpotasse assiduo, ac simul
tuo cum domino?
PHAN   aio.
THEO   quid? is aedis emit has hinc proxumas?
PHAN non aio.
THEO   quadraginta etiam dedit huic quae essent pignori?
PHAN neque istuc aio.
THEO   ei! perdis.
PHAN   immo suom patrem illic perdidit.
980 THEO uera cantas.
PHAN   uana uellem. patris amicu's uidelicet.
THEO eu edepol, patrem eius miserum praedicas!
PHAN   nihil hoc quidem est,
triginta minae, praequam alios dapsilis sumptus facit.
THEO perdidit patrem.
PHAN   unus istic seruos est sacerrumus,
Tranio: is uel Herculi conterere quaestum possiet.
985   edepol ne me eius patris misere miseret, qui quom istaec
sciet
facta ita, amburet ei misero corculum carbunculus.
THEO si quidem istaec uera sunt.
PHAN   quid merear quam ob rem mentiar?
PIN heus uos, ecquis hasce aperit?
PHAN   quid istas pultas ubi nemo intus est?
alio credo comissatum abiisse. abeamus nunciam—
990 THEO puere—
PHAN   —atque porro quaeritemus. sequere hac me.
PIN   ⟨sequor⟩.

984 potest *P*, possiet *Camerarius*
990 sequor *add. Ussing*

PHAN I do.

THEO And that after his father went abroad, he drank nonstop, and that together with your master?

PHAN I do.

THEO Tell me, has he bought that house next to this one?

PHAN No, I don't say that!

THEO Has he also given forty as deposit to the owner?

PHAN I'm not saying that either.

THEO Oh! You're killing me.

PHAN No, that chap killed his father.

THEO Your tale is true.   980

PHAN I wish it weren't. You're obviously a friend of the father.

THEO Goodness, you describe his father as wretched!

PHAN That actually is nothing, the thirty minas, in comparison with the other extravagant expenses he incurs.

THEO He's ruined his father.

PHAN One particular slave is the greatest rascal, Tranio; he could even squander the gains of Hercules himself.[31] Honestly, I feel terribly sorry for his father; once he   985 knows what's been done, a coal will burn this wretched man's poor heart.

THEO If indeed your words are true.

PHAN What would I gain from lying?

PIN (*knocking again*) Hey you, is anyone going to open?

PHAN Why are you knocking there when no one's inside? I think they went elsewhere to have a party. Let's go now—

THEO (*interrupting*) Boy—   990

PHAN (*ignoring the interruption*) —and carry on looking for him. Follow me this way.

PIN Yes.

---

[31] Hercules was proverbially rich because he received the tithes of business profits.

THEO puere, iamne abis?

PHAN   libertas paenula est tergo tuo:

    mihi, nisi ut erum metuam et curem, nihil est qui tergum

       tegam.

IV. v: THEOPROPIDES. SIMO

THEO perii hercle! quid opust uerbis? ut uerba audio,

    non equidem in Aegyptum hinc modo uectus fui,

995   sed etiam in terras solas orasque ultumas

    sum circumuectus, ita ubi nunc sim nescio.

    uerum iam scibo, nam eccum unde aedis filius

    meus emit. quid agis tu?

SIMO   a foro incedo domum.

THEO numquid processit ad forum hodie noui?

1000 SIMO etiam.

THEO   quid tandem?

SIMO   uidi efferri mortuom.

THEO   hem!

SIMO nouom unum: uidi mortuom efferri foras.

    modo eum uixisse aiebant.

THEO   uae capiti tuo!

SIMO quid tu otiosus res nouas requiritas?

THEO quia hodie adueni peregre.

SIMO   promisi foras,

1005   ad cenam ne me te uocare censeas.

THEO hau postulo edepol.

SIMO   uerum cras, nisi ⟨qui⟩ prius

    uocauerit . . . me, uel apud te cenauero.

1006 qui *add. Camerarius*

---

32 Simo takes the inquiry after his well-being literally, as a question about what he is doing.

THEO Boy, are you going already?

PHAN Your freedom is a cloak for your back; I have nothing to cover my back with if I don't fear and look after my master.

Exeunt PHANISCUS and PINACIUM to the right.
Enter SIMO from the right.

THEO I'm dead! What need is there for words? According to what I hear, I've not only traveled to Egypt, but also 995 round deserts and the most distant shores, so that I don't know where I am now. But I'll know in a moment: look, the man who my son bought the house from. (*walking toward Simo*) How are things?

SIMO I'm returning home from the forum.[32]

THEO Has anything new come up at the forum today?

SIMO Yes. 1000

THEO And what?

SIMO I saw a dead man being carried out.[33]

THEO Oh!

SIMO One new thing: I saw a dead man being carried out. They said he'd been alive not long ago.

THEO Curse you!

SIMO Why are you idly inquiring about the news?

THEO Because I've returned from abroad today.

SIMO I have an invitation to eat out, so don't expect me to invite 1005 you to dinner.

THEO I'm not expecting it.

SIMO But tomorrow, unless someone invites . . . me first, I don't mind dining at your place.

[33] Cemeteries were always outside the cities.

THEO ne istuc quidem edepol postulo. nisi quid magis
es occupatus, operam mihi da.

SIMO maxume.

1010 THEO minas quadraginta accepisti, quod sciam,
a Philolachete?

SIMO numquam nummum, quod sciam.

THEO quid, a Tranione seruo?

SIMO ⟨nimis⟩ multo id minus.

THEO quas arraboni tibi dedit?

SIMO quid somnias?

THEO egone? at quidem tu, qui istoc te speras modo
1015 potesse dissimulando infectum hoc reddere.

SIMO quid autem?

THEO quod me apsente hic tecum filius
negoti gessit.

SIMO mecum ut ille hic gesserit,
1018 dum tu hinc abes, negoti? quidnam aut quo die?
−20 THEO minas tibi octoginta argenti debeo.

SIMO non mihi quidem hercle. uerum, si debes, cedo.
fides seruanda est, ne ire infitias postules.

THEO profecto non negabo debere, et dabo;
1025 tu caue quadraginta accepisse hinc te neges.

1026 SIMO quaeso edepol huc me aspecta et responde mihi.
1026ᵃ q *** i argenti minas
1026ᵇ fu ***

THEO ego dicam tibi.
1026ᶜ tantu *** ebeat
1026ᵈ de te aedis.

SIMO i⟨tane? de me⟩ ille aedis emerit?
1026ᵉ ***
1027 SIMO te uelle uxorem aiebat tuo nato dare,
ideo aedificare hic uelle aiebat in tuis.

422

THEO I'm not even expecting that. If you're not too busy, listen to me.

SIMO By all means.

THEO You've received forty minas from Philolaches, as far as I know? 1010

SIMO Never as much as a coin, as far as I know.

THEO Well then, from my slave Tranio?

SIMO Even less so.

THEO Which he gave you as deposit?

SIMO What are you dreaming about?

THEO I? No, you, who are hoping to be able to cancel this by these pretenses. 1015

SIMO Cancel what?

THEO The deal my son made with you here in my absence.

SIMO He should have made a deal with me here while you were away? What deal or on what day? 1020

THEO I owe you eighty silver minas.

SIMO Not me. But if you do, give it to me. A promise has to be kept, don't expect to deny it.

THEO Indeed I won't deny that I owe you, and I'll give it to you; as for you, don't deny that you've received forty from us. 1025

SIMO Please, look at me and answer me. *** silver minas ***.

THEO I'll tell you. This much *** the house from you.

SIMO Do you say so? He should have bought my house? ***

SIMO He said you wanted to give a wife to your son, and he said that was why you wanted to enlarge your own house here.

1012 nimis *add. Fay*
1026a–26e *non inueniuntur in* P
1026d i‹tane? de me› *Schoell et Studemund*
1026e *circiter uiginti uersus exciderunt in* A

THEO hic aedificare uolui?

SIMO   sic dixit mihi.

1030 THEO ei mihi, disperii! uocis non habeo satis.

        uicine, perii, interii!

SIMO   numquid Tranio

        turbauit?

THEO   immo exturbauit omnia.

        deludificatust me hodie indignis modis.

SIMO quid tu ais?

THEO   haec res sic est ut narro tibi:

1035   deludificatust me hodie in perpetuom modum.

        nunc te opsecro ut me bene iuues operamque des.

SIMO quid uis?

THEO   i mecum, opsecro, una simul.

SIMO fiat.

THEO   seruorumque operam et lora mi cedo.

SIMO sume.

THEO   eademque opera haec tibi narrauero,

1040   quis med exemplis hodie eludificatus est.

ACTVS V

V. i: TRANIO. THEOPROPIDES

TRA   qui homo timidus erit in rebus dubiis, nauci non erit;

        atque equidem quid id esse dicam uerbum nauci nescio.

        nam erus me postquam rus misit filium ut suom arcesse-

        rem,

1044 abii illac per angiportum ad hortum nostrum clanculum,

–45 ostium quod in angiporto est horti, patefeci fores,

424

THEO I wanted to enlarge my house?

SIMO So he told me.

THEO Dear me, I'm dead! I'm speechless. Neighbor, I'm ru-   1030
ined, I'm done for!

SIMO Has Tranio stirred up some trouble?

THEO More than that, he's stirred up all the trouble he could.
He's fooled me shamefully today.

SIMO What are you saying?

THEO It's as I'm telling you: he's fooled every inch of me today.   1035
Now I'm asking you to support and help me properly.

SIMO What do you want?

THEO Please come along with me.

SIMO Yes.

THEO Give me your servants' help and some straps.

SIMO Take them.

THEO At the same time I'll tell you how he fooled me today.   1040

Exeunt SIMO and THEOPROPIDES into the former's house.

ACT FIVE

Enter TRANIO from the house of Theopropides.

TRA   Someone who is timid in emergencies won't be worth a
farthing. And I don't know what I should say the word
"farthing"[34] means. After my master sent me to the farm
to fetch his son, I secretly went that way through the alley   1045
to our garden, I opened the wings of the door to the gar-

[34] The Latin word *nauci*, here translated as "farthing," is of obscure
meaning and only occurs in contexts where it denotes something of lit-
tle or no value.

eaque eduxi omnem legionem, et maris et feminas.
postquam ex opsidione in tutum eduxi manuplaris meos,
capio consilium ut senatum congerronum conuocem.

1050 quoniam conuocaui, atque illi me ex senatu segregant.
ubi ego me uideo uenire in meo foro, quantum potest
facio idem quod plurumi alii, quibus res timida aut turbi-
da est:
pergunt turbare usque ut ne quid possit conquiescere.

1054 nam scio equidem nullo pacto iam esse posse haec clam
–55   senem.
non amicus alius quis *** riuabo se ***
aut *** es * ff ***
prosi *** m *** q *** sall ***

1059 ille qui *** ero simul ***
–60   praeoccupabo atque anteueniam et foedus feriam. me
moror.
sed quid hoc est quod foris concrepuit proxuma uicinia?
erus meus hic quidem est. gustare ego eius sermonem
uolo.

THEO ilico intra limen isti astate, ut, quom extemplo uocem,
1065   continuo exsiliatis. manicas celeriter conectite.
ego illum ante aedis praestolabor ludificatorem meum,
quoius ego hodie ludificabor corium, si uiuo, probe.

TRA   res palam est. nunc te uidere meliust quid agas, Tranio.

THEO docte atque astu mihi captandum est cum illo, ubi huc
aduenerit.

1070 non ego illi extemplo hamum ostendam, sensim mittam
lineam.
dissimulabo me horum quicquam scire.

1049 conger(r)onem *AB¹CD*, congeronum *B²*
1056–60 *uersus in P non feruntur*

426

den in the alley, and I led our entire forces out, both the males and the females. After I led all my comrades from siege to safety, I come up with the plan of calling together a senate meeting of debauchees. When I've assembled 1050 them, they exclude me from the senate meeting at once. When I see that I'm being sold in my own market, I do as quickly as possible just what most other people do who are in an emergency or trouble: they carry on perplexing matters so that nothing can calm down. I know that this 1055 matter can no longer be kept behind master's back. No other friend *** or *** benefit *** that one who *** at the 1060 same time to my master ***. I'll get ahead of them, arrive first, and strike a deal. I'm wasting time. But what's the reason that the door has creaked in the next house? This is my master. I want to get a taste of what he's saying. (*steps aside*)

Enter THEOPROPIDES from Simo's house.

THEO (*to the slaves within*) Stand there inside the threshold, so that you can jump out at once when I call. Put the shack- 1065 les together quickly. I'll wait for that trickster of mine in front of the house; I'll play proper tricks on his hide to-day, as truly as I live.

TRA (*aside*) The cat's out of the sack. Now you'd better see what to do, Tranio.

THEO I need to angle for him cleverly and with cunning when he arrives. I won't show him the hook immediately, I'll let 1070 the line down gradually. I'll pretend not to know anything about it.

TRA	o mortalem malum!
	alter hoc Athenis nemo doctior dici potest.
	uerba illi non magis dare hodie quisquam quam . . . lapidi
	potest.
	aggrediar hominem, appellabo.
THEO	nunc ego ille huc ueniat uelim.
1075 TRA	siquidem pol me quaeris, assum praesens praesenti tibi.
THEO	eugae! Tranio, quid agitur?
TRA	ueniunt rure rustici.
	Philolaches iam hic aderit.
THEO	edepol ⟨tu⟩ mi opportune aduenis.
	nostrum ego hunc uicinum opinor esse hominem auda-
	cem et malum.
TRA	quidum?
THEO	quia negat nouisse uos—
TRA	negat?
THEO	—nec uos sibi
1080	nummum umquam argenti dedisse.
TRA	abi, ludis me, credo hau negat.
THEO	quid iam?
TRA	scio, iocaris tu nunc. nam ill' quidem ⟨credo⟩ hau negat.
THEO	immo edepol negat profecto, nec se hasce aedis Philola-
	chi
	uendidisse.
TRA	eho an negauit sibi datum argentum, opsecro?
THEO	quin ius iurandum pollicitust dare se, si uellem, mihi,
1085	nec se hasce aedis uendidisse nec sibi argentum datum.
TRA	*** ⟨datum⟩ est.

1077 tu *add. Sonnenschein*   1081 credo *add. Sonnenschein*
1086 *uersum intercidisse intellexit Acidalius*; *qui uersus exierit in*
datum est

428

TRA   (*aside*) What a sly creature! No second person in Athens can be said to be cleverer. No one can trick him any more than . . . a block of stone.[35] I'll go up to him and address him.

THEO Now I'd like him to come here.

TRA   If you're looking for me, I'm here at your service, present 1075 as you are present.

THEO Hurray! Tranio, how are things?

TRA   The yokels are coming from the country. Philolaches will be here any moment.

THEO You've come in the nick of time. I think our neighbor here is a bold and sly man.

TRA   How so?

THEO Because he denies that he's had any dealings with you—

TRA   (*interrupting*) He denies it?

THEO —and that you've ever given him as much as a silver coin. 1080

TRA   Go away, you're making fun of me, I don't believe he denies it.

THEO Why?

TRA   I know, you're joking now: he doesn't deny it, I believe.

THEO No, he does indeed deny it and says that he didn't sell this house to Philolaches.

TRA   Hey there, he hasn't denied that he was given the money, please, has he?

THEO More than that, he's promised to give me an oath if I so wish that he didn't sell this house and that the money 1085 wasn't given to him.

TRA   *** it has been given.

---

[35] Metaphor for a stupid man.

THEO dixi ego istuc idem illi.

TRA quid ait?

THEO seruos pollicitust dare
suos mihi omnis quaestioni.

TRA nugas! numquam edepol dabit.

THEO dat profecto.

TRA quin cita illum in ius. ibo, inueniam.

THEO mane.

1090 experiar, ut opinor. certum est.

TRA ⟨immo⟩ mihi hominem cedo.

1093 THEO quid si igitur ego accersam homines?

TRA factum iam esse oportuit.

1091 uel hominem aedis iube mancupio poscere.

THEO [immo] hoc primum uolo,

1092 quaestioni accipere seruos.

TRA faciundum edepol censeo.

1094 ego interim hanc aram occupabo.

THEO quid ita?

TRA nullam rem sapis.

1095 ne enim illi huc confugere possint quaestioni quos dabit.
hic ego tibi praesidebo, ne interbitat quaestio.

THEO surge.

TRA minime.

THEO ne occupassis, opsecro, aram.

TRA quor?

THEO scies.
quia enim id maxume uolo, ut illi istoc confugiant. sine:
tanto apud iudicem hunc argenti condemnabo facilius.

1089 et illum in ius si ueniam *P*, cita illum in ius; ibo, inueniam
Ritschl 1090 immo *ex 1091 add. Sonnenschein*
1093 *post 1090 posuit Camerarius*

THEO I told him that same thing.

TRA What did he say?

THEO He promised to give me all his slaves for questioning.[36]

TRA Nonsense! He'll never give them.

THEO He really is giving them.

TRA No, call him to court. I'll go and find him.

THEO Wait. I'll try, I think. I'm resolved.   1090

TRA No, give me the chap.

THEO What if I fetch them then?

TRA You should have done so already. Or rather have your son formally demand the house as his property.

THEO First I want to accept his servants for questioning.

TRA I think that ought to be done. Meanwhile I'll occupy this altar.[37] (*does so*)

THEO Why?

TRA You don't know anything. So that the ones he gives you   1095 for questioning can't flee here. I'll sit on guard for you here so that the questioning won't fall through.

THEO Get up.

TRA No.

THEO Please don't occupy the altar.

TRA Why not?

THEO You'll find out. Because this is what I want most, that they flee there. Let it be: I'll get him condemned to pay damages all the more easily.

[36] The testimony of slaves only counts if obtained under torture.

[37] An altar is in effect also an asylum from which nobody may be dragged away.

1091 iube aedis *P, transp. Mueller* immo *hic del. Sonnenschein*

1100 TRA quod agas, id agas. quid tu porro serere uis negotium?
         nescis quam metuculosa res sit ire ad iudicem?

THEO surgedum huc igitur. consulere quiddam est quod tecum
         uolo.

TRA sic tamen hinc consilium dedero. nimio plus sapio se-
         dens.

         tum consilia firmiora sunt de diuinis locis.

1105 THEO surge, ne nugare. aspicedum contra me.
TRA   aspexi.
THEO   uides?
TRA uideo. huc si quis intercedat tertius, pereat fame.
THEO quidum?
TRA   quia nil ⟨illi⟩ quaesti sit. mali hercle ambo sumus.
THEO perii!
TRA   quid tibi est?
THEO   dedisti uerba.
TRA   qui tandem?
THEO   probe
         med emunxti.
TRA   uide sis, satine recte: num mucci fluont?
1110 THEO immo etiam cerebrum quoque omne e capite emunxti
         meo.

         nam omnia male facta uostra repperi radicitus,

         non radicitus quidem hercle uerum etiam exradicitus.

TRA numquam edepol hodie ⟨hinc⟩ inuitus ⟨surgam.
THEO   surges. nam⟩ tibi
         iam iubebo ignem et sarmenta, carnufex, circumdari.

    1100 uis serere P, transp. Bothe
    1107 illi add. Leo
    1113 inuitus (inditus B²) destinant P, ⟨hinc⟩ inuitus ⟨surgam⟩ et
⟨THEO surges nam⟩ Seyffert et Sonnenschein
    1114 lubeo P, iubebo Pylades

TRA Follow the first plan. Why do you want to give yourself 1100
     extra trouble? Don't you know what a ticklish thing it is to
     go to a judge?

THEO Then get up and come to me. There's something I want to
     discuss with you.

TRA No, I'll give my advice like this, from here. I'm much
     cleverer sitting. Besides, advice from holy places is more
     reliable.

THEO Get up, stop fooling around. Look me in the face. 1105

TRA Okay.

THEO Can you see?

TRA Yes. If a third person were to come between us here, he'd
     starve to death.

THEO How so?

TRA Because he couldn't gain anything. We're both so devil-
     ishly close.

THEO I'm ruined!

TRA What's wrong with you?

THEO You've tricked me.

TRA What's the matter now?

THEO You've blown my nose properly.[38]

TRA Do look and see if I've done a good job: is the snot still
     flowing?

THEO You've even blown my entire brains out of my head as 1110
     well: I've found out about all your bad deeds to the root;
     not just to the root, actually, but to below the root.

TRA I'll never rise from here today against my will.

THEO You will: I'll have fire and brushwood put round you in a
     moment, you hangman.[39]

---

[38] A metaphor for tricking someone.

[39] By burning the place Theopropides can force Tranio to leave the
altar without actually dragging him away.

1115 TRA ne faxis, nam elixus esse quam assus soleo suauior.

THEO exempla edepol faciam ego in te.

TRA   quia placeo, exemplum expetis?

THEO loquere: quoius modi reliqui, quom hinc abibam, filium?

TRA cum pedibus, manibus, cum digitis, auribus, oculis, la-
     bris.

THEO aliud te rogo.

TRA   aliud ergo nunc tibi respondeo.

1120   sed eccum tui gnati sodalem uideo huc ‹nunc› incedere

      Callidamatem: illo praesente mecum agito, si quid uoles.

        V. ii: CALLIDAMATES. THEOPROPIDES. TRANIO

CAL ubi somnum sepeliui omnem atque edormiui crapulam,

      Philolaches uenisse ‹dixit› mihi suom peregre huc pa-
     trem

      quoque modo hominem ad‹uenientem› seruos ludifica-
     tus sit,

1125   ait se metuere in conspe‹ctum sui patris pr›ocedere.

      nunc ego de sodalitate solus sum orator datus

      qui a patre eius conciliarem pacem. atque eccum op-
     tume!

      iubeo te saluere et saluos quom aduenis, Theopropides,

      peregre gaudeo. hic apud nos hodie cenes, sic face.

1130 THEO Callidamates, di te ament. de cena facio gratiam.

CAL quin uenis?

TRA   promitte: ego ibo pro te, si tibi non lubet.

     1120 nunc *add. Redslob*

     1122 omnium *P*, somnum ς, somno *Ritschl* obdormiui *P*, edormiui
Camerarius

     1123 dixit *add. Bothe*

     1124 ad‹uenientem› *Aldus*

     1125 conspe‹ctum sui patris pr›ocedere *Ritschl*

434

TRA Don't do that: I generally taste better boiled than 1115
     roasted.

THEO I'll make an example of you.[40]

TRA Because you approve of me you want others to copy me?

THEO Tell me: what sort of son did I leave when I left this
     place?

TRA One with feet, hands, with fingers, ears, eyes, and lips.

THEO I'm asking you about something different.

TRA Then I'm giving you a reply about something different
     now. But look, I can see your son's chum coming here 1120
     now, Callidamates: deal with me in his presence, if you
     want anything.

Enter CALLIDAMATES from the right.

CAL When I'd buried all my sleep and slept off my drunken-
     ness, Philolaches told me that his father had returned
     from abroad and how his slave had made a fool of him on
     his arrival; he said he was afraid to face his father. Now 1125
     I alone out of our circle of friends have been chosen as
     orator to make peace with his father. And look, here he is
     in the nick of time! (*walking toward Theopropides*) My
     greetings to you, and I'm happy that you've arrived safely,
     Theopropides. Have dinner here with us, please do.

THEO Callidamates, may the gods love you. As for the dinner, 1130
     no thanks.

CAL Why won't you come?

TRA Accept: I'll go for you, if you don't fancy it.

---

[40] *Exemplum* is ambiguous: it can mean a "warning example" as well
as a "model."

THEO uerbero, etiam irrides?

TRA   quian me pro te ire ad cenam autumo?

THEO non enim ibis. ego ferare faxo, ut meruisti, in crucem.

CAL   age mitte ista; ac tu ad me ad cenam—

TRA   dic uenturum. quid taces?

1135 CAL sed tu istuc quid confugisti in aram?

TRA   inscitissumus
      adueniens perterruit me. ‹e›loquere nunc quid fecerim:
      nunc utrisque disceptator eccum adest, age disputa.

THEO filium corrupisse aio te meum.

TRA   ausculta modo.
      fateor peccauisse, amicam liberasse apsente te,

1140   faenore argentum sumpsisse; id esse apsumptum praedi-
      co.
      numquid aliud fecit nisi quod [faciunt] summis gnati ge-
      neribus?

THEO hercle mihi tecum cauendum est, nimis qui es orator ca-
      tus.

CAL   sine me dum istuc iudicare. surge, ego isti assedero.

THEO maxume, accipe hanc ‹tute› ad te litem.

TRA   enim istic captio est.

1145   fac ego ne metuam ‹mihi atque› ut tu meam timeas ui-
      cem.

THEO iam minoris ‹omnia alia fa›cio praequam quibus modis
      me ludificatust.

TRA   bene hercle factum, et factum gaudeo:
      sapere istac aetate oportet qui sunt capite candido.

    1134 ista acto (aito B²) P, ista ac tu *Ernout*, istaec tu *Lindsay*
    1136 ‹e›loquere *Langen*
    1141 faciunt *del. Guyet*
    1144 tute *add. Ritschl*

THEO You whipping post, you're actually laughing at me?

TRA Because I'm saying I'm going to dinner in your place?

THEO No, you won't *go*. I'll make sure you'll *be carried*, to the cross, as you've deserved.

CAL Go on, leave that aside now and say that to my dinner—

TRA (*interrupting*) Say you'll come. Why are you silent?

CAL (*to Tranio*) But why did you flee there onto the altar?   1135

TRA The simpleton scared me when he arrived. (*to Theopropides*) State now what I've done: look, now there's an arbitrator here for the two of us, go on, argue your case.

THEO I say that you've led my son astray.

TRA Just listen. I admit that he's strayed, that he's freed his girlfriend in your absence, and that he's borrowed money   1140 on interest. I'm telling you that it's all been spent. Has he done anything other than what the sons of the best families do?

THEO I must be on my guard against you; you are a terribly clever orator.

CAL (*to Theopropides*) Let me pronounce judgment on this. (*to Tranio*) Get up, I'll sit in your place.

THEO By all means, take this argument into your hands.

TRA (*to Callidamates*) I'm sure there's a trap there. Make sure   1145 that I needn't be afraid for myself and that you are afraid in my place.

THEO (*to Callidamates*) I already care less about everything else compared with how he fooled me.

TRA That was done right and proper and I'm glad it was done: people of your age, who have a hoary head, ought to have more sense.

1145 mihi atque *add. Ritschl*
1146 <omnia alia fa>cio *Ritschl*

437

THEO quid ego nunc faciam?

TRA si amicus Diphilo aut Philemoni es,
1150 dicito is quo pacto tuos te seruos ludificauerit:
optumas frustrationes dederis in comoediis.

CAL tace parumper, sine uicissim me loqui, ausculta.

THEO licet.

CAL omnium primum sodalem me esse scis gnato tuo.
1154 is adit me, nam illum prodire pudet in conspectum tuom
–55 propterea quia fecit quae te scire scit. nunc te opsecro,
stultitiae adulescentiaeque eius ignoscas: tuost;
scis solere illanc aetatem tali ludo ludere.
quicquid fecit, nobiscum una fecit: nos deliquimus.
1160 faenus, sortem sumptumque omnem, qui amica ⟨empta⟩
est, omnia
nos dabimus, nos conferemus, nostro sumptu, non tuo.

THEO non potuit uenire orator magis ad me impetrabilis
quam tu; nec sum illic iratus nec quicquam suscenseo.
immo me praesente amato, bibito, facito quod lubet:
1165 si hoc pudet, fecisse sumptum, supplici habeo satis.

CAL dispudet.

TRA ⟨post⟩ istam ueniam quid me fiet nunciam?

THEO uerberibus, lutum, caedere pendens.

TRA tamen etsi pudet?

THEO interimam hercle ego ⟨te⟩ si uiuo.

CAL fac istam cunctam gratiam:
Tranioni amitte quaeso hanc noxiam causa mea.

1160 empta *add. Ritschl*
1166 post *add. Mueller*
1168 te *add. Guyet*
1169 remitte *P*, amitte *Ussing*

THEO What am I to do now?

TRA If you're a friend of Diphilus or Philemon,[41] tell them   1150
how your slave made fun of you: you'll give them first-
rate stories of imposture in their comedies.

CAL (*to Theopropides*) Be quiet for a while, let me speak in
turn, listen.

THEO Okay.

CAL First of all you know that I'm your son's friend. He ap-   1155
proached me: he's ashamed to come before your eyes be-
cause he did what he he knows you know. Now I ask you
to forgive him for his silliness and youth: he's your own
son. You know that people of that age normally plays this
game. Whatever he did, he did it together with us. *We*
have committed it. Interest, principal, and every expense   1160
through which the girlfriend was bought, all that we'll
give you, we'll scrape it together, from our pockets, not
yours.

THEO A more effective orator than you couldn't have come
to me. I'm not angry with him and I feel no bitterness.
Let him love in my presence, drink, and do what he likes.
If he's ashamed of having wasted money, I'm placated   1165
enough.

CAL He's utterly ashamed.

TRA After that pardon what's going to happen to me now?

THEO You scum of the earth, you'll be hung up and flogged.

TRA Even if I'm ashamed?

THEO I'll kill you, as truly as I live.

CAL Make a complete pardon of it. Please forgive Tranio for
this offense for my sake.

[41] Two of the Greek playwrights whose comedies Plautus adapted.

439

1170 THEO aliud quiduis impetrari a me facilius perferam

      quam ut non ego istum pro suis factis pessumis pessum
        premam.

CAL   mitte quaeso istum.

THEO   ⟨illum ut mittam?⟩ uiden ut astat furcifer?

CAL   Tranio, quiesce, si sapis.

THEO   tu quiesce hanc rem modo

      petere: ego illum, ut sit quietus, uerberibus subegero.

1175 TRA nihil opust profecto.

CAL   age iam, sine ted exorarier.

THEO nolo ores.

CAL   quaeso hercle.

THEO   nolo, inquam, ores.

CAL   nequiquam neuis.

      hanc modo [unam] noxiam unam quaeso ⟨missam⟩ fac
        causa mea.

TRA   quid grauaris? quasi non cras iam commeream aliam
        noxiam:

      ibi utrumque, et hoc et illud, poteris ulcisci probe.

1180 CAL sine te exorem.

THEO   age abi, abi impune. em huic habeto gratiam.

      spectatores, fabula haec est acta, uos plausum date.

1172 illum ut mittam *add. Ritschl* restat *P*, astat *Ritschl*
1173 qui esse sapis *P*, quiesce si sapis *Camerarius*
1177 unam *del. Ritschl* missam *add. Ritschl*

440

THEO I'll let you get anything else from me more easily than me   1170
not getting the upper hand of this fellow for his under-
hand tricks.

CAL Please let him go scot-free.

THEO I should let him go scot-free? Can't you see how the crim-
inal's standing there?

CAL Tranio, you'd do well to be quiet.

THEO Just you be quiet and stop asking for this: I'll subdue him
with blows so that he'll be quiet.

TRA It really isn't necessary.   1175

CAL (*to Theopropides*) Go on now, let yourself be persuaded.

THEO I don't want you to ask.

CAL Please.

THEO I don't want you to ask, I'm telling you.

CAL You don't want it, but in vain. Please, just let this one
offense go unpunished for my sake.

TRA (*to Theopropides*) Why are you making such a fuss? As if
I wouldn't commit some other offense as early as tomor-
row; then you'll be able to punish me properly for both,
this one and that one.

CAL (*to Theopropides*) Let me persuade you.   1180

THEO (*to Tranio*) Go on, go away, go away without punishment.
There, be grateful to this chap. Spectators, this play is
over, give us your applause.

441

PERSA

INTRODUCTORY NOTE

The *Persa* has always been considered one of Plautus' lesser comedies, not because the plot is inferior, but because the tenor of the play is somewhat coarse and unsavory. Thus, while for instance the *Amphitruo* and *Aulularia* have been imitated countless times, the *Persa* has not had any significant influence on European drama at all. Lessing's erroneous belief that the Persian referred to in the title is a woman shows how little attention this comedy has generally received. But even though the play does contain some unpleasant elements, it also has some truly charming and witty exchanges which make its neglect hard to justify.

At the heart of the play is the love between the slave Toxilus and Lemniselenis, a prostitute owned by the pimp Dordalus. Toxilus wants to buy Lemniselenis and set her free but does not have the money the pimp demands. He asks his friend Sagaristio, another slave, to find it for him. Since it is unclear whether Sagaristio will be successful, he also enlists the help of Saturio, his hanger-on, who agrees to a mock sale of his daughter in exchange for food.

The second act begins with a witty exchange between Sophoclidisca, a slave girl in the pimp's household looking after Lemniselenis, and Paegnium, a slave boy working for Toxilus. Sophoclidisca is delivering a letter to Toxilus,

Paegnium one to Lemniselenis. Sophoclidisca, who does not appear in the play again, is characterized as a pleasant and harmless servant, while Paegnium is shown to be a cheeky rascal prone to rudeness and obscenities. Paegnium also meets Sagaristio, with whom he has another entertaining exchange; Paegnium's desire to become free is revealed. The most important element of the second act is the scenes in which Sagaristio states that he has the money Toxilus needs and gives it to him; the money was entrusted to Sagaristio by his master, who wanted him to buy plow oxen with it. Sagaristio is fully aware that if Toxilus cannot pay him back, he himself will suffer at his master's hands.

Now Toxilus could in theory simply pay off the pimp and end the play, but he continues the intrigue he has begun with Saturio, partly in order to punish the pimp and partly in order to pay back Sagaristio. Saturio brings along his daughter, who remains unnamed throughout the play. She does not want to take part in the mock sale because she regards it as dishonorable, but in the end she has to obey her father. He hands her over to Toxilus, who tells Sagaristio to dress up as a Persian merchant, while the girl should play a kidnapped beauty from Arabia. In the meantime, Toxilus gives the pimp the money he got from Sagaristio and receives Lemniselenis in exchange.

Next, Toxilus introduces the pimp to the Persian merchant and the girl from Arabia. The Persian wants to sell the girl to the pimp but tells him that he will not sell her through the formal process of mancipation, which means that he cannot be held accountable should there be anything wrong with the girl. After some hesitation, the pimp agrees to buy her. As soon as the transaction has been carried out, the Persian leaves. Now Saturio comes and states that the girl is his daughter and hence a freeborn Athenian citizen. He takes the pimp to court, where he has to return the girl without receiving compensation. When he comes back, he sees Toxilus and Sagaristio having a drinks party with Lemniselenis. Naturally, he is angry at being deceived, but there is nothing he can do about it; to add insult to injury, Paegnium, Toxilus, Sagaristio, and after some hesitation also Lemniselenis mock and beat him.

A modern audience might feel some pity for the pimp, who has not actually done anything wrong to Toxilus. Admittedly, he is no paragon of virtue: in l. 731 he states that he has given his slaves a brutal beating; however, this seems more like a stock theme inserted by Plautus and is not elaborated any further. In fact, unlike for example the pimp Ballio in the *Pseudolus*, Dordalus appears to be an acceptable, even reliable character. Nevertheless, to a Roman audience the pimp was the enemy par excellence and there could be no exception, so the punishment at the end of the comedy will not have upset the Roman spectators.

The behavior exhibited by Toxilus is probably more shocking: at first he appears as the standard young lover, and when his girl is finally free, he seems overjoyed; but when she does not want to join in the ridiculing of the pimp, he becomes rude and abusive toward her.

The characters in the *Persa* are its most interesting feature. Toxilus embodies both the young lover and the clever slave, an unusual combination because young lovers in comedy are typically free men who lose all their abilities to think rationally when in love. Sagaristio is also a mixed character. On the one hand he is the lover's friend, a role normally played by freeborn men of mediocre intelligence, like Eutychus in the *Mercator*; on the other hand he is also a clever slave willing to cheat his master out of money. Saturio is unusual in that he is the only hanger-on in Plautus who has a daughter; and his participation in the intrigue could indicate that in the Greek original he was a professional informer or sycophant, a job which in l. 62 he says he does not want to have. His daughter is a remarkable character as well. On the one hand she does not want to be part of the intrigue and objects, but on the other, when she cannot avoid helping her father with it, she plays her part professionally.

This playing with standard roles and theatrical conventions indicates that the Greek original was probably one of the later plays of New Comedy. If so, the reference to King Attalus I (269–197 BC) and King Philip V (238–179 BC) in l. 339 is likely to come from the Greek original and is irrelevant for dating the Latin play.

However, there are several purely Plautine elements in the play. Whereas the simple manumission in ll. 438–47 is Greek in character, the reference to the praetor in l. 487 is Roman and not merely the translation of a Greek official; in Greece no such official was needed. Similarly, in ll. 549–672 there are four speakers, an unusual constellation for Greek comedy. It seems that the eavesdropping passage in ll. 549–74 was created by Plautus purely in order to entertain us through the asides; it certainly does not advance the plot. The interrogation in ll. 591–659 also bears all the hallmarks of Plautine expansion; it is an unrealistic element in the dialogue because Toxilus urges the pimp to question the girl after he has already expressed interest in buying her. Moreover, while the young woman is normally described as having been kidnapped and as suitable for regular prostitution, in l. 644 she is supposed to be a prisoner of war to be bought back by her relatives.

I have already indicated that the Greek original probably belongs to the late phase of New Comedy. The Latin play is also likely to be one of Plautus' later plays. In ll. 99– 100 there is a reference to the *epulum Iouis*, a ritual meal instituted in 196, so the Persa must have been written after this date. We can go further if we compare *Persa* 12, *Pseud*. 772, and Persius 1. 77–78: all three passages parody the *Antiopa* of Pacuvius, but since the *Pseudolus* passage corresponds more closely with the Persius passage, we can assume that these two texts are closer to Pacuvius. The more oblique reference in the *Persa* is more readily understood by an audience if they have already watched the *Pseudolus*, which means that in all likelihood the *Persa* is later. The *Pseudolus* was staged in 191, which gives us a *terminus post quem*. The *Persa* is very rich in lyrical passages, a further indication of later composition.

SELECT BIBLIOGRAPHY

Editions and Commentaries

Ammendola, G. (1922), *Il "Persa": testo, introduzione e commento* (Lanciano).

Woytek, E. (1982), *T. Maccius Plautus: Persa; Einleitung, Text und Kommentar* (Vienna).

Criticism

Hofmann, W. (1989), "Plautinisches in Plautus' Persa," in *Klio* 71: 399–407.

Lowe, J. C. B. (1989), "The *virgo callida* of Plautus, *Persa*," in *Classical Quarterly* NS 39: 390–99.

Müller, G. L. (1957), "Das Original des plautinischen Persa" (Ph.D. diss., Frankfurt).

Partsch, J. (1910), "Römisches und griechisches Recht in Plautus Persa," in *Hermes* 45: 595–614.

PERSA

ARGVMENTVM I

Profecto domino suos amores Toxilus
Emit atque curat leno ut emittat manu.
Raptamque ut emeret de praedone uirginem
Subornata suadet sui parasiti filia,
5 **A**tque ita intricatum ludit potans Dordalum.

ARGVMENTVM II

*** tur ‹se›ruu‹s› ***
***
***
***
5 *** fingunt ***
*** ant ‹u›erec ***
***
*** ta *** rsi ***
*** de ‹ui›rgi ***
10 *** cam uen ***
*** ‹pr›etio ‹p›aru ***
***
*** a re‹ci›pit e ***
*** tue ‹l›eno ***

THE PERSIAN

PLOT SUMMARY 1

When his master has left, Toxilus buys his sweetheart and has a
pimp set her free. Toxilus advises him to buy a kidnapped virgin
from her captor after his hanger-on's daughter has been dressed
up for the part, and this is how he entangles the pimp Dordalus 5
and has his fun with him while drinking.

PLOT SUMMARY 2

*** a slave *** *** they invent *** *** for a price *** he takes 10
back *** the pimp ***

---

arg. 1 *om. A*
arg. 1, 3 ui *P*, ut *Valla*
arg. 2 *om. P quae desunt suppleuit Schoell, cuius supplementorum
solum id in textum recepi quod mihi defendi uidetur posse*
arg. 2, 1 ‹se›ruu‹s› *Schoell*

PERSONAE

TOXILVS seruos
SAGARISTIO seruos
SATVRIO parasitus
SOPHOCLIDISCA ancilla
LEMNISELENIS meretrix
PAEGNIVM puer
VIRGO
DORDALVS leno

SCAENA

Athenis

ACTVS I

I. i: TOXILVS. SAGARISTIO

TOX   qui amans egens ingressus est princeps in Amoris uias
       superauit aerumnis suis aerumnas Herculei.[1]

---

[1] Hercules served King Eurystheus for twelve years, during which
he did twelve great labors. Among other things, he killed the Nemean
Lion and the Lernaean Hydra (a snakelike monster) and caught the
Ceryneian Hind. He also captured the Erymanthian Boar, but not
the Aetolian (Calydonian) Boar, as Plautus alleges. The killing of the
Stymphalian Birds is a canonical part of the twelve labors, while the
fight against Antaeus, though done by Hercules, is not one of them.

PERSA

CHARACTERS

TOXILUS a slave; in love with Lemniselenis
SAGARISTIO a slave; friend of Toxilus
SATURIO a hanger-on; sponges off Toxilus
SOPHOCLIDISCA a slave girl; works for the pimp Dordalus
LEMNISELENIS a prostitute; owned by Dordalus
PAEGNIUM a slave boy; works for Toxilus
GIRL Saturio's daughter
DORDALUS a pimp; torn between caution and the desire to
  make a profit

STAGING

The scene represents a street in Athens. On it are two houses:
to the left is the house of Toxilus and his absent master, to the
right the house of Dordalus. There is a little alley between the
houses. To the left the main street leads to the harbor, to the
right to the city center.

ACT ONE

Enter TOXILUS from the right.

TOX   The pennyless lover who first stepped onto the roads of
      Love surpassed the labors of Hercules[1] with his own la-

nam cum leone, cum excetra, cum ceruo, cum apro Aeto-
lico,

cum auibus Stymphalicis, cum Antaeo deluctari maue-
lim

5   quam cum Amore: ita fio miser quaerendo argento mu-
tuo

nec quicquam nisi "non est" sciunt mihi respondere quos
rogo.

SAG   qui ero suo seruire uolt bene seruos seruitutem,

ne illum edepol multa in pectore suo collocare oportet

quae ero placere censeat praesenti atque apsenti suo.

10   ego nec lubenter seruio nec satis sum ero ex sententia,

sed quasi lippo oculo me erus meus manum apstinere
hau quit tamen

quin mi imperet, quin me suis negotiis praefulciat.

TOX   quis illic est qui contra me astat?

SAG   quis hic est qui sic contra me astat?

TOX   similis est Sagaristionis.

SAG   Toxilus hic quidem meus amicust.

15 TOX   is est profecto.

SAG   eum esse opinor.

TOX   congrediar.

SAG   contra aggredibor.

TOX   o Sagaristio, di ament te.

SAG   o Toxile, dabunt di quae exoptes.

17   ut uales?

17ᵃ TOX   ut queo.

SAG   quid agitur?

17ᵇ TOX   uiuitur.

18 SAG   satin ergo ex sententia?

TOX   si eueniunt quae exopto, satis.

bors; I'd rather wrestle with the lion, the snake, the deer, the Aetolian boar, the Stymphalian birds, and Antaeus than with Love, so wretched do I become from looking 5 for money on loan, and the ones I ask only know how to answer "I don't have any."

Enter SAGARISTIO from the left without seeing Toxilus.

SAG   A slave who wants to serve his master well should place many things in his breast which he thinks will please his master when he's present as well as when he's absent. As 10 for me, I don't enjoy being a slave and I'm not sufficiently the way master would want me to be, but nevertheless my master can't keep his hand away from me, as from a sore eye: so he gives me orders and uses me as support for his activities.

TOX   (*noticing Sagaristio*) Who is that standing opposite me?

SAG   Who is this standing opposite me like this?

TOX   He resembles Sagaristio.

SAG   This is my friend Toxilus.

TOX   It's him indeed.   15

SAG   I think it's him.

TOX   I'll approach him.

SAG   I'll step up.

TOX   O Sagaristio, may the gods love you.

SAG   O Toxilus, the gods will grant what you wish. How are you doing?

TOX   As I can.

SAG   How are you?

TOX   Alive.

SAG   More or less as you'd like, then?

TOX   If what I wish happens, yes.

	SAG	nimis stulte amicis utere.
	TOX	quid iam?
	SAG	imperare oportet.
20	TOX	mi quidem tu iam eras mortuos, quia non te uisitabam.
	SAG	negotium edepol—
	TOX	ferreum fortasse?
	SAG	plusculum annum
		fui praeferratus apud molas tribunus uapularis.
	TOX	uetus iam istaec militia est tua.
	SAG	satin tu usque ualuisti?
	TOX	hau probe.
	SAG	ergo edepol palles.
	TOX	saucius factus sum in Veneris proelio:
25		sagitta Cupido cor meum transfixit.
	SAG	iam serui hic amant?
26	TOX	quid ego faciam? disne aduorser?
26ᵃ		quasi Titani cum eis belligerem
27		quibus sat esse non queam?
	SAG	uide modo ulmeae catapultae tuom ne transfigant latus.
29	TOX	basilice agito eleutheria.
29ᵃ	SAG	quid iam?
	TOX	quia erus peregri est.
	SAG	ain tu,
30		peregri est?
	TOX	si tu tibi bene esse
30ᵃ		pote pati, ueni: uiues mecum,
31		basilico accipiere uictu.
32	SAG	uah! iam scapulae pruriunt, quia
32ᵃ		te istaec audiui loqui.

---

² Reference to shackles.   ³ The Titans were gods preceding
the Olympians, who overthrew them.   ⁴ I.e., elm rods.

SAG   You make use of your friends in a terribly stupid way.

TOX   What do you mean?

SAG   You should give them orders.

TOX   To me you were already dead because I couldn't see you.   20

SAG   Indeed, business—

TOX   (*interrupting*) Perhaps iron business?[2]

SAG   For a little longer than a year I was commander of beatings in the mill, shod with iron.

TOX   That military service of yours is already an old one.

SAG   Have you been well throughout?

TOX   No, I haven't.

SAG   That's why you're pale.

TOX   I've been wounded in a battle against Venus: Cupid   25 pierced through my heart with his arrow.

SAG   Are slaves having love affairs here now?

TOX   What should I do? Should I resist the gods? Should I, like the Titans,[3] wage war against those whose equal I couldn't be?

SAG   Just make sure that no elm-wood missiles[4] pierce your side.

TOX   I'm celebrating the Festival of Liberty[5] in grand style.

SAG   How so?

TOX   Because my master is abroad.

SAG   Do you say so? He's abroad?   30

TOX   If you can bear having a good time, come: you'll have the time of your life with me, you'll get a reception with grand food.

SAG   Oh! My shoulderblades are already itching because I've heard you say that.

---

[5] Hyperbole; such a feast would be celebrated if Toxilus were manumitted, but his freedom now is only temporary.

33	TOX	sed hoc me unum excruciat.
	SAG	quidnam id est?
34	TOX	haec dies summa hodie est, mea amica sitne libera
34ª		an sempiternam seruitutem seruiat.
	SAG	quid nunc uis ergo?
35	TOX	emere amicum tibi me potis es sempiternum.
	SAG	quem ad modum?
36	TOX	ut mihi des nummos sescentos
36ª		quos pro capite illius pendam,
37		quos continuo tibi reponam in hoc
37ª		triduo aut quadriduo.
38		age fi benignus, subueni.
	SAG	qua confidentia rogare tu a med argenti tantum audes,
40		impudens? quin si egomet totus ueneam, uix recipi potis est
		quod tu me rogas; nam tu aquam a pumici nunc postulas,
		qui ipsus siti aret.
	TOX	sicin te mi hoc facere?
	SAG	quid faciam?
	TOX	rogas?
		alicunde exora mutuom.
	SAG	tu fac idem quod rogas me.
	TOX	quaesiui, nusquam repperi.
	SAG	quaeram equidem, si quis credat.
45	TOX	nempe habeo in mundo.
	SAG	si id domi esset mihi, iam pollicerer:
		hoc meum est ut faciam sedulo.

34ª ergo et ego *T*, ergo *ceteri Palatini*

39 argenti *T*, argentum *ceteri Palatini*

42 siciare *B*, sitiare *CD¹*, sitiat *D³FZ*, siti aret *Lindsay* hoc te mihi *P*, *transp. Mueller*

TOX	But this one thing is torturing me.
SAG	What is it?
TOX	This is the day that decides whether my girlfriend will be free or serve as a slave forever.
SAG	Then what do you want now?
TOX	You can buy my eternal friendship.
SAG	How?
TOX	By giving me six hundred tetradrachmas[6] which I can pay for her; I'll return it to you within the next two or three days. Go on, be generous, help me out.
SAG	With what nerve dare you ask me for so much money, you shameless creature? If I myself were to be sold entirely, it would scarcely be possible to get in return what you're asking me for: now you're demanding water from a pumice stone that is dry from thirst itself.
TOX	Are you treating me like this?
SAG	What should I do?
TOX	Do you ask? Get it on loan from someone.
SAG	Do the same thing that you ask of me!
TOX	I've looked for it, but found it nowhere.
SAG	I'll look for it, just in case anyone should give me a loan.
TOX	Then I have it in sight, haven't I?
SAG	If I had it at home, I'd promise it now; the only thing I have in my power is to do my best.

35

40

45

[6] The term *nummus* is inherently vague ("coin"), but if we assume that tetradrachmas are meant here, we reach an appropriate price; six hundred sesterces would certainly be too little.

TOX   quicquid erit, recipe te ad me.
         quaere tamen, ego item sedulo.

SAG   si quid erit, ⟨te fac⟩iam ut scias.

48 TOX   *** opsecro te resecroque, operam da hanc mihi
48ᵃ   fidelem.

SAG   ah! odio me enicas.

49 TOX   Amoris uitio, non meo, nunc tibi morologus fio.

50 SAG   at pol ego aps te concessero.

TOX   iamne abis? bene ambulato.
         sed recipe quam primum potes, caue fuas mi in quaes-
            tione.
         usque ero domi dum excoxero lenoni malam rem ali-
            quam.

I. ii: SATVRIO

SAT   ueterem atque antiquom quaestum maio⟨rum meum⟩
         seruo atque optineo et magna cum cura colo.

55   nam numquam quisquam meorum maiorum fuit
         quin parasitando pauerint uentris suos:
         pater, auos, proauos, abauos, atauos, tritauos
         quasi mures semper edere alienum cibum,
         neque edacitate eos quisquam poterat uincere,

60   atque is cognomentum erat uiris Capitonibus.
         unde ego hunc quaestum optineo et maiorum locum.
         nec quadrupulari me uolo, neque enim decet

47 quaere *P*, quaero *Ritschl* ⟨te fac⟩iam *Abraham*

48 *lacunam in initio uersu statuit Schoell* resecroque *T*, resecro *ceteri Palatini*

52 malam rem aliquam *T*, malam *B*, malum *CD*

53 mali *B*, malo *CD*, maiorum meum *Gruterus*

60 neque *P*, atque *Leo* duris *P*, uiris *Woytek*

61 hunc ego *Camerarius*

460

TOX Whatever happens, return to me. Still, look for it, and I'll do the same eagerly.

SAG If I have some, I'll let you know at once.

TOX *** I entreat and beseech you, work loyally on my behalf.

SAG Ah! You're killing me by being so tedious.

TOX It's through Love's fault, not my own, that I'm now talking such rubbish.

SAG Well, I'll get away from you.   50

TOX Are you leaving already? Have a good walk. But return as soon as you can, don't force me to look for you. I'll be at home throughout until I've cooked up some misfortune for the pimp.

Exit SAGARISTIO to the right. Exit TOXILUS into his house. Enter SATURIO from the right.

SAT I continue, keep, and cultivate the old and ancient profession of my ancestors with great care: never was there 55 one of my ancestors who didn't feed his belly by being a hanger-on. My father, grandfather, great-grandfather, great-great-grandfather,   great-great-great-grandfather, and great-great-great-great-grandfather always ate other people's food, like mice; no one could surpass them in voracity and these men had the nickname Mullets.[7] From 60 them I've taken over this profession and the position of my ancestors. I don't want to be a professional informer;[8]

---

[7] *Capito* was a cognomen, but there is also a pun: the *piscis capito*, a type of mullet, corresponds to the Greek *kestreus*, which is not only the name of a fish but also a nickname for a starveling or hanger-on.

[8] A *quadrupulator* is a professional who takes wrongdoers to court, where they have to pay four times as much as the damage they have caused (Paul. Fest. p. 309 Lindsay). Half of this is paid to the court, half to the informer.

	sine meo periclo ire aliena ereptum bona
	neque illi qui faciunt mihi placent. planen loquor?
65	nam publicae rei causa quiquomque id facit
	magis quam sui quaesti, animus induci potest
67	eum esse ciuem et fidelem et bonum.
67ᵃ	sed ***
68	si legerupam qui damnet, det in publicum
	dimidium; atque etiam in ea lege ascribier:
70	ubi quadrupulator quempiam iniexit manum,
	tantidem ille illi rursus iniciat manum,
	ut aequa parti prodeant ad trisuiros:
	si id fiat, ne isti faxim nusquam appareant
	qui hic albo rete aliena oppugnant bona.
75	sed sumne ego stultus qui rem curo publicam
	ubi sint magistratus quos curare oporteat?
	nunc huc intro ibo, uisam hesternas reliquias,
	quierintne recte necne, num infuerit febris,
	opertaen fuerint, ne quis obreptauerit.
80	sed aperiuntur aedes, remorandust gradus.

I. iii: TOXILVS. SATVRIO

	TOX	omnem rem inueni, ut sua sibi pecunia
		hodie illam faciat leno libertam suam.
		sed eccum parasitum quoius mihi auxilio est opus.
		simulabo quasi non uideam: ita alliciam uirum.
85		curate istic uos atque approperate ocius,

67ᵃ–68 sed si *B*, sed *CD*, sed *** / si *Brix*

---

9 As a formal summons to court.

10 The *tresuiri capitales* were responsible for administering justice, imprisoning suspects, and executing criminals.

462

it isn't right for me to carry off other people's property
without risk to myself, and I don't like people who do so.
Am I speaking clearly? Well, I can accept that a man who   65
does so in the public interest more than for his own profit
is a trustworthy and good citizen. But *** if anyone se-
cures the condemnation of a lawbreaker, let him give his
half of the profit into public ownership as well; and what's
more, to this law should be added what follows: when a   70
man bringing criminal accusations has laid his hand on
someone,[9] that other man should in turn lay his hand on
him for the same amount, so that they appear before the
Board of Three[10] in an equal position. If this is done, I bet
those people would disappear who ensnare other peo-
ple's possessions with a white net.[11] But aren't I stu-   75
pid? I'm concerning myself with the common good when
there are magistrates who should concern themselves
with that. Now I'll go in here and see whether yesterday's
leftovers have slept well or not, whether they've caught a
fever, and whether they've been covered, so that no one
could have approached them stealthily. But the door is   80
opening, I need to slow down my step.

Enter TOXILUS from his house.

TOX   I've come up with it all, how the pimp can make her his
freedwoman today at his own expense. But here's the
hanger-on whose help I need. I'll pretend not to see him:
this is how I'll get him interested. (*to servants within*)   85
You there, take care and hurry quickly so that I won't be

---

[11] The net is white because in Athens accusations were made public
on white noticeboards.

ne mihi morae sit quicquam ubi ego intro aduenero.
commisce mulsum, Struthea, calidam appara,
bene ut in scutris concaleat, et calamum inice.
iam pol ille hic aderit, credo, congerro meus.

90   SAT   me dicit, eugae!

TOX   lautum credo e balineis
iam hic affuturum.

SAT   ut ordine omnem rem tenet!

TOX   collyrae facite ut madeant et colyphia,
ne mihi incocta detis.

SAT   rem loquitur meram.
nihili sunt crudae nisi quas madidas gluttias;

95   tum nisi cremore crasso est ius collyricum
nihili est macrum illud epicrocum pellucidum:
quasi birreum esse ius decet collyricum.
nolo in uesicam quod eat, in uentrem uolo.

TOX   prope me hic nescioquis loquitur.

SAT   o mi Iuppiter,

100   terrestris te coepulonus compellat tuos.

TOX   o Saturio, opportune aduenisti mihi.

SAT   mendacium edepol dicis atque hau te decet:
nam Esurio uenio, non aduenio Saturio.

TOX   at edes, nam iam intus uentris fumant focula.

105   calefieri iussi reliquias.

---

87 Struthea *uocatiuum esse intellexit Scaliger* coluthequam *P*, colu-
theaque *ς*, calidam *Woytek*

97 iuream *uel* uiream *BC*, iureseam *D*, birreum *Woytek*

---

[12] Sweet flag was commonly used to flavor wine (see Cato, *Agr.*
105.2).

delayed when I come in. Strutheas, mix the honey-wine, prepare hot water, so that it gets really hot in the pans, and put in sweet flag.[12] That boon companion of mine will be here in a moment, I believe.

SAT (*aside*) He means me, hurray!   90

TOX (*into the house*) I believe he'll be here in a moment, freshly washed in the baths.

SAT (*aside*) How he knows everything from first to last!

TOX (*still into the house*) Make sure that the pasta and the meat are soft,[13] don't give them to me undercooked.

SAT (*aside*) He speaks nothing but the truth. They're useless raw if you can't gobble them up soft; and unless the pasta   95 broth consists of thick gruel, that thin, translucent garb[14] is worthless: pasta broth ought to be like a thick cloak. I don't want something that goes into the bladder, I want something that goes into the belly.

TOX Someone's talking close to me here.

SAT O my dear Jupiter, your earthly table companion is ad-   100 dressing you.[15]

TOX O Saturio, you've come to me in the nick of time.

SAT You're telling a lie and it isn't right of you: I'm coming as Starve-urio, not Sate-urio.

TOX Well, you shall eat: the belly-warmers are already steam-   ing inside. I've had the leftovers warmed up.   105

---

[13] *Collyrae* are a breadlike type of pasta; the *colyphia* are cuts of pork from the haunch.

[14] Saturio compares food with clothes. The *epicrocum* is saffron-colored (Paul. Fest. p. 72 Lindsay), but is mentioned here because it is thin; the *birrus* or *burrus* is a rough cloak with a hood.

[15] Jocular reference to the feast where Jupiter, together with his divine table companions Juno and Minerva, was presented with a meal.

	SAT	pernam quidem
		ius est apponi frigidam postridie.
	TOX	ita fieri iussi.
	SAT	ecquid hallecis?
	TOX	uah, rogas?
	SAT	sapis multum ad genium.
	TOX	sed ecquid meministin, heri
		qua de re ego tecum mentionem feceram?
110	SAT	memini: ut murena et conger ne calefierent;
		nam nimio melius oppectuntur frigida.
		sed quid cessamus proelium committere?
		dum mane est, omnis esse mortalis decet.
	TOX	nimis paene mane est.
	SAT	mane quod tu occeperis
115		negotium agere, id totum procedit diem.
	TOX	quaeso animum aduorte hoc. iam heri narraui tibi
		tecumque oraui ut nummos sescentos mihi
		dares utendos mutuos.
	SAT	memini et scio
		et te me orare et mihi non esse quod darem.
120		nihili parasitus est quoi argentum domi est:
		lubido extemplo coepere est conuiuium,
		tuburcinari de suo, si quid domi est.
		cynicum esse egentem oportet parasitum probe:
		ampullam, strigilem, scaphium, soccos, pallium,
125		marsuppium habeat, inibi paullum praesidi
		qui familiarem suam uitam oblectet modo.
	TOX	iam nolo argentum: filiam utendam tuam
		mihi da.

116 iam *B*, enim iam *CD*, enim *Woytek*
120 cui argentum domideste *B*, cui argentum domi idē *CD*, cui
argentum domi est *Pylades*, qui Argentumdonidast *Schoell*

SAT   But ham should rightfully be served cold the day after.

TOX   That's how I've had it done.

SAT   Is there any fish sauce?[16]

TOX   Bah, you even ask?

SAT   You know very well what's good for you.

TOX   But do you remember at all the matter I mentioned to you yesterday?

SAT   I do: that moray and eel shouldn't be warmed up because   110
they make much better picking cold. But why are we hesitating to commence the battle? While it's early all men should eat.

TOX   It's almost too early.

SAT   A business you begin early proceeds well all day long.   115

TOX   Please pay attention to this. I already told and asked you yesterday to give me six hundred tetradrachmas on loan.

SAT   I remember and know that you asked me and that I didn't have anything to give you. A hanger-on who has money at   120
home is worthless. He's immediately keen to start a banquet, to stuff himself from his own money, if he has any at home. A hanger-on jolly well ought to be a poor Cynic;[17]
he should have a flask, a scraper, a bowl, flat shoes, a cloak, and a wallet, and in it a little support to sustain his   125
own life only.

TOX   I don't want your money anymore; give me your daughter on loan.

---

[16] Pliny the Elder (*Nat. Hist.* 31.93–95) describes how *hallec* is produced. Guts of fish and other refuse are mixed with salt and fermented. The liquid is *garum*; the sediment is *hallec*.

[17] The Cynic school of philosophy, founded by Diogenes of Sinope, aimed at freeing man from unnecessary desires. Cynics were often proverbially poor, like the hangers-on of comedy; but unlike hangers-on the Cynics tried to be self-sufficient.

SAT   numquam edepol quoiquam etiam utendam dedi.

TOX   non ad istuc quod tu insimulas.

SAT   quid eam uis?

TOX   scies.

130   quia forma lepida et liberali est.

SAT   res ita est.

TOX   hic leno nec te nouit nec gnatam tuam?

SAT   me ut quisquam norit nisi ille qui praebet cibum?

TOX   ita est. hoc tu mi reperire argentum potes.

SAT   cupio hercle.

TOX   tum tu me sine illam uendere.

135 SAT   tun illam uendas?

TOX   immo alium allegauero

qui uendat, qui esse se peregrinum praedicet.

sic ut istic leno non sex menses Megaribus

huc est quom commigrauit.

SAT   pereunt reliquiae.

posterius istuc tamen potest.

TOX   scin quam potest?

140   numquam hercle hodie hic prius edes, ne frustra sis,

quam te hoc facturum quod rogo affirmas mihi;

atque nisi gnatam tecum huc iam quantum potest

adducis, exigam hercle ego te ex hac decuria.

quid nunc?

SAT   quid est?

TOX   quin dicis quid facturus sis?

145 SAT   quaeso hercle me quoque etiam uende, si lubet,

dum saturum uendas.

TOX   hoc, si facturu's, face.

140 sedis *P*, edis ς, edes *Bothe*

144 quid est *Saturioni dedit Seyffert*

SAT   I've never given her on loan to anyone yet.

TOX   Not for what you are insinuating.

SAT   What do you want her for?

TOX   You'll find out. Because she has the lovely looks of a free- 130
born girl.

SAT   That's true.

TOX   The pimp here knows neither you nor your daughter?

SAT   Would anyone know me unless he gives me food?

TOX   Yes. That's how you can find money for me.

SAT   I'm eager.

TOX   Then let me sell her.

SAT   You are to sell her? 135

TOX   No, I'll engage someone else to sell her, someone who
should claim to be a foreigner. You see, it's not yet six
months since that pimp moved here from Megara.[18]

SAT   The leftovers are going bad. Your business can be at-
tended to later on just as well.

TOX   Do you know how it can be attended to? Don't fool your- 140
self, you'll never eat here today until you confirm that
you'll do for me what I ask of you. And unless you bring
your daughter here with you as quickly as possible, I'll
throw you out of our gang. Well then?

SAT   What is it?

TOX   Why don't you say what you're going to do?

SAT   Please sell me as well if you wish, so long as you sell me 145
with a full belly.

TOX   If you're going to do this, do it.

---

[18] City to the west of Athens.

SAT faciam equidem quae uis.

TOX   bene facis. propera, abi domum;
praemonstra docte, praecipe astu filiae,
quid fabuletur: ubi se natam praedicet,

150   qui sibi parentes fuerint, und' surrupta sit.
sed longe ab Athenis esse se gnatam autumet;
et ut affleat quom ea memoret.

SAT   etiam tu taces?
ter tanto peior ipsa est quam illam tu esse uis.

TOX lepide hercle dicis. sed scin quid facias? cape

155   tunicam atque zonam, et chlamydem afferto et causeam
quam ille habeat qui hanc lenoni huic uendat—

SAT   eu, probe!

TOX —quasi sit peregrinus.

SAT   laudo.

TOX   et tu gnatam tuam
ornatam adduce lepide in peregrinum modum.

SAT πόθεν ornamenta?

TOX   aps chorago sumito;

160   dare debet: praebenda aediles locauerunt.

SAT iam faxo hic aderunt. sed ego nihil horunc scio.

TOX nihil hercle uero. nam ubi ego argentum accepero,
continuo tu illam a lenone asserito manu.

SAT sibi habeat, si non extemplo ab eo abduxero.

165 TOX abi et istuc cura. interibi ego puerum uolo
mittere ad amicam meam, ut habeat animum bonum
me esse effecturum hodie. nimis longum loquor.

---

[19] Officials supervising buildings and markets, but also games.

SAT I'll do what you want.

TOX Thank you. Hurry up, go home. Instruct your daughter cleverly, teach her smartly what story she should tell: where she should say she was born, who her parents 150 were, what country she was abducted from. But she should say she was born far away from Athens; and she should accompany her words with tears.

SAT Won't you be quiet? She's three times worse on her own than you want her to be.

TOX I'm delighted to hear it. But do you know what you should do? Take a tunic and a belt, and bring a travel 155 cloak and a hat which the man who sells her to the pimp should have—

SAT (*interrupting*) Excellent, splendid!

TOX —as if he were a foreigner.

SAT I praise you.

TOX And you, bring your daughter nicely dressed up in foreign style.

SAT Where should the getup come from?

TOX Take it from the stage manager. He has to give it to you: 160 the aediles[19] have contracted to have it provided.

SAT I'll have it here at once. But I don't understand what all this is about.

TOX No, you don't; when I have received the money, you are to claim her from the pimp as free without delay.

SAT He can have her for himself if I don't take her away from him at once.

TOX Go away and take care of that. In the meantime I want to 165 send a boy to my girlfriend, so that she may be confident that I'll succeed today. I've been talking for far too long.

Exit SATURIO to the left. Exit TOXILUS into his house.

471

PLAUTUS

ACTVS II

II. i: SOPHOCLIDISCA

	SOPH	satis fuit indoctae, immemori, insipienti dicere totiens.
		nimis tandem me quidem pro barda et pro rustica reor
		habitam esse aps te.
170		quamquam ego uinum bibo, at mandata
170ᵃ		non consueui simul bibere una.
171		me quidem iam satis tibi spectatam
171ᵃ		censebam esse et meos mores.
172		nam equidem te iam sector quintum hunc annum, quom interea, credo,
		ouis si in ludum iret, potuisset iam fieri ut probe litteras sciret,
		quom interim tu meum ingenium fans atque infans nondum etiam edidicisti.
175		potin ut taceas? potin ne moneas?
		memini et scio et calleo et commemini.
		amas pol misera: id tuos scatet animus.
		ego istuc pelagus tibi ut sit faciam.
		miser est qui amat. certo is quidem nihili est
180		qui nil amat: quid ei homini opus uita est?
		ire decet me, ut erae opsequens fiam, libera ea opera ocius ut sit.
182		conueniam hunc Toxilum: eius auris,
182ᵃ		quae mandata sunt, onerabo.

II. ii: TOXILVS. PAEGNIVM. SOPHOCLIDISCA

183	TOX	satin haec tibi sunt plana et certa? satin haec meministi et tenes?

178 pelagus *A*, placidum *P*
181 l(ib)era ea *A*, liberam ea *P*, libera mea *FZ*

472

ACT TWO

Enter SOPHOCLIDISCA from the house of Dordalus, carrying a letter.

SOPH (*into the house*) It would have been enough for a fat-witted, forgetful, foolish girl to be told that so often. I think I've been treated too much like an idiot and a country yokel by you. Even though I do drink wine, it isn't my 170 custom to drink down your commands at the same time. I thought that I and my ways had been tested enough by you already: I've been following you for five years now, during which time I believe a sheep would have come to know the alphabet properly if it went to school, while you, human or animal, have still not learned my nature. Can't you be quiet? Can't you stop admonishing me? I re- 175 member, I know, I understand, I keep it in mind. You're in love, poor you: that's what your heart is flowing over from. I'll turn this into the calm sea for you. (*to the audience*) Wretched is the man who is in love. But surely the man who doesn't love at all is worthless. What does such a 180 man need life for? I ought to go in order to show myself obedient to my mistress, so that she may be free more quickly through my collaboration. I'll meet Toxilus here. I'll load up his ears with the commands that I've received. (*walks toward the house of Toxilus*)

Enter TOXILUS from his house, followed by PAEGNIUM, who is carrying a letter; they do not see SOPHOCLIDISCA yet.

TOX Is this sufficiently plain and clear to you? Do you remember and understand this sufficiently?

	PAE	melius quam tu qui docuisti.
	TOX	ain uero, uerbereum caput?
185	PAE	aio enim uero.
	TOX	quid ergo dixi?
	PAE	ego recte apud illam dixero.
	TOX	non edepol scis.
	PAE	da hercle pignus, ni omnia memini et scio,
		et quidem si scis tute quot hodie habeas digitos in manu.
	TOX	egon dem pignus tecum?
	PAE	audacter, si lubido est perdere.
	TOX	bona pax sit potius.
	PAE	tum tu igitur sine me ire.
	TOX	et iubeo et sino.
190		sed ita uolo te currere ut domi sis, quom ego te [esse] illi
		censeam.
191	PAE	faciam.
	TOX	quo ergo is nunc?
	PAE	domum: ut
191ᵃ		domi sim, quom illi censeas.
192	TOX	scelus tu pueri es atque ob istanc rem e-
192ᵃ		go aliqui te peculiabo.
193	PAE	scio fide hercle erili ut soleat
193ᵃ		impudicitia opprobrari
194		nec subigi queantur umquam ut
194ᵃ		pro ea fide habeant iudicem.
195	TOX	abi modo.
	PAE	ego laudabis faxo.
	TOX	sed has tabellas, Paegnium,
196		ipsi Lemniseleni fac des
196ᵃ		et quae iussi nuntiato.

190 esse *del. Kellermann*

474

PAE	Better than you, who taught me.
TOX	Do you say so, you beat-head?
PAE	I do say so indeed.

185

TOX	Then what did I say?
PAE	I'll say it all right at her place.
TOX	You don't know it.
PAE	Make a bet that I don't remember and know everything, and furthermore that you know how many fingers you have on your hand today.
TOX	I should bet against you?
PAE	Boldly, if you're keen on losing.
TOX	Let's have true peace instead.
PAE	Then let me go.
TOX	I order you and let you. But I want you to run so fast that you're already at home when I think you're still there.

190

PAE	I'll do so. (*turns back to his house*)
TOX	Then where are you going now?
PAE	Home, so that I'm at home when you think I'm there.
TOX	You're a rascal of a boy and that's why I'll give you some present[20] today.
PAE	I know how a master's promise tends to be reproached with shamelessness and how they can never be forced to submit to judgment concerning that promise.
TOX	Just go.

195

PAE	I'll make sure you'll praise me.
TOX	But do give these tablets to Lemniselenis in person, Paegnium, and tell her what I told you.

[20] Either something obscene (cf. *Pseud*. 1188) or a beating.

475

197	SOPH	cesso ire ego quo missa sum.
	PAE	eo ego.
	TOX	i sane. ego domum ibo. face rem hanc cum cura geras.
		uola curriculo.
	PAE	istuc marinus passer per circum solet.
200		illic hinc abiit intro huc. sed quis haec est quae me aduor-
		sum incedit?
	SOPH	Paegnium hicquidem est.
	PAE	Sophoclidisca haec peculiarest eius
		quo ego sum missus.
	SOPH	nullus esse hodie hoc puero peior perhibetur.
	PAE	compellabo.
	SOPH	commorandust.
	PAE	‹standum est› apud hanc obicem.
	SOPH	Paegnium, deliciae pueri, salue. quid agis? ut uales?
205	PAE	Sophoclidisca, di . . . me amabunt.
	SOPH	quid me?
	PAE	utrum hercle ‹illis lubet›;
		sed si ut digna es faciant, odio hercle habeant et faciant
		male.
	SOPH	mitte male loqui.
	PAE	quom ut digna es dico, bene, non male loquor.
	SOPH	quid agis?
	PAE	feminam scelestam [te] astans contra contuor.
	SOPH	certe equidem puerum peiorem quam te noui neminem.
210	PAE	quid male facio aut quoi male dico?
	SOPH	quoi pol quomque occasio est.

200 abiit hinc *P, transp. Ritschl*
203 compellabo *Paegnio tribuit Leo* standumst *add. Leo* obieci *P,*
obicem *Valla*   205 illis lubet *add. Lindsay*
208 te *del. Woytek*

SOPH (*to the audience*) I'm delaying to go where I've been sent.

PAE I'm going.

TOX Do go. I shall go home. Do carry this out carefully. Fly running.

PAE That's what an ostrich does in the circus.

Exit TOXILUS into his house.

PAE He's gone in here. But who is that woman who is coming 200 toward me?

SOPH This is Paegnium.

PAE This is Sophoclidisca, the personal slave of the woman I've been sent to.

SOPH It's said that no one is worse than this boy at this time.

PAE I'll address her.

SOPH I need to make him wait. (*positions herself in front of him*)

PAE I need to stop at this barrier.

SOPH Paegnium, you darling of a boy, my greetings to you. What are you up to? How are you?

PAE Sophoclidisca, may the gods love . . . me.   205

SOPH How about me?

PAE Whichever they like; but if they were to act as you deserve, they'd hate and harm you.

SOPH Stop talking badly about me.

PAE Since I'm talking about you as you deserve, I'm talking well, not badly.

SOPH What are you up to?

PAE I'm looking at a bad woman, standing opposite her.

SOPH I certainly don't know any boy worse than you.

PAE What am I doing badly or who am I talking about badly?   210

SOPH About anyone you get a chance to.

477

	PAE	nemo homo umquam ita arbitratust.
	SOPH	at pol multi esse ita sciunt.
	PAE	heia!
	SOPH	beia!
	PAE	tuo ex ingenio mores alienos probas.
	SOPH	fateor ego profecto me esse ut decet lenonis familiae.
	PAE	satis iam dictum habeo.
	SOPH	sed quid tu? confitere ut te autumo?
215	PAE	fatear, si ita sim.
	SOPH	iam abi, uicisti.
	PAE	abi nunciam ergo.
	SOPH	hoc mi expedi, quo agis?
	PAE	quo tu?
	SOPH	dic tu. prior rogaui.
	PAE	at post‹erior› scies.
	SOPH	eo ego hinc hau longe.
	PAE	et quidem ego hau longe.
	SOPH	quo ergo ‹tu is›, scelus?
	PAE	nisi sciero prius ex te, tu ex me numquam hoc quod rogitas scies.
	SOPH	numquam ecastor hodie scibis prius quam ex ted audiuero.
220	PAE	itane est?
	SOPH	itane est.
	PAE	mala es.
	SOPH	scelestu's.
	PAE	decet me.
	SOPH	me quidem addecet.

216 post‹erior› *Acidalius*   217 tu is *add. Ussing*
220 haud decet *P*, addecet *Bothe*

478

PAE No one's ever thought of me like this.

SOPH But many know that it is like this.

PAE Oh tush!

SOPH Oh slush!

PAE You judge other people's ways from your own nature.

SOPH I do indeed admit that I am the way that a member of a
      pimp's household should be.

PAE You've said enough, I've got it.

SOPH But what about you? Do you admit that you're the way I
      claim?

PAE I'd admit it if I were.   215

SOPH Go away now, you've won.

PAE Then go away now.

SOPH Tell me, where are you going?

PAE Where are *you* going?

SOPH You tell me. I asked earlier.

PAE But you'll find out later.

SOPH I'm going somewhere not far from here.

PAE I too am off to somewhere not far from here.

SOPH Then where are you going, you rogue?

PAE Unless I learn it from you first, you'll never learn from me
      what you ask.

SOPH You'll never know it today until I hear it from you.

PAE Really?   220

SOPH Really.

PAE You're bad.

SOPH You're evil.

PAE That's appropriate for me.

SOPH And for me it's very appropriate.

	PAE	quid ais? certum⟨ne⟩ est celare quo iter facias, pessuma?
	SOPH	offirmasti⟨n⟩ occultare quo te immittas, pessume?
	PAE	par pari respondes dicto.
	SOPH	abi iam, quando ita certa rest.
	PAE	nihili facio scire. ualeas.
	SOPH	asta.
	PAE	at propero.
	SOPH	et pol ego item.
225	PAE	ecquid habes?
	SOPH	ecquid tu?
	PAE	nil equidem.
	SOPH	cedo manum ergo.
	PAE	estne haec manus?
	SOPH	ubi illa altera est furtifica laeua?
	PAE	domi eccam. huc nullam attuli.
	SOPH	habes nescioquid.
	PAE	ne me attrecta, subigitatrix.
	SOPH	sin te amo?
	PAE	male operam locas.
	SOPH	qui?
	PAE	quia enim nihil amas quom ingratum amas.
		temperi hanc uigilare oportet formulam atque aetatu-
		lam,
230		ne, ubi [capillus] uorsipellis fias, foede semper seruias.
	SOPH	tuquidem haud etiam es octoginta pondo.

221 certum⟨ne⟩ *Camerarius*
222 offirmasti⟨n⟩ *Camerarius*
223 abi . . . rest *Sophoclidiscae dat Woytek (propter spatium ante*
abi *in* P)
229–30 *uersus dat Sophoclidiscae* P, Paegnio *Woytek*
230 [capillus] uersipellis *Bothe*, uersicapillus *Ritschl*

480

PAE   Well then? Are you resolved to conceal where you're go-
      ing, you most vile of all women?

SOPH Have you decided to hide where you're off to, you worst
      of all boys?

PAE   You're giving me tit for tat.

SOPH Go now, since this is your decision.

PAE   I don't care to know. Goodbye. (*moves away*)

SOPH Stand where you are. (*grabs him*)

PAE   But I'm in a rush.

SOPH So am I.

PAE   Do you have anything?   225

SOPH Do *you*?

PAE   No, nothing.

SOPH Then give me your hand.

PAE   Isn't this a hand? (*stretches out his right hand, holding
      the letter in his left behind his back*)

SOPH Where's the other one, the thieving left?

PAE   At home, look. I didn't bring it here at all.

SOPH You do have something. (*begins to search him*)

PAE   Stop fondling me, you groper.

SOPH What if I'm in love with you?

PAE   You're wasting your effort.

SOPH How so?

PAE   Because your love is in vain when you're in love with
      someone who doesn't requite it. (*pointing at himself*)
      This youthful beauty needs to be on its guard early, so   230
      that you won't disgracefully be a slave forever when your
      looks change.

SOPH You aren't even eighty pounds yet.

PAE   at confidentia
           illa militia militatur multo magis quam pondere.
           atque ego hanc operam perdo.

SOPH   quid iam?

PAE   quia peritae praedico.
           sed ego cesso.

SOPH   mane.

PAE   molesta es.

SOPH   ergo ‹ero› quoque, nisi scio

235   quo agas te.

PAE   ad uos.

SOPH   et pol ego ad uos.

PAE   quid eo?

SOPH   quid id ad te attinet?

PAE   enim non ibis nunc, uicissim nisi scio.

SOPH   odiosu's.

PAE   lubet.

SOPH   numquam hercle istuc exterebrabis.

PAE   tu ut sis peior quam ego siem?

SOPH   malitia certare tecum miseria est.

PAE   merx tu mala es.
           quid est quod metuas?

SOPH   idem istuc quod tu.

PAE   dic ergo.

‹SOPH   edictum est mihi›

240   ne hoc quoiquam homini dicerem, omnes muti ut loque-
            rentur prius.

PAE   edictum est magno opere mihi, ne quoiquam hoc homini
            crederem,
           omnes muti ut ‹e›loquerentur prius hoc quam ego.

234 ero *add. Bothe*

PAE	But that fight is fought with self-confidence much more than weight. But I'm wasting this effort of mine.
SOPH	What do you mean?
PAE	Because I'm telling a woman who knows all about it. But I'm wasting my time. (*tries to move away again*)
SOPH	Wait. (*grabs him*)
PAE	You're being a nuisance.
SOPH	And I'll continue to be one unless you tell me where you're going.
PAE	To your place.
SOPH	And I to your place.
PAE	Why there?
SOPH	Why is this any of your business?
PAE	You won't go now, unless I know in turn. (*grabs her*)
SOPH	You're annoying.
PAE	I enjoy it.
SOPH	You'll never drill it out of me.
PAE	Would you be even worse than me?
SOPH	Competing with you in wickedness is a wretched business.
PAE	You're a bad piece. What is it that you're afraid of?
SOPH	The same as you.
PAE	Then tell me.
SOPH	I was ordered not to tell anyone about this, so that all the dumb should speak before I do.
PAE	And I was ordered explicitly not to entrust this to anyone, so that all the dumb should say it before I do.

235 (at line "And I'll continue to be one unless you tell me where")
240 (at line "I was ordered not to tell anyone about this, so that all the")

---

237 *totum uersum Paegnio dat* P, *prius hemistichium Sophoclidis-cae tribuit Woytek*   239 tu more n T *in fine verso* (*unde* tu: mora *Lindsay*) *finem uersus suppl. Ritschl*   240 dicerem T, edicerem *ceteri Palatini*   242 ‹e›loquerentur *Müller*

SOPH   at tu hoc face:
       fide data credamus.

PAE   noui: omnes sunt lenae leuifidae,
       nec tippulae leuius pondust quam fides lenonia.

245 SOPH dic amabo.

PAE   dic amabo.

SOPH   nolo ames.

PAE   facile impetras.

SOPH tecum habeto.

PAE   et tu hoc taceto.

SOPH   tacitum erit.

PAE   celabitur.

SOPH Toxilo has fero tabellas tuo ero.

PAE   abi, eccillum domi.
       at ego hanc ad Lemniselenem tuam eram opsignatam
          abietem.

SOPH quid istic scriptum?

PAE   iuxta tecum, si tu nescis, nescio;

250   nisi fortasse blanda uerba.

SOPH   abeo.

PAE   et ego abiero.

SOPH   ambula.

II. iii: SAGARISTIO

SAG   Ioui opulento, incluto, Ope gnato,
      supremo, ualido, uiripotenti,
      opes, spes bonas, copias commodanti
      *** lubens uitulorque merito,

---

254 *sic lacuna non indicata* P (A *paene legi non potest sed lacuna
ante* Q *magna fuisse uidetur*)

SOPH But you should do this: let's give each other a promise
and entrust it to the other.

PAE I know: all procuresses are untrustworthy, and a water
spider has more weight than a procuress's promise.

SOPH Tell me, there's a dear.   245

PAE Tell me, there's a dear.

SOPH I don't want to be your dear.

PAE You succeed easily.

SOPH Keep it secret.

PAE And you, be silent about it.

SOPH Silence will surround it.

PAE It will be concealed.

SOPH I'm bringing these tablets to your master Toxilus.

PAE Go, he's at home, look. And I am bringing this sealed fir-
wood tablet to your mistress Lemniselenis.

SOPH What's written there?

PAE If you don't know it, I don't know it any more than you;
but perhaps flattering words.   250

SOPH I'm off.

PAE And I'll be off.

SOPH On your way!

*Exit PAEGNIUM into the pimp's house. Exit SOPHOCLI-
DISCA into the house of Toxilus.*
*Enter SAGARISTIO from the right, with a wallet around his
neck.*

SAG To opulent, glorious Jupiter, son of Ops,[21] the highest,
strong, powerful one providing me with wealth, good
hopes, supplies *** I happily * and sing a song of joy de-

---

[21] Wife of Saturn and goddess of abundance.

255 quia meo amico amiciter hanc commoditatis copiam
danunt, argenti mutui ut ‹ei› egenti opem afferam;
quod ego non magis somniabam neque opinabar nec
censebam,
eam fore mihi occasionem, ea nunc quasi decidit de
caelo.
nam erus meus me Eretriam misit, domitos boues ut sibi
mercarer,
260 dedit argentum, nam ibi mercatum dixit ess' die septumi;
stultus, qui hoc mi daret argentum, quoius ingenium
nouerat.
nam hoc argentum alibi abutar: "boues quos emerem
non erant."
nunc et amico prosperabo et genio meo multa bona fa-
ciam,
diu quo bene erit, die uno apsoluam: tuxtax tergo erit
meo. non curo.
265 nunc amico homini hibus domitis mea ex crumina largiar.
nam id demum lepidum est, triparcos homines, uetulos,
auidos, ardos
bene ammordere, qui salinum seruo opsignant cum sale.
268 uirtus est, ubi occasio
268ᵃ ammonet, dispicere. quid faciet mihi?
269 uerberibus caedi iusserit, compedis impingi. uapulet,
270 ne sibi me credat supplicem fore: uae illi! nil iam mi noui
271 offerre potest quin sim peritus. sed ‹quis hinc exit?›
Toxili
271ᵃ puerum Paegnium eccum.

256 uti egenti *A*, ut legenti *P*, ut ei egenti *Weise*
265 homini bibus *A*, hominibus *P*, homini hibus *Sonnenschein*
271 *lacunam post* sed *indicat Leo supplens* quis hinc exit

servedly, because they give my friend this supply of suc-   255
cess in a friendly way, namely that I can bring him plenty
of money on loan when he's in need. What I didn't dream
of, think of, or believe in, that I would have this opportu-
nity, this has now, as it were, fallen down from heaven:
my master has sent me to Eretria[22] to purchase plow oxen
for him; he gave me the money, because he said there   260
would be a market there a week from now. It was stu-
pid of him to give me this money since he knew my ways;
I'll use this money up elsewhere: "There were no oxen
for me to buy." Now I'll support my friend and do my-
self many good turns. In a single day I'll use up what
will make me happy for a long time. It'll be swish-swash
for my back. I don't care. Now I'll present my friend   265
with these plow animals from my wallet: this is lovely
indeed, to fleece overstingy, elderly, greedy, tightfisted
men properly, who seal up the salt in the saltcellar to stop
the slaves getting it.[23] It's a virtue to see clearly when the
occasion reminds you to. What will he do to me? He'll
have me beaten with blows and have shackles put onto
me. Let him get a beating, so he won't believe I'm going   270
to entreat him: bad luck to him! He can't bring me any-
thing new any longer, anything I haven't experienced.
But who is coming out from here? Look, it's Paegnium,
Toxilus' slave boy.

Enter PAEGNIUM from the pimp's house, running past
SAGARISTIO.

[22] City on Euboea, an island famous for its cattle.
[23] Salt was proverbially cheap, so the action characterizes the miser.

II. iv: PAEGNIVM. SAGARISTIO

PAE pensum meum quod datum est confeci. nunc domum
  propero.
SAG mane, etsi properas.
  Paegnium, ausculta.
PAE emere oportet, quem tibi oboedire uelis.
SAG asta.
PAE exhibeas molestiam, ut opinor, si quid debeam,
275 qui nunc sic tamen es molestus.
SAG scelerate, etiam respicis?
PAE scio ego quid sim aetatis, eo istuc maledictum impune
  auferes.
277 SAG ubi Toxilust tuos erus?
277ᵃ PAE ubi illi lubet, nec
277ᵇ te consulit.
SAG etiam
278 dicis ubi sit, uenefice?
PAE nescio, inquam, ulmitriba tu.
280 SAG male dicis maiori.
PAE prior promeritus perpetiare.
280ᵃ seruam operam, linguam liberam erus iussit med habere.
281 SAG dicisne mi ubi sit Toxilus?
PAE dico . . . ut perpetuo pereas.
SAG caedere hodie tu restibus.
PAE tua quidem, cucule, causa!
  non hercle, si os perciderim tibi, metuam, morticine.
SAG uideo ego te: iam incubitatus es.
PAE ita sum. quid id [attinet] ad te, ‹fatue›?
285 at non sum, ita ut tu, gratiis.
SAG confidens.

284 attinet *del.* Seyffert fatue *add.* Leo

PAE (*to the audience*) I've done the workload given to me.
     Now I'm in a rush to get home.

SAG Wait, even if you're in a rush. Paegnium, listen.

PAE If you want someone to obey you, you ought to buy him.

SAG Stand where you are.

PAE I believe you'd be a real nuisance if I owed you anything,
     since you are annoying enough even now.   275

SAG You criminal, will you look back?

PAE (*turning round*) I know what age I am, that's why you'll
     get away with your abuse unpunished.

SAG Where's your master Toxilus?

PAE Where he likes, and he doesn't ask for your advice.

SAG Will you tell me where he is, you poisoner?

PAE I don't know, I tell you, you elm-exhauster.

SAG You're abusing someone older than yourself.   280

PAE Put up with it, you started it. My master told me to have a
     slave's work, but a freeman's tongue.

SAG Won't you tell me where Toxilus is?

PAE I tell you . . . to perish completely.

SAG You'll be beaten with ropes today.

PAE Because of you, you cuckoo! I wouldn't be afraid if I
     broke into your mouth[24] today, you cadaver.

SAG I can see you: you've already been covered like an egg.

PAE I have. What business of yours is it, idiot? But unlike you 285
     I haven't been covered for nothing.

SAG You're self-confident.

[24] Double entendre: he speaks of beating him as well as forcing him
to be the passive partner in oral sex.

PAE   sum hercle uero.
       nam ego me confido liberum fore, tu te numquam spe-
           ras.

SAG   potin ut molestus ne sies?

PAE   quod dicis facere non quis.

SAG   abi in malam rem.

PAE   at tu domum: nam ibi tibi parata praesto est.

SAG   uadatur hic me.

PAE   utinam uades desint, in carcere ut sis.

290 SAG   quid hoc?

PAE   quid est?

SAG   etiam, scelus, male loquere?

PAE   tandem ut liceat,
       quom seruos sis, seruom tibi male dicere.

SAG   itane? specta
       quid dedero.

PAE   nil, nam nil habes.

SAG   di deaeque me omnes perdant—

PAE   amicus sum, eueniant uolo tibi quae optas.

SAG   atque id fiat,
       nisi te hodie, si prehendero, defigam in terram colaphis.

295 PAE   tun me defigas? te cruci ipsum affigent propediem alii.

SAG   qui te di deaeque—scis quid hinc porro dicturus fuerim,
       ni linguae moderari queam. potin abeas?

PAE   abigis facile.
       nam umbra mea hic intus uapulat.

---

[25] If he is late, he will be beaten; now he is late and his shadow is already suffering, while he himself will suffer soon.

PAE I am indeed: I'm confident I'll be free; you can never hope to be so.

SAG Can you stop being a nuisance?

PAE You can't do what you're telling me to do.

SAG Go and be tortured.

PAE But you, go home: there torture is prepared and ready for you.

SAG He lets me go away on bail.

PAE I hope you won't have people to bail you out, so that you'll be in prison.

SAG What's this? 290

PAE What's what?

SAG Are you still abusing me, you thug?

PAE Since you're a slave, at least a slave should be allowed to abuse you.

SAG Really? Watch what I'll give you. (*clenches his fist*)

PAE Nothing, because you don't have anything.

SAG May all the gods and goddesses ruin me—

PAE (*interrupting*) I'm your friend, I want your wishes to come true.

SAG And may that happen to me, unless I plant you in the ground with my blows if I get hold of you today.

PAE You would plant me? Others will plant you on the cross 295 soon.

SAG May the gods and goddesses—you know what I'd have said further, if I couldn't control my tongue. Can't you go away?

PAE You'll drive me off easily: my shadow is getting a beating in here.[25]

Exit PAEGNIUM into the house of Toxilus.

SAG   ut istunc di deaeque perdant!
        tamquam proserpens bestia est bilinguis et scelestus.
300   hercle illum abiisse gaudeo. foris aperit, eccere autem
        quem conuenire maxume cupiebam egreditur intus.

     II. V: TOXILVS. SOPHOCLIDISCA. SAGARISTIO

TOX   paratum iam esse dicito unde argentum sit futurum,
        iubeto habere animum bonum, dic me illam amare mul-
           tum;
        ubi se adiuuat, ibi me adiuuat. quae dixi ut nuntiares,
305   satin ea tenes?
SOPH   magis calleo quam aprugnum callum callet.
TOX   propera, abi domum.
SAG   nunc huic ego graphice facetus fiam.
        subnixis alis me inferam atque amicibor gloriose.
TOX   sed quis hic ansatus ambulat?
SAG   magnufice conscreabor.
TOX   Sagaristio hicquidem est. quid agitur, Sagaristio? ut uale-
           tur?
310   ecquid, quod mandaui tibi, estne in te speculae?
SAG   adito.
        uidebitur. factum uolo. uenito. promoneto.
TOX   quid hoc hic in collo tibi tumet?
SAG   uomica est, pressare parce;
        nam ubi qui mala tangit manu, dolores cooriuntur.
TOX   quando istaec innata est tibi?

    300 illum *P*, istum *A*
    310 estne in te speculae Ω, in te speculae est *Ritschl*

---

[26] Lit. "I am thicker than a pig's skin," because *callere* means both
"to be thick" and "to be clever," whereas English *thick* means "stupid."

SAG   May the gods and goddesses ruin him! Like a snake he is
evil and has a two-forked tongue. I'm really glad he's left.   300
The door is opening, and look, the man I wanted to meet
most is coming out.

*Enter TOXILUS and SOPHOCLIDISCA from the former's
house.*

TOX   (*to Sophoclidisca*) Tell her that the source of the money
has already been created, tell her to take heart, tell her
that I love her a lot. When she's helping herself, she's
helping me. Have you understood well enough what I   305
told you to report to her?

SOPH   I'm not as thick as pig's skin.[26]

TOX   Hurry up, go home.

Exit SOPHOCLIDISCA into the pimp's house.

SAG   (*aside*) Now I'll become charmingly witty for him. I'll
strut around with arms akimbo and throw my cloak
around myself in a pompous way. (*does so*)

TOX   Well, who is walking here with handles?

SAG   (*aside*) I'll clear my throat in a grand way.

TOX   It's Sagaristio. How are you, Sagaristio? How are you do-
ing? Is there any hope in you concerning my commission   310
to you?

SAG   Approach. It shall be seen to. I want it done. Come. Re-
mind me.

TOX   (*noticing the wallet under the cloak*) What's this swelling
here on your neck?

SAG   It's an abscess, don't press it; it's very painful when some-
one touches it with a rough hand.

TOX   When did you get it?

SAG   hodie.

TOX   secari iubeas.

315 SAG   metuo ne immaturam secem, ne exhibeat plus negoti.

TOX   inspicere morbum tuom lubet.

SAG   ah ah! abi atque caue sis
a cornu.

TOX   quid iam?

SAG   quia boues bimi hic sunt in crumina.

TOX   emitte sodes, ne enices fame; sine ire pastum.

SAG   enim metuo ut possim reicere in bubile, ne uagentur.

320 TOX   ego reiciam. habe animum bonum.

SAG   credetur, commodabo.
sequere hac sis. argentum hic inest quod mecum dudum
orasti.

TOX   quid tu ais?

SAG   dominus me boues mercatum Eretriam misit.
nunc mi Eretria erit haec tua domus.

TOX   nimis tu facete loquere.
atque ego omne argentum tibi hoc actutum incolume re-
digam;

325   nam iam omnis sycophantias instruxi et comparaui
quo pacto ab lenone auferam hoc argentum—

SAG   tanto melior.

TOX   —et mulier ut sit libera atque ipse ultro det argentum.
sed sequere me: ad eam rem usus est tua mihi opera.

SAG   utere ut uis.

317 bini Ω, bimi *Primmer*
319 in bubile(m) reicere Ω, *transp. Bothe*

SAG Today.

TOX You should have it removed.

SAG I'm afraid to remove it too early, or it could create more 315
trouble.

TOX I'd like to have a closer look at your illness. (*touches the
swelling*)

SAG Ouch! Ouch! Go away and beware of the horn, please.

TOX What do you mean?

SAG There are two-year-old oxen here in the wallet. (*removes
it from his neck*)

TOX Do let them out so that you won't starve them to death.
Let them go to feed.

SAG But I'm afraid that I might not be able to drive them back
to their stable and that they might wander off.

TOX I'll drive them back. Take heart. 320

SAG I'll trust you and oblige you. Do follow me this way. The
money you asked me for a while ago is in here. (*hands
over the wallet*)

TOX What are you saying?

SAG My master has sent me to Eretria to buy oxen. Now my
Eretria will be this house of yours.

TOX You're speaking ever so charmingly. And I shall return all
this money to you at once; I've already set up and pre- 325
pared all the tricks by which I can take this money away
from the pimp—

SAG (*interrupting*) All the better of you.

TOX —and how my lady can be free and he himself can volun-
teer to give the money. But follow me: I need your help
for this.

SAG Employ me as you wish.

Exeunt TOXILUS and SAGARISTIO into the former's house.

495

ACTVS III

III. i: SATVRIO. VIRGO

SAT   quae res bene uortat mi et tibi et uentri meo
330   perennitatique adeo huic, perpetuo cibus
        ut mihi supersit, suppetat, superstitet:
        sequere hac, mea gnata, me, cum dis uolentibus.
        quoi rei opera detur scis, tenes, intellegis;
        communicaui tecum consilia omnia.
335   ea causa ad hoc exemplum te exornaui ego.
        uenibis tu hodie, uirgo.
VIRGO   amabo, mi pater,
        quamquam lubenter escis alienis studes,
        tuin uentris causa filiam uendas tuam?
SAT   mirum quin regis Philippi causa aut Attali
340   te potius uendam quam mea, quae sis mea.
VIRGO utrum pro ancilla me habes an pro filia?
SAT   utrum hercle magis in uentris rem uidebitur.
        meum, opino, imperium est in te, non in me tibi[st].
VIRGO tua istaec potestas est, pater. uerum tamen
345   quamquam res nostrae sunt, pater, pauperculae,
        modice et modeste meliust uitam uiuere;
        nam ad paupertatem si ammigrant infamiae,
        grauior paupertas fit, fides sublestior.
SAT   enim uero odiosa es.

330 cibo Ω, cibus *Leo*
343 opinor Ω, opino *Ritschl* tibi A, tibist P

---

[27] An affectionate term for his food.
[28] Philip V of Macedon (238–179) fought against the Ptolemaic and

ACT THREE

Enter SATURIO from the left, accompanied by a GIRL, his daughter.

SAT   May this turn out well for me and you and my belly and   330
also for this perpetuity,[27] so that I'll always have food in
abundance, in readiness, in eternity. Follow me this way,
my daughter, with the goodwill of the gods. You know,
grasp, and understand what purpose this effort is being
made for. I've shared all my counsels with you. That's why   335
I've dressed you up like this. You will be sold today, young
lady.

GIRL   Please, my dear father, no matter how keen you are on
other people's food, would you sell your own daughter for
the sake of your stomach?

SAT   Strange that I'm not selling you for the sake of King   340
Philip or Attalus[28] rather than for my own sake, since
you're mine.

GIRL   Which of the two do you consider me, a slave girl or your
daughter?

SAT   Whichever will seem more advantageous for my belly. I
have authority over you, I believe, not you over me.

GIRL   That's your right, father. But still, father, even though our   345
possessions are on the poor side, it's better to live one's
life with moderation and modesty; if a bad reputation
comes on top of poverty, one's poverty becomes heavier
and one's credit weaker.

SAT   Really, you are annoying.

Seleucid dynasties; Attalus I of Pergamon (269–197) defeated the Gala-
tians.

VIRGO   non sum nec me esse arbitror,
350   quom parua natu recte praecipio patri.
        nam inimici famam non ita ut nata est ferunt.
SAT   ferant eantque maxumam malam crucem;
        non ego inimicitias omnis pluris aestumo
        quam mensa inanis nunc si apponatur mihi.
355 VIRGO pater, hominum immortalis est infamia;
        etiam tum uiuit quom esse credas mortuam.
SAT   quid? metuis ne te uendam?
VIRGO   non metuo, pater.
        uerum insimulari nolo.
SAT   at nequiquam neuis.
        meo modo istuc potius fiet quam tuo.
360 VIRGO attat!
SAT   quae hae res sunt?
VIRGO   cogita hoc uerbum, pater:
        erus si minatus est malum seruo suo,
        tam etsi id futurum non est, ubi captum est flagrum,
        dum tunicas ponit, quanta afficitur miseria;
        ego nunc quod non futurum est formido tamen.
365 SAT   uirgo atque mulier nulla erit quin sit mala,
        quae praeter sapiet quam placet parentibus.
VIRGO uirgo atque mulier nulla erit quin sit mala,
        quae reticet si quid fieri peruorse uidet.
SAT   malo cauere meliust te.
VIRGO   at si non licet
370   cauere, quid agam? nam ego tibi cautum uolo.
SAT   malusne ego sum?

349 me *om. A*   353 pluris existumo Ω, pluris aestumo *Pylades*, plure existumo *Seyffert*
    360 fiat Ω, atat *Palmerius*

GIRL   No, I'm not, and I don't think I am when I, young as I am,   350
       give my father good advice. Well, one's enemies don't
       spread one's reputation the way it really is.

SAT   Let them spread it and go and be hanged. All enmities
       are less important to me than if an empty table were
       placed in front of me now.

GIRL   Father, men's ill repute is immortal; it is alive even at a   355
       time when you think it's died.

SAT   What? Are you afraid that I might sell you for real?

GIRL   I'm not afraid, father. But I don't want any wrong accusa-
       tion to arise.

SAT   But you want it in vain. This will happen my way rather
       than yours.

GIRL   Goodness!   360

SAT   What's this?

GIRL   Consider this saying, father: if a master has threatened
       his slave with a beating, how wretched is the slave when
       the whip has been taken, while he's taking off his tunics,[29]
       even if it's not going to happen. What's not going to hap-
       pen scares *me* nonetheless now.

SAT   There won't be a girl who isn't bad, if she knows more   365
       than her parents like.

GIRL   There won't be a girl who isn't bad, if she keeps quiet
       when she sees something being done the wrong way.

SAT   You'd better look out for trouble!

GIRL   But what if I can't look out, what should I do? I do want to   370
       look out for you.[30]

SAT   I'm trouble, am I?

---

[29] A loose way of saying "his tunic and his undergarment."

[30] The trouble is a beating, but the girl interprets it as Saturio him-
self.

VIRGO		non es nec me dignum est dicere,
	uerum ei rei operam do ne alii dicant quibus licet.	
SAT	dicat quod quisque uolt; ego de hac sententia	
	non demouebor.	
VIRGO		at, meo si liceat modo,

375   sapienter potius facias quam stulte.

SAT   lubet.

VIRGO lubere tibi per me licere intellego;
           uerum lubere hau liceat, si liceat mihi.

SAT   futura es dicto oboediens an non patri?

VIRGO futura.

SAT   scisnam tibi quae praecepi?

VIRGO   omnia.

380 SAT   et [id] ut [ui] surrupta fueris?

VIRGO   docte calleo.

SAT   et qui parentes fuerint?

VIRGO   habeo in memoria.
           necessitate me mala ut fiam facis.
           uerum uideto, me ubi uoles nuptum dare,
           ne haec fama faciat repudiosas nuptias.

385 SAT   tace, stulta. non tu nunc hominum mores uides?
           quoiuis modi hic cum [mala] fama facile nubitur.
           dum dos sit, nullum uitium uitio uortitur.

VIRGO ergo istuc facito ut ueniat in mentem tibi
           me esse indotatam.

SAT   caue sis tu istuc dixeris.

390   pol deum uirtute dicam et maiorum meum,
           ne te indotatam dicas quoi dos sit domi:

377 liceat si liceat *A*, liceat si lubeat *P*
   380 id ut *P*, ut ui *A*, ut *Leo*   386 cuius *A*, quoius *B*, quo uis
CD, quoiuis *Guyet* mala *del. Camerarius*

GIRL No, you aren't, and it isn't proper for me to say so, but I'm making an effort so that others who could say so don't say so.

SAT Everybody can say what he wants; I won't be moved from this decision.

GIRL But if you'd let me have my way, you'd act wisely rather than stupidly. 375

SAT I like it like this.

GIRL I realize that I must let you like it; but if you were to let me have my way, I wouldn't let you like it.

SAT Will you obey your father or won't you?

GIRL I will.

SAT Do you know the instructions that I gave you?

GIRL All of them.

SAT And how you were abducted? 380

GIRL I understand it totally.

SAT And who your parents were?

GIRL I have it in my memory. You're forcing me to become bad. But make sure that this reputation won't make my wedding repudiable when you want to give me in marriage.

SAT Be quiet, silly. Can't you see the ways of people nowadays? A girl can marry here with any type of reputation. So long as she has a dowry, no fault is found fault with. 385

GIRL Then do bear in mind that I'm without dowry.

SAT Please don't say that. Thanks to the gods and my ancestors I'll tell you, so that you won't call yourself without dowry when you have a dowry at home: look, I have a 390

      librorum eccillum habeo plenum soracum.
      si hoc accurassis lepide, quoi rei operam damus,
      dabuntur dotis tibi inde sescenti logi
395   atque Attici omnes; nullum Siculum acceperis:
      cum hac dote poteris uel mendico nubere.
VIRGO quin tu me ducis, si quo ducturu's, pater?
      uel tu me uende uel face quid tibi lubet.
SAT   bonum aequomque oras. sequere hac.
VIRGO   dicto sum audiens.

III. ii: DORDALVS

400 DOR quidnam esse acturum hunc dicam uicinum meum,
      qui mihi iuratust sese hodie argentum dare?
      quod si non dederit atque hic dies praeterierit,
      ego argentum, ille ius iurandum amiserit.
      sed ibi concrepuit foris. quisnam egreditur foras?

III. iii: TOXILVS. DORDALVS

405 TOX curate isti intus, iam ego domum me recipiam.
DOR   oh,
      Toxile, quid agitur?
TOX   oh, lutum lenonium,
      commixtum caeno sterculinum publicum,
      impure, inhoneste, iniure, illex, labes popli,
      pecuniai accipiter auide atque inuide,
410   procax, rapax, trahax—trecentis uersibus
      tuas impuritias traloqui nemo potest—
      accipin argentum? accipe sis argentum, impudens,
      tene sis argentum, etiam tu argentum tenes?

---

31 Normally the dowry had to be higher if the husband was richer;
here Saturio says that her dowry will be sufficient to live on for both
husband and wife.

hamper full of books. If you nicely sort out the business
we're giving our attention to, you'll get six hundred witty
words from there, and all of them Attic ones; you needn't   395
take a single Sicilian word. With this dowry you'll be able
to marry even a beggar.[31]

GIRL Why don't you take me now if you're going to take me
anywhere, father? You can sell me or do whatever you
like.

SAT What you say is good and fair. Follow me this way.

GIRL I'm obeying you.

Exeunt SATURIO and the GIRL into the house of Toxilus.
Enter DORDALUS from his house.

DOR What should I say this neighbor of mine is going to do?   400
He gave me an oath that he'd give me the money today. If
he doesn't give it to me and this day passes, I'll lose my
money and he his oath. But the door has creaked there.
Who is coming out?

Enter TOXILUS from his house, carrying a wallet.

TOX (*into the house*) Take care of it in there, I'll return home   405
in a moment.

DOR Oh, Toxilus, how are you?

TOX (*holding out the wallet, but removing it quickly every
time the pimp tries to grab it*) Oh, you pimp dirt, you pub-
lic dungheap mixed with filth, dirty, dishonest, unjust,
unlawful creature, downfall of the people, greedy and
hateful money hawk, daring, stealing, thieving—in three   410
hundred verses no one could list your dirty tricks com-
pletely—won't you take the money? Take the money, will
you, you impudent person! Have the money, will you

503

possum te facere ut argentum accipias, lutum?
415 non mihi censebas copiam argenti fore,
qui nisi iurato mihi nil ausu's credere?
DOR sine respirare me, ut tibi respondeam.
uir summe populi, stabulum seruitricium,
scortorum liberator, suduculum flagri,
420 compedium tritor, pistrinorum ciuitas,
perenniserue, lurcho, edax, furax, fugax,
cedo sis mi argentum, da mihi argentum, impudens,
possum a te exigere argentum? argentum, inquam, cedo,
quin tu mi argentum reddis? nilne te pudet?
425 leno te argentum poscit, solida seruitus,
pro liberanda amica, ut omnes audiant.
TOX tace, opsecro hercle. ne tua uox ualide ualet!
DOR referundae ego habeo linguam natam gratiae.
eodem mi pretio sal praehibetur quo tibi.
430 nisi me haec defendet, numquam delinget salem.
TOX iam omitte iratus esse. id tibi suscensui
quia te negabas credere argentum mihi.
DOR mirum quin tibi ego crederem, ut idem mihi
faceres quod partim faciunt argentarii:
435 ubi quid credideris, citius extemplo a foro
fugiunt quam ex porta ludis quom emissust lepus.
TOX cape hoc sis.
DOR quin das?
TOX nummi sescenti hic erunt,
probi, numerati. fac sit mulier libera
atque huc continuo adduce.

423 a *om. A*
435 a *om. A*

have the money now? Can I make you take the money,
you piece of dirt? You didn't think that I'd have the op- 415
portunity to get hold of money, did you? You didn't dare
trust me until I gave you an oath.

DOR Let me catch my breath so that I can reply to you. (*very
loudly*) You most respected man of the people, brothel
for slave girls, liberator of prostitutes, sweating chamber
of the whip, wearer-away of shackles, inhabitant of the 420
mills, eternal slave, swilling, guzzling, thieving runaway,
give me my money, will you, give me my money, you im-
pudent person! Can I get the money out of you? Give me
my money, I insist! Why won't you give me my money?
Don't you have any shame at all? The pimp is demanding 425
money from you, you embodiment of slavery, for setting
your girlfriend free, so that everybody can hear.

TOX Be quiet, please. Your voice is really powerful!

DOR I have a tongue that was made for returning thanks. I get
salt for the same price as you. If my tongue won't defend 430
me, she'll never lick any salt.

TOX Stop being angry now. I was upset with you because you
refused to trust me with the money.

DOR Strange that I didn't trust you, so that you'd do the same
to me that the bankers do in part: when you entrust 435
something to them, they immediately run away from the
forum faster than a hare when it's let out of its hutch at
the games.

TOX Take this, will you? (*holds out the wallet, but removes it
quickly*)

DOR Why won't you give it to me?

TOX (*handing it over*) There will be six hundred tetradrach-
mas here, good ones and counted. Free the woman and
bring her here at once.

DOR	iam faxo hic erit.
440	non hercle quoi nunc hoc dem spectandum scio.
TOX	fortasse metuis in manum concredere?
DOR	mirum ni citius iam a foro argentarii
	abeunt quam in cursu rotula circumuortitur.
TOX	abi istac trauorsis angiportis ad forum;
445	eadem istaec facito mulier ad me transeat
	per hortum.
DOR	iam hic faxo aderit.
TOX	at ne propalam.
DOR	sapienter sane.
TOX	supplicatum cras eat.
DOR	ita hercle uero.
TOX	dum stas, reditum oportuit.

ACTVS IV

IV. i: TOXILVS

TOX	si quam rem accures sobrie aut frugaliter,
450	solet illa recte sub manus succedere.
	atque edepol ferme ut quisque rem accurat suam,
	sic ei procedit postprincipio denique:
	si malus aut nequam est, male res uortunt quas agit;
	sin autem frugi est, eueniunt frugaliter.
455	hanc ego rem exorsus sum facete et callide,
	igitur bene prouenturam confido mihi.
	nunc ego lenonem ita hodie intricatum dabo,
	ut ipsus sese qua se expediat nesciat.
	Sagaristio, heus, exi atque educe uirginem

442 quin Ω, ni *Langen*

DOR I'll have her here in a minute. I don't know who I should   440
give this to now for checking.

TOX Perhaps you're afraid to entrust it to the banker directly?

DOR It's a wonder if the bankers don't leave the forum more
quickly now than a wheel turns on its travel.

TOX Go to the forum along there, through the back alleys.
Have the woman come to me on the same way through   445
the garden.

DOR I'll have her here in a moment.

TOX But not in public.

DOR Quite wise of you.

TOX Tomorrow she should go to pray.[32]

DOR Absolutely.

TOX You should have returned in the time that you've been
standing here.

Exit DORDALUS between the houses.

ACT FOUR

TOX If you look after something soberly or properly, it usually   450
shapes up well under your hands.[33] And as everybody
looks after his own business, so is his result afterward; if
he's bad or useless, the things he does turn out badly, but
if he's decent, they turn out properly. I've started this   455
business cleverly and smartly, so I trust it'll be a success
for me. Now I'll make sure that the pimp gets so entan-
gled today that he won't know how to disentangle him-
self. (*into the house*) Sagaristio, hey, come out and bring

---

[32] After manumission it was customary in Greece to thank the gods
in an official ceremony.   [33] A metaphor from pottery.

460   et istas tabellas quas consignaui tibi,
           quas tu attulisti mi ab ero meo usque e Persia.

IV. ii: SAGARISTIO. TOXILVS

SAG numquid moror?
TOX   eugae, eugae! exornatu's basilice;
          tiara ornatum lepida condecorat schema.
          tum hanc hospitam autem crepidula ut graphice decet!
465   sed satin estis meditati?
SAG   tragici et comici
          numquam aeque sunt meditati.
TOX   lepide hercle adiuuas.
          age, illuc apscede procul e conspectu, tace.
          ubi cum lenone me uidebis colloqui
          id erit adeundi tempus. nunc agerite uos.

IV. iii: DORDALVS. TOXILVS

470 DOR quoi homini di propitii sunt, aliquid obiciunt lucri;
          nam ego hodie compendi feci binos panis in dies.
          ita ancilla mea quae fuit hodie, sua nunc est: argento ui-
            cit.
          iam hodie alienum cenabit, nil gustabit de meo.
          sumne probus, sum lepidus ciuis, qui Atticam hodie ciui-
            tatem
475   maxumam maiorem feci atque auxi ciui femina?
          sed ut ego hodie fui benignus, ut ego multis credidi!
          nec satis a quiquam homine accepi: ita prorsum crede-
            bam omnibus;

---

[34] The *crepidula*, a type of footgear that was in between a sandal and a more stable shoe, actually came from Greece rather than Persia or Arabia.   [35] Despite the reference to the Athenian state, we are dealing with Roman law here: only in Rome, not in Athens, did manumitted slaves get citizens' rights.

out the girl and those tablets which I sealed up for you 460
and which you brought to me from my master from as far
away as Persia.

Enter SAGARISTIO and the girl from the house of Toxilus, both
in exotic outfits, the former also carrying a letter which he hands
over to TOXILUS.

SAG I'm not delaying you, am I?
TOX Splendid, splendid! You're dressed up magnificently!
The tiara sets off your getup in a nice fashion. And how
beautifully the sandals[34] suit this girl from abroad! But 465
have you two rehearsed well enough?
SAG Tragic and comic actors have never rehearsed so well.
TOX You're supporting me nicely. Go on, step over there, out
of sight, and be quiet. When you see me talking with the
pimp, that will be the time to approach. Now, you two,
get away. (*they obey*)

Enter DORDALUS from the right.

DOR (*to the audience*) If the gods are well disposed toward 470
someone, they throw some profit his way: as of today, I've
saved two loaves of bread per day; the girl who was my
slave today belongs to herself now. (*pointing at the house*
of Toxilus) He's bought his victory. Now she'll have an-
other's dinner today, she won't taste anything out of my
pocket. Aren't I a decent chap, a charming citizen? I've
made the Athenian state a lot bigger today and increased 475
it with a female citizen.[35] But how generous I've been to-
day, how many people I've trusted! I didn't take security
from anyone; I trusted everyone entirely. I'm not afraid

509

		nec metuo, quibus credidi hodie, ne quis mi in iure abiu-
		rassit:
		bonus uolo iam ex hoc die esse . . . quod nec fiet nec fuit.
480	TOX	hunc hominem ego hodie in trasennam doctis deducam
		dolis,
		itaque huic insidiae paratae sunt probe. aggrediar uirum.
		quid agis?
	DOR	credo.
	TOX	unde agis te, Dordale?
	DOR	credo tibi.
		di dent quae uelis.
	TOX	eho, an iam manu emisisti mulierem?
	DOR	credo edepol, credo, inquam, tibi.
	TOX	iam liberta auctu's?
	DOR	enicas.

485–
86

		quin tibi me dico credere.
	TOX	dic bona fide: iam libera est?
	DOR	⟨s⟩ol⟨ide⟩.
		i ad forum ad praetorem, exquire, siquidem credere mihi
		non uis.
		libera, inquam, est: ecquid audis?
	TOX	at tibi di bene faciant omnes!
		numquam enim posthac tibi nec tuorum quoiquam quod
		nolis uolam.
490	DOR	abi, ne iura, satis credo.
	TOX	ubi nunc tua liberta est?
	DOR	apud te.
	TOX	ain, apud me est?
	DOR	aio, inquam, apud te est, inquam.

485–86 *olet* A *ut uidetur, om.* P, solide *Woytek*

that any of the people I've trusted today will deny this on oath in court. From this day onward I want to be good . . . which won't happen and never has happened.

TOX   (*aside*) I'll lead this chap into the net with my clever   480
tricks today, since a plot has been prepared against him properly. I'll approach him. (*to Dordalus*) How are you?

DOR   I trust you.[36]

TOX   Where are you coming from, Dordalus?

DOR   I trust you. May the gods grant what you wish.

TOX   Tell me, have you set the woman free?

DOR   I trust you, I do indeed trust you, I'm telling you.

TOX   Are you one freedwoman the richer now?

DOR   You're killing me. I'm telling you that I trust you.   485

TOX   Tell me in good faith: is she free now?

DOR   Thoroughly. Go to the forum to the praetor,[37] inquire, if you won't trust me. I'm telling you, she's free: can you hear me?

TOX   May all the gods bless you! From now on I'll never wish for anything you don't want for yourself or for anyone of your people.

DOR   Go away, stop making oaths, I trust you enough.   490

TOX   Where's your freedwoman now?

DOR   At your place.

TOX   Do you say so? She's at my place?

DOR   Yes, I'm telling you, she's at your place, I'm telling you.

---

[36] Ambiguous; Dordalus wants to express his trust in matters of finance, but the phrase is also used in reply to congratulations in order to show that one believes them to be genuine. Dordalus thinks that this is his lucky day.

[37] A high-ranking Roman magistrate with mainly judicial functions.

511

TOX ita me di ament ut ob istanc rem tibi multa bona instant a
me.

nam est res quaedam quam occultabam tibi dicere: nunc
eam narrabo,

und' tu pergrande lucrum facias: faciam ut mei memine-
ris, dum uitam

495 uiuas.

DOR   bene dictis tuis bene facta aures meae auxilium ex-
poscunt.

TOX tuom promeritum est merito ut faciam. et ut me scias esse
esse ita facturum,

tabellas tene has, pellege.   istae quid ad me?

DOR   istae quid ad me?

TOX   immo ad te attinent et tua refert:

nam ex Persia sunt haec allatae mi a meo ero.

DOR   quando?

TOX   hau dudum.

DOR quid istae narrant?

TOX   percontare ex ipsis: ipsae tibi narrabunt.

500 DOR cedo sane [mihi].

TOX   at clare recitato.

DOR   tace, dum pellego.

TOX   [recita,] haud uerbum faciam.

DOR "salutem dicit Toxilo Timarchides

et familiae omni. si ualetis, gaudeo.

ego ualeo recte et rem gero et facio lucrum

neque istoc redire his octo possum mensibus,

505 itaque hic est quod me detinet negotium.

Chrysopolim Persae cepere urbem in Arabia,

497 hae Ω, istae *Bach*

512

TOX	As truly as the gods may love me, because of this a lot of good things are coming your way from me: there's a certain matter I was keeping to myself; now I'll tell you about it, so that you can make a great profit from it. I'll make sure you remember me as long as you live.
DOR	My ears demand some kind actions in support of your kind words.
TOX	You deserve that I should give them to you deservedly. And so that you may know that I'll act accordingly, take these tablets and read them through. (*offers the pimp the letter, but he does not take it*)
DOR	How do they concern me?
TOX	They do concern you and matter to you: they were brought to me from Persia from my master.
DOR	When?
TOX	Not long ago.
DOR	What do they tell you?
TOX	Ask them in person: they'll tell you in person.
DOR	Do give them to me.
TOX	(*handing them over*) But read them out clearly.
DOR	Be quiet while I'm reading through them.
TOX	I won't utter a word.
DOR	"Timarchides gives his greetings to Toxilus and the entire household. If you are well, I rejoice. I am doing well, am busy, and am making a profit, and in the next eight months I can't return to you, such is the business which keeps me here. The Persians have taken the city of Chry-

495

500

505

---

498 sunt istaec allatae mi a meo ero *A*, ad me allatae modo sunt istae a meo domino *P* istae(c) Ω, haec *Bach*

500 mihi *del. Müller* pellico *P*, pelligo recito *uel* pelligo recita *A*

plenam bonarum rerum atque antiquom oppidum:
ea comportatur praeda, ut fiat auctio
publicitus; ea res me domo expertem facit.

510 operam atque hospitium ego isti praehiberi uolo
qui tibi tabellas affert. cura quae is uolet,
nam is mihi honores suae domi habuit maxumos."
quid id ad me aut ad meam rem refert Persae quid rerum
    gerant
aut quid erus tuos?

TOX   tace, stultiloque; nescis quid te instet boni

515 nec quam tibi Fortuna faculam lucrifera[m] allucere
    uolt.

DOR quae istaec lucrifera est Fortuna?

TOX   istas quae norunt roga.
ego tantundem scio quantum tu, nisi quod pellegi prior.
sed, ut occepisti, ex tabellis nosce rem.

DOR   bene me mones.
fac silentium.

TOX   nunc ad illud uenies quod refert tua.

520 DOR "ist' qui tabellas affert adduxit simul
forma expetenda liberalem uirginem,
furtiuam, abductam ex Arabia penitissuma;
eam te uolo curare ut istic ueneat.
ac suo periclo is emat qui eam mercabitur:

525 mancupio nec promittet nec quisquam dabit.
probum et numeratum argentum ut accipiat face.
haec cura et hospes cura ut curetur. uale."

TOX quid igitur? postquam recitasti quod erat cerae credi-
    tum,
iam mihi credis?

515 lucriferam *A*, lucificam *P*, lucrificam *Z*, lucrifica *Ritschl*

514

sopolis[38] in Arabia, an ancient town full of riches. This booty is being collected so that a public auction can be held. This is the matter which keeps me from home. I 510 want the man who brings you these tablets to receive your attention and hospitality. Take care of what he wants, for he has treated me with the greatest honor in his house." What does it matter to me or to my business what the Persians are doing, or your master for that matter?

TOX   Be quiet, idiot. You don't know what harvest awaits you and what torch profitable Good Fortune wants to light 515 for you.

DOR   What profitable Good Fortune is that?

TOX   Ask those tablets, they know it. I know as much as you, except that I read through them first. But as you've begun, learn the matter from the tablets.

DOR   You're giving me good advice. Be silent.

TOX   Now you'll come to the part that matters to you.

DOR   "The man who's carrying these tablets has brought a free- 520 born virgin with him, of desirable appearance, kidnapped, abducted from the heart of Arabia; I want you to take care that she's sold there. And the person who purchases her is to buy her at his own risk. No one will prom- 525 ise to sell her formally[39] and no one will hand her over that way. Make sure that our man gets good money duly counted out. Take care of this and take care that the guest is taken care of. Farewell."

TOX   Well then? Do you believe me, now that you've read out what was entrusted to the wax?

---

[38] Invented name, "Goldtown" or "Eldorado."

[39] I.e., in a procedure in which the buyer lays his hands on the merchandise in the presence of witnesses.

DOR   ubi nunc ille est hospes qui hasce huc attulit?

530 TOX   iam hic credo aderit: arcessiuit illam a naui.

DOR   nil mi opust
litibus nec tricis. quam ob rem ego argentum enumerem
    foras?
nisi mancupio accipio, quid eo mihi opust mercimonio?

TOX   tacen an non taces? numquam ego te tam esse matulam
    credidi.
quid? metuis?

DOR   metuo hercle uero. sensi ego iam compluriens,

535 nec mi haud imperito eueniet tali ut in luto haeream.

TOX   nil pericli mihi uidetur.

DOR   scio istuc, sed metuo mihi.

TOX   mea quidem istuc nil refert: tua ego hoc facio gratia,
ut tibi recte conciliandi primo facerem copiam.

539– DOR gratiam habeo. sed te de aliis quam alios de te suauiust
40   fieri doctos.

TOX   ne quis uero ex Arabia penitissuma
persequatur. etiam tu illam destinas?

DOR   uideam modo
mercimonium.

TOX   aequa dicis. sed optume eccum ipse aduenit
hospes ille qui has tabellas attulit.

DOR   hicine est?

TOX   hic est.

545 DOR haecine illa est furtiua uirgo?

TOX   iuxta tecum aeque scio,
nisi quia specie quidem edepol liberali est, quisquis est.

DOR   sat edepol concinna est facie.

TOX   ut contemptim carnufex!
taciti contemplemus formam.

DOR   laudo consilium tuom.

516

DOR Where's that guest now who brought these tablets here?

TOX I believe he'll be here in a moment. He went to fetch the 530
girl from the ship.

DOR I don't need any lawsuits or complications. Why should I
count out money to an outsider? What do I need this
merchandise for unless I buy it formally?

TOX Will you be quiet or not? I never thought you'd be such a
chamber pot. What? You're afraid?

DOR I am indeed afraid. I've suffered many times already, and 535
it won't be a new experience for me if I get stuck in a
mudhole.

TOX There doesn't seem to be any danger to me.

DOR I know that, but I'm afraid for myself.

TOX It's none of my business. I've been doing this for your
sake, so that you could be the first I give the opportunity
to make a bargain.

DOR Thank you. But it's more pleasant if you learn a lesson 540
from others than if they learn it from you.

TOX (*with irony*) Watch out that no one follows her here from
the heart of Arabia. Will you buy her now?

DOR At least I should see the merchandise.

TOX What you say is fair. (*looking around*) But perfect, look,
the guest who's brought these tablets is coming in person.

DOR Is that him?

TOX It is.

DOR Is this that kidnapped virgin? 545

TOX I know as little as you, except that she has the beautiful
appearance of a freeborn woman, whoever she is.

DOR She has quite a pretty face.

TOX How full of contempt the criminal is! Let's watch her appearance in silence.

DOR I praise your plan.

IV. iv: SAGARISTIO. VIRGO. TOXILVS. DORDALVS

SAG satin Athenae tibi sunt uisae fortunatae atque opiparae?

550 VIRGO urbis speciem uidi, hominum mores perspexi parum.

TOX numquid in principio cessauit uerbum docte dicere?

DOR hau potui etiam in primo uerbo perspicere sapientiam.

SAG quid id quod uidisti? ut munitum muro tibi uisum oppi-
    dum est?

VIRGO si incolae bene sunt morati, id pulchre moenitum arbi-
    tror.

555   perfidia et peculatus ex urbe et auaritia si exulant,

   quarta inuidia, quinta ambitio, sexta optrectatio,

   septumum periurium—

TOX   eugae!

VIRGO   —octaua indiligentia,

   nona iniuria, decumum, quod pessumum aggressu est,
    scelus:

   haec unde aberunt, ea urbs moenita muro sat erit sim-
    plici;

560   ubi ea aderunt, centumplex murus rebus seruandis pa-
    rum est.

TOX quid ais tu?

DOR   quid uis?

TOX   tu in illis es decem sodalibus: .

   te in exilium ire hinc oportet.

DOR   quid iam?

TOX   quia periurus es.

DOR uerba quidem haud indocte fecit.

TOX   ex tuo, inquam, usu est: eme hanc.

DOR edepol qui quom hanc magis contemplo, magis placet.

TOX   si hanc emeris—

565   di immortales!—nullus leno te alter erit opulentior.

   euortes tuo arbitratu homines fundis, familiis;

SAG (*approaching with the girl, apparently without noticing the two men conversing with each other*) Did Athens seem happy and prosperous to you?

GIRL I've seen the outward appearance of the city; the charac- 550
ter of its people I've studied too little.

TOX Did she hesitate at all to say a clever word right at the start?

DOR I couldn't verify her wisdom in her first word yet.

SAG What about what you've seen? How did the city appear to be fortified with its wall?

GIRL If its inhabitants have a good character, I consider it beautifully fortified. If perfidy and embezzlement and 555
greed have gone into exile from this city, fourth envy, fifth corruption, sixth vilification, seventh perjury—

TOX (*still aside*) Hear, hear!

GIRL —eighth carelessness, ninth injustice, and tenth wicked-
ness, which is most difficult of all to tackle: a city from which these are absent will be fortified sufficiently with a simple wall; where they are present, a hundredfold wall 560
is too little to preserve its contents.

TOX What do you say?

DOR What do you want?

TOX You are among those ten comrades; you ought to go into exile.

DOR What do you mean?

TOX Because you're a perjurer.

DOR She hasn't spoken stupidly.

TOX It's to your advantage, I tell you: buy her.

DOR Indeed, the more I look at her, the more I like her.

TOX If you buy her—immortal gods!—no pimp will be better 565
off than you. You'll turn men out of their estates and households as you please; you'll have dealings with men

519

cum optumis uiris rem habebis, gratiam cupient tuam:
uenient ad te comissatum.

DOR   at ego intro mitti uotuero.

TOX at enim illi noctu occentabunt ostium, exurent fores:
570   proin tu tibi iubeas concludi aedis foribus ferreis,
ferreas aedis commutes, limina indas ferrea,
ferream seram atque anellum; ne sis ferro parseris:
ferreas tute tibi impingi iubeas crassas compedis.

DOR i [sis] in malum cruciatum.

TOX   i sane tu . . . hanc eme; ausculta mihi.

575 DOR modo ut sciam quanti indicet.

TOX   uin huc uocem?

DOR   ego illo accessero.

TOX quid agis, hospes?

SAG   uenio, adduco hanc ad te, ut dudum dixeram.
nam heri in portum noctu nauis uenit. ueniri hanc uolo,
si potest; si non potest, iri hinc uolo quantum potest.

DOR saluos sis, adulescens.

SAG   siquidem hanc uendidero pretio suo.

580 TOX atqui aut hoc emptore uendes pulchre aut alio non potis.

SAG esne tu huic amicus?

TOX   tam quam di omnes qui caelum colunt.

DOR tum tu mi es inimicus certus. nam generi lenonio
numquam ullus deus tam benignus fuit qui fuerit propi-
    tius.

SAG hoc age. opusne est hac tibi empta?

DOR   si tibi uenisse est opus,
585   mihi quoque empta est; si tibi subiti nihil est, tantundem
    est mihi.

SAG indica, fac pretium.

574 sis A, *om.* P

	of the highest rank, they'll be keen on your favor and come to you for their drinks parties.	
DOR	Well, I won't let them in.	
TOX	Well, they'll serenade your door at night and burn down its panels. So you should have your house closed with an iron door, you should change your house to an iron one, put in an iron lintel and threshold and an iron bar and door ring. Please don't be economical with iron: you should have heavy iron shackles put on yourself.	570
DOR	Go and be hanged.	
TOX	No, you go . . . and buy her; listen to me.	
DOR	At least I should know what price he's setting for her.	575
TOX	Do you want me to call him?	
DOR	I'll step over there. (*does so*)	
TOX	(*to Sagaristio*) What are you up to, my guest?	
SAG	I'm coming, I'm bringing the girl to you, as I'd said a while ago: my ship came into the harbor last night. I want her to be sold, if possible. If it's not possible, I want us to leave as quickly as possible.	
DOR	May you be well, young man.	
SAG	I will be if I sell her for the price she deserves.	
TOX	Either you'll sell her nicely with this purchaser or you won't be able to with any other purchaser.	580
SAG	Are you his friend?	
TOX	As much as all the gods who live in heaven.	
DOR	Then you're a true enemy of mine: no god has ever been so kind as to have been well disposed toward the class of pimps.	
SAG	Pay attention. Do you need to buy her?	
DOR	If you need to sell her, I also need to buy her; if you aren't in a rush, I'm in no rush either.	585
SAG	Put a price on her, make a bid.	

521

DOR	tua merx est, tua indicatio est.
TOX	aequom hic orat.
SAG	uin bene emere?
DOR	uin tu pulchre uendere?
TOX	ego scio hercle utrumque uelle.
DOR	age, indica prognariter.
SAG	prius dico: hanc mancupio nemo tibi dabit. iam scis?
DOR	scio.

590 indica minimo daturus qui sis, qui duci queat.

TOX tace, tace. nimis tu quidem hercle homo stultus es pueri-
 liter.

DOR quid ita?

TOX quia enim te ex puella prius percontari uolo
 quae ad rem referunt.

DOR atque hercle tu me monuisti hau male.
 uide sis, ego ille doctus leno paene in foueam decidi,
595 ni hic adesses. quantum est adhibere hominem amicum
 ubi quid geras!

TOX quo genere aut qua in patria nata sit aut quibus parenti-
 bus,
 ne temere hanc te emisse dicas me impulsore aut illice,
 uolo te percontari.

DOR quin laudo, inquam, consilium tuom.

TOX nisi molestum est, percontari hanc paucis hic uolt.

SAG maxume,
600 suo arbitratu.

TOX quid stas? adi sis tute atque ipse itidem roga
 ut tibi percontari liceat quae uelis; etsi mihi
 dixit dare potestatem eius; sed ego te malo tamen
 eumpse adire, ut ne contemnat te ille.

DOR It's your merchandise, you have to put a price on her.

TOX (*to Sagaristio*) What he says is fair.

SAG (*to Dordalus*) Do you want to buy her for a good price?

DOR And you, do you want to sell her for a fine figure?

TOX I know that each of you is keen.

DOR (*to Sagaristio*) Go on, put a price on her clearly.[40]

SAG I'll tell you in advance: no one will convey her to you formally. Do you know that already?

DOR I do. Tell me the lowest price for which you're going to   590
give her to me, for which she can be had.

TOX Be quiet, be quiet. You're terribly stupid, in a childish way.

DOR What do you mean?

TOX Because I want you first to ask the girl all the important questions.

DOR That's good advice. Just look, I, that clever pimp, almost
fell into a pit, if you hadn't been present. How important   595
it is to consult a friend when you're doing business!

TOX I want you to ask in what family, in what country, and to
what parents she was born, so that you won't say you
bought her rashly because I urged or enticed you to.

DOR Yes, I praise your plan, I tell you.

TOX (*to Sagaristio*) Unless it's a nuisance, he wants to question the woman briefly.

SAG Absolutely, at his own discretion.   600

TOX (*to Dordalus*) Why are you standing around? Do go to
him in person and ask him yourself in the same way to be
allowed to ask her what you want; to be sure, he told me
he'd allow you to ask her, but I still prefer you to approach him in person so that he won't look down on you.

---

[40] I am following Festus (p. 84 Lindsay), who interprets the obscure *prognariter* as "clearly."

```
DOR                                        satis recte mones.
      hospes, uolo ego hanc percontari.
SAG                                  a terra ad caelum, quidlubet.
605 DOR  iubedum ea huc accedat ad me.
SAG                                    i sane ac morem illi gere.
      percontare, exquire quiduis. age, age nunc tu, in proe-
         lium
      uide ut ingrediare auspicato.
VIRGO                           liquidum est auspicium, tace.
      curabo ut praedati pulchre ad castra conuortamini.
TOX   concede istuc, ego illam adducam.
DOR                              age, ut rem esse in nostram putas.
610 TOX  ehodum huc, uirgo. uide sis quid agas.
VIRGO                              taceas, curabo ut uoles.
TOX   sequere me. adduco hanc, si quid uis ex hac percontarier.
DOR   enim uolo te adesse.
TOX                    hau possum quin huic operam dem hospiti,
      quoi erus iussit. quid si hic non uolt me una adesse?
SAG                                        immo i modo.
TOX   do tibi ego operam.
DOR                  tibi ibidem das, ubi tu tuom amicum adiuuas.
615 SAG  exquire.
TOX            heus tu, aduigila.
VIRGO              satis est dictum: quamquam ego serua sum,
      scio ego officium meum, ut quae rogiter uera, ut accepi,
         eloquar.
TOX   uirgo, hic homo probus est.
VIRGO                        credo.
```

605 ea Ω, eam *Redslob*
606–7 age . . . auspicato *Toxilo dat P, Sagaristioni Woytek*
613 una adesse *A*, adesse una *P*

DOR (*to Toxilus*) You're giving me decent advice. (*to Sagaris-tio*) Stranger, I want to question her.

SAG Anything you like, from earth to heaven.

DOR Have her come here to me.   605

SAG (*to the girl*) Do go and obey him. (*to Dordalus*) Ask her, inquire about anything you like. (*to the girl, quietly*) Go on, go on now, take care that you enter battle with a good omen.

GIRL (*quietly*) The omen is unmistakable, be quiet. I'll make sure that you return to the camp after acquiring booty in fine style.

TOX (*to Dordalus*) Step over there, I'll bring her to you.

DOR Go on, as you think is to our advantage.

TOX Over here, girl. (*quietly*) Do watch out what you're do- 610
ing.

GIRL (*quietly*) Be quiet, I'll sort it out the way you want.

TOX (*to the girl*) Follow me. (*to Dordalus*) I'm bringing her to you, in case you want to ask her anything.

DOR I want you to be present.

TOX I can't help supporting my guest, whom my master told me to support. What if he doesn't want me to be present with you?

SAG No, do go along.

TOX (*to Dordalus*) I'm at your service.

DOR You're at your own service when you help your friend.

SAG Question her.   615

TOX (*to the girl*) Hey there, be alert.

GIRL Enough has been said: even though I'm a slave girl, I know my duty: to say the truth about what I'm asked, the way I've heard it.

TOX My girl, this is a decent chap.

GIRL I believe so.

TOX   non diu apud hunc seruies.

VIRGO ita pol spero, si parentes facient officium suom.

DOR   nolo ego te mirari, si nos ex te percontabimur

620   aut patriam tuam aut parentes.

VIRGO   quor ego hic mirer, mi homo?

        seruitus mea mi interdixit ne quid mirer meum malum.

DOR   noli flere.

TOX   ah, di istam perdant! ita cata est et callida.

        ut sapiens habet cor, quam dicit quod opust!

DOR   quid nomen tibi est?

TOX   nunc metuo ne peccet.

VIRGO   Lucridi nomen in patria fuit.

625 TOX nomen atque omen quantiuis iam est preti. quin tu hanc
            emis?

        nimis pauebam ne peccaret. expediuit.

DOR   si te emam,

        mihi quoque Lucridem confido fore te.

TOX   tu si hanc emeris,

        numquam hercle hunc mensem uortentem, credo, serui-
            bit tibi.

DOR   ita uelim quidem hercle.

TOX   optata ut eueniant operam addito.

630   nihil adhuc peccauit etiam.

DOR   ubi tu nata es?

VIRGO   ut mihi

        mater dixit, in culina, in angulo ad laeuam manum.

TOX   haec erit tibi fausta meretrix: nata est in calido loco,

---

41 Ambiguous; she wants to make the pimp believe that her father
will buy her back, but she also hints at being liberated by force and with-
out pay for the pimp.

42 The name sounds as if it were derived from *lucrum*, "profit."

TOX You won't be a slave for long at his place.

GIRL I do hope so, if my parents do their duty.[41]

DOR I don't want you to be surprised if we ask you about your 620
country or your parents.

GIRL (*sobbing*) Why should I be surprised, my dear fellow? My
slavery has forbidden me to be surprised at any misfortune of mine.

DOR Don't cry.

TOX (*aside*) Ah, may the gods ruin her! She's so sly and smart.
What a clever heart she has, how she says what's necessary!

DOR (*to the girl*) What's your name?

TOX (*aside*) Now I'm afraid that she might make a mistake.

GIRL (*to Dordalus*) In my country my name was Lucris.[42]

TOX (*to Dordalus*) The name and omen are already worth any 625
price. Why don't you buy her? (*aside*) I was terribly afraid
that she might make a mistake. She's got it right.

DOR (*to the girl*) If I buy you, I trust you'll be a lucrative Lucris
for me as well.

TOX If you buy her, she won't be your slave for this revolution
of the moon, I believe.[43]

DOR That's how I'd like it.

TOX Add your effort so that your wishes come true. (*aside*) 630
She hasn't made any mistake so far.

DOR (*to the girl*) Where were you born?

GIRL As my mother told me, in the kitchen, in the corner at the
left-hand side.

TOX (*to Dordalus*) She'll be a lucky prostitute for you; she was

---

[43] Ambiguous. Toxilus seems to be saying that she will earn so much
that she can buy her freedom soon, but he also hints at her liberation
through her father.

ubi rerum omnium bonarum copia est saepissuma.
tactus leno est; qui rogaret ubi nata esset diceret,
635   lepide lusit.

DOR   at ego patriam te rogo quae sit tua.

VIRGO quae mihi sit, nisi haec ubi nunc sum?

DOR   at ego illam quaero quae fuit.

VIRGO omne ego pro nihilo esse duco quod fuit, quando fuit:
tamquam hominem, quando animam efflauit, quid eum
quaeras qui fuit?

TOX   ita me di bene ament, sapienter! atque eo miseret tamen.

640 DOR sed tamen, uirgo, quae patria est tua, age mi actutum ex-
pedi.
quid taces?

VIRGO   dico equidem: quando hic seruio, haec patria est mea.

TOX   iam de istoc rogare omitte—non uides nolle eloqui?—
ne suarum se miseriarum in memoriam inducas.

DOR   quid est?
captusne est pater?

VIRGO   non captus, sed quod habuit [id] perdidit.

645 TOX haec erit bono genere nata: nil scit nisi uerum loqui.

DOR quis fuit? dic nomen.

VIRGO   quid illum miserum memorem qui fuit?
nunc et illum Miserum et me Miseram aequom est nomi-
narier.

DOR quoius modi is in populo habitust?

VIRGO   nemo quisquam acceptior:
serui liberique amabant.

634 tactus leno est *A*, tactus est leno *P*
644 id *del. Bothe*

born in a warm place, where there's a very regular supply
of all good things. (*aside*) That's one for the pimp! She
charmingly tricked the man who asked her to say where   635
she was born.

DOR (*to the girl*) But I'm asking you what your country is.

GIRL What should it be except the one where I am now?

DOR But I'm asking about the one that used to be yours in the
past.

GIRL I reckon everything in the past as nothing, once it's in the
past; like a man who has breathed his last, why would you
ask who he was?

TOX (*to Dordalus*) As truly as the gods may love me, an intelli-
gent reply! I do pity her, though.

DOR But even so, my girl, do tell me at once what your country   640
is. Why are you silent?

GIRL I *am* telling you: since I'm a slave here, this is my country.

TOX (*to Dordalus*) Stop asking about this now—can't you see
she doesn't want to tell?—so that you won't remind her of
her misfortunes.

DOR (*to the girl*) Well then? Is your father a prisoner of war?

GIRL Not a prisoner, but he lost what he had.

TOX (*to Dordalus*) She'll be from a good family; she knows   645
how to speak nothing but the truth.

DOR (*to the girl*) Who was he? Tell me his name.

GIRL Why should I recall the wretched man who is no more?
Now it's right to call him Mister Wretched and me Miss
Wretched.

DOR What was his standing among the people?

GIRL No one was more welcome;[44] slaves and freeborn loved
him alike.

---

[44] Ambiguous; she states that he was popular, but the audience also
understands that he was a hanger-on.

TOX   hominem miserum praedicas,

650   quom et ipsus probe perditust et beneuolentis perdidit.

DOR emam, opinor.

TOX   etiam "opinor"? summo genere esse arbitror;

diuitias tu ex istac facies.

DOR   ita di faxint!

TOX   eme modo.

VIRGO iam hoc tibi dico: [iam] actutum ecastor meus pater, ubi me sciet

ueniisse, ipse aderit et me aps te redimet.

TOX   quid nunc?

DOR   quid est?

655 TOX audin quid ait?

VIRGO   nam etsi res sunt fractae, amici sunt tamen.

DOR ne sis plora; libera eris actutum, si crebro cades.

uin mea esse?

VIRGO   dum quidem ne nimis diu tua sim, uolo.

TOX satin ut meminit libertatis? dabit haec tibi grandis bolos.

age si quid agis. ego ad hunc redeo. sequere. redduco hanc tibi.

660 DOR adulescens, uin uendere istanc?

SAG   magis lubet quam perdere.

DOR tum tu pauca in uerba confer: qui datur, tanti indica.

SAG faciam ita ut te uelle uideo, ut emas. habe centum minis.

DOR nimium est.

SAG   octoginta.

DOR   nimium est.

SAG   drachuma abesse hinc non potest

quod nunc dicam.

650 prope *P*, probe *Bothe*   653 iam[2] *del. Guyet*
654 uenisse ipse aderit *A*, uenisse huc aderit hic *P*

TOX	You describe him as wretched indeed, since he is completely lost himself and has lost his well-wishers.	650
DOR	I'll buy her, I think.	
TOX	Still "I think"? I believe she comes from a noble family; you'll make a fortune from her.	
DOR	May the gods grant it!	
TOX	Just buy her.	
GIRL	I'm telling you now: as soon as my father knows I've been sold, he'll be here in person and buy me back from you.	
TOX	(to Dordalus) Well then?	
DOR	What is it?	
TOX	Can you hear what she's saying?	655
GIRL	Well, even if his position is ruined, he still has friends.	
DOR	Please stop crying. You'll be free at once if you fall back often enough. Do you want to be mine?	
GIRL	As long as I'm not yours for too long, I do.	
TOX	(to Dordalus) Doesn't she remember her freedom well enough? She'll give you great profit. Act now if you're going to act at all. I'm returning to this chap. Follow me. (to Sagaristio) I'm bringing her back to you.	
DOR	(to Sagaristio) Young man, do you want to sell her?	660
SAG	I prefer that to losing her.	
DOR	Then keep it short: state the price I can get her for.	
SAG	I'll do as I can see you desire, so that you can buy her. Have her for a hundred minas.	
DOR	It's too much.	
SAG	Eighty.	
DOR	It's too much.	
SAG	Not one drachma can be deducted from what I'll say now.	

---

663 nummus *P*, drachuma *scripsi rhythmi causa* (*cf. Rud. 1330*)

	DOR	quid id est ergo? eloquere actutum atque indica.
665	SAG	tuo periclo sexaginta haec datur argenti minis.
	DOR	Toxile, quid ago?
	TOX	di deaeque te agitant irati, [et] scelus,

qui hanc non properes destinare.

	DOR	habebo.
	TOX	abi, argentum effer huc.
668		non edepol minis trecentis cara est. fecisti lucri.
668ᵃ	DOR	***.
	SAG	⟨habeto.⟩
	TOX	eu! praedatu's probe.
669	SAG	heus tu, etiam pro uestimentis huc decem accedent

minae.

670	DOR	apscedent enim, non accedent.
	TOX	tace sis, non tu illum uides
671		quaerere ansam, infectum ut faciat? abin atque argen-

tum petis?

671ᵃ		*** atque ut dignust perit.
672	DOR	heus tu serua istum.
	TOX	quin tu is intro?
	DOR	abeo atque argentum affero.

IV. V: TOXILVS. VIRGO. SAGARISTIO

	TOX	edepol dedisti, uirgo, operam allaudabilem,

probam et sapientem et sobriam.

	VIRGO	si quid bonis
675		boni fit, esse id et graue et gratum solet.
	TOX	audin tu, Persa? ubi argentum ab hoc acceperis,

simulato quasi eas prorsum in nauem.

	SAG	ne doce.

666 et *del. Pylades*   667 habebo *CD*, habeto *B*
668ᵃ eu . . . probe *post* habeto / habebo (667) *exhibet P*, habeto *add.*
Lindsay

DOR   What is it, then? Tell me at once and state it.

SAG   You can have her at your own risk for sixty silver minas. 665

DOR   Toxilus, what am I to do?

TOX   The gods and goddesses are after you in their anger, you criminal, since you aren't making haste to buy her.

DOR   (*to Sagaristio*) I'll have her.

TOX   Go, bring the money out here. She wouldn't expensive at three hundred minas. You've made a profit.

DOR   ***.

SAG   Have her.

TOX   (*to Dordalus*) Hurray! You've made booty properly.

SAG   (*to Dordalus*) Hey you, another ten minas will be added for her clothing.

DOR   They'll be subtracted, not added.   670

TOX   Be quiet, will you? Can't you see that he's looking for a handle to undo it? Won't you go and get the money? *** and he's perishing as he deserves.

DOR   Hey, you keep watch over him.

TOX   Why don't you go in?

DOR   I'm going and bringing the money.

Exit DORDALUS into his house.

TOX   Young lady, you've done a praiseworthy, decent, wise, and sober job.

GIRL If a good turn is done to good people, it's generally valued 675
      and appreciated.

TOX   Can you hear me, Persian? When you've taken the money from him, pretend to return straight to the ship.

SAG   Stop lecturing me.

---

669 accedent *CD*, accedant *B*
671ᵃ *non fertur in Palatinis*

TOX   per angiportum rursum te ad me recipito
      illac per hortum.
SAG   quod futurum est praedicas.
680 TOX   at ne cum argento protinam permittas domum
      moneo te.
SAG   quod te dignum est, me dignum esse uis?
TOX   tace, parce uoci: praeda progreditur foras.

      IV. vi: DORDALVS. SAGARISTIO. TOXILVS

DOR   probae hic argenti sunt sexaginta minae,
      duobus nummis minus est.
SAG   quid ei nummi sciunt?
685 DOR   cruminam hanc emere aut facere ut remigret domum.
SAG   ne non sat esses leno, id metuebas miser,
      impure, auare, ne crumillam amitteres?
TOX   sine, quaeso. quando leno est, nil mirum facit.
DOR   lucro faciundo ego auspicaui in hunc diem:
690   nil mihi tam parui est quin me id pigeat perdere.
      age, accipe hoc sis.
SAG   hu[n]c in collum, nisi piget,
      impone uero.
DOR   fiat.
SAG   numquid ceterum
      me uoltis?
TOX   quid tam properas?
SAG   ita negotium est:
      mandatae quae sunt, uolo deferre epistulas;
695   geminum autem fratrem seruire audiui hic meum,
      eum ego ut requiram atque uti redimam uolo.

691 hunc *P*, huc *Gruterus et Ritschl quadrante spatio in* A
692 uero *dat Sagaristioni* F, *Dordalo* A (*ut uidetur*), *spatium deest*
in P

TOX   Return to me through the alley again, that way through the garden.

SAG   You're foretelling what's going to happen.

TOX   But don't go home with the money directly, I warn you.   680

SAG   Do you want me to deserve what you deserve?

TOX   Be quiet, spare your voice: our booty is coming out.

Enter DORDALUS with a wallet.

DOR   There are sixty decent silver minas here, minus two obols.[45]

SAG   What can these obols do?

DOR   They can buy this wallet or make it return home.   685

SAG   You wretch, to make sure you'd be enough of a pimp you were afraid to let go of a paltry wallet, you dirty, greedy creature?

TOX   Let it be, please. He's not acting out of character for a pimp.

DOR   (*to Sagaristio*) I took auspices for today for making a profit; nothing is of such little value to me that I wouldn't   690 regret losing it. Go on, take this please.

SAG   Put it here onto my neck, if you're not loath to do so.

DOR   Yes. (*does so*)

SAG   Do you two want anything else from me?

TOX   Why are you in such a rush?

SAG   Business. I want to deliver letters that were entrusted to me; what's more, I've heard that my twin brother is a   695 slave here: I want to find him and set him free.

---

[45] Here *nummus* ("coin") must refer to a very small sum, hence my translation as "obol."

TOX	atque edepol tu me commonuisti hau male.
	uideor uidisse hic forma persimilem tui,
	eadem statura.
SAG	quippe qui frater siet.
700 DOR	quid est tibi nomen?
TOX	⟨sciscita⟩ quod ad te attinet.
DOR	quid attinet non scire?
SAG	ausculta ergo, ut scias:
	Vaniloquidorus Virginesuendonides
	Nugiepiloquides Argentumexterebronides
	Tedigniloquides Nuncaesexpalponides
705	Quodsemelarripides Numquameripides. em tibi!
DOR	eu hercle! nomen multimodis scriptum est tuom.
SAG	ita sunt Persarum mores, longa nomina,
	contortiplicata habemus. numquid ceterum
	uoltis?
DOR	uale.
SAG	et uos, nam animus iam in naui est mihi.
710 TOX	cras ires potius, hodie hic cenares.
SAG	uale.

IV. vii: TOXILVS. DORDALVS. VIRGO. SATVRIO

TOX	postquam illic abiit, dicere hic quiduis licet.
	ne hic tibi dies illuxit lucrificabilis;
	nam non emisti hanc, uerum fecisti lucri.
DOR	illequidem iam scit quid negoti gesserit,
715	qui mihi furtiuam meo periclo uendidit,
	argentum accepit, abiit. qui ego nunc scio

700 sciscita *add. Leo*
703 Argentumextenebronides Ω, Argentumexterebronides *Pius*
704 Nugides Palponides *A*, Nundesexpalponides *B*, Numdesexpalponides *CD*, Nuncaesexpalponides *Woytek*

TOX	You haven't given me a bad hint. I seem to have seen a man of very similar appearance to you here, of the same figure.
SAG	Naturally, since he's my brother.
DOR	What's your name? 700
TOX	Mind your own business.
DOR	Why isn't it my business to know?
SAG	Then listen so that you may know: Vainspeakerpresent Girlsellerson Nonsenseadderson Silverdiggerson Serve-yourighttalkerson Moneywheedlerson Whativegrabbed- 705 onceson Youllnevergetbackson. There you go!
DOR	Goodness! Your name takes a lot of writing.
SAG	That's the Persian tradition: we have long, complicated names. Do you two want anything else?
DOR	Farewell.
SAG	You two as well: my mind is already on the ship.
TOX	You should have gone tomorrow instead and dined here 710 today.
SAG	Goodbye.

Exit SAGARISTIO to the left; he enters the house of Toxilus from behind.

TOX	Now that he's left, I can say anything I like here. This day has shone upon you as a profitable one: you didn't buy her, you made a profit of her.
DOR	He already knows what sort of business he's done: he's 715 sold me a kidnapped girl at my own risk, has taken the money, and has left. How do I know now if she'll soon be

an iam asseratur haec manu? quo illum sequar?
in Persas? nugas!

TOX   credidi gratum fore
beneficium meum apud te.

DOR   immo equidem gratiam

720   tibi, Toxile, habeo; nam te sensi sedulo
mi dare bonam operam.

TOX   tibin ego? immo sedulo.

DOR   attat! oblitus sum intus dudum edicere
quae uolui edicta. asserua hanc.

TOX   salua est haec quidem.

VIRGO   pater nunc cessat.

TOX   quid si ammoneam?

VIRGO   tempus est.

725   TOX   heus, Saturio, exi. nunc est illa occasio
inimicum ulcisci.

SAT   ecce me. numquid moror?

TOX   age, illuc apscede procul e conspectu, tace;
ubi cum lenone me uidebis colloqui,
tum turbam facito.

SAT   dictum sapienti sat est.

730   TOX   tunc, quando abiero—

SAT   quin taces? scio quid uelis.

IV. viii: DORDALVS. TOXILVS

DOR   transcidi loris omnis adueniens domi,
ita mi supellex squalet atque aedes meae.

claimed as free? Where should I follow him? To Persia?
Nonsense!

TOX   I thought my good turn would earn me your gratitude.

DOR   Yes, I am indeed grateful to you, Toxilus: I knew that you   720
were supporting me eagerly.

TOX   I you? (*correcting himself*) Yes, eagerly.

DOR   Goodness! A while ago I forgot to give the orders indoors
which I wanted to give. Watch over her.

TOX   She's safe.

Exit DORDALUS into his house.

GIRL   My father isn't doing anything.

TOX   What if I remind him?

GIRL   It's time.

TOX   Hey, Saturio, come out. Now's the best opportunity to   725
take revenge on your enemy.

Enter SATURIO from the house of Toxilus.

SAT   Here I am. I'm not wasting time, am I?

TOX   Go on, step over there, far out of sight, and be quiet;
when you see me talking with the pimp, that's the time to
make a commotion.

SAT   A word is enough for the wise.

TOX   Then, when I've left—   730

SAT   (*interrupting*) Why won't you keep quiet? I know what
you want. (*steps aside*)

Enter DORDALUS from his house.

DOR   On my arrival at home I thoroughly beat everyone with
straps; my furniture and house are positively filthy.

TOX	redis tu tandem?
DOR	redeo.
TOX	ne ego hodie tibi bona multa feci.
DOR	fateor, habeo gratiam.
735 TOX	num quippiam aliud me uis?
DOR	ut bene sit tibi.
TOX	pol istuc quidem omen iam ego usurpabo domi, nam iam inclinabo me cum liberta tua.

IV. ix: SATVRIO. VIRGO. DORDALVS

SAT	nisi ego illunc hominem perdo, perii. atque optume eccum ipsum ante aedes.
VIRGO	salue multum, mi pater.
740 SAT	salue, mea gnata.
DOR	ei! Persa me pessum dedit.
VIRGO	pater hic meus est.
DOR	hem, quid? pater? perii oppido! quid ego igitur cesso infelix lamentarier minas sexaginta?
SAT	ego pol te faciam, scelus, te quoque etiam ipsum ut lamenteris.
DOR	occidi!
745 SAT	age ambula in ius, leno.
DOR	quid me in ius uocas?
SAT	illi apud praetorem dicam. sed ego in ius uoco.
DOR	nonne antestaris?
SAT	tuan ego causa, carnufex, quoiquam mortali libero auris atteram qui hic commercaris ciuis homines liberos?

738 illum Ω, illunc *Camerarius*

TOX Are you returning at last?

DOR I am.

TOX I've really done you many good turns today.

DOR I admit it and I thank you.

TOX Do you want anything else from me?   735

DOR Only that you're well.

TOX I'll accept and carry out that omen at home now: I'll re-
cline with your freedwoman at once.

Exit TOXILUS into his house.

SAT (*walking toward the pimp*) Unless I kill that person
I'm dead. Perfect, look, the man himself in front of the
house.

GIRL Many greetings, my dear father.

SAT My greetings, my dear daughter.   740

DOR No! The Persian has sent me to perdition!

GIRL This is my father.

DOR Eh? What? Your father? I'm completely ruined! Dear
me, then why don't I lament my sixty minas?

SAT I'll make sure that you lament yourself too, you criminal.

DOR I'm dead!

SAT Come on, go to court, pimp.   745

DOR Why are you summoning me to court?

SAT I'll tell you there in front of the praetor. But I'm sum-
moning you to court.

DOR Won't you take a witness?

SAT You hangman, should I wear off any free man's ears[46] for
your sake, you who traffic free citizens here?

---

[46] In order to make someone an official witness, one had to touch his
ear.

750	DOR	sine dicam.
	SAT	nolo.
	DOR	audi.
	SAT	surdus sum. ambula.

        sequere hac, scelesta feles uirginaria.

        sequere hac, mea gnata, me usque ad praetorem.

VIRGO   sequor.

ACTVS V

V. i: TOXILVS. LEMNISELENIS. SAGARISTIO

TOX   hostibus uictis, ciuibus saluis, re placida, pacibus perfec-
        tis,

        bello exstincto, re bene gesta, integro exercitu et praesi-
        diis,

755   quom bene nos, Iuppiter, iuuisti, dique alii omnes caeli-
        potentes,

        eas uobis gratis habeo atque ago, quia probe sum ultus
        meum inimicum.

        nunc ob eam rem inter participes diuidam praedam et
        participabo.

758   ite foras: hic uolo ante ostium et ianuam

758ᵃ   meos participes bene accipere.

759   statuite hic lectulos, ponite hic quae assolent.

759ᵃ   hic statui uolo primum aliqua,

760   unde ego omnis hilaros, ludentis, laetificantis faciam ut
        fiant,

        756 grates habeo *BT*, habeo grates *CD*

        759ᵃ pri mihi aliqua mihi *B¹*, primum aliquam *B²*, primum aquila
mihi *CD*, primum aliqua *scripsi ut an⁴^ fiat*

DOR	Let me speak!	750
SAT	No!	
DOR	Listen!	
SAT	(*to Dordalus*) I'm deaf. Move. Follow me this way, you criminal maiden-mouser. (*to his daughter*) Follow me this way, my dear daughter, to the praetor.	
GIRL	Yes.	

Exeunt SATURIO, DORDALUS, and the GIRL to the right.

ACT FIVE

Enter TOXILUS from his house.

TOX   Now that the foes are conquered, the citizens safe, the state tranquil, peace treaties concluded, war come to an end, the affair successfully concluded, the army and garrisons intact, I say and give thanks to you, Jupiter, and to   755 all other gods inhabiting heaven, for supporting us well, because I have taken proper revenge on my enemy. Now because of this I'll divide and share the booty among all those who have taken part. (*into the house*) Come out! I want to receive them well here in front of the door and entrance.

Enter LEMNISELENIS and SAGARISTIO from the house of Toxilus, followed by PAEGNIUM and other servants.

TOX   (*to servants*) Place couches here, put here what one usu-ally does. Here I first want something to be placed from   760 which I shall make you all happy, joyous, and cheerful;

       quorum opera mi facilia factu facta haec sunt quae uolui
          effieri.

       nam improbus est homo qui beneficium scit accipere et
          reddere nescit.

    LEM Toxile mi, quor ego sine te sum, quor tu autem sine
         me es?

    TOX   agedum ergo
       accede ad me atque amplectere sis.

    LEM   ego uero.

    TOX   oh, nil hoc magis dulce est.

765   sed, amabo, oculus meus, quin lectis nos actutum com-
          mendamus?

766 LEM omnia quae tu uis, ea cupio.

766ᵃ TOX mutua fiunt a me. age, age [age] ergo,

767   tu Sagaristio, accumbe in summo.

767ᵃ SAG ego nil moror: cedo parem, quem pepigi.

768 TOX temperi.

    SAG   mihi istuc "temperi" sero est.

768ᵃ TOX hoc age, accumbe. hunc diem suauem

769   meum natalem agitemus amoenum.

769ᵃ   date aquam manibus,

769ᵇ   apponite mensam.

770   do hanc tibi florentem florenti. tu hic eris dictatrix nobis.

    LEM age, puere, ab summo septenis cyathis committe hos lu-
          dos.

772 TOX moue manus, propera.

772ᵃ   Paegnium, tarde cyathos mihi das;

773   cedo sane. bene mihi, bene uobis,

766ᵃ age age age *P* (*etiam T*), age age *W*

through your hard work the things I wanted done be-
came easy for me to do. A man who knows how to receive
a good turn, but doesn't know how to return it, is worth-
less. (*the servants bring couches, a table, jugs of wine and
water, and garlands*)

LEM My dear Toxilus, why am I without you, and why are you
without me?

TOX Come on then, come to me and embrace me please.

LEM Yes, I will. (*does so*)

TOX Oh, nothing is sweeter than this. But please, apple of my   765
eye, why don't we commit ourselves to the couches at
once?

LEM I desire everything you want. (*she reclines in the middle,
Toxilus at the lower end*)

TOX It's mutual. Go on, go on then, you, Sagaristio, must lie at
the head.

SAG I don't care for that; give me the partner I've settled for.

TOX In due course.

SAG That "due course" of yours is too late for me.

TOX To business! Lie down. (*Sagaristio obeys*) Let's celebrate
this sweet birthday[47] of mine as a pleasant one. (*to ser-
vants*) Give us water for our hands, put down a table.
(*handing a garland to Lemniselenis*) I'm giving flowers to   770
you, my flower. You will be our commander here.

LEM (*to Paegnium*) Come on, boy, begin these games at the
head of the table with seven ladles.

TOX (*to Paegnium*) Move your hands, hurry up. Paegnium,
you're giving me the ladles slowly; get on with it. (*propos-
ing a toast*) Good health to me, good health to you (*nods

---

[47] His birthday because he feels as if born again now that his girl is
free.

773ᵃ		bene meae amicae,
773ᵇ		optatus hic mi
774		dies datus hodie est ab dis, quia te licet liberam med amplecti.
775	LEM	tua factum opera.
	TOX	bene omnibus nobis.
775ᵃ		hoc mea manus tuae poclum donat,
775ᵇ		ut amantem amanti
776		decet.
	LEM	cedo.
	TOX	accipe.
	LEM	bene ei qui inuidet mi
776ᵃ		et ei qui hoc gaudet.

V. ii: DORDALVS. TOXILVS. SAGARISTIO.
PAEGNIVM. LEMNISELENIS

777	DOR	qui sunt, qui erunt quique fuerunt quique futuri sunt posthac,
		solus ego omnibus antideo facile, miserrumus hominum ut uiuam.
779– 80		perii, interii! pessumus hic mi dies hodie illuxit corruptor,
		ita me Toxilus perfabricauit itaque meam rem diuexauit.
		uehiclum argenti miser eieci [amisi] neque ‹illuc› quam ob rem eieci, habeo.
		qui illum Persam atque omnis Persas atque etiam omnis personas
		male di omnes perdant! ita misero Toxilus haec mi conciuit.
785		quia ei fidem non habui argenti, eo mihi eas machinas molitust:

at the audience), good health to my girlfriend; this day of my desire has been given to me today by the gods, since I can embrace you as a free woman.

LEM   Thanks to your own hard work.   775

TOX   Good health to all of us. My hand is giving this cup to yours, as a lover should to his lover.

LEM   Give it to me.

TOX   Take it. (*passes it on*)

LEM   Good health to the man who envies me and to the one who is happy about all this.

Enter DORDALUS from the right.

DOR   (*not yet seeing the banquet*) In living as the most wretched man I alone easily surpass all those who live, who will live, who have lived, and who are going to live hereafter. I'm ruined, I'm destroyed! This awful day has 780 shone upon me as a disastrous one today, given how Toxilus finished me off and ravaged my possessions. Poor me, I've thrown away a cartload of money and I don't have the object for which I threw it away. May all the gods ruin that Persian and all Persians and all stage characters! Toxilus has stirred up this trouble for me, wretch that I am. Because I didn't trust him about the money he 785 set these machinations in motion against me. For me not

---

782 amisi *del. Acidalius* illuc *add. Ritschl*

quem pol ego ut non in cruciatum atque in compedis co-
    gam, si uiuam!
siquidem huc umquam erus redierit eius, quod spero—
    sed quid ego aspicio?
hoc uide, quae haec fabula est? hic quidem pol potant.
    aggrediar. o bone uir,

789–
90   TOX   salueto, et tu, bona liberta.   Dordalus hicquidem est.

    SAG   quin iube adire.

    TOX   adi, si lubet.

    SAG   agite, applaudamus.

    TOX   Dordale, homo lepidissume, salue.

792   locus hic tuos est, hic accumbe.

792ᵃ   ferte aquam pedibus.

792ᵇ   praeben tu, puere?

793   DOR   ne sis me uno digito attigeris, ne te ad terram, scelus,
         affligam.

    PAE   at tibi ego hoc continuo cyatho oculum excutiam tuom
         ⟨iam actutum⟩.

795   DOR   quid ais, crux, stimulorum tritor? quo modo me hodie
         uorsauisti!
        ut me in tricas coniecisti! quo modo de Persa manus mi
         adita est!

    TOX   iurgium hinc auferas, si sapias.

798   DOR   at, bona liberta, haec sciuisti et

798ᵃ   me celauisti?

    LEM   stultitia est,

799   quoi bene esse licet, eum praeuorti

800   litibus. posterius ted istaec

801   magis par agere est.

    DOR   uritur cor mi.

to force him into torture and shackles, if I live! If his master ever returns here, as I hope—but what do I see? Look at this! What business is this? Here they're drinking. I'll approach them. Oh my good man, my greetings, and also to you, my good freedwoman.   790

TOX   It's Dordalus.

SAG   Have him come here.

TOX   Come here if you like.

SAG   Go on, let's give him a big hand. (*applauds*)

TOX   Dordalus, most charming chap, my greetings. This is your place, recline here. (*to servants*) Bring water for his feet. (*to Paegnium*) Are you bringing it, boy?

DOR   Don't touch me even with one finger, mind, so that I don't smash you to the ground, criminal.

PAE   But I will knock out your eye with this ladle at once.

DOR   (*to Toxilus*) What do you say, you gallows tree, whip eradicator? How you've fleeced me today! How you've thrown me into difficulties! How I've been tricked about the Persian!   795

TOX   You'd do well to stop your abuse.

DOR   But you, my good freedwoman, knew all this and kept it from me?

LEM   It's stupidity if someone who can have a good time turns to fights instead. It's more appropriate if you deal with that later.   800

DOR   My heart is burning.

---

788 pol hic quidem *P, transp. Müller*

794 iam actutum *add. Thomsen*

798 ea *P,* et *Camerarius*

800 ista h(a)ec te *P,* ted istaec *O. Skutsch*

801ª	TOX	da illi cantharum. exstingue ignem, si
802		cor uritur, caput ne ardescat.
	DOR	ludos me facitis, intellego.
	TOX	uin cinaedum nouom tibi dari, Paegnium?
805		quin elude, ut soles, quando liber locust hic.
		hui, babae! basilice te intulisti et facete.
	PAE	decet me facetum esse et hunc irridere
		lenonem lubido est, quando dignus est.
	TOX	perge ut coeperas.
	PAE	hoc, leno, tibi.
810	DOR	perii! perculit me prope.
	PAE	em, serua rursum.
	DOR	delude, ut lubet, erus dum hinc abest.
	PAE	uiden ut tuis dictis pareo?
		sed quin tu meis contra item dictis seruis
		atque hoc quod tibi suadeo facis?
	DOR	quid est id?
815	PAE	restim tu tibi cape crassam ac suspende te.
	DOR	caue sis me attigas, ne tibi hoc scipione
		malum magnum dem.
	PAE	tu utere, te condono.
	TOX	iam iam, Paegnium, da pausam.
819	DOR	ego pol uos eradicabo.
	PAE	at
819ª		te ille, qui supra nos habitat,
820		qui tibi male uolt maleque faciet.
820ª		non hi dicunt, uerum ego.

815 suspende te *P, transp. Ritschl*
817 tu *T, omm. ceteri Palatini*

550

TOX   (*to a slave*) Give him a goblet. (*to Dordalus*) Extinguish the fire, if your heart is burning, so that your head doesn't catch fire.

DOR   You're mocking me, I realize.

TOX   Do you want to get a new catamite, Paegnium? Have 805 your fun, as you always do, since you have a free field here. (*as Paegnium dances toward the pimp and hits him*) Hey, wow! That was a fantastic, fine movement!

PAE   I ought to be fine and I'm keen to make fun of this pimp, since he deserves it.

TOX   Continue the way you began.

PAE   Take this, pimp. (*hits him again*)

DOR   I'm dead! He almost knocked me over. 810

PAE   There, watch out again. (*hits again*)

DOR   Have your fun with me as you like while your master's away.[48]

PAE   Can you see how I obey your words? (*hits again*) But why don't you reciprocate and follow my words in turn and do what I advise you?

DOR   What's that?

PAE   Take a thick rope and hang yourself. 815

DOR   Mind you don't touch me so that I don't give you a big thrashing with this cane.

PAE   Have it for yourself, I grant that to you.

TOX   Give it a break now, Paegnium.

DOR   I'll exterminate the lot of you.

PAE   But you will be exterminated by the one who lives above us and who has harsh feelings for you and will treat you 820 harshly. Not they are saying so, but I.

---

[48] The master is not Toxilus, who is of course present, but the master of Toxilus.

821	TOX	age, circumfer mulsum, bibere da usque plenis cantha- ris.
		iam diu factum est, postquam bibimus; nimis diu sicci su- mus.
	DOR	di faciant ut id bibatis quod uos numquam transeat.
	SAG	nequeo, leno, quin tibi saltem staticulum olim quem He- gea
825		faciebat. uide uero, si tibi satis placet.
	TOX	me quoque uolo
		reddere Diodorus quem olim faciebat in Ionia.
	DOR	malum ego uobis dabo, ni[si] abitis.
	SAG	etiam muttis, impudens?
		iam ego tibi, si me irritassis, Persam adducam denuo.
	DOR	[iam taceo hercle.] atque tu Persa es, qui me usque am- mutilauisti ad cutem.
830	TOX	tace, stulte: hic eius geminust frater.
	DOR	hicine est?
	TOX	ac geminissumus.
	DOR	di deaeque et te et geminum fratrem excrucient!
	SAG	qui te perdidit;
		nam ego nil merui.
	DOR	at enim quod ille meruit, tibi id opsit uolo.
	TOX	agite hunc sultis ludificemus.
	LEM	nisi si dignust, non opust.
		et me hau par est.
	TOX	credo eo quia non inconciliat, quom te emo.
835	LEM	at tamen non—tamen—

827 nisi *P*, ni *Reiz*
829 iam taceo hercle *del. Leo*
833 sultis hunc *P, transp. Guyet*

TOX   Go on, pass the honey-wine round, give us to drink from full goblets. It's been a long time since we had a drink; we've been dry for far too long.

DOR   May the gods make you drink something that will never pass through you.[49]

SAG   Pimp, I can't refrain from dancing the lascivious dance for you that Hegea used to dance long ago.[50] But see if 825 you like it well enough. (*dances toward him and hits him*)

TOX   And I want to stage the one that Diodorus used to dance in Ionia long ago. (*dances toward him and hits him*)

DOR   I'll give you a beating unless you leave me.

SAG   You're still muttering, you shameless creature? If you annoy me, I'll bring you the Persian back.

DOR   You are the Persian who fleeced me down to the quick.

TOX   Be quiet, idiot! He's his twin brother.   830

DOR   Is he?

TOX   Yes, the twinniest twin ever.

DOR   (*to Sagaristio*) May the gods and goddesses torture both you and your twin brother!

SAG   He's the one who ruined you: I haven't done anything.

DOR   But I'd like you to suffer for what he did.

TOX   (*to all banqueters*) Go on, please, let's have our fun with him.

LEM   There's no need to if he doesn't deserve it; and it isn't appropriate for me.

TOX   (*with sarcasm*) No doubt because he didn't create any trouble when I bought you.

LEM   But still, I don't—still—   835

---

[49] I.e., poison.

[50] Nothing is known about the dancers Hegea and Diodorus from Ionia, the west coast of what is Turkey today.

	TOX	caue ergo sis malo et sequere me.
		te mihi dicto audientem esse addecet, nam hercle apsque me
		foret et meo praesidio, hic faceret te prostibilem prope-diem.
838		sed ita pars libertinorum est:
838ᵃ		nisi patrono qui aduorsatust,
839		nec satis liber sibi uidetur
839ᵃ		nec satis frugi nec sat honestus,
840		ni id effecit, ni ei male dixit,
840ᵃ		ni grato ingratus repertust.
841	LEM	pol bene facta tua me hortantur
841ᵃ		tuo ut imperio pareant.
842	TOX	ego sum tibi patronus plane qui huic pro te argentum dedi.
		⟨nunc⟩ graphice hunc uolo ludificari.
	LEM	meo ego in loco sedulo curabo.
	DOR	certo illi homines mihi nescioquid mali consulunt, quod faciant.
	SAG	heus uos!
845	TOX	quid ais?
	SAG	hicin Dordalus est leno qui hic liberas uirgines mer-catur?
		hicin est qui fuit quondam fortis?
	DOR	quae haec res est? ei! colapho me icit.
		malum uobis dabo.
	TOX	at tibi nos dedimus dabimusque etiam.
	DOR	ei! natis peruellit.
	PAE	licet: iam diu saepe sunt expunctae.
	DOR	loquere tu etiam, frustum pueri?
	LEM	patrone mi, i intro, amabo, ad cenam.
850	DOR	mea Ignauia, tu nunc me irrides?

554

TOX   Do watch out for trouble then and follow me. You ought to be obedient to me, because if it hadn't been for me and my protection, he'd have turned you into a prostitute without delay. But that's how some freedmen are: unless one has opposed his patron, he doesn't consider himself free enough or useful enough or decent enough, unless   840 he's done this, unless he's been rude to him, unless he's been found to be ungrateful to his benefactor.

LEM   Yes, your good turns spur me on to obey your command.

TOX   I am clearly your patron as I have paid him for you. Now I want him mocked beautifully.

LEM   For my part I'll do my best.

DOR   (*as they approach him menacingly*) Those people are definitely planning to do something bad to me.

SAG   Hey, you two!

TOX   What do you say?   845

SAG   Isn't this the pimp Dordalus, who deals in free virgins here? Isn't this the one who used to be powerful? (*attacks him*)

DOR   What's this? Ouch! He's given me a smack. I'll give the lot of you a beating!

TOX   But we have already given you one and will give you another.

DOR   (*as Paegnium attacks*) Ouch! He's pinched my arse.

PAE   That's okay: it's been pricked often enough for years.

DOR   Are you still speaking, you fragment of a boy?

LEM   (*also hitting him*) My dear patron, please go in to dinner.

DOR   My dear Idleness, are you mocking me now?   850

---

843 nunc *add. Leo*   844 quid *P*, quod *Aldus*
846 colaphum *P*, colapho me *Lambinus*

851	LEM	quiane te uoco, bene ut tibi sit?
851ª	DOR	nolo mihi bene esse.
	LEM	ne sit.
852	TOX	quid igitur? sescenti nummi
852ª		quid agunt, quas turbas danunt?
853	DOR	male disperii! sciunt referre probe inimico gratiam.
	SAG	satis sumpsimus supplici iam.
855	DOR	fateor, manus uobis do.
855ª	TOX	et post dabis sub furcis.
856	SAG	abi intro . . . in crucem.
	DOR	an me hic parum exercitum hisce habent?
	TOX	conuenisse te Toxilum me‹mineris›. spectatores, bene ualete. leno periit.
	GREX	plaudite.

857 me‹mineris› *Camerarius*

LEM Because I'm inviting you to enjoy yourself?

DOR I don't want to enjoy myself.

LEM Then don't.

TOX Well then? What are the six hundred tetradrachmas do-
ing, what trouble are they making?

DOR I'm totally ruined! These people know how to give
proper thanks to an enemy.

SAG We've punished you enough now.

DOR I admit it, I'm giving you my hands.[51]   855

TOX And you'll do so later under the fork.[52]

SAG Go in . . . for crucifixion.

DOR Haven't they given me enough exercise?

TOX Remember that you've met Toxilus. Spectators, farewell.
The pimp has perished.

TROUPE Give us your applause.

---

[51] A submissive gesture; Dordalus is willing to be tied up.

[52] An instrument of torture; a forked frame to which a slave's hands
were tied.

METRICAL APPENDIX

MERCATOR

arg. 1 + 2, 1–110 ia^6
111–116 ia^8
117 tr^7
118–128 ia^8
129–131 tr^7
132–133 ia^8
134 ia^6
135–136 ia^4
137–140 ia^8
141–224 tr^7
225–334 ia^6
335–336 ba^4
337 an^4
338 ba^c + ba^2
339 an^4
340 ba^2 + ba^c

341 tr^8
342 ba^c + ba^2
343–355 ba^4
356 tr^8
357–358 ba^4
359 tr^8
360–361 ba^4
362–363 tr^8
364–498 tr^7
499–543 ia^7
544–587 ia^6
588–666 tr^7
667–829 ia^6
830–884 tr^7
884^a extra metrum
885–1026 tr^7

MILES GLORIOSVS

arg. 1 + 2, 1–155 ia^6
156–353 tr^7
354–425 ia^7

426–480 tr^7
481–595 ia^6
596–812 tr^7

813–873 ia^6

874–946 ia^7

947–1010 tr^7

1011–1093 an^7

1094–1136 ia^6

1137–1215 tr^7

1216–1283 ia^7

1284–1310 ia^6

1311–1377 tr^7

1378–1393 ia^6

1394–1437 tr^7

MOSTELLARIA

arg., 1–83 ia^6

84–87 ba^4

88 ba^2 + ba^c

89 ba^4

90 ia$^{4\wedge}$

91–93 ba^4

94 an^4

95–97 ba^4

98 ia$^{4\wedge}$

99–101 ba^4

102 ia$^{4\wedge}$

103–104 ia^8

105–106 cr^4

107 ia^8

108–109 cr^2 + cr^c

110 cr^4

111–112 cr^c + cr^2

113 cr^2 + cr^c

114 cr^c + cr^2

115 tr^7

116 cr^2 + cr^c

117 tr^7

118–119 ia^8

120–122 ba^4

123 an^4

124 ba^4

125 ba^2 + ba^c

126 ba^4

127 ia$^{4\wedge}$

128 ia^8

129 tr^7

130 ia^4

131–132 ia^8

133–136 cr^2 + cr^c

137 cr^4

138 cr^c + cr^2

139–140 cr^4

141 cr^2 + cr^c

142–143 ia^8

144 cr^4

145 tr^7

146–148 ia^8

149 cr^2 + cr^c

150 cr^4

151 cr^4 ?

152 cr^c + cr^c

153 cr^2

154–156 tr^7

157–247 ia^7

248–312 tr^7

313–314 ba^2 + bac

315 cr^c + cr^2

316 ba^4

317–318 ba^2 + bac

319 ba^3

320 cr^2

321 ba^3

322 an^4

323 an^2 + c^r

324 cr^2 + cr^c

325–325^a tr$^{4\wedge}$

326 cr^2 + cr^c

327 cr^4

328 cr^c + tr$^{4\wedge}$

329 cr^2 + cr^c

330 v^r

331–333 an^4

334 ia^4

335–335^a an$^{4\wedge}$

336–338 cr^2 + cr^c

339–341 cr^2 + thy

342–343 cr^2 + cr^c

344 cr^c + thy

345 cr^c + cr^c

346 tr$^{4\wedge}$ + c^r

347 v^r

348–408 tr^7

409–505 ia^6

506 extra metrum

507–689 ia^6

690–692 cr^2 + cr^c

693 cr^2 + thy

694–695 cr^2 + cr^c

696–697 cr^2 + thy

698–701 cr^2 + cr^c

702–703 cr^2 + thy

704–705 cr^2 + cr^c

706 cr^2 + thy

707–708 cr^2 + cr^c

709 cr^c + cr^c

709^a ?

710–712 cr^2 + cr^c

713 cr^4

714 cr^2 + cr^c

715–716 cr^4

717 cr^2 + cr^c

718–720 cr^4

721 gl

721^a-723 cr^4

724 ?

725 cr^c + cr^2

726 ?

727 tr^7

728–731 cr^4

732 $cr^2 + tr^2$

733 $cr^c + cr^2$

734–736 cr^4

737 tr^4

738 $cr^c + cr^2$

739 $cr^2 + sp^2$

739^a $cr^1 + cr^c$

740 tr^7

741–745 ia^8

746 ia^7

747–782 ia^6

783–785 $ba^2 + ba^c$

786–789 ba^4

790 $ba^c + ba^2$

791 ba^4

792 $ba^2 + ba^c$

793 ba^4

794 $ba^c + ba^2$

795 ba^4

796 $ba^2 + ba^c$

797 ba^4

798 $ba^2 + ba^c$

799–803 ba^4

804 tr^8

805–857 tr^7

858 v^r

859 $an^{4\wedge}$

860 $an^4 + an^2$

861 $an^{4\wedge}$

862 an^8

863 tr^7

864–865 $ba^2 + ba^c$

866 ?

867 ith

868–869 $c^r + c^r$

870–871 ba^4

872 $ba^2 + ia^2$

873 ba^4

874 $c^r + c^r$

875 ba^4

876 $c^r + c^r$

877 $ia^{4\wedge}$

878 an^8

879 cr^4

880 $gl + cr^c$

881 cr^4

882 wil

882^a ith

883–884 tr^7

885–887 $tr^{4\wedge}$

887^a ba^4

888 tr^8

889 an^4

890–891 $ba^c + c^r$

892 v^r

893 $tr^{4\wedge} + c^r$

894–895 $ia^4 + ith$

896 an^8

897–898 tr^7

899 $ia^4 + cr^c$

900 ia^6

901 $an^{4\wedge}$

902 an^4 904–992 tr^7

902^a ia^4 993–1040 ia^6

903 an^4 1041–1181 tr^7

PERSA

arg. 1 + 2 ia^6 48^a ia^4

1 ia^4 + tr$^{4\wedge}$ 49–52 ia^7

2 ia^7 53–167 ia^6

3–6 ia^8 168–169 an^8

7–8 ia^7 170–171 an^4

9–12 ia^8 171^a an$^{4\wedge}$

13–16 tr^8 172–174 an^8

17 cr^1 175–180 an^4

17^a cr^2 181 an^7

17^b cr^1 182 an^4

18 tr^7 182^a tr^4

19–22 ia^7 183–190 tr^7

23–25 ia^8 191–191^a tr$^{4\wedge}$

26–27 tr sy^{6metr} 192–194^a tr sy^{12metr}

28 tr^7 195 tr^7

29 wil   196–197 tr sy^{6metr}

29^a-32^a tr sy^{12metr} 198–199 tr^7

33 ia^4 200–202 tr^8

34 tr^7 203–250 tr^7

34^a-35 ia^c 251 cr^1 + cr^c

36–37^a tr sy^{8metr} 252 ba^3

38 ia^4 253 ba^4

39–41 ia^c 254 ? + ith

42 ia^8 255–256 ia^8

43–46 ia^7 257–259 tr^8

47–48 ia^8 260–262 tr^7

263–264 tr^8

265 tr^7

266 tr^8

267 tr^7

268 cr^c + cr^1

268^a ith + cr^c

269–271 ia^8

271^a ith

272 an^8

273 tr^8

274–276 tr^7

277 ia$^{4\wedge}$

277^a-277^b c^r

278 ia^4

279 cr^1 + cr^c

280–328 ia^7

329–469 ia^6

470–471 tr^7

472 tr^8

473 tr^7

474 tr^8

475–477 tr^7

478 tr^8

479–484 tr^7

485–486 an^7

487–488 tr^8

489 tr^7

490 an$^{4\wedge}$

491 an^8

492 an^7

493–494 an^8

495 an^7

496–500 an^8

501–512 ia^6

513–519 tr^7

520–527 ia^6

528–672 tr^7

673–752 ia^6

753–755 an^8

756 an^7

757 an^8

758 cr^4

758^a an$^{4\wedge}$

759 cr^4

759^a an$^{4\wedge}$

760–765 an^8

766–769 an^4

769^a an^2

769^b c^r

770–771 an^7

772 an^2

772^a-773 an^4

773^a an^2

773^b c^r

774 an^7

775–775^a an^4

775^b c^r

776 an^4

776^a c^r

777–778 an^7

779–781 an^8

782–784 an^7

785–791 an^8

792 an^4

792^a an^2

792^b c^r

793–796 an^8

797 an$^{4\wedge}$

798–802 an sy$^{14\text{metr}}$

803 cr^3

804 cr^4

805–806 cr^3 + tr^2

807 ba^4

808 ba^2 + ba^c

809 ba^c + ba^c

810 ba^4

811–812 ia^4

813–814 ba^4

815 ba^c + tr$^{4\wedge}$

816–817 ba^4

818 ba$^{3\wedge}$

819–820^a tr sy$^{8\text{metr}}$

821–837 tr^7

838–841^a tr sy$^{16\text{metr}}$

842 tr^7

843–847 an^8

848 an^7

849 c^r + c^r

850 an^4

851–852^a tr sy$^{8\text{metr}}$

853 tr^7

854–855^a ia$^{4\wedge}$

856 ba^4

857 ba^2 + ia$^{4\wedge}$

858 tr^7

INDEX OF PROPER NAMES

The index is limited to names of characters in the play, and of characters, persons, towns, countries, regions, peoples, languages, works of literature, mythical creatures, and deities mentioned in the plays. Names for which established English forms or translations exist are listed under the English forms, for instance, *Jupiter* or *Underworld*.

INDEX OF PROPER NAMES